The Russian Revolution, 1917

Rex A. Wade presents here a new account of one of the pivotal events of modern history, combining his own long study of the revolution with the best of contemporary scholarship. Within an overall narrative that provides a clear description of the 1917 revolution, he introduces several new approaches on its political history and the complexity of the October Revolution. Wade clears away many of the myths and misconceptions that have clouded studies of the period. He also gives due space to the social history of the revolution and incorporates people and places too often left out of the story, including women, national minority peoples, peasantry and front soldiers, enabling a richer and more complete history to emerge. Now appearing in a second edition, this highly readable book has been thoroughly revised and expanded. It will prove invaluable reading to anyone interested in Russian history.

REX A. WADE is Professor of Russian History at George Mason University. He is the author of numerous books and articles on Russian history.

D0209213

NEW APPROACHES TO EUROPEAN HISTORY

Series editors
WILLIAM BEIK *Emory University*
T. C. W. BLANNING *Sidney Sussex College, Cambridge*

New Approaches to European History is an important textbook series, which provides concise but authoritative surveys of major themes and problems in European history since the Renaissance. Written at a level and length accessible to advanced school students and undergraduates, each book in the series addresses topics or themes that students of European history encounter daily: the series embraces both some of the more "traditional" subjects of study, and those cultural and social issues to which increasing numbers of school and college courses are devoted. A particular effort is made to consider the wider international implications of the subject under scrutiny.

To aid the student reader scholarly apparatus and annotation is light, but each work has full supplementary bibliographies and notes for further reading: where appropriate chronologies, maps, diagrams and other illustrative material are also provided.

For a list of titles published in the series, please see end of book.

The Russian Revolution, 1917

Second Edition

REX A. WADE

George Mason University

CAMBRIDGE
UNIVERSITY PRESS

CAMBRIDGE UNIVERSITY PRESS
Cambridge, New York, Melbourne, Madrid, Cape Town, Singapore, São Paulo, Delhi

Cambridge University Press
The Edinburgh Building, Cambridge CB2 8RU, UK

Published in the United States of America by Cambridge University Press, New York

www.cambridge.org
Information on this title: www.cambridge.org/9780521602426

First published 2005
Third printing 2008

Printed in the United Kingdom at the University Press, Cambridge

A catalogue record for this publication is available from the British Library

Library of Congress Cataloguing in Publication data
Wade, Rex A.
The Russian Revolution, 1917 / Rex Wade.
    p.   cm. – (New approaches to European history)
Includes bibliographical references.
ISBN 0 521 84155 0 (hb) – ISBN 0 521 60242 4 (pb)
1. Soviet Union – History – Revolution, 1917–1921.
I. Title: Russian Revolution.   II. Title.   III. Series.
DK265.W24   2000
947.084′1 – dc21   99–056317

ISBN 978-0-521-84155-9 hardback
ISBN 978-0-521-60242-6 paperback

Contents

Plates

Maps

Preface

The Russian Revolution remains without doubt one of the most important events of modern history. It has been central to the shaping of twentieth-century world history and its legacy continues to be influential to the present. The collapse of the Soviet Union has made it easier to put the Russian Revolution into better historical perspective. Moreover, writing about it no longer involves an implied judgment on an existing government and system, as it often did during the era of the Soviet Union's existence. At the same time, however, the renewed struggle over democracy and political forms, class and social-economic issues, the autonomy or independence of the non-Russian peoples, Russia's great-power status and other issues that have wracked the region since 1991 reaffirm the importance of the Russian Revolution of 1917, when these very issues were first fought out. The outcome was then, as it is now, important to the world as well as to Russia and its neighbors.

Despite its importance and the tremendous amount written about the revolution, reliable general histories, especially relatively brief ones, have been rare. This book attempts to provide such a history in a new account of the Russian Revolution that also reflects recent scholarship. It brings together both my own long study of the revolution and the fruit of the many recent specialized studies. While writing, I found myself rethinking our narrative and interpretation of several major features of the revolution. The result, I hope, is a book accessible and interesting to general readers while also introducing new perspectives that my colleagues in the field of Russian studies will find stimulating.

Within an overall narrative that seeks to provide a clear account of the revolution, several new approaches and interpretations are introduced. For one, this book recasts the political history of the revolution. It emphasizes the importance of the political realignments that accompanied the revolution and the significance of the new political blocs that were, in many ways, more important during the revolution than traditional party labels. This allows proper focus on the role of the Revolutionary Defensist, "moderate socialist" bloc in the leadership of the revolution during the early months. It similarly allows proper recognition of the importance of the radical left bloc – not just Bolsheviks – during the period of the October Revolution. This study also stresses the importance of the slogan "All Power to the Soviets" and the idea of "Soviet power" in paving the way for the October Revolution. It emphasizes the complexity of the October Revolution and the degree to which it was part of a genuinely popular struggle for "All Power to the Soviets" and only later a "Bolshevik revolution." This allows the clearing away of many myths and misconceptions that have long clouded that important upheaval. It was neither a simple manipulation by cynical Bolsheviks of ignorant masses nor the carefully planned and executed seizure of power under Lenin's omniscient direction that the traditional myth of October has so often portrayed.

At the same time the book gives due space to the social history of the revolution, stressing the importance of popular activism and of social and economic issues in shaping the course and outcome of the revolution. The aspirations of various segments of the population and the many organizations they created to advance their interests are central to the story. Historians in recent years have debated the social versus the political history of the revolution – this work suggests that the two are inseparable. No understanding of the revolution is complete without a consideration of popular aspirations and activism and how they interacted with political parties and leadership.

This history also incorporates people and places all too often left out of the story of the revolution. It moves beyond the capital, Petrograd, and without ignoring the centrality of events there it treats the revolution in the provinces as important and integral parts of the revolution. In particular it includes the national minorities and the importance of the revolution to them and of them to the revolution. It gives attention to the peasantry, to front soldiers, to women and to events in provincial Russia, groups and places that are often given cursory treatment or omitted from histories of the revolution. The result, I believe, is a richer as well as more complete history.

Finally, there is the issue of where to end a book on the revolution; books on "the Russian Revolution" have been published encompassing very different time periods. Each of these has some validity, depending on the story one wishes to tell. The October Revolution has traditionally been a popular date, but it overstates the importance of that event by itself. Most people at the time did not see October as such a sharp break. It also misses the importance of political events in Petrograd and elsewhere during the next two months in transforming the revolution for "Soviet power" into the Bolshevik regime that followed and in paving the road to civil war. Another popular date has been 1921, and this has good logic. However, it does not adequately distinguish between revolution and civil war, which seems to me an important distinction. Other dates up to 1930 have also been used to define the revolution. I suggest that early January 1918, and specifically the dispersal of the Constituent Assembly on January 6, is a good point to take as the end of the revolution. A number of trends come together at the 1917/18 year transition and are given a punctuation by the dispersal of the Constituent Assembly to most clearly mark the end of the revolution, turning the struggle over Russia's future into a civil war which would be decided by armies rather than politics. Revolution strictly defined ends and civil war begins.

This book is directed at the general reader as well as the specialist and that has determined many stylistic features. It assumes that readers do not know Russian. I have therefore sought to use the English counterparts of Russian terms where possible. Thus, for example, city *duma* is rendered city council, which is what they were in effect. Similarly, after much internal debate and conflicting external advice, I have used the English version of first names of major figures and persons well known to readers in that form – Nicholas and Alexandra, Alexander Kerensky, Leon Trotsky and even Paul Miliukov – rather than strict transliteration of the Russian spelling (Nikolai, Aleksandr, Lev, Pavel), but the Russian form for people less well known and for names less common in English. In many instances I have used the Russian convention of two initials instead of a first name. Similarly, cities and places are given in the manner most familiar to contemporary readers. Thus they are usually given in their Russian variant rather than in the various nationality language forms (Kharkov rather than Kharkiv). I use the name familiar today rather than the official Russian names of 1917 for some cities (Tallinn rather than Revel, Helsinki instead of Helsingfors). While producing some inconsistencies in usage, I think that this commonsense approach to names and terms will make it easier for the reader unfamiliar with Russian and already confronted by numerous new names. Those who read Russian will not find any difficulty with understanding these and, where desired, transposing them to the Russian original. Family names and Russian words are in the standard Library of Congress transliteration with the common slight modifications such as omission of the soft sign (Lvov rather than L'vov) and the ending "sky" rather than "skii" (Kerensky rather than Kerenskii). Strict transliteration is used for notes and the further reading section, and for some titles in the text (such as the newspapers *Den'* and *Rech'*).

The same considerations dictated certain other features. Where possible I have drawn illustrative quotations from English-language sources, including secondary works, rather than the Russian originals on the assumption that this provides some guidance as to where interested readers can expect to find more information on that subject. The work is lightly footnoted, primarily for direct quotations, to acknowledge specific borrowing of data or to guide readers to especially important works on a topic. In contrast to the limited footnoting, the further reading list is extensive and intended to give readers a wide-ranging reference to the literature available in English. I have included most of the secondary literature and documentary collections. The memoir literature, especially of foreign observers, is less thoroughly represented; for those and other works readers should consult Murray Frame, *The Russian Revolution, 1905–1921: A Bibliographic Guide to Works in English*. Both the informational footnotes and the further reading section are limited to English-language works, for the reasons already given. Those interested in the voluminous Russian-language literature (and skilled in the problems of its use, especially for Soviet-era publications) can find extensive guidance in the bibliographies of the specialized studies given in the further reading.

A word should be said about the use of "Russia" and "Russian." The population of the Russian Empire in 1917 (and Russians today) used two different words to distinguish between "Russian" (*russkii*) meaning that language, nationality and culture, and "Russian" (*rossiiskii*) when referring to the state or territory. English and most other languages do not make that distinction. This can create confusion for those unfamiliar with the dual meaning of "Russian." In this book, as in almost all writing on the history of Russia, the term "Russian" is used in both meanings and sometimes fuses them. Thus references to the aspirations of "Russian society" or that "Russians felt" something, unless otherwise indicated, usually means the population as a whole, but especially the ethnically Russian or the Orthodox Slavic (Russians, Ukrainians and Belorussians). Such usages are impossible to avoid in writing about the history of the Russian Empire and Soviet Union, but have also become more problematic since the breakup of that state and the rise of newly assertive nationalisms in its former territories. This double meaning of "Russian," coupled with my greater attention to nationality and provincial issues, has led me to use "All-Russia" rather than the more traditional "All-Russian" in the names of congresses and assemblies such as the "All-Russia Congress of Soviets." "All-Russia" provides a clearer reference to something pertaining to the state (*rossiiskii*) and all the peoples of the state, in contrast to Russians (*russkii*) as a specific nationality or linguistic group. It makes more comprehensible the demands of some groups, Ukrainians or Estonians for example, for autonomy and self-determination, but within the authority of an "All-Russia" Constituent Assembly.

All dates are in the Russian calendar of that time, which was thirteen days behind the Western and modern Russian calendar. Thus the February Revolution and the October Revolution (Russian calendar in use in 1917) are called the "March Revolution" and the "November Revolution" (Western calendar) in some books.

My narrative and interpretations have taken form over many years of reading, listening, conversing and teaching. I owe intellectual debts to many more people than can be named and in more ways than I could possibly recall. I have had the good fortune to participate in academic conferences with most of the leading scholars in the field; their presentations, comments and conversations (and publications) have certainly, and in more ways than I could ever identify, influenced my knowledge of and thinking about the revolution. If I have inadvertently borrowed, unconsciously and without acknowledgment, too directly from any of those I have interacted with, I do apologize and hope they accept it as testimony to their own scholarship and persuasiveness.

Several colleagues have read all or parts of the manuscript, and to them I owe an enormous debt of gratitude: Olavi Arens, Barbara Engel, Daniel Graf, Tsuyoshi Hasegawa, Michael Hickey, Semion Lyandres, Michael Melancon, Daniel Orlovsky, Scott Seregny, Philip Skaggs and Ronald Suny. My thanks to Jonathan Sanders for advice and help on photos. Mollie Fletcher-Klocek ably prepared the maps. Kathleen Ward helped with keyboarding the further reading section and technical aspects of finishing off the typescript. Nathan Hamilton helped track down materials and also read the manuscript. In addition I owe thanks to some of my undergraduate and MA students at George Mason University, who read and critiqued early versions of the manuscript from a student perspective. My wife, Beryl, has been a rock of support throughout, amiably tolerating a frequently distracted writer-husband. This book is lovingly dedicated to her.

Preface to the second edition

I have been gratified by the positive responses to the original edition, not only from formal reviews but also from the more informal responses of academic colleagues (many of whom have found it useful in their classes), students, and general readers. At the same time, however, my own continued reading and reflection on the revolution, combined with new research and the suggestions of readers, has convinced me that there are sufficient changes that would improve the book and thus its usefulness to readers to justify a new edition. Some changes are minor stylistic improvements, others clarify or extend a passage, some allow me to strengthen an argument made in the first edition or to insert new material altogether. I also have incorporated recent scholarly publications into the "Further Reading."

What is new? I have strengthened the discussion of political developments on the eve of the October Revolution and have augmented the sections on the role of the Constituent Assembly, cross-party political co-operation, peasants, nationalities, and religion and the church. Without going all the way with some of the claims of the "linguistic turn" and cultural anthropology, I have expanded significantly the treatment of the role of language, symbols, and festivals, which so obviously were an important part of the revolution and which give the reader a better sense of the texture of life during these stirring days. Smaller modifications have been made in some other places. Finally, in response to some colleagues' suggestions, I have drawn some of the conclusions more explicitly, both in the final chapter and within earlier chapters. These changes do not alter the basic contours and themes of the book, but hopefully will make it better and more useful to readers seeking to understand the Russian Revolution.

Rex A. Wade

Chronology

Feb. 9–22	Rising tide of strikes in Petrograd.
Feb. 23	Women's Day demonstrations.
Feb. 24–25	Demonstrations in Petrograd grow in size daily; troops show reluctance to act against demonstrators; political parties become more involved.
Feb. 26	Demonstrations continue; government barricades streets and orders troops to fire on demonstrators.
Feb. 27	Garrison mutiny; Petrograd Soviet formed; Temporary Committee of the State Duma formed and announces assumption of authority.
Mar. 1	Order No. 1.
Mar. 2	Provisional Government formed; abdication of Nicholas II; spread of revolution to other cities.
Mar. 14	Soviet "Appeal to the People of the World" for a "peace without annexations or indemnities."
Mar. 20	Tsereteli arrives in Petrograd from Siberian exile.
Mar. 21–22	Tsereteli and Revolutionary Defensists establish leadership of Petrograd Soviet.
Mar. 20	Provisional Government abolishes all discriminations based on nationality or religion.
Apr. 3	Lenin arrives in Petrograd from Switzerland.
Apr. 4	Lenin issues "April Theses."
Apr. 18–21	April Crisis.
May 2–5	Government crisis and reorganization to include Soviet leaders in the government: "coalition government."
June 3–5	First All-Russia Congress of Soviets of Workers' and Soldiers' Deputies.
June 10	Ukrainian Central Rada issues First Universal.
June 18	Russian military offensive begins.
June 18	Soviet-sponsored demonstration in Petrograd turns

	into massive antiwar and antigovernment demonstration.
July 1	Provisional Government delegation and Central Rada reach agreement on limited self-government for Ukraine.
July 2	Kadet ministers resign over Ukrainian issue – new government crisis begins.
July 3–5	July Days: street demonstrations demand that the Soviet take power; Soviet leaders refuse; Bolsheviks belatedly assume leadership; Lenin and others forced to flee.
July 5	German counteroffensive and collapse of Russian offensive.
July 5	Second Universal of Ukrainian Central Rada; Finnish parliament votes to assume governing authority in Finland.
July 8	Kerensky becomes minister-president.
July 17	Tsereteli, as acting minister of the interior, orders measures against land seizures by peasants.
July 18	General Kornilov appointed supreme commander of army.
July 20	Provisional Government extends right to vote to women.
July 21–23	New government crisis, leading to second coalition government.
Aug. 12–15	Moscow State Conference.
Aug. 21	New German offensive takes key city of Riga.
Aug. 27–31	Kornilov Affair.
Aug. 31	Bolshevik resolution passes in Petrograd Soviet for first time.
Sep. 1	"Directory," a five-man government headed by Kerensky, established.
Sep. 5	Bolshevik resolution passes in Moscow Soviet.
Sep. 9	Petrograd Soviet confirms Bolshevik resolution and the old Revolutionary Defensist leadership resigns.
Sep. 14–22	Democratic Conference to find a new base of support for Provisional Government; debates forming an all-socialist government but fails to reach agreement.
Sep. 25	Trotsky elected chairman of Petrograd Soviet as Bolshevik-led radical bloc takes control.
Sep. 25	Third coalition government formed under Kerensky.
Oct. 7	"Preparliament" opens; Bolsheviks walk out.

Oct. 10–16	Bolshevik leadership debates seizing power.
Oct. 11–13	Congress of Soviets of the Northern Region.
Oct. 22	"Day of the Petrograd Soviet" with rallies for Soviet power.
Oct. 21–23	Military Revolutionary Committee challenges military authorities over control of garrison.
Oct. 24	Kerensky moves to close Bolshevik newspapers, sparking the October Revolution.
Oct. 24–25	Struggle for control of key points in Petrograd between pro-Soviet and pro-government forces; the former prevail.
Oct. 25	Provisional Government declared deposed; Kerensky flees to front seeking troops; Second Congress of Soviets opens in evening.
Oct. 26	Provisional Government members arrested early morning.
Oct. 26	Second session of Second Congress of Soviets passes decrees on land, on peace and on formation of a new government – Council of People's Commissars.
Oct. 27	Decree establishing censorship of press.
Oct. 27–30	Kerensky–Krasnov attack; it and armed Petrograd opponents defeated.
Oct. 29	Vikzhel appeals for broad socialist government and forces negotiations.
Oct. 26–Nov. 2	First wave of spread of Soviet power across country, culminating in victory in Moscow on Nov. 2.
Nov. 2	Declaration of the Rights of the Peoples of Russia.
Nov. 7	Third Universal proclaims Rada the government of Ukraine.
Nov. 10	Abolition of ranks and titles.
Nov. 12	Elections to Constituent Assembly begin.
Nov. 19	Formal armistice negotiations with Germany and Austria-Hungary, but informal armistices already begun between troops.
Nov. 20	Bolsheviks take over army general staff headquarters.
Nov. 28	Arrest of Kadet Party leaders ordered.
Dec. 2	Formal armistice with Germany and Austria-Hungary.
Dec. 7	Cheka established.
Dec. 11–12	Lenin's theses against the Constituent Assembly.
Mid-Dec.	Further spread of Soviet power in south and at front.
Dec. 12	Left SRs join the government.

Dec. 16, 18	Decrees on divorce, marriage, civil registration.
Jan. 4	Soviet government officially accepts Finnish independence.
Jan. 5	Constituent Assembly opens.
Jan. 6	Constituent Assembly closed by force.

1   The coming of the revolution

The Russian Revolution suddenly broke out in February 1917. It was not unexpected. Russians had long discussed revolution and by late 1916 a sense existed across the entire political and social spectrum that some kind of upheaval could happen at any time. The crisis in Russia was obvious even abroad. "In December, 1916 and still more markedly in January, 1917, there were signs that something important and significant was going on . . . [in Russia that] required exploration, and the rapidly growing rumors of coming political changes called for more accurate knowledge and fuller interpretation."[1] Thus wrote Nicholas Murray Butler of the Carnegie Endowment for International Peace in the United States of the decision to send the Norwegian, Christian Lange, on a fact-finding mission to Russia at the beginning of 1917. Still, when the new year dawned no one inside or outside Russia expected that within two months not only would the old regime be overthrown, but that this would set in swift motion the most radical revolution the world had yet seen. This fast-moving and far-reaching revolution grew out of a complex web of long- and short-term causes which also helped shape its direction and outcome. The latter in turn profoundly affected the global history of the century to follow.

The autocracy

The Russian Revolution was, first, a political revolution that overthrew the monarchy of Nicholas II and made the construction of a new governmental system a central problem of the revolution. At the beginning of the twentieth century Russia was the last major power of Europe in which the monarch was an autocrat, his power unlimited by laws or institutions. Since at least the early nineteenth century the Russian tsars had fought the increasing demands for political change. Then, in 1894, the strong-willed Alexander III died unexpectedly, leaving an ill-prepared Nicholas II as Emperor and Tsar of all the Russias.

Nicholas came to the throne at a time when a rapidly changing world demanded vigorous and imaginative leadership to steer Russia through turbulent times. Nicholas and those he chose to administer his government were unable to provide that. Part of the problem was the very structure of government. The ministers and other high officials were each appointed individually by Nicholas and each reported directly and individually to him. A "government" in the sense of a group of people organized into a unified body of policy makers and executors did not exist. Therefore the emperor had to provide coherence and overall direction. This even more capable men such as his father and grandfather found difficult. For Nicholas, mild-mannered, of limited ability, disliking governance and drawn more to the trivia of administration than to major policy issues, it was impossible. Yet Nicholas clung stubbornly to his autocratic rights, supported vigorously in this by his wife, Alexandra. Alexandra constantly exhorted him to "Never forget that you are and must remain authocratic [sic] emperor," to "show more power and decision," and shortly before the revolution, to "Be Peter the Great, John [Ivan] the Terrible, Emperor Paul – crush them all under you."[2] All her exhortations, however, could not make Nicholas a decisive, much less effective, ruler. They could only reinforce his resistance to needed reforms. Government drifted, problems remained unsolved, and Russia suffered two unsuccessful wars and two revolutions during Nicholas' two decades of rule. A personally kind man and loving husband and father, he became known to his subjects as "Nicholas the Bloody."

   Not only was Nicholas' government poorly run, but it gave little in the way of civil or other rights to the population, who were subjects, not citizens. The government closely controlled the right to form organizations for any purpose, even the most innocuous. Censorship meant an almost complete absence of open political discourse, forcing it into illegal, often revolutionary channels. Alexander II, as part of the Great Reforms of the 1860s, had allowed the formation of zemstvos, noble-dominated local elected councils. These exercised limited rights of self-government at the local level, including working to improve roads, primary education, health and medical care, agricultural practices and other local affairs. However, the monarchs resolutely refused to share supreme political power with popular institutions and after 1881 re-stricted the zemstvos' authority. Shortly after coming to the throne in 1894 Nicholas dismissed hopes for creation of a national zemstvo, a national elected assembly, as "senseless dreams." Rather than create a more modern political system in which the populace became citizens instead of subjects, with at least a modest stake in political life and the future of the state, Nicholas clung to an outmoded autocratic view of God-given ruler and loyal subjects.

Nowhere was the outdated vision of Nicholas' government more apparent than in its treatment of the many non-Russian peoples of the empire. The Russian Empire was a vast multiethnic state in which nationalist sentiments stirred in the late nineteenth and early twentieth centuries. These initially focused on demands for cultural and civil rights and nationality-territorial autonomy. The government responded with repression and "Russification," a variety of policies limiting use of local languages, forcing use of Russian, discriminating on religious grounds, imposing changes in local administrative structures and in other ways attempting to "Russify" non-Russian populations. These measures temporarily hindered development of nationality-based movements while increasing resentments. When the means of repression were removed in 1917, nationalism burst forth as a significant part of the revolution.

The economy and social classes

The Russian Revolution was also, and profoundly, a social revolution. One reason Russia so needed good leadership was that both the economic and social systems were in transition and placing tremendous stresses on the population. Shaken by defeat in the Crimean War of 1854–56, Alexander II launched Russia on a cautious path of reform and modernization known as the Great Reforms. The centerpiece of the reforms was the emancipation of the serfs in 1861. Emancipation gave the peasants their personal freedom and a share of the land, which amounted to about half overall. The peasants, however, were dissatisfied with the emancipation settlement, believing that by right all the land should be theirs. Their claim on the rest of the land remained a source of rural discontent and drove peasant revolution in 1905 and 1917.[a]

In an effort to sustain stable relationships in the countryside and to prevent the peasants from losing control over their newly acquired land, the emancipation of 1861 vested peasant land ownership, in most cases, in the peasant commune rather than in individual families. The reforms preserved the peasant village as a largely self-contained economic and administrative unit. The key decision-making body was the village assembly, composed of heads of households. The assembly elected the village elder and other officials, who dealt with the government and

---

[a] Extremely diverse rural systems existed in Russia: the landless agrarian laborers of the Baltic regions, the relatively prosperous emigrants of West Siberia and German farmers of the Volga, the nomadic herding cultures of Central Asia, the Cossack communities and others. Discussion in this work centers on the Russian and Ukrainian peasantry, who made up a majority of the rural population, upon whom both government and revolutionaries focused their attention, and who drove the peasant revolt of 1917.

outside world. Within the village the assembly settled disputes and dealt with all matters affecting the village as a whole. This included joint responsibility for taxes and, in the Russian heartland, the periodic redistribution of land among the village families. These traditional practices provided a certain equality and security among villagers, but also worked against initiative and improvements in agricultural productivity. They also perpetuated a tradition of collective action that then carried over into the later industrial work force and the soldiers of the revolutionary era.

Emancipation did not bring the expected prosperity for either the peasants or the state. Rapid population growth – the population more than doubled between 1860 and 1914 – in the absence of increased productivity created new hardships. The condition of the rural peasantry varied, but overall little if any per capita economic gain was made. Moreover, the peasantry, over 80 percent of the population at the turn of the century, lived always at the edge of disaster. Families could be pushed over by illness, bad luck or local conditions, while great disasters periodically swept large regions: the famine of 1891–92 alone claimed 400,000 lives. Peasant poverty, the persistence of disparities in land, wealth and privileges between peasants and landowning nobles, and the peasant lust for the land still held by private landowners fueled peasant violence in the revolutions of 1905 and 1917.

By the 1880s many Russian leaders came to realize that Russia could not remain so overwhelmingly agrarian. Industrialization of the country was essential if Russia were to sustain great-power status in a world in which power and industry were increasingly linked. In the 1880s the government took steps to spur industrial development, augmenting efforts of private entrepreneurs through tariffs, fiscal policies and direct investment. Russia enjoyed phenomenal growth. During the 1890s Russian industrial growth rates averaged 7–8 percent annually, and for the period 1885–1914 industrial production increased by an average of 5.72 percent annually, exceeding the American, British and German rates for those years. Percentage growth rates, however, told only part of the story. While Russian iron smelting grew rapidly in percentage terms, total output was still far below those same three countries. Moreover, labor productivity grew only slowly and per capita income fell in the second half of the nineteenth century compared with West European countries.[3] Russia underwent an industrial revolution in the last three decades of imperial Russia, but the economic picture could be seen in either optimistic or pessimistic light, depending on how and against what one measured.

Industrialization brought with it enormous strains on the society.

Tariffs, higher prices and higher taxes held down the standard
of an already poor population who had to wait for any future be
might bring them. Sergei Witte, minister of finance from 1892
and chief architect of the system, acknowledged the stresses in
memorandum to Nicholas in 1899: while Russia was developing "an
industry of enormous size" to which the entire economy's future was
tied, "Its services cost the country too dearly, and these excessive costs
have a destructive influence over the welfare of the population, particularly in agriculture."[4] Moreover, with industrialization came a social
transformation with enormous political implications. The old hierarchy
of legally defined estates (*sosloviia*) – noble, clergy, merchant, peasant
and other – lost much of its meaning and was being replaced by a newer
social structure based on profession and economic function in the new
industrial age. This emerging class structure created identities and
aspirations that played a major role in the coming of the revolution and
in its outcome.

A key part of the new social structure was the industrial work force.
This critically important class did not even exist as a classification under
the old estate system, which grouped them according to the estate from
which they had come, usually as peasants or one of the categories that
included urban lower classes such as artisans or day laborers. Despite
such outdated classifications the industrial workers were a very identifiable new class and several important features made them a potent
revolutionary force. One was the wretched condition in which they
worked and lived. The social tensions inherent in adjusting to the new
urban and factory conditions were great enough, but the terrible
circumstances under which the working class labored and lived made
them even worse. The factories offered long hours (twelve or more), low
pay, unsafe conditions, a harsh and degrading system of industrial
discipline and a total absence of employment security or care if ill or
injured. Housing was overcrowded, unsanitary and lacked privacy.
Many workers lived in barracks, some employing the "ever warm bed"
system by which two workers shared the same bunk, moving between it
and their twelve- to thirteen-hour shifts. Families often shared single
rooms with other families or single workers. The conditions of industry
not only left them poor, but also robbed them of personal dignity.
Alcoholism was rampant, as was disease: cholera epidemics swept
through St. Petersburg every few years. Their social-economic plight
was reflected even in the differences between the middle- and upper-
class districts of the city center with their paved streets, electric lights
and water system, and the outlying workers' districts where dirt (or
mud) streets, kerosene lamps, and filth and disease prevailed.

Efforts by workers and their champions from among the educated classes to organize to improve their lives generally met repression by the government. Indeed, government industrialization policies depended on the economic advantages of cheap labor, of which there seemed an inexhaustible supply. It reflected also the mentality of a ruling class accustomed to thinking of poverty and hard labor as the natural condition of peasants (as most workers were or had recently been). The government failed to create an arena for labor organizing where workers could try to redress their grievances through legal means. This contributed to political radicalization. Because the regime mostly denied workers the right to organize and pursue economic interests legally, they were forced to resort to illegal actions and linkage with the revolutionary parties. The emerging working class was not merely a deeply aggrieved, growing segment of the population, but one that increasingly saw a connection between the political system and their own wretched condition.

An important feature of this new industrial working class was its concentration in a relatively small number of industrial centers, including St. Petersburg and Moscow. This enhanced workers' ability to have an impact politically if they were organized. Within the cities the factories provided a potent focus for organization and mobilization. This was reinforced by the fact that Russian factories tended to be much larger than their Western counterparts. The industrial system brought them together not only in the larger factory, but also in smaller workshops and foundries within it, giving them an inherent organizational structure. The factories thus functioned as natural organizing centers and as bases for revolutionary activity before and during 1917. Factory identity was strong and workers often characterized themselves and recognized others by factory: *Putilovtsy* (workers of the Putilov factory), *Obukhovtsy* (Obukhov factory workers), etc.

Many of the new industrial workers retained close ties to the peasantry, a connection reinforced by the steady flow of recruits from the villages. Some workers returned annually to participate in the harvest and general village life, while others worked in the city only a short time before returning permanently to the village, where their wives and children had often remained. Organized brotherhoods (*zemliachestva*) based on rural regions of origin played an important role in the lives of many urban workers. These ties helped keep alive among urban workers the peasant values of egalitarianism and collective action, as well as a shared hostility to the "masters," whether landowners or industrialists. This helped create the broad lower-class versus upper-classes mentality that played so important a role in 1917.

While peasant attitudes and ties continued to be important, equally or even more significant was the emergence of a specifically working-class identity and values. By the early twentieth century a layer of permanent, more highly skilled, better-educated workers emerged. They led the way in attaining literacy, forming study circles, organizing strikes and demonstrations, and even turning to politics by linking up with the revolutionary parties and by reading their political tracts. The revolutionaries explained the political world and its importance to them. These parties, through their reading circles and discussion groups, opened for some workers a window into a different, better world. Moreover, they explained how to achieve it. Marxism in particular gave an explanation of why factories had emerged, why they had become workers, why their condition was what it was, and told them why and how it must change. A working-class identity developed, not merely as a result of social-economic circumstances, central as those were, but also because of the efforts of revolutionary parties to cultivate a working-class identity among them. This reinforced the lessons of their labor experience, where the state aided employers in suppressing strikes, blocking unions, and enforcing workplace subservience, leading some workers to draw the conclusion that economic improvement required political change. Out of these experiences came the worker-activists who provided leadership for their fellow workers and a linkage between the revolutionary parties and the mass of workers. A cadre of politically oriented worker-activists emerged, their class and political identities hardened by the police and employer persecution that followed activism. They played a central role in the revolution.

The industrial revolution also combined with social and economic forces at work since mid-century to produce a diverse and growing middle class – middle classes might be a better term – different from the traditional legally defined merchant and urban dweller categories. An important part of these new middle classes grew out of the professions, which blossomed in Russia in the second half of the century: teachers, doctors, pharmacists, lawyers, agronomists and others. Industrialization added a new and diverse middle class of engineers, bookkeepers, technicians, managers and small entrepreneurs. To these could be added the growing number of white-collar employees. These middle-class elements came from diverse social origins and not only suffered from a relatively weak sense of common identity and goals, but also lacked political movements devoted to developing a middle-class identity. Indeed, the primary political party spokesman for the interests of these groups after 1905, the liberal Constitutional Democrats, always insisted that the party stood "above classes." An identity was growing, however, encouraged especially in the twentieth century by the growth of professional associations as well as of social, cultural, leisure and sporting clubs that served the new middle classes – more than 600 were listed in Moscow in 1912.[5] These provided forums for exploring their common interests and discussing broader social and political issues. The education and the social-economic significance of this growing middle class gave it importance and provided the social basis for the emergence of a liberal movement demanding political rights and constitutionalism.

Another way to look at the changing society is through the concept of "educated society," which roughly corresponds to what the Russians called *obshchestvo*. "Educated society" encompassed both the new middle classes and large portions of the old nobility and even part of the government bureaucracy. It cut across the traditional legal castes and to some extent even the new economic classes, and its "sense of identity rested on a keen perception that the Russian 'nation' differed from the Russian 'state'" and reflected the "presence of educated Russians determined to work for the common good, for 'progress.'"[6] They led the way in demanding a voice in public affairs for themselves as spokesmen for society at large, and asserted that the old imperial regime could no longer properly manage the affairs of state, at least not as well as they could. The bungled handling of the famine of 1891–92 was especially important in energizing them and in confirming their view that the old regime was bankrupt, and later the Revolution of 1905 and handling of the war effort after 1914 reinforced that belief. Increasingly the spokesmen of the new educated class were referred to as "public men," a reflection of a new self-image. Their view of themselves as new leaders of society against a corrupt regime was hampered, however, by the fact that for the lower classes the notion of "educated society" largely overlapped with that of "privileged Russia." Educated Russians of the upper, middle and professional classes were, to the peasants and workers of the lower classes, "them." This helped set the stage for the sharp social antagonisms of 1917 between "educated" or "privileged" society and "the masses" of workers, peasants, soldiers and even some of the urban lower middle class.

An important subset of educated society, and one reason for the middle class's poor sense of identity, was the "intelligentsia." This primarily intellectual element had evolved out of small circles of nobles in the middle of the nineteenth century discussing public issues to become the most politically involved part of educated society. The intelligentsia was generally characterized by opposition to the existing order in Russia and a strong desire to change it. Out of its radical wing emerged the revolutionary parties, and from the more moderate wing came the political reformers and liberal parties. One of the fundamental beliefs of the nineteenth-century intelligentsia was hostility to "the bourgeoisie," an idea growing out of both noble contempt and West European socialist thought. This mentality persisted, despite the fact that by the early twentieth century the intelligentsia came from all legal classes and were in fact primarily middle class in social-economic terms; mostly they were professionals and white-collar employees of all types. Nonetheless, the ongoing negative image of "bourgeoisie" hampered development of a clear and positive middle-class identity and political movement. Indeed, the term was used as a pejorative in 1917 by both the industrial workers and radical intelligentsia leaders of the socialist parties.

In addition to these social class developments, many other changes were sweeping through Russia of the early twentieth century, consciously or unconsciously challenging the old order and preparing grounds for revolution. A rapid expansion of education by the early twentieth century led to both increased basic literacy and a rapid growth in the number of graduates from university and higher technical institutes. Education, at all levels, opened access to a wide range of information and ideas that directly or indirectly challenged traditional beliefs and social structures, introducing a powerful force for instability in the Russian Empire. Rapid urbanization uprooted people of all classes from established patterns and relationships and created new ones. People saw their world increasingly defined by the jobs they held and by new kinds of social, economic, professional, cultural and other organizations to which they belonged. For the educated elites, major new directions in arts and literature not only confirmed a cultural flowering but spoke to the sense of rapidly changing times. The emergence of a feminist movement, a proliferation of art galleries and museums, impressive new shopping arcades and other features of a changing urban society reinforced that sense. Russia on the eve of war and revolution was a rapidly changing society, with all the attendant dislocations and anxieties. Little wonder that some writers described it as a rapidly modernizing country of immense potential, while others saw a society hurtling toward disaster.

The revolutionary movement

The conjuncture of the development of the intelligentsia, the monarchy's refusal to share political power, and the social and economic problems of Russia produced organized revolutionary movements of exceptional persistence and influence. The most important early revolutionary movement, Populism (*Narodnichestvo*), grew out of the conditions of the middle of the nineteenth century and called for the overthrow of the autocracy and a social revolution that would distribute the land among the peasants. The Populists' problem was how to find a way to mobilize and organize the scattered peasant masses to make a revolution. This led some revolutionaries, organized as "The People's Will," to turn to terrorism. In 1881 they assassinated Alexander II. The result, however, was that the revolutionary movement was temporarily crushed and the governments of Alexander III and then Nicholas II turned toward ever more reactionary policies and away from even the moderate reforms of Alexander II. The revolutionary intelligentsia in turn was forced to rethink revolutionary theory and practice. From this emerged the main revolutionary parties of twentieth-century Russia, the ones that played the key roles in 1917: the Socialist Revolutionaries (SRs) and the Social Democrats (SDs), the latter soon dividing into two major parties, the Bolsheviks and the Mensheviks.

The SR Party organized in 1901 as a party stressing a broad class struggle of all toilers (peasants and urban workers) against exploiters (landowners, factory owners, bureaucrats and middle-class elements). This helped them develop a following among urban industrial workers as well as among peasants. They gave special attention to the peasantry, however, with a demand for socialization of the land and its equal distribution among those who worked it. This guaranteed the SRs the support of the overwhelming mass of the population, the peasants (and thus of the soldiers in 1917). Beyond that they called for a variety of social, economic and political reforms, including the abolition of monarchy and its replacement by a democratic republic. Indeed, their program was often summarized in the slogan "Land and Liberty," a slogan that figured prominently on banners in 1917. Two major problems, however, made it difficult for the SRs to use their peasant support in a revolutionary situation such as 1917: the difficulty of effectively mobilizing widely dispersed peasants for political action, and the party's own loose organizational structure and disagreements on specifics of the general program. Indeed, in 1917 the party split into right, center and left wings.

The rethinking of revolutionary tactics after 1881 led some Russian radicals to Marxism and the Social Democratic movement. Looking at the beginning of industrialization in Russia, G. V. Plekhanov worked out a theory explaining that Russia was becoming capitalist and thus was ripe for the beginning of a socialist movement that focused on the new industrial working class rather than the peasants. Vladimir Lenin carried this a step further in 1902 with *What Is To Be Done?*, in which he argued for forming a small party of professional revolutionaries from the intelligentsia that would both cultivate the necessary revolutionary consciousness among industrial workers and provide leadership in the revolution. Simultaneously several Marxist groups, divided by ideology and strategy, developed in the Russian Empire. In 1903 one group, including Plekhanov, Lenin and Iulii Martov, organized the Second Congress of the Russian Social Democratic Labor Party (RSDLP or, more commonly, SDs). It opened in Belgium, but under police pressure moved on to London. There the organizers split. Lenin demanded a more restrictive party membership, while Martov argued for a broader (but still restricted) one. Lenin and what became the Bolshevik Party put a greater emphasis upon leadership, while Martov and the Mensheviks gave a greater role to the workers themselves.

In the years after 1903 the Bolsheviks and Mensheviks fought over many points of doctrine and became in fact separate parties, the two main Marxist parties, each claiming to be the true voice of the Social Democratic movement. Underlying the specific differences between the two parties were fundamentally different outlooks about party organization and relationship to the workers, which significantly affected behavior in 1917. Lenin proceeded to create a party emphasizing a higher degree of centralization and discipline and which exalted the importance of leadership and distrusted initiative from below. Martov, Plekhanov and others slowly developed Menshevism as a somewhat more diffuse, often divided, movement. By 1917 Menshevism emerged as more genuinely democratic in spirit and with a moderate wing willing to cooperate with other political groups for reform. Personal animosities from the years of partisan ideological squabbling among the Social Democratic intelligentsia, especially the emigres, would carry over into the actions in 1917. Indeed, in 1917 as in 1903 and after, Lenin's hard line and domineering personality would polarize political life.

Soon after the socialist parties took form, new issues emerged that divided them in the years before 1917. Two were especially significant for the history of the revolution. One set of issues involved the debate over whether to abandon underground revolutionary activity in favor of legal work and the closely related question of relations with the liberal parties and the middle classes they were assumed to represent. This became especially important with the legalization of political parties after the Revolution of 1905 and was a major source of division among Mensheviks and between Mensheviks and Bolsheviks. The SRs were also torn by these issues, which produced several small splinter parties as well as divisions within the SR Party. Lenin turned the Bolshevik

Party resolutely against cooperation with liberals and toward the idea of moving swiftly through revolutionary stages to a "proletarian" revolution, while some Mensheviks and SRs accepted the importance of legal political work and even cooperation with liberals in the early stage of the revolutionary transformation. This dispute helped shape the image of the Mensheviks as the more moderate wing of social democracy and the Bolsheviks as the more radical and uncompromising. It also had important implications for the question of cooperation with liberals and of "coalition" governments in 1917.

The second major controversy to divide socialists was the appropriate response toward national defense in World War I. Most European socialists, but only a minority of Russian socialists, supported their countries' war efforts and were dubbed "Defensists." Russian Defensists stressed solidarity with the Western democracies and insisted that they supported only defense against German domination. Other socialists, including most Russian socialists, refused to support their national war efforts, repudiated the war as an imperialist venture and called for socialist unity to find a way to end it; they came to be called Internationalists. The Defensist versus Internationalist controversy split all the Russian revolutionary parties, the Mensheviks and the SRs especially but the Bolsheviks as well. Although often obscured by the continued use of party labels, this Defensist–Internationalist alignment was fundamental. It often was more important than party affiliations and carried into and became central to the politics of 1917.

Alongside the emergence of the revolutionary socialist parties, a liberal and reformist political movement developed in the early twentieth century. Drawing upon the ideas of West European liberalism and the emergence of a larger urban middle class, liberalism belatedly took hold in Russia. It emphasized constitutionalism, parliamentary government, rule of law, and civil rights, within either a constitutional monarchy or a republic. It also stressed the importance of major social and economic reform programs, but rejected both socialism and the radical intelligentsia's traditional call for sweeping revolution. Liberalism first took organized political form as the Union of Liberation, founded in 1903–04. Then during the Revolution of 1905 the Constitutional Democratic Party (Kadets) emerged.[b] The Kadets developed as the major voice of political liberalism and for the aspirations of the growing middle classes. In 1917 they would become the only important non-

[b] Kadet (also spelled Cadet) was an acronym based on the first syllables of the party's name; it should not be confused with military cadets (junkers), who played a role later in 1917. The party's official name in February 1917 was Party of the People's Freedom, although that name is rarely met in writings about them.

socialist party and their leader, Paul Miliukov, a history professor at Moscow University, one of the men responsible for the formation of the Provisional Government.

By the early 1900s Russia was undergoing rapid social-economic changes, suffering from old and new discontents, and witnessing the emergence of political movements devoted to transforming Russia. This combination set the stage for a revolutionary upheaval. That came in 1905 when, in the midst of an unpopular and unsuccessful war against Japan, a particular event provided the spark to ignite discontents into revolutionary turmoil. That spark was Bloody Sunday.

The Revolution of 1905 and the Duma era

The Russian government, in an attempt to cope with worker discontents, experimented with allowing formation of workers' unions under police supervision and with a limited range of activities. One such was the Assembly of Russian Factory Workers, organized in St. Petersburg by a priest, Father Gapon. Under pressure from workers for more forceful action, Gapon and the assembly organized a great demonstration for Sunday, January 9, 1905. Workers would march to the Winter Palace, carrying religious icons and portraits of Nicholas, to present a petition asking for redress of grievances. The government decided to block the demonstration. Troops and police fired into the packed masses of men, women and children, killing and wounding hundreds.

"Bloody Sunday" shocked Russia. Riots and demonstrations broke out across the country, continuing through the spring and summer despite both repressive measures and minor concessions from the government. Workers struck and clashed with police. In the countryside the peasants attacked landlords and government officials. Students and middle-class elements demanded civil rights, constitutional government and social reform. Mutinies broke out in the armed forces, the most spectacular being the revolt on the cruiser *Potemkin* in June. A general strike in October immobilized the country. Workers' soviets (councils), which were combination strike committees and political forums, emerged in many cities in the summer and fall, including St. Petersburg and Moscow. Overall, however, the many revolts occurring simultaneously lacked unified leadership and direction.

Confronted by the seemingly endless waves of disorders, Nicholas' government wavered between compromising and attempting to suppress them by massive force. Finally Nicholas' advisors convinced him to make much more sweeping concessions than he wished. On October 17,

1905, Nicholas signed a manifesto promising expanded civil rights and the election of a legislature, the Duma. The "October Manifesto" divided the opposition. Some accepted it as a new beginning, but others vowed to fight on until the complete overthrow of the monarchy. Indeed, rural and industrial unrest grew after October, joined by demonstrations among non-Russian minorities demanding greater civil rights. The government, however, felt that it could now reassert control. In November it easily arrested the leaders of the St. Petersburg Soviet, but suppressed the revolution in Moscow and the Moscow Soviet in December only after bitter street fighting in which hundreds died. Army detachments subdued rebellious peasants across the countryside, with thousands killed and tens of thousands exiled. At the same time right-wing groups known as "Black Hundreds" attacked non-Russians and radicals and launched pogroms against Jews in many cities. In 1906 the government gradually reasserted control over the country.

The Revolution of 1905 produced mixed results. It forced major changes in the political system, including limited civil rights and an elected legislature with the right to approve all laws. The traditional autocracy was ended, though Nicholas retained very extensive power. On the other hand, the imperial government soon chipped away at the changes made in 1905, while demands for a full parliamentary democracy, distribution of land to peasants, basic improvements in the lives of industrial workers and other reforms remained unfulfilled. Nicholas ruled over a sullen populace of permanently politicized workers and of peasants who expressed their discontent through petty harassment of landlords and officials, and sometimes more violently. Moreover, the major ingredients of the revolt persisted after 1905. These included worker discontents, peasant unrest, middle-class aspirations for civil rights and a larger voice in governance, and the government's own determination to hold on to power. Thus if the other key ingredient of 1905, war and soldier discontent, was again added into the mix, all the elements of that revolution would again be present.

In many respects whatever chance Russia had of avoiding another revolution rested with the new legislative system. If it functioned well it could not only address the demands of the growing middle class for political participation, but also perhaps could produce a government sufficiently attuned to popular aspirations to be able to address some of the more pressing social and economic discontents of the lower classes. These were big ifs. They depended not only on the Duma, but first of all on the behavior of Nicholas II.

Nicholas and his closest advisors, once they survived the revolutionary turmoil, regretted the October Manifesto. Some wanted Nicholas to repudiate it, but he refused to violate his solemn word – this was a point of honor. Therefore Nicholas provided for elections to the Duma and issued the Fundamental Laws outlining the structure of the new government. It provided for a sharing of power among Nicholas, his government ministers and the two houses of the legislature, the Duma and the State Council. The Duma was elected on a broad if not entirely representative franchise. The State Council was intended as a conservative check on the popularly elected Duma, with half the Council's members appointed by Nicholas and the other half elected mostly by the clergy or wealthy groups. The arrangement, which probably would have been greeted joyously a year earlier, was a sore disappointment to the liberals and their middle-class constituency after 1905. They saw its chief defect to be the absence of parliamentary responsibility, i.e., that the government, the Council of Ministers, be responsible to a majority in the legislature, in the British pattern. Instead the monarch appointed and dismissed the members of the Council of Ministers, issued emergency decrees, dismissed the Duma when it pleased him and generally still dominated the machinery of government, including the secret police. Nicholas retained the title "autocrat" and continued to think of himself as such rather than as a constitutional monarch. The Duma's main authority was that its approval was necessary for all new laws. It was, however, unable to enact new legislation that might address basic social or other problems, as all new laws required the approval of the conservative State Council and of Nicholas himself.

The first two Dumas contested political power with Nicholas. When the first Duma elections returned a liberal majority led by the Kadet Party, the latter determined to push for immediate reform of the government structure to include ministerial responsibility. When the Duma opened in April 1906 the Duma leaders clashed with Nicholas' government over a number of specific issues, especially land reform, but the underlying question was the balance of power. In July Nicholas exercised the monarch's right to dissolve the Duma and call new elections. Nicholas and his advisors hoped that the new elections, farther removed from the turmoil of 1905, would return a more conservative majority. The first Duma had only a weak conservative wing to match a similarly weak radical left wing (most socialist parties officially boycotted the elections). New elections for the second Duma did indeed alter its composition, but not in the way the government had hoped. The socialist parties entered the elections in force and made impressive gains at the expense of the liberals, while conservatives did not gain; the second Duma was politically well to the left of the first. When it opened on March 6, 1907, bitter conflict quickly proved that there were no grounds for fruitful work between the radicalized Duma and the ever more resistant and ultraconservative government.

The government now took drastic steps under the energetic leadership of the newly appointed minister-president, Peter Stolypin. In June he had Nicholas again dissolve the Duma and call new elections. The government then took advantage of a provision in the Fundamental Laws under which the government could pass laws while the Duma was not in session, but which then required approval by the Duma at its next session. Using this, Stolypin changed the electoral system to effectively disenfranchise most of the population through a complex system of indirect and unequal voting that gave large landowners and wealthy individuals vastly disproportionate strength. One percent of the population now elected a majority of the Duma. By this maneuver Stolypin produced a third Duma with a conservative majority which then sanctioned the changes and worked with the government. The Duma retained some authority, but the predominance of power clearly rested with Nicholas and his ministers.

The strike at the Duma had profound consequences for revolution in Russia. First, the prospects for meeting the political, social and economic aspirations of Russian society peacefully and through measured change waned, while the likelihood of a new revolution increased dramatically. Second, these actions underscored the extent to which Nicholas still saw himself as an autocrat rather than as a constitutional monarch, thus keeping alive a broad popular belief in the necessity of revolution. Third, the unrepresentative nature of the transformed Duma meant that, although the Duma leaders could play a significant role in the February Revolution, the Duma would be unsuitable as the country's government after the February Revolution, thus launching Russia on a more radical and uncertain political path than it might have had the Duma remained more representative.

While Nicholas' government successfully manipulated the Duma to avoid the immediate political threat to its authority, it was unsuccessful in reducing economic and social problems. The government did, to its credit, make an imaginative effort to deal with peasant discontent. Stolypin undertook to break up the traditional peasant communal landholding and strip-farming system and replace it with a system in which each peasant held his land in full ownership. This, he hoped, would introduce a much needed improvement in agricultural productivity and produce a class of prosperous, conservative small farmers who would one day provide a social-political base of support for the monarchy. Stolypin's death in 1911 and the outbreak of war in 1914 cut short the "Stolypin reforms" and left the peasant problem unresolved. Indeed, whatever the government's efforts – and they were halting and their efficacy debatable – the underlying reality was that the years before 1914 were not peaceful ones in the Russian countryside. Peasant disturbances, suppressed by force after 1905, revived. The years 1910–14 saw 17,000 in European Russia alone.[7] While both government and political parties debated the nature of peasant distress and how to deal with it, for the peasants the answer remained simple: the redistribution of all land to themselves.

The government made even less effort to address the grievances and growing alienation of the industrial workers and the urban lower classes generally. About 1910 a new spurt of industrial growth began. This led to a rapid growth of the industrial work force and, from 1912, of industrial tensions. After the Lena Goldfield massacre of 1912, in which about 200 striking workers were killed, a much more assertive strike and labor protest movement emerged. The growing strike movement led finally to a great strike in July 1914 that was both violent and widespread. These strikes were a mixture of economic, social and political protests, tightly commingled. The regime's traditional support for employers in labor disputes had long ago taught the industrial workers the close connections between economic and political issues. By this time it was a common view that a change of the political regime, probably including the overthrow of the monarchy, was essential to attaining the general goals of bettering their condition. Indeed, the strike movement of 1912–14 appears to have led to a political radicalization of industrial workers and an orientation toward more radical wings of the revolutionary parties. Where the strike movement might have led – some saw a new revolution looming – is unknown, for it was suddenly choked off by the outbreak of war in August 1914.

World War I and its discontents

The war was central both to the coming of the revolution and to its outcome. It put enormous strains on the population and dramatically increased popular discontent. It undermined the discipline of the Russian army, thereby reducing the government's ability to use force to suppress the increased discontent. Whether Russia, absent the war, might have avoided revolution is a question that is ultimately unanswerable. What is certain is that, even if a revolution was probable or inevitable, the war profoundly shaped the revolution that did occur.

Russia was poorly prepared for the war, militarily, industrially and politically. The first campaigns of 1914 revealed the Russian shortcomings in weaponry, especially the inadequate number of new weapons such as machine-guns and the disastrous shortage of artillery shells. Russia's weak industrial base, compared to other combatants, had a difficult time overcoming these shortages. The 1914 campaign also revealed serious weaknesses in the command staff and culminated in shattering defeats, although there were successes to the south against the Austro-Hungarian armies.

The battles of early 1915 only reinforced awareness of these shortcomings. A horrified British military attache, General Alfred Knox, observed that because of a shortage of rifles "Unarmed men had to be sent into the trenches to wait till their comrades were killed or wounded and their rifles became available."[8] German heavy artillery bombardments, to which the Russians lacked the guns and shells to reply, buried Russian units before they ever saw an enemy. The Russian armies were routed in a chaotic retreat. The minister of war, General A. A. Polivanov, reported to the Council of Ministers on July 16, 1915, that "The soldiers are without doubt exhausted by the continued defeats and retreats. Their confidence in final victory and in their leadership are undermined. Ever more threatening signs of impending demoralization are evident."[9] To add to the catalogue of problems, the military high command applied a scorched-earth policy as the Russian armies retreated, thus sending hordes of refugees eastward where they overtaxed communication lines and became a permanent source of problems and discontents in Russia's cities.

By the end of 1915 Russia had lost a large and rich slice of empire in the west: all of Poland and parts of Ukraine, Belorussia and the Baltic region. Even worse, Russia's armies in 1915 lost about two and half million men in addition to the million and a half already killed, wounded or taken prisoner in 1914. Although in 1916 the Russian army was better equipped than previously, the campaigns of that year failed to see any major Russian breakthrough and losses were heavy. By the end of 1916 Russia had lost about 5,700,000 men, 3,600,000 of them dead or seriously wounded, the rest prisoners of war.[10] Even the military high command, which had squandered lives recklessly, began to realize that Russia was approaching the end of what had earlier appeared to be an almost bottomless supply of manpower. The horrendous losses shattered the morale of the soldiers. The suffering inflicted on the soldiers, their families, refugees and other segments of the population are important to understanding the revolt of the soldiers in 1917 and the impatient demand for an end to the war that dominated politics during the revolution.

The outbreak of the war initially caused a political rallying to defense of the country and an end of strike activities, but that very quickly changed.[c] Defeat and government mismanagement led to widespread discontent among all segments of society. Particularly important was the emergence of growing hostility to the government from within educated society, drawing on conservative as well as liberal political circles. They based their opposition to the government both on a patriotic demand for a more efficient prosecution of the war and on an attempt to use the war crisis to force fundamental changes in the political system (as had happened in 1905). This opposition expressed itself through both the Duma and a variety of organizations and societies where politically oriented members of educated society could gather, exchange opinions and work for change.

Among the many nongovernmental organizations that provided vehicles for educated society to voice its growing frustration with the government's handling of the war effort, the War Industries Committee and Zemgor were particularly important. The Central War Industries Committee (hereafter, the WIC) and its local branches were created by industrialists for the purpose of coordinating and increasing war production, and sanctioned by the government. In July 1915 Alexander Guchkov, leader of the moderate conservative Octobrist Party, became chairman and A. I. Konovalov, a leader of the liberal, business-oriented Progressist Party, vice-chairman. Zemgor, the joint effort of the All-Russia Union of Towns and the All-Russia Union of Zemstvos, headed by Prince G. E. Lvov, undertook to organize aid for the wounded, sick and displaced, as they had during the Russo-Japanese War a decade earlier. Because of the extended nature of the war and heavy casualties, both the WIC and Zemgor soon took on important public and political roles. They brought together a broad circle of politically active moderate conservatives and liberals from the industrial and business community, the academic world, the landowning nobility and city and local government.

There were many other organizations in which men with a concern for public affairs and holding similar beliefs could come together to discuss events. One was a revived Freemason movement. Masonic lodges in Moscow and Petrograd included prominent political figures and provided vehicles for discussion across party and nonparty lines. Membership even included politically active royalists such as Grand Duke Nikolai Mikhailovich. Several members of the first Provisional Government were members, many of them also in the WIC, Zemgor or the State Duma. Less overtly political but still important places where

---

[c] During this early patriotic surge the capital's name was changed from the Germanic sounding St. Petersburg to the Russian Petrograd, which remained its name for 1914–24 and will be used for the rest of this book.

blic could discuss the issues of the day were the many
ιd professional associations such as the Free Economic
ε Pirogov Medical Society, the Russian Technological
Russian Society of Engineers and others, as well as social
the universities and polytechnical institutes. All of these
ρ.. εhicles for members of educated society to meet each other,
discuss issues and find the extent to which they shared broad values and
outlooks on political matters.

These and other public organizations, working with the approval of
and often in co-operation with government bureaucracies to mobilize
resources for the war effort, created a "parastatal complex," a network
of professional and public organizations closely intertwined with the
state.[11] These became more important than political party organizations, which tended to wither during the war. Participation in these
parastatals also encouraged a more vigorous identification with the
Russian state – but not the current government thereof – among the
educated classes, across party lines. This greater state-consciousness
had important consequences for their behavior when they became the
governing class in 1917. The very existence and activity of these
parastatal groups was a rebuke to the government and an implied
assertion that educated society could better manage Russia's affairs.
Moreover, they represented a potential replacement government.
Indeed, men active in these organizations became an important part of
the first Provisional Government in 1917: Lvov became its head, two
other members had been active in Zemgor, and four came from the
leadership of the WIC, including Guchkov and Konovalov.

The same social and political strata also pressured the government
through the Duma. Dismayed by the early military defeats and mismanagement, moderate conservatives and liberal political leaders in the
Duma formed the "Progressive Bloc" in the summer of 1915. This was
a broad coalition of all factions except the extreme left and extreme
right, based especially on the Octobrist, Kadet and Progressist Parties.
The Progressive Bloc called for a series of measures that its members
felt were essential for the successful conclusion of the war. First and
foremost was the creation of a government enjoying "public confidence"
and which would work with the Duma. They also called for "decisive
change in the methods of administration," greater civil rights for non-
Russian nationalities, meeting the pressing needs of workers and other
reforms.[12] Some government ministers supported their position.

It appeared for a moment in 1915 that the government's critics might
successfully use the war and attendant problems to force Nicholas II to
agree to significant reform of the political system. Pressure from the

Duma and from industrial circles led in the summer of 1915 to the dismissal of some of the more ultraconservative and anti-Duma ministers. So confident were the reformers that speculation about the membership of a new government began to circulate; on August 13th and 14th the newspaper *Utro Rossii* published two lists of a possible new government, both dominated by the Octobrists, Kadets and Progressists from the Duma, the WIC and Zemgor. Most of the men on these and similar lists circulated in 1915 actually did become members of the Provisional Government in 1917, revealing the general consensus in educated society about the basic political contours and membership of a desirable future government.

These reform hopes of 1915 were soon disappointed. Nicholas saw the demands of the Progressive Bloc as a threat to his authority. Instead of appointing the kind of government it expected, he dismissed the pro-Duma members of the government and suspended the Duma session in September. This followed his decision in August 1915, against the advice of his ministers, to go to the front and take personal command of the army. This decision in turn allowed Empress Alexandra to play a larger role in government affairs in Petrograd, and she was an adamant foe of any kind of political concession. Indeed, she had a visceral hatred of the Duma and reform leaders. She wrote to Nicholas that she would "quietly and with a clear conscience . . . have sent *Lvov* to Siberia, . . . *Miliukov, Guchkov & Polivanov* also to Siberia."[13]

The quality of the government deteriorated rapidly as more competent ministers, many of whom had supported working with the Duma or opposed Nicholas' decision to go to the front, were dismissed in early 1916. A rapid succession of lesser men replaced them, often appointed at the urging of Empress Alexandra. The latter in turn relied increasingly on the advice of Gregory Rasputin, the disreputable semi-literate peasant "holy man," who in her letters to Nicholas she called "our Friend." His influence grew because of Alexandra's belief that only he could save the life of her son and the heir to the throne, Alexis, who suffered from the incurable disease of hemophilia. This was reinforced by her own increasingly hysterical conviction that only she and Rasputin could guide Nicholas to the right decisions. "And guided by Him [Rasputin] we shall get though this heavy time. It will be hard fighting, but a Man of God [Rasputin] is near to guard yr. [your] boat safely through the reefs – little Sunny [Alexandra] is standing as a rock behind you, firm and unwavering."[14] Besides his insidious influence on Alexandra and government, Rasputin's sordid personal life, which was common knowledge, tarnished the royal family and alienated many conservatives, even imperial relatives. Equally important, rumors of his having had intimate relations with Alexandra or Nicholas' daughters circulated widely, discrediting Nicholas in the eyes of many of the common people, including soldiers and-lower rank officers.[15] Rasputin's assassination in December 1916 by ultraconservatives, including a relative of Nicholas, not only was inadequate to solve Russia's political problems, but also underscored Nicholas and Alexandra's growing isolation and weakness.

As hopes to use the war crisis to reform the government ran into the intransigence of Nicholas, the Progressive Bloc members and reform advocates moved in three directions. One group, represented by Miliukov, continued to pressure the government from within the Duma, hoping that military reverses and the rising tide of popular discontent would force Nicholas to make concessions as they had in 1905. On November 1, 1916, Miliukov, speaking in the Duma, attacked the government bitterly and demanded change. He asserted that, if the Germans wanted to stir up trouble and disorder, "they could not do better than to act as the Russian Government has acted." Describing both the failures of the government and the "dark rumors of treachery and treason" circulating in the country, he posed the question of "What is it, stupidity or treason?"[16] The speech electrified public opinion. Miliukov's sentiments were echoed soon afterwards by V. M. Purishkevich, a leader of the extreme right in the Duma, underscoring the breadth of political hostility to the current group of government ministers and, indirectly, to Alexandra. Both speeches reflected how widespread was the belief that many high government and court officials were pro-German or even in German pay.[d]

At the same time other important political and military figures were coming to the conclusion that some kind of palace revolution might be necessary to remove Nicholas – and with him Alexandra – from the throne and direction of Russia's affairs. They believed that only such a drastic move could improve the government's ability to prosecute the war, head off a popular revolt and save the Russian state. Alexander

---

[d] By the end of 1916 the idea of a pervasive pro-German treason at the highest levels had permeated all strata of society as an explanation for defeats and government mismanagement. Rumors circulated of "German officers" (many Russian noble families and officers had German names, mostly dating from the eighteenth-century annexation of the Baltic region) deliberately sending Russian peasant soldiers to their deaths. Empress Alexandra was of German birth and several court and government officials had German names, which gave rise to rumors of pro-German sentiment, even betrayal, at the highest level. By 1916 even some aristocrats referred to Alexandra as "the German woman." These charges were untrue. Belief in a German hand behind Russia's political and military problems continued to affect politics through the year 1917, long after the overthrow of the Romanovs, but with different groups now identified as the "German agents."

Guchkov, who figured prominently in talks about a coup, wanted a palace revolution because he feared that if political change came because of a popular revolt, then "the streets would rule" instead of "responsible" public figures, leading to the collapse of authority, Russia and the front.[17] Other individuals, including Prince Lvov and members of the royal family, were engaged in similar discussions. Some key generals were aware of these talks. At a gathering of political figures at Rodzianko's house in January 1917, General A. M. Krymov declared that "The feeling in the army is such that all will greet with joy the news of a coup d'etat. It has to come . . . we will support you."[18] Bruce Lockhart, the British consul in Petrograd, reported to the British ambassador in December 1916 that "Last night I dined alone with the Chief of Staff [probably G. I. Gurko]. He said to me that 'the Emperor will not change. We shall have to change the Emperor.'"[19] The February Revolution preempted these discussions, but they helped prepare military and political circles for the idea of Nicholas' abdication as a way to solve Russia's political problems. This proved to be important in February 1917.

The third strategy of some Progressive Bloc and WIC leaders was to forge links with the moderate socialists and to use the growing popular discontent to force political change. Konovalov and Nikolai Nekrasov, a leader of the left wing of the Kadets, represented this approach. Impressed on the one hand by Nicholas' intransigence and on the other by rising popular discontents, they sought a way to link their own political objectives to popular discontents in a liberal–socialist alliance. They hoped this could be accomplished via the Workers' Group of the WIC. Founded in 1915 to enlist cooperation from the industrial workers in the war effort, the Workers' Group was under the leadership of moderate and Defensist socialists, mostly Mensheviks. Some of the Workers' Group, notably K. A. Gvozdev, a Menshevik, seemed willing to cooperate with the liberals, although they were also under pressure from the workers to adopt more aggressive tactics in connection with the strikes of late 1916 and early 1917. This tentative wartime alliance of liberals and moderate socialists facilitated the later negotiations leading to the formation in 1917 of the Provisional Government and even later of the "coalition" governments.

What precipitated the overthrow of Nicholas' government was none of these strategies, although each contributed to the outcome of the February Revolution, but a popular revolt that arose out of the severe social and economic problems that predated the war and which it exacerbated. The war created serious dislocations in the economy as the government drafted fifteen million men and diverted resources, production and transport to war needs. This deprived the population of necessary manufactured goods and stimulated inflation. The railroad system, already suffering from rolling stock shortages in 1914, was in near collapse by late 1916 and unable to move adequate amounts of industrial or civilian goods. By late 1916 the population suffered from a shortage of goods of "prime necessity" such as soap, kerosene, firewood, textiles, boots and sugar. Food shortages in the major cities added to the problems and the government was forced to introduce some rationing of foodstuffs. A police agent wrote that "Resentment is felt worse in large families, where children are starving in the most literal sense of the word."[20]

The shortages of food and other goods produced riots as early as 1915, riots which sometimes took on political dimensions when crowds abused and threw rocks at police, who were the visible daily representation of the tsarist government. Soldiers' wives, the *soldatki*, had a special sense of entitlement because their husbands were at the front, and were particularly active in food disorders across Russia. In July 1916 rioting soldiers' wives in the Don Cossack territory tore down the tsar's portrait and trampled it while pillaging a local merchant's shop. More ominously for the regime, Cossacks restrained an official in the Don territory who threatened Cossack wives during food riots in August 1916 – asserting that he had no right to threaten women whose husbands were at the front.[21] These Cossack attitudes foreshadowed soldier behavior in February 1917 toward demonstrators.[e] Women predominated in these goods riots, and the February Revolution would begin in no small part out of a women workers' protest demanding bread, while the food supply and other economic dislocations continued to be a serious source of popular discontent throughout the revolution.

Life in the cities, especially Petrograd, became harder. Millions of refugees from the western regions flooded in. They, plus the influx of new workers for expanding industry and of soldiers into the garrisons, overtaxed housing and municipal services, which worsened even beyond the wretched prewar conditions for the lower classes. By winter 1916–17 a serious fuel shortage confronted the populace. A report of

---

[e] Cossacks were a special military caste who received certain legal and economic privileges in return for military obligations, mostly as cavalry. Because of their privileges, military spirit and traditional contempt for peasants and townsmen, they had come to be regarded as reliable supporters of the monarchy and were often used to suppress demonstrations. Hence their actions here and in February 1917 had special significance, which the population immediately recognized. Throughout 1917 the political left feared and the political right hoped that the Cossacks would be a conservative force; both left and right misread the complex impulses of the Cossacks in the revolution and the civil war that followed.

February 1917 stated that in Petrograd apartments the temperature rarely rose above 52–59 degrees Fahrenheit (9–12 °Celsius), while in many public and work places it was even lower, about 44–50 degrees Fahrenheit (6–8 °Celsius).[22] Police in 1916 reported that complaints "against the intolerable conditions of daily existence have begun to be heard . . . The impossibility of even buying many food products and necessities, the time wasted standing idle in queues to receive goods, the increasing incidence of disease due to malnutrition and unsanitary living conditions."[23] Some women workers found new job opportunities in a male-depleted work force, but many more, with husbands taken to the army, found themselves the sole or main support of families while faced with impossible work and household toil. Police reports insisted that "mothers, exhausted from standing endlessly at the tail of queues, and having suffered so much in watching their half-starving and sick children, are perhaps much closer to a revolution than" the Duma leaders.[24] A thick tension hung in the air, tinged with more than a little desperation. "The mood of anxiety," wrote a police agent, "growing daily more intense, is spreading to ever wider sections of the populace. Never have we observed such nervousness as there is now."[25]

The war and its economic problems both mobilized and radicalized the industrial workers. Wartime production pressures led to deteriorating working conditions, longer hours and harsher punishments for strikes or labor infractions (including being drafted and sent to the front), while the deterioration of urban services and the scarcity of foodstuffs and consumer goods affected workers as well as others of the poorer urban population. Moreover, the social, industrial and political sources of conflict that had led to the great upsurge of strikes on the eve of the war still existed. Strikes again increased as workers were able, despite wartime suppression, to use underground unions and strike organizations as well as the few legal organizations available to them as a means to keep struggling to improve their lives. The figures for those factories under the supervision of the factory inspectorate tell the story dramatically. January–July 1914 saw 1,327,897 strikers. This dropped to 9,561 for August–December 1914, after the war broke out. In 1915 the number rose to 539,528 and in 1916 to 957,075.[26] As 1917 opened a new strike wave exploded. On January 9, the anniversary of Bloody Sunday, 186,000 workers, most of them in Petrograd, struck. Strikes continued at a furious pace in January and February 1917, far beyond that in 1916. Not only were the numbers of strikes increasing, but their character was more threatening. For one thing, an increasing percentage was classified by authorities as "political" in nature. Antiwar sentiments became more pronounced. Slogans and speeches reflected a growing perception that their problems could not be remedied without radical political change. This meant that both workers and educated society agreed about the need for a change of political regimes, although they perhaps had different changes in mind. A second key feature of the strikes was that they were especially concentrated in the largest industrial centers, and Petrograd in particular. This focused the explosion of political, social and economic anger where it could have the greatest political effect.

The deteriorating conditions in society drew the attention of the revolutionary parties as well as that of the police. The strikes of 1915–16 energized the socialist parties to capitalize on popular discontents to try to promote, even lead, any revolution that might be developing. All the socialist parties increased their activity at the factories and also at higher educational institutions and even in army garrisons. By late 1916 this had grown, in Petrograd and other large cities, into a significant presence, although broader organizational structures and leadership remained fragile even where existent at all. They also managed to issue an increasing number of manifestos, leaflets and other antiregime propaganda. Some of these were distributed by hand, but they were also read aloud or used as the basis for speeches. In January 1917 Workers' Group socialists got a good reception when they read out a typewritten leaflet in Petrograd factories blaming the government for the enormous war casualties, the food crisis and other problems.[27] The series of strikes in January–February 1917 leading up to the revolution were a combination of unplanned actions sparked by worker grievances or circumstances (such as the labor dispute and lockout at the Putilov plant on February 19–22), and demonstrations planned ahead by the socialist parties (those of January 9 and February 14, for example).

The major socialist party leaders and theoreticians were in exile, but significant numbers of second-level leaders were in Petrograd. These leaders struggled to organize themselves and find a common approach to the gathering crisis. Meetings in Petrograd in November 1916 included both Defensists and Internationalists from all parties. These led to creation of an Interparty Informational Bureau, which debated the prospects for revolution and tactics, and especially whether or not to cooperate with the Progressive Bloc and the WIC in a broad antiregime alliance. Despite inability to agree on specific tactics, they continued to meet and to try to stimulate and influence the rising strike movement. They believed that any major strike or demonstration *might* be the event starting revolution and therefore pressed for continuation of strikes in late 1916 and early 1917. The nature and amount of activity by the socialist parties on the eve of the revolution, the extent of their contact with factory-level activists and how much influence they had on events remain frustratingly unclear. Post-Soviet archival revelations suggest that it may have been more extensive and more important than previously thought, especially by parties other than the Bolsheviks. Certainly the activity and visibility of many of the participants in the interparty meetings – including the Duma deputies Alexander Kerensky (Trudovik[f]) and Nicholas Chkheidze (Menshevik), Workers' Group leaders like K. A. Gvozdev, and radicals like Alexander Shliapnikov of the Bolsheviks and Peter Alexandrovich of the SRs – help explain their leadership in the formation of the Petrograd Soviet on February 27.[28] Still, the extent to which the socialist parties helped start the revolution or merely capitalized on a popular revolt remains uncertain.

The war added yet a new social factor to the restive workers and educated society: discontented soldiers. After the devastating casualties of 1914–16, anger and despair at their dangerous lot drove them to the brink of rebellion. Several small-scale unit mutinies and refusals to return to front-line positions took place in 1916. Self-wounding and desertion rates rose. Front soldiers wanted out of the carnage, new draftees at the rear garrisons dreaded marching orders, while recuperating wounded desperately hoped to avoid being sent back to the fighting. To these natural fears were added social tensions within the military. The rank and file of the army were composed mainly of peasants, with workers and other urban lower-class elements making up the rest. The officer corps was drawn mostly from educated society, noble and non-noble. For the peasants and workers of the army rank and file, the harsh and degrading terms of service seemed a continuation of serfdom, of a servitude in which they were at the complete mercy of the officer, whom they saw as an extension of the "lord," the "master." Between officers and men a vast gap loomed. To compound the social division, the very purpose of the war divided them. Educated society adopted a strongly nationalist outlook after 1914. The peasant and worker masses, on the other hand, quickly lost interest in the goals of the war, seeing it as a purposeless slaughter, a heavy burden they carried for the benefit of others. Their alienation, fears and resentments prepared them for their role in the revolution.

Moreover, the defeats and the political situation politicized the soldiers, especially the rear garrisons and the capital. The expansion of the army during the war meant that many conscripts brought their civilian

---

[f] The Trudoviks (Toilers) were moderate agrarian socialists, a parliamentary offshoot of the Socialist Revolutionaries (SRs); Kerensky in 1917 was usually referred to as simply an SR.

political beliefs with them. Many new junior officers from educated society held liberal or socialist political beliefs, and some were party members. Lower-class draftees likewise brought their social grievances and political attitudes with them into the ranks. Many soldiers of the Petrograd garrison were of local, often working-class background – some had been drafted for striking – and maintained extensive contacts with the local population. These preexisting party affiliations and continued contact with the civilian population provided a natural conduit for political agitation in the army, including even the forming of small socialist party cells. The SR Party managed to create a Northern Military Organization, of unclear size, in the Petrograd garrison and other garrisons behind the Northern Front. Given that the ultimate loyalty of the army had allowed the crushing of the 1905 Revolution, the socialists were aware of the importance of revolutionary agitation among soldiers. Widespread discussion of events – strikes, Duma criticism of the government, war casualties, other topics – took place in the barracks involving officers, noncommissioned officers and ordinary soldiers (probably separately). These increased dramatically during the February days, contributing to the soldiers' revolt on February 27.

By 1917 the conditions for revolution were present: incompetent government, a discredited and obstinate monarch, divisions within the political elite, alienation of educated society from the regime, deteriorating economic conditions, a revival of prewar social-economic tensions and industrial strikes, an extreme war-weariness, resentful soldiers, a revival of activity by revolutionary parties, and widespread anxieties and a sense that something had to break soon. Meanwhile Nicholas, on whom any attempt to head off revolution through political reform depended, waved away all warnings of approaching disaster. On February 24, 1917, even as revolution began, he wrote to Alexandra: "My brain is resting here [at military headquarters] – no ministers, no troublesome questions demanding thought."[29]

2   The February Revolution

The popular revolt

As 1917 opened, the many and widespread popular discontents were caught up on a wave of industrial strikes and popular demonstrations that suddenly surged and swept away the imperial regime. It began with a great strike on January 9, the anniversary of Bloody Sunday. About 140,000 workers from at least 120 factories – 40 percent of the industrial workers of Petrograd – struck that day. On February 14, while educated society focused anxiously on political clashes between the reopened Duma and Nicholas' government, another major strike brought out about 84,000 workers and idled fifty-two or more factories.[1] Strikes and demonstrations became daily events, with student demonstrations at Petrograd's higher educational institutions and strikes in other cities adding to the growing turmoil. Then on February 22 a labor dispute at the giant Putilov plant, the largest in Russia, led to a general lockout of workers by the Putilov management. This threw approximately 30,000 workers onto the streets, inflaming tensions in the city. Some Putilov workers attempted a demonstrative march toward the governmental center of the city on the 22nd, but police blocked them. They disrupted work at nearby factories and some of the Putilov women workers demonstrated at food warehouses over the shortage of bread. Moreover, the strike immediately took on a clearly political nature as groups of Putilov workers attempted to contact two Duma socialist leaders, Nicholas Chkheidze and Alexander Kerensky. They did meet with the latter, warning him that the strike might be the beginning of a big political movement and that "something very serious might happen."[2]

The "something very serious" suggested by the Putilov workers happened the next day across the city in the heavily industrial and traditionally restive Vyborg district. February 23 was "International Women's Day," a socialist holiday. The Russian socialist factions had argued about what kind of activities to plan for that day, but did not agree on what to do. Nonetheless, some issued appeals for meetings and

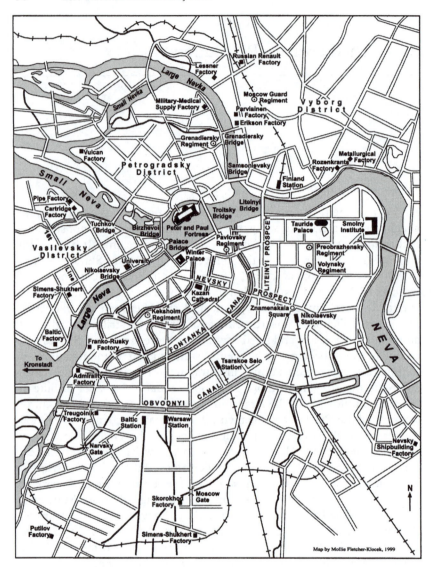

Map 1 Petrograd, 1917

demonstrations, in keeping with general socialist strategy to use all worker holidays or anniversaries to promote strikes and demonstrations in the belief that one of them would provide the spark for revolution. Given the level of strikes and tensions in February 1917, they could hardly ignore Women's Day, even though there was no specific expectation, much less a plan, that this particular day would lead to revolution. Therefore, it did not seem a cause for either unusual alarm by the authorities or exceptional revolutionary hopes when women at several textile factories in the Vyborg district held illegal protest meetings that morning. Although they expressed general discontents, their main complaint was the food supply. The women were angry that after working ten to twelve hours they then had to wait in lines at the food stores without assurance of getting any bread or other provisions. They now marched out of their factories shouting for "bread."

The women demonstrators headed for nearby metalworking factories, demanding that the men come out and join them. One male worker at the New Lessner Factory described the scene:

women's voices were heard in the alley onto which the windows of our department opened, shouting "Down with the war! Down with the high cost of living! Down with hunger! Bread for the workers!" . . . Throngs of militant women workers filled the alley. Those who spotted us began waving their arms and yelling "Come out! Stop work!" Snowballs pelted the windows. We decided to join the demonstration.[3]

A rapidly swelling demonstration flowed through the Vyborg district as factory after factory ceased work under the cajoling of the crowds. The strikes and demonstrations quickly spread from Vyborg across the Large Nevka River to the Petrogradsky district, while scattered strikes broke out elsewhere. More than 100,000 workers, a third of the city's industrial work force, were out by the end of the day.[4] Although most striking workers soon simply went home, a determined minority pressed the demonstration. The more militant tried to cross the Neva River and reach the government and upper-class centers on the left bank, especially the symbolically important Nevsky Prospect and the major squares.[a] Two large demonstrations nearly reached Nevsky Prospect before being broken up by the police. Smaller ones did reach it. The Russian Revolution had begun.

The strikes and demonstrations on the 23rd erupted out of the women workers' demand for "bread," but they were more than mere food riots, pressing as the food supply problem was. The call for bread was a symbol of general grievances and could unite a broad spectrum of

---

[a] The geography of Petrograd affected the revolution in February and afterward. The Neva River and its branches divided the city into several areas, while canals further sliced up the land of the city. The industrial areas surrounded the governmental and upper-class center of the city, of which Nevsky Prospect was the symbol. Therefore worker demonstrations tended to take the form of marches from the surrounding areas toward the center and Nevsky Prospect. To do so and to link up with each other, those in the Vyborg, Petrogradsky and Vasilevsky districts had to cross the rivers, while others had to cross canals. Hence control of bridges was important in the February and October Revolutions and during other demonstrations.

the population against the authorities. It activated the already restive industrial workers, garnered support from broader circles of lower- and even middle-class elements of the population, and elicited sympathy from the soldiers. Moreover, it raised the question of the overthrow of the regime. As a police agent reported that day, "the idea that an uprising is the only means to escape from the food crisis is becoming more and more popular among the masses."[5] The years of the state's intervention on behalf of management in industrial disputes, as well as its obvious role in the food, war and other problems bedeviling them, had firmly fixed in their minds the close connection between economic and political issues. Once the women started the demonstrations, workers at the metalworking factories eagerly took them up, with more overtly political slogans and goals. The metalworkers had a long tradition of militancy and of channeling explosions of anger into demonstrations and strikes. The revolutionary parties had managed to maintain illegal organizations in some factories.

Especially important were the factory activists, both party and non-party. Drawing on lengthy strike experience they quickly moved to the fore and provided the organizational skills and leadership for the demonstrations of the next few days. They organized the columns of workers as they marched from the factories and exhorted workers to demonstrate rather than simply going home. They gave impassioned speeches articulating worker grievances and demanding the overthrow of the regime. These activists helped organize the strike committees, factory committees and, on February 27 and 28, the workers' militias and other revolutionary organizations. They, especially those with ties to political parties, also supplied the political sophistication to link economic grievances to political change. Although not providing any overall leadership or mapping a strategy for revolution, they furnished the primary political and organizational leadership in the demonstrations of February 23–27 which led to the collapse of the old regime. Only with the revolution's initial triumph on the 27th did major political figures step forward late that day to consolidate it.[6]

Particularly notable, a harbinger of things to come, was the behavior of troops who were called out to help control the demonstrations on the 23rd. The troops displayed a reluctance to act and a tendency to try to evade the actual implementation of orders. The official in charge of city police forces, General A. P. Balk, has left a memorable account of what happened when he ordered Cossacks, who had been watching "indifferently," to help the police disperse a large crowd on Nevsky Prospect:

The officer, still quite young, perplexedly looked at me, and gave the command with a sluggish voice. The Cossacks formed a platoon formation and . . . moved slowly. Going together with them several steps, I shouted: "On gallop!" The officer turned his horse "on motion," and the Cossacks did the same, but the closer they got to the crowds, the slower their gallop became and finally they completely stopped.[7]

Such reticence by the soldiers, and especially the much-feared Cossacks, did not escape notice. It emboldened the crowds. Over the course of the next few days the passiveness, reluctance to obey orders and even friendliness of the troops became even more obvious. This encouraged the crowds and helped the buildup of revolutionary pressures.

Few government officials or socialist party leaders attached exceptional significance to that day's activities. Government authorities in Petrograd dismissed their importance, assuming them to be primarily bread disorders that would quickly dissipate. The socialists had taken heart from the great wave of strikes in January and February and hoped that these strikes would spread across the country, perhaps leading eventually to a revolutionary situation such as 1905. They were not, however, expecting them to lead to such a quick collapse of the old regime as was about to occur. Most socialist intelligentsia memoirs agree with O. A. Ermansky, a Menshevik, that to interpret the events of February 23 "as an overture to mighty events was something that really did not enter my head at the time."[8] Nonetheless, they were exactly that, as both excited workers and many socialist activists agitated for a continuation of the strike, reflecting both popular anger and the general socialist belief that any strike *might* be the one that sparked revolution.

On the morning of February 24 the factories were the scenes of innumerable meetings and speeches. The workers gathered at the factories, but instead of working they held meetings, listened to orators and exchanged information and impressions. Their long-simmering anger could no longer be contained. The factories became organizing points for revolutionary activity, assuming a function they would continue to play throughout 1917 – sites that workers could instantaneously transform from work place into a meeting hall or mobilization point. Both veteran socialist party members and newly emerging activist-leaders urged the workers to strike and helped organize the columns of workers as they marched out for the demonstrations. One such was Peter Tikhonov, an otherwise anonymous worker, whom police agents recorded as giving the following speech at his factory:

So, comrades, we must quit our work today, support union with other comrades and go to get bread by ourselves. Comrades, my opinion is this. If we cannot get a loaf of bread for ourselves in a righteous way, then we must do everything: we must go ahead and solve our problems by force. Only in this way will we be able to get bread for ourselves. Comrades, remember this also. Down with the government! Down with the war![9]

The continuation of the strikes on the 24th was of the greatest importance, turning the demonstrations of the 23rd into more consciously revolutionary activity, although few would have dreamed that it would lead to the result of the next week. The strikes and demonstrations of the 24th spread to most of the working-class districts, resulting in upwards of 200,000 strikers, the largest number since the outbreak of the war. By noon, despite the efforts of the police to block them, large groups of demonstrators began to reach Nevsky Prospect – for the first time since the Revolution of 1905 – and other main thoroughfares of central Petrograd. Students, housewives, and the broad but unorganized population of day laborers, shop clerks and residents of all descriptions joined the workers in the demonstrations. Several major rallies took place, with speaker after speaker denouncing the regime. Transportation was disrupted as tram drivers walked away from their cars. There was some looting of food stores.

Throughout the city mounted police and military repeatedly charged into crowds, whips flailing, dispersing them temporarily, only to have them re-form elsewhere. Many of the troops showed confusion and reluctance to act, sometimes even encouraging the crowd to "push on." Cossacks ordered to charge a crowd sometimes instead rode single file through the hole opened by their officers. Troops blocking a street let demonstrators slip by. Demonstrators appealed to soldiers not to shoot, often in the name of common bonds. Many soldiers were recent recruits from the working-class population of the Petrograd region and identified closely with the demonstrators. Women were especially effective in pleading with soldiers in the name of husbands, fathers and sons at the front and in reminding them that their own womenfolk suffered also from the deprivations of the war. These conversations undermined military discipline. The disintegration of the discipline of the soldiers, reflecting both the large number of new recruits and the antiwar sentiment of veterans and recruits alike, was one of the most important of the many unplanned, even spontaneous, aspects of the February Revolution.

The socialist parties, none of which had major leaders present, were divided on how to respond to the events of February 23–24. During the war right and left blocs had emerged, based on different approaches to the war and various political and economic issues. The right (moderate) socialists were skeptical of the chances for any positive outcome from the demonstrations. Their organizations in the factories opposed strikes on the 23rd and 24th and had even held some factories back. The more radical left socialists insisted on encouraging strike activity. The Interdistrictites (*Mezhraiontsy*, a small grouping of Social Democratic intellectuals standing between the Mensheviks and Bolsheviks) issued a proclamation on February 23 urging strikes and another on the 24th calling for continued strikes and preparations for a popular revolt. Their leaflet also appealed to soldiers to join the revolt, recognition perhaps of the faltering discipline that had been observed on the streets. What role these proclamations may have played is hard to measure. To the extent they were known they certainly encouraged, but did not cause, the demonstrations. Moreover, while the socialist parties could hope that strikes and demonstrations would lead to full revolution, they as yet had not found a way to turn that hope into institutionalized leadership. Many of the socialist intelligentsia felt marginal to events, although others plunged into what A. A. Peshekhonov called the "thicket" of revolution.[10]

In contrast the government treated the demonstrations as simply another in a long chain of disorders. General S. S. Khabalov, commander of the Petrograd Military District, insisted that this was primarily a bread disorder and issued a statement assuring the population that sufficient flour for bread existed. Officials took minor steps to improve crowd control. The Council of Ministers meeting on the afternoon of the 24th did not even discuss the disturbances.

The level of confrontation, and violence, escalated on February 25, a Saturday.[11] When the workers assembled at their factories the mood was much more aggressive. Many had prepared for battle with the police by putting on thick clothing and by arming themselves with knives, crude weapons and pieces of metal which they could hurl at authorities. Work was out of the question. The mood was hard and determined. The marchers carried banners with "Down with the Tsar," "Down with the War" and other revolutionary slogans as they moved toward the city center. At the Liteinyi Bridge across the Neva River the Vyborg workers again met mounted police under the command of police Colonel M. G. Shalfeev, who had driven them back the two previous days. This time the workers surged around Shalfeev, pulled him from his horse and killed him. Now began general attacks on police stations in the Vyborg district and on individual policemen throughout the city.

On February 25, larger numbers of students and middle-class elements swelled the demonstrations. Students from St. Petersburg University and the various technical institutes abandoned their studies for the streets, where they mingled with the workers and general crowds. Individual students often provided leadership or inspiration during the confusion of the next few days, as speech makers, organizers and leaders. Middle-class citizens of various professions also became more noticeable in the crowds, thus bringing virtually the entire social spectrum of the capital into the "movement" against the tsarist regime. In addition to the relatively disciplined columns of marching industrial workers, socially diverse crowds of men, women and youths milled about listening to orators, harassing policemen and adding to the general turmoil. The ongoing street demonstrations were facilitated by the relatively good weather that began on February 23 and continued for several days, after a period of bitter cold and harsh winds.

As the crowds became more assertive, soldiers and Cossacks increasingly showed reluctance to take action. A police agent reported that "Among the military units sent to quell the disorders, a tendency to play around with the demonstrators has been observed, and some units relate to [the strikers] protectively . . . [and] have encouraged the crowds by calling to them to 'press on harder.'"[12] Cases of outright refusal to help the police quell mobs grew in frequency. The most spectacular event occurred at Znamenskaia Square on Nevsky Prospect, where Cossacks not only refused to assist police in breaking up the demonstration, but attacked the police and killed their commander.[13] Most troops still obeyed orders, however, even if reluctantly, and sometimes fired at crowds. Still, many in the crowds – and some police agents reporting on them – sensed the shifting loyalties of the troops and with that the prospects for a successful uprising. The balance rested with the troops: could the government maintain control of the fundamental means of coercion?

This question was at the heart of discussions late on the 25th as both government officials and various political leaders and groups debated the meaning of events and what steps to take. The persistence of the strikes and evidence of worker determination impressed, even surprised, intelligentsia socialists. Observers realized that an unusually sharp political and social crisis was underway, the outcome of which was uncertain but which had definite revolutionary potential. The moderate socialist leaders now swung to a more radical stance. Their support for the demonstrations created a united socialist front in favor of keeping the strike movement alive in the hope that it might have a significant political impact, and some began to think that this might, indeed, be the beginning of a successful revolution. Even so, however, they remained divided in their assessment of events and future courses of action. Factory- and district-level activists were more aggressive than higher party leaders. While some stressed continued street action and demanded arms, others, such as Alexander Shliapnikov, the most prominent Bolshevik leader in the city, urged the workers to focus instead on drawing the soldiers into the movement as the only way to guarantee success. The problem for all party leaders at this point was to keep up with the aggressiveness of the workers themselves.

The activities of the liberal and moderate conservative parties, themselves alienated from the regime, centered on the State Duma rather than the streets. When the demonstrations began the Duma was, ironically, debating the food supply problem. In assessing the strikes and street demonstrations the Duma members were very concerned about their effect on the war effort and this influenced both their initial inaction and their eventual decision to act on the 27th. Their first response to the demonstrations was to use them to intensify criticism of the government and to demand a new government responsible to the Duma. Alarmed at the course of events, M. V. Rodzianko, the Duma chairman, sent Nicholas II a telegram once more urging formation of a government enjoying public confidence, as the Progressive Bloc had called for since 1915. Nicholas, however, dismissed it: "Again this fat Rodzianko has written me lots of nonsense, to which I shall not even deign to reply."[14] The Duma leaders were in a quandary. They wanted the government reformed, not overthrown. Yet, they feared that events were spinning out of control. Only a minority, the handful of socialists and some liberals, were interested in linking up with the street demonstrators against the government. The majority could only watch, powerless to affect the outcome of events in the streets even as they pressed the government for reform.

The government officials, however, decided on forceful action. Up to this time General S. S. Khabalov, the military commander of Petrograd, had employed strategies for dealing with the disturbances that called for minimal use of force. It appears that he planned to let the demonstrations run their course and gradually die out from exhaustion and futility, without risking a major confrontation by his shaky troops. However, his report to military headquarters on the 25th detailing the disturbances provoked a terse telegram from Nicholas II at military headquarters: "I order you to bring all of these disorders in the Capital to a halt as of tomorrow. These cannot be permitted in this difficult time of war with Germany and Austria. Nicholas."[15] In response the Petrograd authorities determined to take decisive action. The government arrested some dozens of revolutionary activists that night and began preparations to control the streets the next day with a massive show of troops to intimidate demonstrators. Khabalov issued a proclamation forbidding street gatherings and warning that they would be dispersed by force. The discipline of the troops, and specifically their willingness to fire on the crowds, would now be fully tested.

Plate 1 Street barricade during the February Revolution, probably February 26. Prints and Photographs Division, Library of Congress.

Sunday, February 26, dawned clear and crisp upon a city turned into an armed camp. The fresh light snow that had fallen during the night softened but did not fundamentally alter the impression created by the sight of large numbers of soldiers positioned to control the main streets of the city center. When demonstrators moved into the city center they were met in several instances by gunfire, as the troops were ordered to fire into the crowds. The most serious incident took place at Znamenskaia Square and involved the Volynsky Regiment training detachment (detachments composed of men selected for training as noncommissioned officers and therefore presumed to be more reliable than most garrison units). Its commander, Captain Lashkevich, first tried to use sabers and whips to disperse the crowds, and then, after the warning bugle, ordered the soldiers to fire into the crowds. Although some fired into the air above the crowds, enough fired directly that they killed approximately forty people and wounded others. A second round of firing killed more.[16] In addition police, sometimes firing from rooftops or high windows, used machine-gun fire to break up crowds. Through such use of force the government managed to control Nevsky Prospect and some other streets in the center, although demonstrations continued elsewhere. By the end of the 26th hundreds had been killed.

The question at day's end was whether the shootings would dishearten the crowds and lead to the gradual end of the demonstrations. Would this new "bloody Sunday" end the demonstrations or, like its famous predecessor in 1905, turn them into full-fledged revolution?

February 27 – the revolt of the soldiers

What effect continued and determined use of force might have had on the workers and their demonstrations can never be known because of the impact the shooting on the 26th had on the troops themselves. The soldiers of 1917 were not the same ones who had suppressed revolution in 1905. Most were new recruits, only partially accustomed to military discipline. Many were from the Petrograd region. Recently they had been in the same position as those on whom they were being ordered to fire. Even "veterans" among them were wartime draftees, often embittered by wounds and front experiences. During February 23–26 there had been hundreds of conversations between these soldiers and the crowds in which the former were reminded of their common interests with the latter, of the general injustice and the hardships of the population (including the soldiers' own families), and of the common desire to end the war. The experience of firing on the crowds seriously disturbed them. Heated discussions about events were going on in many units. Indeed, some of the Pavlovsky Guard Regiment had briefly mutinied on the 26th, but were quickly arrested.

The actual soldiers' revolt of February 27 began with the noncommissioned officers of the training detachment of the Volynsky Guard Regiment. After inflicting heavy casualties on the crowds at Znamenskaia Square, the detachment returned to its barracks badly shaken. In their barracks that night the soldiers feverishly debated the day's events. Anger over their role in the shootings combined with longer-term discontents, such as hatred of the harsh terms of military service and war-weariness, to drive them to the brink of mutiny. During the night some of the noncommissioned officers met and resolved to refuse any order to take up positions the next day or to fire on the crowds. The next morning Sergeant T. I. Kirpichnikov, who along with Sergeant Markov emerged as their leader, informed the assembled Volynsky training detachment of this and received their shouted assent.

At about 8:00 a.m. on the 27th, when the officers arrived to commence the day's activities, the Volynsky soldiers rebelled. They shot their commanding officer – the same Captain Lashkevich who had ordered firing on the crowds the day before – as he fled the building. They then poured from the barracks and rushed to nearby regiments and urged those soldiers to join them. This threw those regiments, already agitated by the events of previous days, into disarray. The mutineers spread their message to other barracks and throughout the day other units revolted, often after being "invaded" in a process reminiscent of that in the factories on February 23–24. Although only a minority of soldiers actually joined the rebels on the streets, the military effectiveness of all regiments for suppressing disorders was destroyed. Many officers went into hiding that morning, either fleeing from their units or simply staying away. Memory of this flight of the officers reinforced later distrust of officers by soldiers, a key feature of the military-political situation throughout 1917.

The soldiers' revolt started as physically separate from the workers' demonstrations, beginning in the early morning hours in the center of the city while the workers' demonstrations were still assembling in the outlying districts. Then during the late morning and afternoon the two flowed together. By afternoon mixed crowds of soldiers, workers, students and others, now armed, dominated the streets. In the face of the revolt of the soldiers and the general support for revolution, governmental authority in Petrograd collapsed.

A kind of nervous exaltation swept the city, an excitement such as characterizes a large crowd engaged in thrilling, exhilarating, yet at the same time dangerous or forbidden activities. Indeed, at this point there could be little assurance that tsarist retribution might not soon appear – a fear felt especially by the mutinied soldiers – yet the awareness that they were perhaps achieving the long-held dream of revolution and the liberties it would bring buoyed the crowds. An additional uncertainty was added by the absence of printed news; newspapers ceased publication the 25th and resumed only after March 1.

Much of the crowd's destructive energy was directed against symbols of tsarist authority, such as the police, prisons and royal emblems. Tearing down and destroying portraits of Nicholas and the imperial two-headed eagle were especially popular. Enthusiastic crowds "arrested" tsarist officials. Trucks and cars filled with armed soldiers, workers and students and emblazoned with red ribbons careened through the streets. The city was the scene of innumerable demonstrations, impassioned speeches, skirmishes with the few remaining police and impromptu celebrations. Here and there individuals emerged out of the crowds to provide temporary leadership in this or that action, such as attacking a police station, and then disappeared again from the limelight.

A curious example of these unknown temporary leaders is the young man in a leather jacket and student's cap – seemingly from the Mining Institute – who appears in photos directing one of the many volunteer

Plate 2 Crowd burning the Romanov royal insignia – destruction of royal symbols was a part of the February Revolution. Prints and Photographs Division, Library of Congress.

Plate 3 A voluntary militia (white arm bands) with two arrested policemen who had attempted to hide by changing out of uniform. The man in the leather jacket with arm raised appears in several pictures of the February Revolution and represents the many unknown individuals who stepped forward to provide local leadership. The Hoover Institution.

armed bands which came into being during the revolution; apparently a friend accompanied him with a camera and recorded both this unknown person and some of the best pictures of street scenes during the February Revolution. Many of these street leaders, both old activists and new men, became activist-leaders in the numerous organizations that sprang up in the next few days and weeks; some have their names recorded in membership rolls and newspaper accounts, but most remain anonymous to us.

The long-awaited revolution had come swiftly, arising out of strikes and popular demonstrations and without apparent preparation or leaders, contrary to the expectations of both the government authorities and the revolutionary parties. That the revolution came so directly from the collective actions of the industrial workers and then of the soldier masses in their gray greatcoats, guided by factory-level activists and noncommissioned officers and supported by the general population, left a permanent stamp on the revolution's character and subsequent development. Popular self-assertion became a dominant feature of the entire revolution of 1917. How to organize, channel and ultimately control that newfound self-assertiveness of the worker, soldier and peasant masses became a major dilemma for all of the would-be leaders of the new, but as yet undefined, order. Efforts to assert leadership and control began in earnest on the 27th, and with it the political revolution that could consolidate the popular street revolution. The popular revolution had triumphed; consolidating it was the next task and fell to different people.

Consolidating the revolution, February 27–March 2

By midday on February 27 the popular revolution in the streets had swept away imperial authority in the capital. Where this would lead no one knew, and no leadership had yet emerged to establish a new political authority and consolidate the revolution. The revolt of the soldiers made these pressing issues, and serious efforts to provide overall leadership from above began on the afternoon of the 27th. By that time also the crowds in the streets had begun to seek a leadership that could organize their efforts and consolidate their triumph. In a process that was to have tremendous consequences for the development of the revolution, this effort took two channels, one via the Temporary Committee of the State Duma and the other via creation of the Petrograd Soviet. The two met in opposite wings of the Tauride Palace, the meeting place of the State Duma, which now became the physical focal point of the revolution.

The Duma members had anxiously watched the spread of street

disorders the previous days. Pressed by events the Duma leaders decided on February 26 to convene a "private," unofficial meeting of deputies on the 27th (the Duma was scheduled to meet again the 28th). By the time they gathered the morning of the 27th, however, the situation had changed radically because of the revolt of the troops. To further complicate matters, during the night Nicholas II had sent an order recessing the Duma until April, leaving it without any legal grounds for acting. This reduced the possibility of the Duma leaders being able to use the disturbances to force Nicholas to accept major political reforms. It also fundamentally changed the circumstances under which the Duma operated and its possible role in resolving the crisis. Moreover, the Duma leaders found that the Tauride Palace was already becoming the magnet for almost everyone: political figures of all colorations, mutinied soldiers seeking direction, even workers' demonstrations. By late afternoon thousands filled the halls of the palace, while Duma leaders were summoned constantly to address the still larger crowds outside. The revolution had come to the Duma. This was, however, hardly a body of revolutionaries. The reluctance and anguish of the conservatives of the Duma were well summed up by the plaintive protest of M. V. Rodzianko, the Duma's chairman: "I have no desire to revolt. I am not a rebel. I made no revolution and do not intend to make one. If it is here it is because they would not listen to us. But I am not a revolutionist."[17]

Revolutionaries or not, the Duma leaders realized that action of some kind was necessary. Led by the liberals and more reform-oriented elements, the party leaders of the Duma, in a "private" meeting, decided about 5 p.m. to form a "Temporary Committee of the State Duma" (hereafter, Duma Committee) to act on their behalf. Toward midnight, prodded by news of the formation of the Soviet in another part of the palace, it announced that it "found itself compelled to take responsibility for restoring state and public order" and for forming a new government that could command popular confidence.[18] It sent special "commissars" to government offices and to take over communication centers such as the telegraph office and railroads. It took in and held the main officials of the old government, who were brought to the Duma by crowds that had "arrested" them; the minister of the interior, A. D. Protopopov, actually came to the Duma to seek safety by turning himself in. The Duma Committee began efforts to organize the mostly leaderless soldiers and establish control over those units that had not mutinied. Its actions on the 27th guaranteed the Duma Committee a key role in the creation of a new Provisional Government in the following days, although a very different one than they expected. The participation of these respectable leaders also legitimized the revolution in the eyes of educated society and, especially important, in the view of the front generals, thereby helping deflect efforts to suppress the revolution by force (see pp. 51–52). Although the Duma Committee became the center of political authority for the next few days, and many thought that it had become the new government, the Duma leaders were thinking in terms of a very circumscribed revolution. Most hoped to limit the authority of Nicholas or his successor and to move toward some kind of Duma-based government within a constitutional monarchy.[19]

While the Duma moved reluctantly, socialist leaders moved with more enthusiasm to try to secure the revolution they had so long awaited. As the strikes and demonstrations unfolded the need for broader coordination became obvious. Some factory activists and local party leaders harked back to the experience of 1905, when a Soviet of Workers' Deputies had emerged from a strike movement as a sort of combination strike committee and revolutionary council (soviet – *sovet* – means simply council), and the idea of its recreation was raised from at least February 25 onwards. The rapid press of events and absence of effective leadership, however, prevented its creation before the 27th. The revolt of the troops put more pressure on the socialist leaders to create a revolutionary body to organize and wield the political power that the revolution in the streets was creating. About 2:00 p.m. on the 27th a group of thirty to forty socialist leaders gathered at the Tauride Palace to discuss recreating the soviet. Most of those attending were Mensheviks of the more moderate wing of the party, including two Menshevik members of the Duma, Chkheidze and Mikhail Skobelev. Some were Menshevik members of the Workers' Group of the Central War Industries Committee, who came directly from prison, from which the street revolt had just released them. These socialists formed a Temporary Revolutionary Committee of the Soviet of Workers' Deputies and issued an appeal to workers *and soldiers* to elect deputies for a Soviet meeting that evening.

About 9:00 p.m. approximately 250 workers, soldiers and socialist intellectuals gathered in one room of the Tauride Palace to form the Soviet. The intellectuals were in the majority and clearly in control. Chkheidze was chosen as chairman, a post he held until September. Two other Duma deputies, Skobelev and Kerensky, were elected as vice-chairmen. An Executive Committee was elected, also composed mostly of socialist intellectuals. It met almost constantly during the hectic first days after February 27 and quickly became actual wielder of the power of the Soviet. The inclusion of soldiers transformed the

Soviet from a purely workers' body and radically affected the distribution of power in the city. By including soldiers – they changed the
title on March 1 to Petrograd Soviet of Workers' and Soldiers' Deputies
– the socialist leaders bound the armed forces in the city to the Soviet.
The implications for the later unfolding of the revolution were enormous.[20]

During the night of February 27–28 the Soviet sat in one part of the
Tauride Palace while the Duma Committee worked in the other wing.
The two organizations grappled with many of the same problems and
soon found themselves working together via special commissions or
agents. Both turned to the pressing problems of public security, maintaining food supply and municipal services, what to do about the
thousands of soldiers on the streets and how to organize them into an
effective resistance to the expected tsarist counterattack from the front.
This impromptu cooperation of political leaders across the political
spectrum was both a reflection of the urgency all felt and a harbinger of
the political structure to come. This was facilitated by the fact that most
Soviet leaders were from the more moderate wing of the socialist parties
that accepted cooperation with the liberals. A political leadership began
to emerge and the process of consolidating the revolution commenced.
How insecure they felt, however, was described a few weeks later by Iuri
Steklov, one of the Soviet's initial leaders:

You, comrades, who were not here in Petrograd and did not experience the
revolutionary fever cannot imagine how we lived: surrounded by various
soldiers' units that did not even have noncommissioned officers . . . There were
rumors that five regiments were marching on us from the north and that
General Ivanov was leading twenty-six echelons [against us]. Shooting
resounded in the streets, and we could only conclude that the weak forces
surrounding the Tauride Palace would be routed. From minute to minute we
expected that they would arrive and if not shoot us, take us away.[21]

Despite such fears, the process of consolidating the revolution proceeded rapidly. This required four major actions: (1) defending the
revolution against an expected attack by loyalist troops from the front,
(2) forming a new government, (3) assuring the support of the rest of
the country and obtaining the acquiescence of the army high command
and (4) the removal of Nicholas II.

Organizing to defend against an expected attack by Nicholas from the
front was the first pressing concern. On February 28 and March 1 those
Petrograd military units that had not joined the revolution the previous
day did so. Increasingly the soldiers converged on the Tauride Palace,
sometimes whole units marching in order, with bands, led by their
officers (although whether the officers so much led as went along is

debatable). Nonetheless, an *organized* force to defend the capital did not exist. Most soldiers were either a part of the unruly crowds in the streets or in their barracks without effective leadership.

The Duma Committee quickly attempted to assert control over the troops, with disastrous results. A Military Commission under Colonel B. A. Engelhardt began issuing orders early on the morning of the 28th in an attempt both to limit the breakdown of military discipline and to organize the soldiers of the garrison into a force which could defend the revolution and maintain order in Petrograd. These included many calls for restoration of order and discipline in military units. The emphasis upon getting the troops to return to their barracks and to resubmit to their officers and traditional military discipline struck a sour note among the soldiers; theirs had been in part a revolt against the harsh disciplinary and hierarchical system of the old army and they were not going to accept the reimposition of the old military order. Thus when the rumor spread that the Military Commission intended to disarm the soldiers, it drove them into a rage. The result was "Order No. 1," issued March 1 by the Soviet at soldier insistence. This ordered a fundamental restructuring of relations between officers and rank-and-file soldiers, and provided for elected soldiers' committees. It solidified soldier support for the Soviet and marked the beginning of the end of the old army (see chapter 4 for a fuller account of the origins, content and significance of Order No. 1).

Ironically, the Military Commission's efforts to restore discipline in the garrison, which provoked Order No. 1 and contributed to the ultimate disintegration of military command authority, proved unnecessary for the defense of the revolution. Petrograd's and the revolution's military protection lay, although few could have understood that then, in several other factors: the very size of the popular demonstrations and that they included all layers of society; the rapid spread of the revolution to other cities; the extent to which Nicholas and his government were discredited even among the upper classes; and the concern about the war effort which led to the willingness of the military commanders to accept a new government based on the Duma in preference to trying to suppress the revolution. These considerations led the generals to cancel the order to suppress the revolt with troops from the front, which guaranteed the initial survival of the revolution. An organized military defense turned out not to be necessary after all.

The second task was forming a new government, which took all political leaders into uncharted territory. There had long been talk of a government based on the Duma, which assumed a major but still limited reform within the overall old political system. The role of the massive street demonstrations in precipitating the political crisis and the appearance of the Soviet (and its rapid gathering of popular support) made such a moderate, even nonrevolutionary, change impossible. At the same time the leaders of the Soviet rejected attempting to use the street demonstrations to build a radical revolutionary government, as some leftists wanted. They felt that they lacked the strength and experience to form such a government and feared that any such attempt would only provoke a counterrevolution and destroy all prospects for a successful revolution. Therefore the Soviet leaders turned toward working with the Duma liberals to negotiate the question of forming a new government. The Soviet was represented primarily by Chkheidze and by N. D. Sokolov, Iu. M. Steklov and N. N. Sukhanov, three independent radical Social Democrats. Paul Miliukov, the Kadet leader who was beginning to emerge as the acknowledged leader of the Duma Committee, was its primary spokesman in the negotiations.

In three days of negotiations beginning February 28 and running to March 2, they groped toward creation of a new "Provisional Government." Discussions centered on two main questions: the composition of the government, and its initial statement of policy. Regarding composition, both groups agreed that this should be a government drawn primarily from liberal political circles in the Duma and public organizations such as the War Industries Committee and Zemgor. Rodzianko and many others had assumed a government based on and responsible to the Duma. However, the popular demands for radical change and the fact that the Duma's membership was based on undemocratic elections quickly undermined this idea. Sentiment swiftly arose among some liberal and socialist politicians that the new government should be composed of the liberal political elements and based on the revolution itself. Miliukov, speaking of the composition of the government to the crowd at the Tauride Palace on March 2, responded to the taunt "Who elected you?" with "We were elected by the Russian Revolution."[22] Miliukov and the Duma Committee negotiators began to emphasize the need to create a strong *national* government, one independent of all parties and institutions and owing its origins to the revolution itself. In freeing itself of Duma tutelage (and the taint of its undemocratic electoral base), the new government would also presumably be independent of the Petrograd Soviet, despite the latter's role in its creation. They believed that only such a government, invested with a "plentitude of power," could safeguard Russia's national interest and steer it to a Constituent Assembly. The latter, based on a universal franchise, would determine the future government and political structure for Russia.

Following from this the Duma Committee proposed a government list drawn primarily but not exclusively from the Duma and dominated by liberals but including two socialists, Chkheidze and Kerensky. The Soviet leaders, however, had already decided against allowing any of their members to enter the new government. Their reasoning was based in part on a Marxist-derived ideology about revolutionary stages and that this was the "bourgeois" stage of revolutionary development. Therefore the government must be "bourgeois," i.e., composed of middle- and upper-class liberals. Their refusal also rested in part on a belief that this new government could not possibly pursue social policies which, as socialists, they would have to insist upon. The socialists also feared that their participation might prevent important conservative and wealthy elements from supporting the revolution, and they considered such support essential to its survival. Therefore they would remain outside the government, vigilant revolutionary watchdogs. Although they had yet to work out a clear theory of the role of the Soviet in the revolution, they did not see it as taking governmental authority (although a minority view advocated such a role).

Alexander Kerensky partially upset this neat scheme when he dramatically burst into the Soviet meeting of March 2 and, opening with an electrifying "Comrades! Do you trust me?," emotionally appealed for the deputies to show their faith in him by allowing him to accept the position of minister of justice.[23] He received a rousing ovation and left to join the government. Kerensky thus became the only socialist in the new government – "democracy's hostage," as he dramatically styled himself – and found himself in the strategic position of being the only person to be in both the Provisional Government and the Soviet Executive Committee. This put him in a position to exercise enormous influence, beyond what his flamboyant personality promised for him anyway. The new government therefore was composed of liberals and moderate conservatives, plus Kerensky, who was in fact a very moderate socialist.

Agreeing on an initial programmatic statement of the new government proved quite easy. The Soviet negotiators presented a list of minimum demands that were, for the most part, guarantees of civil liberties and a promise to convene a Constituent Assembly. These were readily acceptable to the Duma leaders, fit well with their own outlook and formed the basis of the first proclamation of the new Provisional Government. In return the Soviet promised to support the new government "in so far as" the government pursued policies of which the Soviet approved. The conditional nature of this support, and the instinctive suspicion by the socialists of their nonsocialist counterparts which underlay it, was an early expression of the problems of cooperation that would plague the democratic elements in 1917.

Late on March 2 the negotiators agreed on the new government and issued an announcement of its formation, membership and program. The members of the new government came primarily from the liberal and moderate members of the Duma, but it drew on some from outside, including its head, the minister-president, Prince G. E. Lvov. A liberal nobleman well known for his work in public and charitable organizations and as head of the Union of Zemstvos, Lvov's appointment emphasized the new government's separation from the old Duma. The Kadet Party, the principle liberal party, was the most important party in the new Provisional Government and the Kadet leader, Paul Miliukov, was expected to be the effective guiding spirit of the new government. Events quickly proved otherwise, but for now the important thing was that they had formed a new government, created by the two most important political institutions in the country, and that it was generally acceptable both to the general populace and to the military leaders.[24] Significant for the future was that it was formed as a compromise of the more moderate center – liberals and socialists – against the wishes of the extremes, both ultraconservatives and radical socialists; this fore-shadowed the political coalitions that dominated political life for most of 1917.

By March 2, when the Provisional Government was formed, it was obvious that the two remaining problems would be resolved favorably: the acceptance of the revolution across Russia, and the acquiescence of the high command and the abdication of Nicholas II. These took place essentially simultaneously.

The revolution spread from Petrograd to the major cities of the country by telegraph. On March 1 commissars of the Duma Committee took over the Petrograd Telegraph Agency and sent an account of events in Petrograd to the newspapers of provincial cities. This telegram on March 1 was the first news of the revolution received in most cities, although some heard as early as February 28 and others as late as March 2–3. At first many local authorities tried to hold up such information, even, as in Kharkov, suppressing the newspaper that first printed news of revolution in Petrograd. Such actions proved futile, however, and usually within hours of the first news the process of local revolution began. A general pattern emerged as the February Revolution spread across the country much more swiftly and much more uniformly than would be the case later with the October Revolution.

Typically this revolutionary process began on March 1 and was completed March 2–3, and included at least three types of revolutionary activity. First, some kind of Public Committee was formed quickly after receipt of the news from Petrograd.[b] This typically included representatives of political parties and various "public organizations" – professional and middle-class organizations, legal workers' organizations such as the medical fund offices, and others – and sometimes members of the old city councils (city duma, elected on a restricted franchise). The Kadets usually emerged as the leaders of these, much as they did of the Provisional Government in Petrograd. The Public Committees then quickly moved to replace the old imperial officials as the local governmental authority. Second, at about the same time or slightly later, local socialists undertook to form a local soviet of workers' (and sometimes soldiers') deputies, which supported and usually participated in the work of the Public Committee. Often they formed a soviet in one section of the local city council building while the Public Committee was meeting in another part of the building, in a curious echoing of the Tauride Palace scene. Third, crowds of demonstrators swiftly took to the streets in support of the revolution coming from Petrograd. The local garrison (if there was one) either was quiet or joined the demonstrations and supported the new revolutionary local government. All three of these actions tended to happen within the first twenty-four to forty-eight hours after receipt of news of events in the capital. They were the local parallels to the street crowds, Duma Committee, Soviet and Provisional Government in Petrograd, although locally street demonstrations usually came after the formation of new political authorities, a reversal of the Petrograd pattern.

The revolution spread easily and quickly to the provincial cities and then the countryside. Generally the local revolutions triumphed so easily, and there was such a feeling of them being a general action by all the population against a handful of impotent old officials, that in many cities there was something of a festive air to it all. In most places the revolution prevailed with little or no violence, but there were exceptions such as Tver, where the revolution was accompanied by extensive violence against officials and officers.[25] Some of the naval garrisons also witnessed violence. The rapid spread helped secure the revolution by undermining any possibility that the "country" might support the old regime against the capital. It also set the stage for the emergence of a vigorous local political life which sometimes mimicked the capital, but often pursued its own issues. From the major provincial cities the

---

[b] These had a variety of names: Public Executive Committee, Committee of Public Organizations, Committee for Public Safety, Provisional Executive Committee and others. The term "Public Committee," which catches their essential intent and spirit, will be used here for all of them.

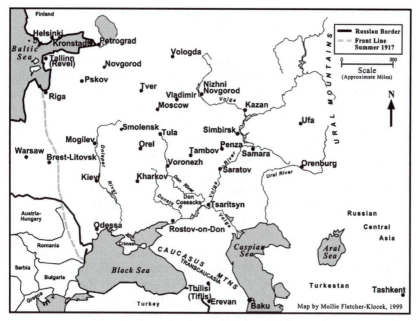

Map 2 European Russia, 1917

revolution spread to smaller towns and the villages over the next few days and weeks.

The final task to set the seal of success on the revolution was obtaining the acquiescence of the military high command and the abdication of Nicholas II.[26] Throughout the February Revolution the imperial authorities in Petrograd consistently sent falsely optimistic reports to Nicholas and the military high command at Mogilev (front head-quarters). Only on February 27 did they finally admit the true gravity of events, appealing for troops from the front. The evening of February 27 General N. I. Ivanov, at Nicholas' order, prepared to lead a military expedition to Petrograd the next day to crush the revolt. The military leaders, however, had good relations with the moderate reform elements in the Duma, especially with conservatives such as Rodzianko and Guchkov. Military and Duma leaders had a common interest in restoring order in Petrograd quickly and with as little disruption to the war effort as possible. Both were willing to accept major political restructuring, including a government based on the Duma leadership, to achieve that. Indeed, before the revolution they had discussed restricting Nicholas' power or even removing him from the throne in the interests of the war effort. Therefore, once Rodzianko and the Duma leaders were able to convince General M. V. Alekseev, the chief of staff, and other generals that the Duma leaders had asserted their control in the capital and were creating a "responsible" government, military suppression of the Petrograd revolt became unnecessary. Moreover, news of the beginning of revolution in Moscow and elsewhere reinforced the generals' desire for a political solution by increasing doubts about the feasibility of a purely military one. Therefore, they countermanded Nicholas' order and suspended efforts to suppress the revolt by force.

Nicholas, who had left military headquarters to go to Tsarskoe Selo and his family, spent the critical days of February 28 and March 1 in relative isolation as his train was shunted about by rail dispatchers. By the morning of March 2 he was stranded at Pskov. There his senior military officers, reacting to news from Petrograd and elsewhere and in the belief that the Duma was in control, confronted him with the demand that he grant a government of the Duma. After a long discussion Nicholas gave in to the arguments of his generals. Hardly had he done so, however, than new information arrived from Rodzianko and Petrograd: now the streets demanded the abdication of Nicholas. The army command quickly accepted this as the price of keeping the country and army able to defend the front, and sent telegrams to Nicholas to that effect. After reading them that afternoon Nicholas announced his intention to abdicate in favor of his young son, Alexis. At the last minute Nicholas decided to abdicate in favor of his brother Michael instead of his son, being unable to bear the thought of separation from the incurably ill Alexis and of the burdens that would fall on the boy.

By this time, however, a strong sentiment had developed within the Petrograd political leadership that the monarchy itself had to be dropped. This reflected how rapidly the revolution – and especially popular demands – were moving. Grand Prince Michael met with Duma and Provisional Government leaders on the morning of March 3 and, after listening to them and their refusal to assure him that they could protect his life if he accepted the crown, declined to ascend the throne. The Romanov dynasty, begun when the first Michael, a frightened boy of sixteen, accepted the crown three centuries earlier, now ended when a second frightened Michael refused it.

3 Political realignment and the new political system

A fundamental political realignment accompanied the formation of the Provisional Government and the emergence of the Petrograd Soviet, a realignment that reshaped political parties in 1917 into multiparty blocs that dominated the politics of 1917. This complex realignment had three aspects, understanding of which is essential to comprehending the politics of the Russian Revolution. First, the revolution completely altered the political spectrum. It swept away the old right wing of Russian politics as represented by the monarchist and truly conservative political parties. The liberal parties, previously on the left, became the "new conservatives" of the revolutionary era and made up most of the right wing of the new political spectrum, leaving the socialist parties alone on the left wing of the new political system. Second, at the same time both the new left (socialists) and the new right (nonsocialists, mostly liberals) split into subfactions, with centrist and more extreme wings. Third, a broad centrist coalition emerged composed of the "center-left" of more moderate socialists and the "center-right" from the nonsocialists. The cooperation of these two centrist groups, left center and right center, produced the broad political coalition that dominated Russian politics from February to September–October. The overall result of this realignment was a new political and governmental system, what might be called the "February System," quite different from that which anyone would have predicted. This realignment and these political blocs continued to color revolutionary politics through 1917, including the rise to political power of a radical left bloc in the fall. Moreover, a similar political realignment took place in the major provincial cities, making it a national phenomenon.

The Provisional Government

The Provisional Government formed on March 2 seemed to represent the triumph of liberal, reform Russia over autocratic Russia, setting the country firmly on the road to parliamentary democracy and moderate

Plate 4 "The Provisional Government at Work," a cartoon stressing the temporary nature of the Provisional Government – its table rests on suitcases. Prince Lvov is standing in the center, with Kerensky and Tereshchenko to his right, Miliukov and Nekrasov to his left. Prints and Photographs Division, Library of Congress.

social reform. The government certainly saw itself that way. Its head, the minister-president, was Prince George Lvov, a liberal aristocrat. The core of the government came from the main liberal party, the Kadets, led by Paul N. Miliukov, the new minister of foreign affairs. Most of its members represented the reform-oriented professional and business elite of the country. As the government's very name suggested, it considered itself a transitional regime with its primary duty being to hold the country together, prosecute the war, and maintain public order and services until it could hand over authority to a government created by a Constituent Assembly. The Provisional Government, influenced by Kadet thinking, stressed the distinction between state and government. The former was permanent and had broad, long-term interests. The latter could come and go and pursued specific partisan programs. The Provisional Government, they believed, being temporary, could legitimately use state power only in the interests of the state and in ways that transcended partisan programs and interests: defending the country, reviving the economy, mediating especially pressing social conflicts, and convening the Constituent Assembly. As William Rosenberg has noted, "Its essential task was to nurture political democracy, not to resolve the question of Russia's future political economy, social order or even its specific political forms."[1]

Central to the Provisional Government and the February System was the underlying assumption that only a government created by the Constituent Assembly, itself elected by a universal, equal, secret and direct ballot, was truly legitimate and had the moral right to decide basic political and social issues. Indeed, the ideal of a Russia reconstituted via a Constituent Assembly, which became an integral part of the mentality of the intelligentsia during the nineteenth and early twentieth centuries, seemed to have triumphed entirely in March 1917. This had, however, a paradoxical effect, both legitimizing and undermining the Provisional Government. On the one hand, the Constituent Assembly was the central democratic ideal that provided a fragile political unity for the country in 1917. All four compositions of the Provisional Government – March, May, July, and September – made its convocation a central part of their programs, and both General Lavr Kornilov on the right and Vladimir Lenin on the left justified their attempts to seize power (unsuccessfully in August and successfully in October, respectively) as essential to guaranteeing the convening of the Constituent Assembly. Even the Bolshevik government formed by the October Revolution initially declared its decrees to be in effect until the Assembly met, as did some provincial soviets after October.

On the other hand, the idea of the total authority of the Constituent Assembly undermined and immobilized the Provisional Government. That the government should not predetermine important issues was an article of faith for all political groups. It became both a cause of and justification for inaction, as well as a basis for criticizing the government when it did try to act (or even threatened to do so). The government's problem was compounded by the fact that during 1917 at least two conflicting views of the Constituent Assembly emerged, roughly along social class lines. For the upper and middle strata its task was to create a law-governed state while solving the problems facing the country within a constitutional, peaceful, reformist framework, but for the lower strata the Constituent Assembly was attractive as a means of carrying out and legitimizing a radical social-economic revolution and meeting their aspirations. Moreover, many nationality spokesmen saw the assembly as the means of ratifying their rights or autonomy. The aspirations of different groups determined what they expected from the Constituent Assembly, and through that their perception of its importance. To add to the problems, organization of elections proved more difficult than initially expected and took place only in November, after the Provisional Government had already been overthrown.[2]

The Provisional Government's sense of temporariness also contributed to its failure to build a strong administration. Lvov, who as both minister-president and minister of the interior had key responsibility for the basic administrative apparatus of the state (including the police), failed to push vigorously to create a strong administrative structure. "There was," V. D. Nabokov wrote about Lvov and his administration, "a strange faith that everything would somehow take care of itself and would start working in a correct and organized way."[3] Kerensky, who became minister-president in July, also showed little appreciation of the importance of government structure and administration. This nonchalance about administrative structures was typical of the Russian intelligentsia, but perhaps also reflected a sense that this government was only temporary and thus such administration-building activity was not terribly pressing. At the same time it probably grew at least in part out of Lvov's belief in the importance of strengthening local self-government and reducing somewhat the highly centralized political authority of the old Russian government, a belief he brought with him from his long association with the zemstvos.

The Provisional Government's problems in governing were accentuated by the fact that although it acquired the central bureaucracies reasonably intact, it had little means of enforcing its decisions beyond verbal exhortation. In both Petrograd and the provinces the old police force was gone, replaced by a weak and decentralized "militia" system under the control – often nominal – of city governments. The garrison soldiers were unreliable enforcers of government decrees. Thus, when the Provisional Government ordered changes that met the aspirations of major segments of the population, such as legalizing trade unions or peasant use of idle land, such laws were carried out. However, whenever it acted in a manner that was at odds with the ambitions or interests of any important groups, they ignored its laws. In the provinces commissars appointed by the Provisional Government to head local government exercised less real power than either the reformed local city government (Public Committee), the local soviet or, in some places, new nationalist-based organizations.

Perhaps most serious of all, the soviets and other new institutions challenged the authority of the Provisional Government. The power of the Petrograd Soviet, which grew steadily because of its support from the Petrograd workers and soldiers, was the greatest threat. Quickly political commentators began to speak of the *dvoevlastie*, the "dual authority." The Duma Committee soon faded as a significant institution after the Provisional Government was formed, but the Petrograd Soviet not only remained but grew stronger, becoming an alternative political authority. Some participants quickly perceived the actual power relationship between the two institutions: Alexander Guchkov, minister of war, told a conference of army commanders on March 13 that "We do not have authority, but only the appearance of authority; the real power lies with the Soviet."[4] Many Soviet members, fearful of government intentions, quickly asserted a dominant role for the Soviet. A deputy named Romanov, during discussion of government–Soviet relations on March 10, asserted that "The Provisional Government should be the secretary of the Soviet . . . and nothing more." Another deputy, Manerov, argued that the government should fulfill the Soviet's will "unquestioningly."[5] Indeed, events would soon prove that, in a conflict with the Petrograd Soviet, the Provisional Government was helpless. The government had formal authority but limited power, while the Soviet had real power but no formal responsibility for government. Similar situations developed elsewhere, as local soviets soon came to wield more authority than local government officials. Moreover, thousands of other new organizations – political parties, trade unions and professional associations, nationality-based organizations, community associations, educational and cultural clubs, and others – came into existence after February and asserted their right to participate in public affairs in a way never possible before. These further undermined, rather than bolstered, the central government's authority.

Once the weakness of the Provisional Government became apparent, it sparked a demand for a fundamental government restructuring in which the Soviet leaders would take a greater share of government responsibility. This led to the "coalition" governments, Provisional Government cabinets composed of socialists and nonsocialists, which became a central part of the political ideology of the February System. Bringing the Soviet members into the Provisional Government in a "coalition" government in May changed neither this fundamental reality of government weakness vis-à-vis the Soviet, nor the existence of two main institutions of political authority. Nor did it halt the devolution of political authority to the provinces and to nongovernmental organizations. Indeed, it proved only the first reshuffling of government membership in what became a milieu of almost permanent political instability that would see six to eight governments (depending on how one counts them) between March and December 1917.

The term "Provisional Government" obscures that it was really several successive governments and that in 1917 Russians lived in a world of continual governmental crisis and turnover. Moreover, one of the important features of the political situation in 1917 that is often overlooked is that none of the governments had the legitimizing authority of being elected or based on a universally elected assembly, but rather were the products of agreements among small groups of political leaders in Petrograd. This is true of the first Provisional Government formed in February and of the several later reorganizations and re-formations of it, and of the two Bolshevik governments formed in 1917 after the October Revolution (the first of which initially termed itself "provisional").

The political realignment on the right

The Provisional Government was the product of and main arena for a major political realignment on the right side of the new political spectrum. Although the new government appeared at first to be the triumph of liberal Russia, the February Revolution caused such a dramatic shift of the political spectrum to the left that the new "liberal" government was immediately transformed into a conservative one. The February Revolution so completely swept away the traditional conservative political parties and movements that they temporarily disappeared from the scene as significant actors. Yesterday's liberals, personified especially by the Kadet Party, became today's conservatives, not only in their place on the right wing of the newly truncated political spectrum but even in their political stance. For them, the first objective of the revolution – the overthrow of the autocracy – had been achieved. The present task was to consolidate its political gains, namely a democratic parliamentary government and the guarantee of civil rights, while containing the further revolutionary impulses of the masses. Other goals, such as fundamental social and economic reforms, would await the end of the war. They became true moderate conservatives and made up the nonsocialist – or, in the parlance of 1917, the "bourgeois" – part of the governments and political alignments of 1917. They were always, however, a distinct minority in the various popular elections of 1917, drawing votes primarily from Russia's small white-collar employee, professional and commercial classes.

Although there were differences among them, overall several beliefs characterized these old liberals/new conservatives:

(1) They were strongly nationalist in outlook and committed to continuation of the war and to cooperation with the Allies, although the

more centrist wing came to accept the Soviet policy of a negotiated peace, albeit out of necessity and with reservations.

(2) They saw the revolution as above all a political revolution, not a social revolution, and its main objective to be the securing of a democratic, parliamentary political system and government. For them the problem was to secure the political achievements of February, not to forge ahead with major new reforms and changes in the near future.

(3) They accepted the importance of major social and economic reforms, including some kind of land distribution, but believed that these had to await the end of the war. They also believed these reforms must take place within a framework of private property and enterprise; they rejected socialism.

(4) They objected to the socialists' emphasis upon class-based politics and took an "above classes" posture, stressing instead the needs of Russia as state, although in fact they represented the outlook of the small professional and business middle class concerning Russia's interests.

(5) Once the power of the Soviet became obvious they divided over just how to work with the Soviet while insisting on the authority of the government. Some, such as Miliukov, the Kadet leader, never reconciled themselves to the Soviet and its role, while others, such as Konovalov of the Progressist Party and Nekrasov of the left wing of the Kadets, favored working with the socialists and soviets and soon committed themselves to "coalition" government and politics.

(6) They feared civil war, which was one reason for their reluctant acceptance of coalition, but they saw the rash social policies and class-war rhetoric of the socialists – which even the moderate socialists indulged in constantly – as its most likely source.

(7) A "restoration of order," whatever that meant specifically, became an increasingly attractive slogan as the year wore on and they became ever more alarmed by economic breakdown and fearful of popular anarchy. The rise of the radical left, the Bolsheviks especially, worried them and many would have been willing to use repressive measures against the radicals if their moderate socialist allies had allowed it. A more assertive government, even a little counterrevolution, became acceptable to many by summer.

(8) Although committed to full civil rights for and respect of the customs of the various minority peoples, they opposed separatism and insisted on the territorial integrity of the Russian state.

The old liberals, or new conservatives, with the Kadets at their core, generally shared the above values and initially dominated the Provisional Government. This was deceptive, however, for the two issues of the war and relations with the Soviet deepened divisions among them, splitting them into more conservative and more centrist wings. Most Kadets, symbolized by Miliukov, were increasingly nationalist in outlook, stressing the importance of the interests of "the state" above all class, nationality or other sectional interests, and were deeply committed to continuing the war. They now saw the war as one between democracies and autocratic monarchies, Russia having left the latter for the former. Miliukov and many others argued that the revolution had come in no small part because of the inability of the old regime to conduct the war successfully. This idea led them to a ruinous error: that the first task of the new government was to prosecute the war more effectively to a complete victory. Miliukov also resisted sharing authority with the Soviet, which he saw as a class-based organization improperly intruding on the government's authority. Inherent in the Kadet stress on "interests of state" was also an implied acceptance of the social and economic status quo while national aims were pursued. Miliukov and his supporters soon became the right wing of the new conservatives.[6]

In opposition to Miliukov a more centrist viewpoint quickly emerged among some Kadets and other nonsocialists, which stressed cooperation with the more moderate socialists of the Soviet, as well as a willingness to consider a way out of the war other than by total victory. This group included several political leaders of a generally liberal but also somewhat romantically populist outlook for whom party labels were less important than a set of shared, if vague, attitudes. The key members of this grouping within the government were Prince Lvov, Nekrasov, Konovalov and M. I. Tereshchenko, a young nonparty liberal from the War Industries Committee. Within the political realignment underway they represented a loosely defined center-right bloc which quickly came to dominate the government. These men reflected an outlook that had emerged in liberal political circles just before and during the war which stressed the importance of creating connections with the more moderate socialists and through them with the broad masses of workers and peasants. This, they felt, was essential to achieve the classic liberal objective of a government based on parliamentary democracy and civil rights. This set of attitudes was one reason for the offer to Chkheidze and Kerensky to join the government and the emergence within the government of a group anxious to work with the Soviet. It helped pave the way for the later "coalition" governments of socialists and nonsocialists, the heart of the February System.

Prince Lvov was the initial focal point and symbol of this group within the government (and Russian liberalism). Lvov was a liberal aristocrat who had devoted himself to humanitarian projects and the extension of local self-government. His prominence increased during the war in part because of his willingness to press Nicholas II for reforms (unsuccessfully, like everyone else). He had long been considered a possible member of a reformed, more democratic government, although he was not a member of the Duma nor active in a political party. Lvov also had a romantic, almost mystical, faith in the peasants and common people of Russia. This was combined, in 1917, with a vague internationalism and a quixotic vision of the great role the Russian people – and revolution – would play in world history. This combination was well expressed in a speech he gave on April 27:

The great Russian revolution is truly miraculous in its majestic, quiet progress under the red glow of the World War . . . The miraculous thing about it is not the fairylike unbelievableness of the change itself, not the colossal alterations that have taken place . . . but the very essence of the guiding spirit of the revolution. The freedom won by the Russian revolution is permeated by elements of a world-wide, universal nature . . . The soul of the Russian democracy has turned out to be, in its very nature, the soul of the world democracy. It is ready not only to merge with the world democracy but also to take a position of leadership and guide the world democracy on the road of human development laid out by the principles of liberty, equality and fraternity.[7]

These were phrases which fit readily with the Internationalist views of the socialists, who also stressed the worldwide importance of the Russian Revolution (even if to different ends), and they underscored the intellectual bases for cooperation between the Lvov group of the government and the Soviet leaders. The outlook of the Lvov group also helps explain why Alexander Kerensky, the lone socialist of the government, joined them in the internal policy disputes with the Miliukov group and why, in a matter of weeks, Kerensky was able to become the actual leader of this group and the hinge on which hung the political coalitions of 1917.

If the Miliukov and the Lvov–Nekrasov groups were the "new conservatives," the defenders of the political regime created by the February Revolution, what of the traditional conservative parties and groupings? Initially swept from the political stage, with the passage of time and the sharpening of social and political conflict they reemerged in mid-summer. With a very small popular base in 1917 they were never able to exercise much influence through the voting that took place, primarily for city governments and the Constituent Assembly, but their

Plate 5 Prince G. E. Lvov. Prints and Photographs Division, Library of Congress.

Plate 6 Alexander Kerensky. Prints and Photographs Division, Library of Congress.

strength far exceeded any electoral base. It lay in part in their political experience, education and wealth. It also grew out of the possibility of a military-based counterrevolutionary seizure of power supported by what remained of the old political right and by disillusioned members of the upper and middle classes. An even more fundamental source of their political influence was the psychological sway they held over the political left. The socialists in 1917 had an exaggerated notion of the strength of "the bourgeoisie" and the political right, and an obsessive fear of counterrevolution. It was an article of faith on the political left that the bourgeoisie *must* be strong and *must* be actively counterrevolutionary. This belief profoundly influenced the behavior of the left, thus giving the right an influence over their actions far out of proportion to any real strength. In fact the right was politically very weak in 1917, the "Kornilov Affair" of August notwithstanding, and not until civil war became a reality in 1918 did the old conservative right again become a significant political force.

The Petrograd Soviet

The Petrograd Soviet of Workers' and Soldiers' Deputies rapidly emerged as the dominant political power in the capital – and perhaps the most influential in the country as a whole – while local soviets quickly became the dominant force in the cities and towns of the country.[a] Effective wielding of that power, however, meant that the Soviet had to develop clear leadership and policies. This took about three weeks and involved the arrival of the first wave of major socialist party leaders from exile. More broadly it involved a major realignment of the parties on the left of the new political spectrum, which, with that on the right, completed the political realignment caused by the February Revolution.

Initially the activity, organization and leadership of the Petrograd Soviet were erratic and often chaotic. As newly elected factory and army deputies flooded in, the Soviet grew to almost 3,000 members by the end of March. Its meetings took on the atmosphere of a mass rally.

---

[a] The word Soviet by itself and capitalized refers to the Petrograd Soviet, and terms such as "Soviet leadership" refer to the leadership of the Petrograd Soviet and the All-Russia Soviet leadership established later by the Congress of Soviets. When not capitalized, soviet or soviets refers to the phenomenon of soviets or to soviets (and their leadership) generally. The word "soviet" (*sovet*) simply meant "council" and was widely used for many Russian political and other institutions. However, it soon came to have a definite political connotation for this one particular political institution and so has passed into general historical use to refer to these particular "councils," the political soviets of the Revolutions of 1905 and 1917, as well as the latterday Soviet Union.

Plate 7 A meeting of Soldiers' Section of the Petrograd Soviet. Prints and Photographs Division, Library of Congress.

Because of its size it was from the beginning mainly a sounding board for policies decided in the Executive Committee (which in turn grew too large and later found most of its decisions made in a yet smaller bureau, and then in informal meetings of its leadership group). During the first days of the revolution the Executive Committee met almost around the clock, with whomever was in attendance deciding whatever issues came up. Moreover, decisions were made in the name of the Soviet by individual members in response to specific situations. Since the leaders were a diverse collection of socialists, ranging from very moderate to very radical and with a variety of opinions on specific issues, it was difficult to establish any clear policy line of the Soviet. Events crowded in upon the Soviet leaders in dizzying succession and they responded as best they could, often with only a vague idea of how these related to long-term objectives, or even what the latter might be.

The initial vagueness also was in part a result of uncertainty about the purpose of the Soviet and what kind of power it should exercise. The institution of soviets originated in 1905 out of a strike movement within a revolutionary situation and led a short life as a vehicle for defending worker interests. Memory of it had lived on, especially among activist industrial workers themselves, but it had not been integrated into the ideologies of the various revolutionary parties as an institution that might play a role in a future revolution or the creation of a new society afterward. Then, in February 1917 it arose so quickly and so much out of the circumstances of the revolution, in which a strike movement again played a key role, that there was not any well-articulated notion of its political purpose beyond the immediate securing of the revolution. What, then, would be the Soviet's role as a "power," as an "authority" or perhaps even as a government?

Two very different viewpoints quickly emerged. Some radicals saw it as a potential revolutionary government. On the afternoon of February 27 leaflets were issued by some socialists calling for a Soviet which would create a "Provisional Revolutionary Government." This appeal was not successful in February, but the notion of the Soviet as a revolutionary government did not disappear. It remained as an idea of great potency which would be revived, after the initial period of optimism and social cooperation passed, in the immensely appealing slogan of "All Power to the Soviets" or, more simply, "Soviet power."

A more restricted view of the role of the Petrograd Soviet and of soviets in general prevailed in early 1917. This view saw the soviets as vehicles for organizing and mobilizing the workers (and soldiers and peasants), preparing them for a future revolution. This reflected the intellectual dominance of Marxist, especially Menshevik, intellectuals in the soviet leadership. These Marxists saw this as the "bourgeois stage" of the revolution with an attendant liberal, middle-class government. During this period the soviets would keep close tabs on the government, guard against the betrayals that they believed "the bourgeoisie" must commit against the revolution, serve to reflect and protect the interests of the "revolutionary democracy" (lower classes) and prepare the workers for a future socialist revolution. While doing so it would support the government within limits. This was the Petrograd Soviet's own restrictive view of its function, parallel to the Provisional Government's restricted vision of its role.

Such a narrow view of the Soviet's role was difficult to sustain. The very predominance of the Soviet in terms of raw power in Petrograd, based on its ability to summon the backing of the soldiers and worker masses, made that impossible. Moreover, the Soviet's role inevitably changed when the major party leaders returned from exile. Most of the latter were admitted directly into the Soviet on their return, many of them also being coopted into the Executive Committee. These men expected to play a leading role in the affairs and direction of Russia – and did. They moved quickly to redefine the policies of the Soviet, and in the process completed the realignment of socialist politics begun by the war and of Russian politics started by the revolution. Because popular political loyalty in 1917 was more to the Petrograd and other soviets than to individual socialist political parties, the struggle for control of the soviets proved to be key to who would lead Russia to its future.

The realignment on the left: the moderate socialists

The realignment on the right among nonsocialists was accompanied by a parallel realignment on the left among socialist parties. With the shift of liberals from left-of-center to right-of-center on the post-February political spectrum, the left wing was composed entirely of socialist parties. The socialist parties themselves were in flux, having been torn apart first by the questions arising out of how to respond to the war in 1914 and now by the new issues called forth by revolution in 1917. As V. Bazarov, a former Bolshevik and now independent leftist Social Democrat, noted in May: " 'Bolshevik,' 'Menshevik,' 'Socialist-Revolutionary' – to a considerable extent these are historical relics; the programmatic differences which really exist between Russian socialists do not fit into these divisions bequeathed to us from the past."[8] Indeed, the socialist intelligentsia shared a general body of ideas and rhetoric that cut across party lines and allowed movement between parties and forging of multiparty blocs. As a result of these shared ideas and the

Plate 8 Irakli Tsereteli. *12, 14 i 15 avgusta v Moskve; Risunki Iu. K. Artsybusheva na zasedaniiakh Gosudarstvennago soveshchaniia (1917)* (Moscow, 1917).

Plate 9 Vladimir Lenin. Prints and Photographs Division, Library of Congress.

wartime issues that divided them, a new socialist political alignment quickly took shape in the wake of the February Revolution.

Two returning political leaders with fundamentally different programs of revolutionary action by the Soviet drove the realignment on the left and Soviet policies: Irakli Tsereteli and Vladimir Lenin. Tsereteli was a Georgian Menshevik who had played a prominent role in the Second Duma and been exiled to Siberia after its dismissal. Morgan Phillips Price described him in June as he spoke to the All-Russia Congress of Soviets as "a spare, thin man with the dark complexion and the deep kindly eyes of a Caucasian [Georgian], he bore upon him the signs of former physical suffering."[9] Tsereteli returned from Siberian exile on March 20 and led a group which forged a Menshevik–SR bloc of "moderate socialists" under the banner of "Revolutionary Defensism." This bloc dominated the Petrograd Soviet until September and most provincial soviets until then or later. Vladimir Lenin, founder and leader of the Bolshevik Party, returned two weeks after Tsereteli and staked out a position on the extreme left. At the same Congress of Soviets Price described him as "a short man with a round head, small pig-like eyes and close-cropped hair. The words poured from his mouth, over-whelming all in a flood of oratory. One sat spellbound at his command of the language and the passion of his denunciation."[10] Lenin focused the radical left opposition to the Provisional Government, the Tsereteli leadership of the Soviet, and the February System.

Central to the realignment on the left, and indeed to the whole political realignment, was the emergence of the moderate socialist bloc. This was composed mostly of Mensheviks and SRs but included smaller socialist parties as well. It began to take form in early March, but took clear identity only with the return of Irakli Tsereteli and the enunciation of the policy of "Revolutionary Defensism." Tsereteli and his Siberian associates were the first important group of exiled political leaders to return to the capital. They arrived in Petrograd on March 20, to be met with bands, crowds and speeches of welcome (a pattern which became common for the next couple months of the revolution). Tsereteli quickly emerged as one of the most important leaders during the revolution and a pivotal figure in the political realignment underway. In Siberia Tsereteli and a group of socialists – SRs, Mensheviks and Bolsheviks – had come together to discuss socialist politics and the war and formed the crossparty alliance that provided the nucleus for the future Revolutionary Defensist leadership of the Soviet. On returning to Petrograd the Tsereteli group immediately joined with some of the existing leaders of the Petrograd Soviet, especially Chkheidze and Skobelev, and established their leadership over the Soviet, ousting in the process the slightly more radical early leaders such as Sukhanov and Steklov. One of the original Soviet leaders, Vladimir Stankevich, later wrote that the history of the Soviet could be divided into two periods: before and after Tsereteli's return. The former period was characterized by disorganization, lack of consistent policy and each member of the Executive Committee following his own ideas, while the latter period saw orderly functioning, clear and consistent policy and a well-defined leadership.[11]

The issue which established the new leadership was the war. Tsereteli arrived in Petrograd in the midst of a major debate within the Soviet leadership about the war and a peace policy. He immediately plunged into the debate and laid out what would become the official Soviet position on the war. Tsereteli addressed the widespread desire for an end to the war by putting forth the idea – developed in Siberian exile – of rallying the splintered international socialist movement to pressure the warring governments to end the war. At the same time he spoke to the still patriotic soldiers by stressing the need to defend the country *and the revolution* from destruction at the hands of imperial Germany. Moreover, he argued, the new Russian government, pressured and supported by the Soviet, should take the lead in the effort to find a general negotiated peace based on the principle of "peace without annexations or indemnities, self-determination of peoples." This combination of peace efforts and defense quickly came to be called Revolutionary Defensism. It was a bold, dramatic program, perfectly suited for the moment. It catapulted Tsereteli and his group into the leadership of the Soviet and provided a coherent policy for the latter on the most pressing issue of the time and was key in defining the political realignment of 1917.[12]

Around Tsereteli a talented leadership group coalesced which reflected the new political alignments and which was held together by common outlook on the major issues rather than by party affiliation. Of the original Petrograd Soviet leadership, Chkheidze and Skobelev (who remained chairman and vice-chairman, respectively) were the two most important among the new leadership group. Both were, like Tsereteli, Menshevik Duma deputies from the Caucasus. Several key members were from the Siberian exile group, including Fedor Dan (Menshevik), Abram Gots (SR) and Vladimir Voitinsky (former Bolshevik). Dan played an important role in keeping the Mensheviks lined up behind the Revolutionary Defensist policies, while Gots played the same role for the SRs. Other key leaders included A. V. Peshekhonov, the leader of the Popular Socialists (moderate agrarian socialists), N. D. Avksentiev, the SR who soon became chairman of the All-Russia Soviet of Peasants' Deputies, and Mark Liber of the Bund (Jewish Workers' Union). One of the noteworthy characteristics of this Revolutionary Defensist leadership was that almost all spent the war years in Russia, either in Siberian exile or living a legal existence (in contrast, most of the leaders of the more radical groupings had spent long periods, including the war years, abroad). This new Soviet leadership group met each morning at Skobelev's apartment (where Tsereteli lived) to discuss the issues, make decisions and work out how these would be implemented through the Soviet or other institutions. Here, in informal discussions in a private apartment, the basic decisions were taken on the policies and affairs of the Soviet and, therefore, to a very great degree those of the Provisional Government as well. This was the heart of Revolutionary Defensism and the Menshevik–SR bloc, the "moderate socialists" who dominated political affairs for a critical half-year in 1917.

The defining positions of the new moderate socialist alignment were: (1) a general negotiated peace to end the war; (2) active defense of the country until that could be achieved; (3) cooperation with the Provisional Government and, from May onward, commitment to a "coalition" policy, i.e., a government based on a centrist bloc of socialist and nonsocialist parties and groups that united "all the vital forces of the country" in a government of moderate socialists and liberals; (4) socialism and a broad range of social reforms, including land distribution for the peasants and industrial reforms, but also a willingness to postpone the more controversial ones until either the Constituent Assembly or after the war; (5) a belief in electoral democracy in which all people had an equal right to vote and those votes were binding. They were also characterized by (6) a preference for settling political disputes with the liberals by negotiation and a reluctance to call on mass politics such as street demonstrations because of a fear of civil war if the socialist elements pushed too fast for radical social-economic reforms; (7) a constant fear of counterrevolution which made it difficult to take vigorous action to restore public order or military discipline for fear this might be used by "counterrevolutionaries"; (8) a belief that there could be "no enemies to the left," that however distressing and disruptive the activities of fellow socialists such as the Bolsheviks might be, only the right could threaten the democratic revolution; and (9) a general belief, especially strong among the Mensheviks, that this was the "bourgeois" stage of the revolution and therefore all their activity must take place within that framework – the socialist stage would come later. These general policies and values defined the new moderate socialist bloc, the center-left of the new political alignment.

Moreover, in almost every city of Russia a similarly oriented Menshevik–SR, moderate socialist bloc emerged by the end of March or early

April to dominate the soviet and local politics. These varied in detail and each came into being independently, but the general pattern prevailed, reflecting national political trends. Revolutionary Defensism provided a platform which local soviets could adopt, giving them a position on the key issues of the war and relations with the government, both local and national. By late spring these blocs controlled most soviets and, after elections in the summer, most city councils. With this local support the new Menshevik–SR bloc dominated the first All-Russia Congress of Soviets which met in June and the Central Executive Committee (CEC) elected by it, thus forging a national political alliance.

In April, May and June 1917 Tsereteli and the Revolutionary Defensists were at the height of their power. Through the Petrograd Soviet and the CEC their influence spread across the breadth of the Russian state. Because of their influence in the coalition governments formed from May to September, it could be argued that they became the dominant force in determining government policies as well. In many respects the success or failure of the February Revolution rested with them, and depended on their success in steering Russia through the difficult months to follow and establishing a stable, democratic government that could reasonably hope to meet popular aspirations.

The realignment on the left: the radical left

What then made up the radical left in the new alignment? Several distinct groups quickly emerged, sharing a general opposition to the February System, i.e., the Provisional Government, the moderate socialist leadership of the Petrograd Soviet and their efforts to work together. Ironically, the original leadership of the Soviet included several radicals, men such as Sukhanov and Steklov, who played an important role in it until they were pushed out of key positions after the return of the Revolutionary Defensists. The radical left, however, was ill defined, disorganized and lacking strong leadership until the return of major political leaders from abroad. The most important of these, certainly, was Lenin, but included others such as Iulii Martov among the left Mensheviks (Menshevik–Internationalists), Leon Trotsky (who first joined the Interdistrictites and then the Bolsheviks in July) and Mark Natanson and Maria Spiridonova of the Left SRs. After their return a better-defined left wing of the political spectrum emerged, dominated by the Bolsheviks but including also the Menshevik–Internationalists, the Left SRs and the anarchists.

The revolution found many of the radical left socialist leaders in Switzerland. Because it was surrounded by the warring powers, the

Allied governments found it easy to hinder the efforts to return to Russia of groups or individuals considered to be antiwar. Among those were Lenin and Martov. Finally the frustrated Lenin and some other radicals, mostly Bolsheviks, worked out an arrangement whereby they would pass through Germany on the way to neutral Sweden and thence to Russia. The Germans, after all, had an interest in helping the radical antiwar Russian socialists get home where they might help disrupt the government and war effort, just as Britain and France had an interest in hindering them. This led to the famous and much misunderstood "sealed train," where the Russian radicals, in an effort to defuse the inevitable charges of cooperation with the enemy in wartime, were given a special status whereby no German would enter their car during the trip across Germany and all contact would be via a Swiss intermediary. Feeling that the need to return to Russia and participate in the politics of the revolution outweighed the dangers of being labeled a "German agent," Lenin made the trip. Martov, Natanson and other socialist emigres made the same trip later. The return of the leftist leaders, especially the Lenin group, galvanized the radical left and made it a force.

Lenin arrived at the Finland Station in Petrograd on the evening of April 3, to the now regular ceremony of greetings given to returning political leaders. Lenin quickly ruined the ceremonial atmosphere, however, by delivering a speech attacking both the Provisional Government and the Petrograd Soviet leadership. It contained the basic points which soon became known as the "April Theses." Striking a note fundamentally different from not only that of the moderate socialist leaders of the Petrograd Soviet but even that of the Bolshevik leaders in Petrograd, he disavowed the policies of the Soviet and called for Soviet power and a new revolution:

(1) In our attitude towards the war . . . not the slightest concession to "revolutionary defensism" is possible . . .

(2) The specific feature of the present situation in Russia is that the country is *passing* from the first stage of the revolution . . . to its *second* stage, which must place power in the hands of the proletariat and the poorest sections of the peasants . . .

(3) No support for the Provisional Government; the utter falsity of all its promises should be made clear . . .

(4) . . the necessity of transferring the entire state over to the Soviets of Workers' Deputies . . .

(5) Not a parliamentary republic – to return to a parliamentary republic from the Soviets of Workers' Deputies would be a retrograde step – but a republic of Soviets of Workers', Agricultural Laborers' and Peasants' Deputies throughout the country, from top to bottom.[13]

Lenin's theses outraged the political leadership of Petrograd, marked the emergence of a vigorous left opposition, and laid out the strategy Lenin would successfully ride to victory. Lenin now led the Bolshevik Party into a position of absolute opposition not only to the Provisional Government, but also to the leadership and policies of the Petrograd Soviet. At the Seventh Party Conference of April 24–29 he won Bolshevik commitment to the idea of preparing for a socialist revolution, although when and how remained sufficiently vague to accommodate both the more impatient and the more cautious party members – and set the stage for later disagreements within the party in October. The Bolshevik position might be summarized as: (1) overthrow of the Provisional Government and its replacement with a socialist government based on the soviets; (2) rejection of cooperation with nonsocialist political groups and criticism of the Soviet leadership on this score, especially after the coalition government was formed in May; (3) emphasizing their difference from the moderate socialists and completing the split between Bolsheviks and Mensheviks in those places where united Social Democratic movements still existed; (4) a demand for an immediate end to the war; (5) a demand for immediate implementation of a wide range of social and economic reforms in their most radical form (immediate land distribution without compensation, workers' control of factories, reduction or even abolition of the economic role of the "bourgeoisie," extensive government role in running the economy); (6) an emphasis on class differences and antagonisms; (7) although sharing the general fear of counterrevolution, an unwillingness to temper policies in order to lessen the prospect of provoking it (in contrast to the moderate socialists); (8) less concern than the other parties about the prospect of civil war, and perhaps even welcoming it; and (9) a broad interpretation of the Russian Revolution as the first of a series of European-wide revolutions to come out of the war.[14]

Initially Lenin's program of extreme social and political antagonisms was out of keeping with the mood of the country. The spirit of optimism following the fall of the autocracy and a patriotic sense of the need to defend the country and revolution from Germany still prevailed. Therefore Lenin's program at first cast the party into the position of ineffectual opposition. Some observers believed that poor Lenin simply had not yet made the transition from emigre politics to the new realities of revolutionary Russia. Whatever Lenin's understanding of Russian politics, his stance positioned the party to become the beneficiary of any failures of the government and Soviet leadership to solve the many problems facing the country. The Bolsheviks became the magnet for those discontented with the policies and actions (or inaction) of the government or soviet. Their radical policies became ever more appealing as political and social tensions rose in the summer and fall.

The Bolsheviks were not alone on the radical left, although they proved to be the most important party there, and a loose radical left bloc played an increasingly important role in the summer and fall. Both the SR and Menshevik Parties had left wings which did not accept Revolutionary Defensism. The leftist SRs and Mensheviks both were, at first, simply minority points of view within their larger parties. They were critical of the policy of cooperation with the nonsocialists – especially the Kadets – in the Provisional Government and pressed for more rapid and more radical social and economic reforms. They also pressed for more vigorous efforts to end the war. However, they generally were less strident and less extreme, and lacked Lenin's single-minded drive and willingness to simplify and to appeal to discontents. Moreover, the leftist wings of the SRs and Mensheviks had a difficult time establishing a clear identity and a clear policy alternative to the Soviet leadership, which was, after all, made up of Mensheviks and SRs. A separate party of Left SRs emerged only later, at the time of the October Revolution. The Menshevik–Internationalists took on a loose form after Martov's return from immigration in May and clearer identity in October, but remained always within the Menshevik Party. The absence of a clear identity different from their parent parties made it difficult for the left Mensheviks and SRs to establish themselves either as challengers to the Soviet leadership or as an alternative to Bolshevism on the radical left. For a worker or soldier dissatisfied with governmental or Soviet policy the Bolsheviks were a clearer alternative than the left-wing Mensheviks and SRs.[15]

In addition there were yet other radical left parties and organizations. One was the Interdistrict Group (*Mezhraiontsy*), an association of Social Democratic intellectuals standing between the Mensheviks and Bolsheviks. Active in the February Revolution, they received an infusion of prominent leaders returning from foreign exile, most notably Leon Trotsky. In July they finally joined the Bolsheviks en masse, giving that party an important injection of leadership talent. The other important radical left element were the anarchists. They were splintered into several groups, most importantly the Anarcho-Syndicalists and Anarchist-Communists, and never able to pose an organized threat. Nonetheless their sweeping rejection of authority struck a popular responsive chord and they exercised significant influence among workers and soldiers at the lower levels of political life, at the factory and army unit. Moreover, they were effective agitators and played a significant role in the summer and fall in stirring popular discontent into action. Their organizational weakness belied their influence.[16] Other small parties and groups existed as well.

Although historical attention has, for reasons having to do with later developments, focused primarily on the Bolsheviks, the history of 1917 cannot be understood without recognizing the importance of the emergence of a radical left bloc. Bolsheviks, Left SRs, Menshevik–Internationalists, anarchists and others all criticized Revolutionary Defensism and the Provisional Government. They frequently worked together and many of the resolutions of the summer and fall described as "Bolshevik" were in fact the work of radical left blocs voting together in soviets, factory and army committees, and elsewhere. Moreover, in some provincial cities local SR and Menshevik Parties were to the left of their national leadership, giving broad leftist alliances influence in or even control of local soviets and institutions earlier than in Petrograd.

Kerensky, the centrist coalition and the basis for coalition

The final piece in the new political realignment was the emergence to prominence of Alexander Kerensky and his increasingly central role in politics, the realignment, and, especially, the new centrist coalition. Kerensky, the lone socialist in the government, quickly joined with the Lvov–Nekrasov–Konovalov–Tereshchenko grouping. He immediately established himself as the indispensable man, the only person initially holding offices in both the Provisional Government and the Soviet. Kerensky belonged to the Trudovik faction in the Duma, and in 1917 was usually described as a Socialist Revolutionary. He was the mildest of socialists, however, even in Russia, where a socialist identity was often taken on as a badge of one's opposition to the autocracy. Tsereteli later called him "by nature a nonparty individualist" and argued that "In his views he was less close to the socialist than to the democratic intelligentsia on the borderline between the socialist and bourgeois democracy."[17] Sukhanov, who knew him well before 1917, said that "by conviction, taste and temperament he was the most consummate middle-class radical" who only believed he was a socialist.[18] Indeed, in outlook and politics Kerensky was in many ways closer to the Lvov–Nekrasov group than to the leaders of the Soviet and the socialist parties. He stood at the point where moderate socialism blended into the left wing of the liberals and thus was a perfect symbol of the emerging political center and of coalition politics. Kerensky became the political hinge on which hung the two wings of the new political alignment, center-right and center-left. He was the essential man.

Kerensky soon proved to be the major personality of the Provisional Government in general. In May he became minister of war, and in July minister-president, the head of the government. In these offices he moved to position himself as a man above parties and factions. On May 22 Kerensky declared to the Petrograd Soviet that "parties do not exist for me at the present moment because I am a Russian [government] minister; for me only the people exist and one sacred law – to obey the majority will."[19] Kerensky soon became the government's commanding figure to the point of making it almost his personal regime by late summer (ever since the Provisional Government has sometimes been called the "Kerensky government"). He came to see himself as the embodiment of democratic revolution to such an extent that he could no longer separate his own career from the fate of the revolution.

Only thirty-four at the time of the February Revolution, Kerensky had made a reputation as a defense lawyer in political trials and as an outspoken critic of the old government in the Duma. During the February Revolution he seemingly was everywhere – haranguing crowds outside the Tauride Palace and elsewhere, dramatically "arresting" officials of the old regime, rushing about on urgent errands and popping in and out of meetings of the Duma Committee, the Soviet and the Provisional Government – and emerged with a heroic reputation. One conservative rival admiringly if reluctantly wrote that "He grew in this new revolutionary bog, in which he was used to running and jumping, while we had not yet learned to walk."[20] Many saw him as personifying the best of the revolution and its ideals. He enjoyed an immense popularity, even adulation, during the early months of the revolution and a personality cult grew up around him. His picture hung in shop windows and adorned postcards and medallions, crowds cheered his appearance, the press praised him lavishly, and both individuals and groups addressed petitions to him. Some even proposed to elect him tsar.[21] Thin, pale, with flashing eyes, theatrical gestures and vivid verbal imagery, he was a dramatic and mesmerizing speaker with a remarkable ability to move his listeners. A journalist described the effect of his speeches in May: "Not only does he burn, he kindles everything around him with the holy fire of rapture. As you listen to him you feel that all your nerves have reached out to him and intertwined with his nerves to form one knot. You feel as if you yourself were speaking."[22] The SR leader Victor Chernov, not a political admirer, testified that "In his best moments he could communicate to the crowd tremendous shocks of moral electricity; he could make it laugh and cry, kneel and soar, for he himself surrendered to the emotion of the moment with complete self-forgetfulness."[23] This ability, however, was to lead him to grievous overestimation of his own success in governing, and ultimately to a reputation as an empty babbler. Kerensky was the popular hero, almost a demigod, of the first months of the revolution, but by fall his name was attached to the new paper currency issued by his government, the "Kerenki" as they were dubbed, and became a synonym for worthless.[24]

In the short run, however, Kerensky was a key part of the new political realignment, which took clear form by April. On the right the liberals, the "new conservatives," dominated the Provisional Government. On the left the moderate socialists of the Menshevik–SR bloc dominated the Soviet. This set the stage for what quickly became the key feature of Russian politics, the working alliance of the center-left and center-right. The emergence of the Tsereteli-led Revolutionary Defensist bloc in the Soviet and the Lvov–Kerensky grouping in the Provisional Government laid the basis for closer cooperation and eventual restructuring of the Provisional Government as a centrist coalition of moderate socialists and the liberal/moderate new conservatives. Both looked ahead to some kind of parliamentary system in which all elements of society could play a role according to their popular support. Until then the Soviet would play an essential role in mobilizing mass support for government policies, while at the same time supervising the government to ensure that it acted in a "democratic" manner. The newly emergent Lvov–Kerensky–Nekrasov leadership in the government, although they preferred to downplay the supervisory role of the Soviet, could work with such a vision. This, they hoped, would forge the union of educated society and masses which had long been an objective of many Russian political figures.

Indeed, the new Soviet leaders and the Lvov–Kerensky–Nekrasov bloc in the government had much in common, despite the socialist/nonsocialist division. These men were all members of the small educated and politically active sector of Russian society and shared many values. They easily spoke the same language of national unity and faith in "the people." At the All-Russia Conference of Soviets in April, Tsereteli stressed the importance of uniting "all the vital forces of the country" in order to solve its problems. Lvov, Kerensky and Nekrasov – but not Miliukov or Lenin – could and did make similar statements in speeches. They also found a common ground in their stress on defense of the country and revolution. The right wing of the SRs had become more nationalist during the war and the revolution strengthened their Defensist posture. The revolution also brought some of the previously Internationalist center wing of the party over to the new Revolutionary Defensism. This created a newfound compatibility with the Kadets and liberals, who were already strongly nationalist and defensist by 1917.

Defensist Mensheviks trod a somewhat similar path. Most Menshevik and SR intellectuals also shared with the liberals a belief in the Western ideals of democracy, constitutionalism, and a law-governed society; building a democratic order in Russia was their common objective. Moreover, governmental responsibility (national and local) in the spring and summer brought an increasingly "statist" outlook for the moderate socialists, a concern for the "interests of state" and for public order, which also brought them closer to the Kadets. Indeed, the Revolutionary Defensists, especially the Mensheviks, were in many aspects of mentality closer to the Kadets than to their fellow socialists, the Bolsheviks. Tsereteli later described the right SRs as "Kadets in disguise,"[25] but his description could be expanded to include many of the Menshevik Revolutionary Defensists as well. Moreover, the Menshevik theory of this as the "bourgeois-liberal" stage of the revolution (and SR acquiescence to it) facilitated, even demanded, cooperation with the liberals in governance.

The Tsereteli and Lvov blocs also shared similar views on the revolution's world significance: at the same meeting where Prince Lvov spoke glowingly of the revolution's universal mission, Tsereteli responded that he listened "with great pleasure" to Lvov's statement that "he does not regard the Russian revolution simply as a national revolution, but that a similar revolutionary movement may be expected in the entire world as a result of the Russian revolution."[26] Their shared values and tacit understandings facilitated cooperation and laid the foundation for the coalition government formed in May and, even more important, for the "coalition mentality" which dominated political thought until the October Revolution.

Yet, the Soviet leadership's attitude toward the government contained important ambiguities. By maintaining their opposition on key issues, their ideological prejudices against "the bourgeoisie" and the organizational dichotomy of political authority represented by the *dvoevlastie*, the dual authority, the Soviet leaders ensured a continued political instability. Despite their shared values and stated desire to cooperate, the policies and ideology of the socialists, especially the Marxists, made meaningful cooperation difficult. This was not helped by the vituperative attacks on the "bourgeois" parties and politicians which were the daily fare of the socialist press and speeches, both moderate and radical. The socialists, even the moderates, could never quite stop seeing counterrevolution behind every action of the nonsocialist parties; at the high point of Revolutionary Defensist influence in May they warned, at the All-Russia Congress of Soviets, that "Counterrevolutionaries have not yet given up hope of preventing the establishment of a democratic republic in Russia."[27] Over time the conspicuous contradiction in the posture of the moderate socialists – their pragmatic commitment to coalition with the nonsocialists but their ideological hostility toward them – undermined both the moderate socialists and the government. This was further complicated by the Soviet leadership's ambiguity about the Soviet's function in the new political structure. They were adamantly opposed to having it assume full governmental authority, although by summer that was being put forward by many of their supporters in the slogan of "All Power to the Soviets." Yet, neither were they willing to relinquish to the government any of the real power they wielded. That power, and the dilemma it posed for both government and Soviet leaders, was starkly revealed in the controversy over foreign policy and the war, and led to the collapse of the first government and the formation of a coalition ministry for the Provisional Government.

Foreign policy, the April Crisis and coalition government

Through all these political realignments and political instability the war was the dominant reality of life in Russia in 1917, profoundly affecting the course of the revolution. It touched the life of virtually every person, usually for the worse. It, and the enormous army, was a major cause of the social and economic dislocations that plagued the country. It loomed as a nearly insurmountable obstacle to any efforts to solve the massive problems of the economy or meet popular aspirations for social and economic reforms and land distribution. Moreover, the war spun off new controversies that riled politics in the spring and summer. Financial needs forced the government to try to float a "liberty loan," which not only failed to meet its goals but also divided society along broad class lines, the upper and middle classes supporting it and lower classes opposing. Efforts to send units of the Petrograd garrison to the front as replacement units in April also became embroiled in the political debate about the war, and further alienated the garrison soldiers. The Provisional Government, the Petrograd Soviet and all political parties had to develop positions regarding it, and it was central to the political realignment. A program for ending the war was the cornerstone of Revolutionary Defensism and of the ascendancy of the moderate socialist leadership group of the Petrograd Soviet, and their political future depended on their success in meeting popular aspirations in this regard. The war became the main issue in the first major political crisis of the revolution, leading to the collapse of the first cabinet of the government and to the policy of coalition government.

The political conflict over the war emerged quickly. Paul Miliukov, the foreign minister of the new government, believed that the revolution did not change Russia's essential foreign policy interests. The latter, he argued, required that Russia continue to prosecute the war alongside its allies to a final victory. The defeat of Germany, he felt, was essential to Russia's interests. Moreover, victory would bring the annexation of Constantinople and the Straits, promised to Russia by the secret treaties with the Allies. This territory would allow Russia unhindered access to the Mediterranean Sea and thus was of immense economic and military value to Russia. This view initially became the official policy of the new government.

A fundamentally opposite view quickly unfolded in Soviet circles as the early Soviet leaders came out against Miliukov's war-until-victory position. On March 3 N. N. Sukhanov, one of the early Soviet leaders, raised the idea of the Soviet issuing an appeal to the European socialist parties and workers to unite to force a peace agreement on their governments. This resulted in the "Appeal" of March 14 by the Soviet. In ringing tones it called for a new era and an end to the war: "appealing to all people who are being destroyed and ruined in the monstrous war, we announce that the time has come to start a decisive struggle against the grasping ambitions of the governments of all countries . . . Toilers of all countries: We hold out to you the hand of brotherhood across the mountains of our brothers' corpses, across rivers of innocent blood and tears." To appease uncertain soldiers, it also promised that "the Russian revolution . . . will not allow itself to be crushed by foreign military force."[28] A mixture of optimism as to what the revolution could achieve, internationalist socialist rhetoric, protest against the war and a pledge to defend the country, it gained wide acceptance in Russia and helped cement the allegiance of the garrison soldiers to the soviets and their socialist leaders. The early Petrograd Soviet leaders, however, lacked a strategy for implementing their appeal.

The elaboration and implementation of a Soviet peace policy was taken up by the new Revolutionary Defensist leaders of the Soviet. Tsereteli wanted to work *with* the government to get it to renounce all imperialist war aims and accept the idea of a negotiated peace. This approach to the peace issue began a general strategy of emphasizing quiet negotiation and reasoned settlement with the government on outstanding issues rather than calling for mass demonstrations and direct confrontation (as the radical left wing tended to favor). For this purpose Tsereteli was able to use the Soviet Executive Committee's Liaison Commission, which had been set up as a vehicle for Soviet leaders to meet with the government to resolve issues. The desire to cooperate did not keep moderate socialist newspapers, including the Soviet's *Izvestiia*, from publishing a steady barrage of articles hostile to government policy, or prevent the Soviet leaders from using the threat of street actions to back their arguments. It did, however, mean that the Soviet leadership preferred to deal with the government through negotiation rather than confrontation.

Tsereteli's strategy, and the entire peace policy, was threatened by the actions of Miliukov. Irritated by a steady stream of criticism in the socialist press, Miliukov lashed out at his critics. He labeled the "peace without annexations" slogan of the Soviet a "German formula that they endeavor to pass off as an international socialist one" and reaffirmed the importance of Russia's acquisition of Constantinople and the Straits.[29] Miliukov's attack created a political furor and tested Tsereteli's strategy of working with and through rather than against the government. On March 24 the Liaison Commission met with the government to try to resolve the conflict. Tsereteli argued that the government's desire to improve morale in the army could be achieved by reassuring the country that the war was purely defensive and not being prolonged by ambitions for annexation of foreign territory. This required, he argued, that the government explicitly renounce imperialist war aims – and the secret treaties which affirmed them – and announce that it would take positive steps to bring about a negotiated general peace.

Miliukov flatly rejected the Soviet proposals, but it quickly became evident that the majority of the cabinet members favored some sort of compromise with the Soviet. It was at this time that the Lvov–Kerensky–Nekrasov bloc within the cabinet clearly emerged. On March 27 the Provisional Government agreed to make a new statement of principles of foreign policy to the Russian people. It was a compromise document, with some passages stressing the Soviet theme of renunciation of annexations and indemnities while other sections stressed defense and treaty obligations, Miliukov's theme. Nonetheless, the resolution was an important success for the Soviet leaders. They emerged victorious in the first major policy battle between the two institutions, validating the widely held opinion that they held the preponderance of actual power. The outcome also seemed to vindicate Tsereteli's strategy in dealing with the government through compromise and negotiation.[30]

The Soviet leaders took advantage of their victory to push further on the peace issue, utilizing the All-Russia Conference of Soviets of Workers' and Soldiers' Deputies. A conference of delegates from soviets from around the country, it strengthened the hand of the Revolutionary Defensist leaders in that they, but not the Provisional Government, could now claim to speak on behalf of a national constituency and organization. At the opening session on March 29 Tsereteli, after describing the successes of the "revolutionary democracy" in gaining government acceptance of its foreign policy program, stepped up the level of demands on the government. He insisted that now the Russian government must go beyond renouncing its own annexationist ambitions and must enter into negotiations with the Allied governments to get them to join in drawing up a general Allied declaration of war aims renouncing all annexations. The Soviet leadership now pressured the government to send the declaration of March 27, with its "no annexations" clauses, to the Allied governments as a formal diplomatic note. The pressure on the government intensified with the return of other prominent socialist emigres, especially Victor Chernov, the SR leader. After his arrival on April 8 Chernov immediately began a series of newspaper attacks on Miliukov. At the same time, however, the Soviet leaders rejected more radical demands that the secret treaties be published immediately, arguing that to push too hard too fast would rupture the working relationship with the government. Negotiation, not confrontation or street demonstrations, was the Revolutionary Defensists' preferred strategy.

Under Soviet pressure the government reluctantly agreed to send the declaration of March 27 to the Allies, but Miliukov insisted upon being allowed to send a covering note as well. He hoped thereby to insure that the declaration would be interpreted by the Allies in the way he wished and with Russia's interests protected. The declaration and Miliukov's note were sent to the Allies on April 18. The latter gave a decidedly one-sided interpretation to the declaration. It ignored those sections that referred to renunciation of annexations and stressed those that talked of defense of the country and loyalty to the alliance and treaty obligations. Moreover, it spoke of prosecution of the war to a "decisive victory" and ended with a statement that the "leading democracies will find a way to establish those guarantees and sanctions which are required to prevent new bloody encounters in the future."[31]

The note, and especially the passage about "guarantees and sanctions," a phrase widely understood as code for endorsing the very annexations that the declaration supposedly repudiated, enraged the left. Large numbers of people poured into the streets on April 20 in protest, some carrying placards demanding Miliukov's resignation. Some soldiers proposed arresting the entire government. The anti-Miliukov demonstrations stimulated smaller pro-Miliukov demonstrations in response, and on the 21st there were a number of clashes between rival demonstrators, with loss of life. Both the Soviet and government leaders were frightened by the specter of civil war and hastened to find some kind of peaceful solution. Neither wanted the overthrow of the Provisional Government. A compromise finally was cobbled together by which the government issued an explanation that the passages in the note of April 18 about decisive victory referred to defense of the country, while "by 'guarantees and sanctions' . . . [was meant] the limitation of armaments, international tribunals, etc."[32] It was hardly convincing, but it was sufficient to paper over the disagreements, end the street demonstrations and avert the danger of greater armed conflict. It left pending both a final resolution of the conflict over foreign policy and the underlying problems inherent in the existing political system with its two centers of political authority.

The April Crisis stimulated a debate in political circles about the need for a fundamental restructuring of the government to reflect the realities of political power in the country. The *dvoevlastie*, the dual authority, had become ever more apparent rather than fading away as some hoped. It was firmly institutionalized in the Provisional Government–Petrograd Soviet duality, but the two institutions in turn reflected deep-seated divisions in society. The Provisional Government represented especially the educated and propertied classes, whereas the Soviet represented the lower classes. The Provisional Government attempted to bring order out of the revolution and create a new era of *political* liberty within the existing social and economic order, whereas the Soviet represented the determination of the lower classes to continue the revolution to a sweeping *social and economic* overturn. From the workers' and soldiers' view the soviets were "ours" while the Provisional Government and other government agencies were in some way "theirs" and not to be entirely trusted. The socialist intellectuals reinforced this by articulating a role for the soviets a vehicles for organizing "the democracy," the lower classes, during the "bourgeois stage" of the revolution and by constantly asserting that the Provisional Government must be closely, suspiciously watched. All of this made the Provisional Government– Soviet relationship unworkable. By late April it was clear that the original government could no longer function effectively.

Discussion turned with increasing frequency to overcoming the *dvoevlastie* and political crisis by the creation of a "coalition government" which would bring leading Soviet members into the Provisional Government. The increasing call for coalition government was based not only on a desire to bring Soviet leaders and the power they represented into the government, but a sense that only a government resting on broad popular support could be strong enough and have sufficient moral authority to guide Russia through this difficult period. A coalition government, buttressed by the socialist leaders of the Petrograd Soviet and representing "all the vital forces" of the country, presumably would have that authority. Moreover, this would reflect the political realignment (itself partly driven by the peace issue) by bringing together the two new "center" blocs, the center-right of the Lvov–Nekrasov group of the Provisional Government and the center-left of the Tsereteli group of the Soviet, in a "coalition" government of the center. This, it was hoped, would end the conflict between the two bodies and strengthen the government.

Some of the socialist leaders, Tsereteli in particular, resisted entering the government. He argued that if the Soviet leaders joined the government it would arouse great expectations among their followers for the quick solution to the many social and economic problems of the country as well as for the rapid end of the war. Such expectations, he argued, were bound to be disappointed and those socialist parties that entered the government would see their support fade away to the more extremist parties such as the Bolsheviks. However, on May 1 Lvov informed Tsereteli that the Soviet leaders would again be asked to join the government and that if they refused he would resign, forcing a governmental crisis. At this Tsereteli capitulated and the Soviet Executive Committee voted to join the government, with the Bolsheviks, leftist SRs and Menshevik–Internationalists voting against.

On May 5 a new, "coalition" government was announced.[b] Five additional socialists, including Tsereteli, Skobelev and Chernov, joined Kerensky in the government. Ten nonsocialists, including four Kadets, completed the government. Lvov remained head of the government. Miliukov and Guchkov, the two men originally expected to be the dominant figures of the Provisional Government and who had been especially critical of the Soviet's role in politics, exited. Kerensky took over the Ministry of War and Tereshchenko assumed the sensitive post of foreign minister. The difficult task of dealing with the expectations of industrial workers and peasants fell to two Soviet leaders, Skobelev (Menshevik) as minister of labor and Chernov (SR) as minister of agriculture. Tsereteli, who joined the government reluctantly, took the minor position of minister of posts and telegraphs so as to be able to devote his energies to political affairs of the Soviet.

The formation of the coalition Provisional Government put great

[b] It is indicative of the power of ideology and class terminology that the very idea of having socialists and nonsocialists together in a government was termed a "coalition." "Coalition" in 1917 always meant having socialists and nonsocialists in the government, never merely a coalition of parties.

pressure on the moderate socialists to solve a wide range of problems. Indeed, the Soviet leaders now faced an intractable dilemma. For the Soviet constituency the real reason for coalition was to ensure vigorous implementation of the Soviet programs, including peace, land reform, major social reforms in favor of industrial workers, greater control over the economy to ensure employment and fixed prices on essential goods, and speedy convocation of the Constituent Assembly. Although Chernov would describe the new political situation as one in which "the Soviet of Workers' and Soldiers' Deputies will, in effect, make state decisions and the ministers will only carry them out,"[33] the situation was much more complex, and treacherous. There were major policy differences between the socialists and nonsocialists, and within each, on many of the most fundamental issues. If the Soviet leaders pushed hard for their resolution, especially social and economic reform, they would alienate their coalition partners and reveal divisions within their own ranks. If they did not they would alienate their own supporters. The only other option was to strike out boldly for "Soviet power" and take over the government themselves. However, their fear of civil war, plus their own genuine moderation, prevented such a course of action. Instead, the responsibilities of government led them into a policy of compromise on social reforms while pursuing their peace program, the resolution of which they hoped would free them to face domestic issues. Sharing power sobered the Soviet leaders and converted them into advocates of caution, order and authority. This was in direct conflict with the aspirations of their constituencies.

4   The aspirations of Russian society

The February Revolution opened an unprecedented opportunity for the people of the Russian Empire to express their aspirations and to organize for their fulfillment. Released from the old regime's censorship and controls over organizations and public life, they burst forth with a dazzling display of self-assertiveness, public meetings and creation of new organizations. Announcements of conferences, congresses, committees, meetings, organizations being formed and other manifestations of a newly unfettered public life filled the newspapers. Speeches became the order of the day in a society that had previously been gagged but now could and did speak, not only freely but constantly. In some ways Russia in 1917 was simply a vast and ongoing meeting. A young woman recalled later a Moscow in which "everywhere there were meetings, on every corner someone was talking. Everyone ate lots of sunflower seeds the whole time, so all the pavement was covered with sunflower seeds and husks. Everyone was talking, talking, talking and there was always a meeting."[1] A new verb, *mitingovat'*, "to meeting," entered the language. Amid all the meetings, speeches, posters, newspaper editorials and other clutter of untrammeled free expression, one can perceive the process by which the various strata of society voiced their aspirations and struggled to fulfill them. Through a staggering multitude of new organizations they put forth their vision of what the revolution meant, its purpose, what should be its outcome. Everyone measured the revolution by the extent to which it fulfilled or threatened their aspirations.

Initially the mood was extremely optimistic that all problems could be solved and all aspirations met. After the overthrow of Nicholas, everything seemed possible. Pictures of members of the new government and of popular heroes of the revolution, such as Sergeant Kirpichnikov, the leader of the revolt of the Volynsky regiment in February, hung in store windows. During the first few weeks a festive atmosphere swept Petrograd and other cities, with huge rallies, constant parades, singing of revolutionary songs, bands playing (the *Marseillaise*, the song of the French Revolution, was especially popular), all amidst a sea of red flags, red banners and red ribbons. Moreover, the traditional Orthodox Easter celebrations reinforced the revolutionary euphoria, as people used the traditional Easter kisses and greetings of rebirth and salvation to express revolutionary as well as religious hopes for the future. Russia did indeed seem reborn, and the future limitless. Nor was the optimistic mood limited to Russians: the spirit of the times was well caught in far away Tashkent by the Muslim poet Sirājiddin Makhdum Sidqi, in a long poem, "The New Freedom," published in 10,000 copies in March 1917: "Praise be that the epoch of freedom has come. The sun of justice has lit the world . . . The time of love and truth has arrived . . . Now, we have to set aside our false thoughts; . . . the most important aim must be to give thought to how we will live happily in the arena of freedom."[2]

Despite such optimism, the reality was that the varied aspirations of society were not easily satisfied. The Russian Empire not only faced serious political, economic and social problems, but also was an enormously diverse society, divided by wealth, occupation, education, nationality, religion, legal status, regional characteristics and in various other ways. Therefore we will take some of the more important social groupings, outline their aspirations, explore how they undertook to achieve those aspirations in the new world of revolutionary turmoil, and assess their impact on the revolution. We should always keep in mind that these large groups were made up of many smaller subgroups as well as millions of individuals and contained great diversity. Nor should we forget the multiplicity of identities a single person might have. A recent rural recruit to a Moscow factory could well harbor continuing aspirations for a share of the land in his home village alongside his new industrial concerns. Many urban workers in 1917 maintained a complex identity as workers (in general and in particular factories), as citizens, and as recent peasants, as well as identities based on gender, religion, region, nationality and politics. Soldiers shared the aspirations of their social class – usually peasant – and of other identities such as nationality. What then of a Ukrainian peasant soldier? Did he have more sense of common interest with other Ukrainians regardless of class or with peasants of whatever ethnicity against all landlords? How did his situation as a soldier threatened with possible death if the war continued affect these other identities? Which predominated? Interests were often multiple, sometimes complementary and sometimes competing.

Nonetheless, identifiable important groupings with shared grievances and aspirations did exist. Moreover, mobilization to fulfill those aspirations took place along certain group lines. In this chapter we will examine the initial reactions and demands of the urban workers, the soldiers, the middle class, and women, both as a gender and as members of their particular social grouping. Two other important groups, the peasants and minority nationality peoples, whose responses to February and whose impact on the revolution unfolded somewhat differently, will be taken up in the next chapters.

The urban workers

Central to the history of the revolution, key players in all stages of its development, were the urban, especially industrial, workers.[3] There were about 3.5 million factory and mine workers at the time of the February Revolution. Petrograd and Moscow each had slightly over 400,000. The majority were concentrated in large factories employing over 500 workers, and many factories employed several thousand workers. Adding construction workers, railway workers, longshoremen and various kinds of wage laborers to the above number brings the total to about 18.5 million workers, or about 10 percent of the population.[4] Although they formed only a small portion of the population, the workers' aspirations and actions were exceptionally important because of their concentration in the major cities, their organization by the industrial process, the attention political parties devoted to them and the role they played in the February Revolution and after. The revolution began as a demonstration of industrial workers and they never relinquished their leading role in both political and social revolution in 1917. They represented a potent force for further revolutionary upheaval if their aspirations were not met – as they almost certainly would not be, at least not in full. While there was a wide range of differences among workers based on skill, trade, income, length of service, place of employment and other variables, these ultimately were less important than their shared need to improve their circumstances as well as a generalized distrust of the educated and privileged classes.

The workers' aspirations might be divided into two broad groupings: (1) economic and workplace issues and (2) broader political and social questions.[5] The two were linked, as they well realized. This was illustrated by the demand for an eight-hour working day, which emerged during the February Revolution. The eight-hour day brought together demands for better working conditions and personal dignity with a sense of being a citizen participating in the new civic life. Workers saw the eight-hour day as essential to all of these, arguing that without the limited work day they could not pursue a civic, political life as citizens. The eight-hour day also connected to issues as diverse as workplace safety, health and opportunity for educational improvement and leisure activities. The industrial workers began unilaterally to institute the eight-hour day immediately after the February Revolution, disregarding political calls for moderation based on either economic or defense (arms production) reasons. The workers, however, did acknowledge the problem of production of supplies for the army and therefore often agreed to work longer hours, but as overtime beyond an official eight-hour day. They insisted on the *principle* of the eight-hour day as sacrosanct, even when they compromised in practice. Most employers in Petrograd, faced with an accomplished fact, yielded. Even the socialist intelligentsia leaders of the Petrograd Soviet had to yield to worker insistence on this point. On March 10 the Petrograd Soviet and the Petrograd Association of Manufacturers formally signed an agreement on implementing an eight-hour day, which ratified what workers had already instituted. In the provincial cities local industrialists resisted the eight-hour day more vigorously, but even there gains were made.

Another major demand was for wage increases. There had been a significant inflation during the war and by February 1917 wages in real terms had fallen seriously behind. The initial struggle over wages was carried on locally, factory by factory, and the details and results varied. In general, however, in Petrograd during March monthly earnings rose 30–40 percent and by July were double or treble January wage rates.[6] These early wage gains soon were negated by inflation, however, prompting renewed wage demands in the summer and fall and fueling new industrial and political conflict.

A whole series of demands reflected a desire to ameliorate the unsafe, harsh and degrading working conditions. Workers demanded safety improvements, meal breaks, sick leave, reform of hiring and firing procedures and other improvements in the workplace. Labor contracts and factory rule books, with their lists of fines, punishments and often humiliating rules, were torn up or burned, sometimes ceremoniously. The workers moved immediately to get rid of unpopular and abusive managers and foremen. Usually the latter were simply expelled, but sometimes this was done in a more ritualistic, humiliating way. A particularly unpopular supervisor might be put in a wheelbarrow, carted out of the factory and dumped outside the factory gate or in a particularly unpleasant place. Among those so treated at the Putilov factory was one Puzanov, who was tossed in a wheelbarrow, had red lead powder poured over him, and then was carted out and dumped in the street.[7] At the Thornton Mills (textiles) workers in one shop called in foremen one by one, then made them stand on a table and explain their past actions and promise to behave differently in the future.[8] These kinds of actions were in part symbolic and associated with the insistence on being treated with a reasonable degree of dignity and respect. That insistence was one of the broad themes running through the actions of many social groups in the course of the revolution. At the same time these actions certainly contained an element of revenge against bosses for past mistreatment.

While their own economic, working and personal conditions were their most pressing concern, broader political issues also animated the workers. The war was intensely unpopular among them. They expressed themselves politically in calls for a quick convening of the Constituent Assembly, in favor of a democratic republic (i.e., formal abolition of the monarchy), universal and direct suffrage, land distribution and other issues. In putting forth these broader political demands, workers were asserting their role as "free citizens" of a newborn "democratic Russia" as well as part of and speaking for a broad "laboring people." Much of the revolutionary political rhetoric, especially that of SRs, talked precisely of this broad laboring population that included factory workers, peasants, and all types of hired labor, urban and rural.

Workers were aware that the government played a major role in social and economic questions as well as political ones, and were determined that the new one would be as favorable to their interests as the old had been hostile. They were ambivalent toward the Provisional Government and many worker resolutions expressed distrust of any government composed of members of the upper classes. Even after "coalition" governments of socialists and nonsocialists were formed, "down with the capitalist ministers" was a popular slogan. This attitude reflected not only social hostility and the influence of the socialist parties, but that in the eyes of many workers real legitimacy and authority rested with the soviets, Petrograd and local. They often ignored the government altogether, with factory resolutions more likely to call on the Soviet than the government to deal with issues. From there it was only a short step to resolutions calling for a government based on the soviets, for "Soviet power."

The Petrograd and other city soviets were, of course, especially important as institutions through which the workers could and did pursue their aspirations. The soviets were the political agency whereby the socialist parties came together with the workers (and soldiers) and through which they could advance their programs for change and future revolution. The soviets had enormous popular support because they were class-based organs that could pursue unabashedly class objectives. As such they had an authority which even socialist-dominated multiclass institutions such as city councils did not. The soviets also were the primary institutions where working-class activism interacted with the political parties, yet also existed independent of specific parties. They were, as Don Raleigh has noted regarding Saratov, "a marketplace for revolutionary ideas" and served as "a distribution point for revolutionary language (the 'privileged bourgeoisie' and the 'revolutionary democracy'); for revolutionary imagery (counterrevolutionary forces conspiring, always conspiring, to arrest the deepening of the revolution); and for revolutionary symbols (red bunting and ribbons, workers' caps and soldiers' greatcoats)."[9] They were a potent expression of worker empowerment, both as a vehicle for achieving their demands and as an institutional authority emanating from them. To the working class, the soviets were "ours."

In addition the workers moved swiftly during and immediately after the revolution to create other organizations, closer to them and more directly controlled by them, to give voice to their aspirations and muscle to their demands. Intensely local in orientation as well as organization, they were the primary vehicles for worker self-assertion. They were also a key point where workers intersected with the political parties. Here, in these organizations, the parties influenced the workers and the workers decided the popularity of the parties (and with that the political fate of the revolution).

The factory committees were the most important of these initially. They emerged during the February Revolution as the most direct way for workers to organize to advance their aspirations and defend their interests. They grew out of a long tradition of elected "elders" in both the village and factory who represented their collective interests to landlord or factory boss. In 1917 they were elected by the workers in their shops and factories, and kept a close relationship with them. They became the focal point for efforts to implement the eight-hour day, to reform the internal working of the factory (hiring and firing of workers, replacement of foremen, new work rules, labor discipline), wage increases and other worker demands. Management, while forced to accept the committees, bitterly resented this intrusion into management prerogatives. The factory committees were among the first targets when in late summer management felt strong enough to attempt to reassert more traditional authority over the workers.

A key function of the factory committees was "workers' supervision."[a] This meant basically a right to have some kind of supervisory or

---

[a] By tradition the term is usually translated "workers' control", taking the Russian word *kontrol'* directly into English. Often there is a note that "control" is not an accurate translation, the Russian *kontrol'* having the meaning of supervision, checking, oversight or observation rather than the English "control." I will use "workers' supervision" as closer to the Russian meaning, but readers should be aware than in many English-language books the term "workers' control" is used.

inspection function over factory production and working conditions. This demand emerged soon after the February Revolution, especially in state-owned factories where managers fled or were ousted during the revolution. Factory committees, usually in cooperation with remaining or new administrative personnel, therefore took on a role in keeping factories operating. Workers' supervision continued in both private and state factories as worker–management conflicts escalated in the summer. Conflict over wages prompted demands to inspect the factory account books. Layoffs on the basis of lack of orders or raw materials sparked calls to supervise the flow of materials in and out of the factory. These demands often met refusal by management, which only increased worker suspicions that something was amiss and worker supervision necessary. Workers' supervision was more than a response to immediate issues, however. It was seen also as part of a democratic revolution inside the factory accompanying that outside, as the overthrow of autocratic rule in the factory as well as in the state.[10] It was in many ways analogous at the factory level to the Petrograd Soviet's supervision of the actions of the government.

The Provisional Government opposed, and the Soviet leadership failed to support wholeheartedly, workers' supervision; this became a major source of friction with the workers. The factory committees, alienated by lack of support from the moderate socialists, turned to the radicals. Curiously, the top radical party leaders – Bolsheviks, left Mensheviks and Left SRs – were themselves slow to recognize the factory committees' political significance. The early political support came from the lower-level party activists at the factory. Only later, in May, did Lenin and other top radical party leaders begin to pay attention to the importance of supervision to the workers and the factory committees and to give support to it.

The trade unions were a second important worker organization. Only weak, usually illegal, unions had existed before the revolution. After the February Revolution they developed somewhat slower than the factory committees, but over 2,000 were created in 1917,[11] indicative of both the urge to organize and the unions' importance to workers. Socialist intelligentsia played a more important role in both starting and running them than they had in the factory committees. Most unions formed along industrial lines, organizing all the workers in a given industry (such as metalworking plants or textile plants) regardless of the specific jobs of individual workers. This allowed them by late spring to undertake industry-wide wage contract bargaining in a given city, which was preferred also by the government, by the soviets and by some industrialists' associations. There was some tension between them and the factory

Plate 10 Workers' demonstration headed by armed Red Guards. Note that they have put on their best clothes, which was typical for demonstrations after February, to show their newly asserted dignity. *Proletarskaia revoliutsiia v obrazakh i kartinakh* (Leningrad, 1926).

committees over which would do what. Gradually the unions took over most wage negotiations while the factory committees dealt with production issues within each factory and other matters concerning the workers on a daily basis. Within the trade unions especially, but also the factory committees, there was a tension between an urge to focus on economic issues and demands from political activists to play a more aggressive political role. The latter reflected the realization of the importance of politics in economic decision making and to hopes for fulfilling their workplace aspirations.

The district soviets of workers' (and soldiers') deputies provided a third organizational framework in the major cities, especially Petrograd and Moscow. They were based on administrative subdivisions within larger cities. Being smaller and more accessible than the city soviet, they were more directly responsive to worker aspirations. As avowedly political bodies they translated local worker sentiments into political statements and action. Being closer to the grass-roots they more quickly reflected worker needs and sentiments, and also were effective in mobilizing workers from a number of plants to put pressure on management, the Petrograd Soviet and other organizations. Their closeness to the workers allowed them to reflect shifting political allegiances in the summer, earlier than did the Petrograd or Moscow city soviets.[12]

Volunteer workers' armed bands, the workers' militias and (later) Red Guards, were an important form of workers' organization. They first emerged at factories during the February Revolution and continued to form throughout 1917. Some were self-organized; others formed under the sponsorship of factory committees or other worker organizations. They signaled a willingness by at least the more assertive elements to pursue their aspirations by force if necessary. Sometimes they worked with the factory committees to put pressure on management, providing muscle behind worker demands. They increasingly saw themselves as having a political purpose to "protect the revolution" and advance the interests of the working class against its enemies. They reflected a psychology on the part of industrial workers that this was their revolution and, by some, a willingness to use arms to enforce their vision of it. Not surprisingly, they tended to be in the forefront of radical sentiment among workers. Efforts by factory management and even the Soviet leaders – who distrusted the Red Guards' radicalism and self-assertiveness – to suppress them were unsuccessful. Although nonparty, they increasingly allied with the most radical parties, especially the Bolsheviks but also the Left SRs. They survived and grew in size and radicalism as political and social tensions heightened later in the year. They had both symbolic and practical importance.[13]

The *zemliachestva* were yet another form of worker organization. These were informal brotherhoods of workers who had migrated to the city from a given province or district and which functioned to help new arrivals negotiate the transition to urban life. After the revolution many were transformed into formal organizations that carried on cultural, educational and political activities, often via clubs they organized. As such they became important organizing units within factories and across factory lines, by linking workers from a region. Soldiers, especially those assigned to factory work, often joined these. Utilizing their dual identity as urban workers and as peasants or former peasants with ties to their home villages, the brotherhoods played an important role in linking the urban and rural revolutions. Although some individuals returned to their home villages to take local leadership roles, mostly the influence of the brotherhoods was through spreading information about the revolution in Petrograd and Moscow and helping interpret the larger revolution for peasants at home, both informally and as speakers at peasant meetings. Politically, they usually stressed their nonparty character and their leadership blended SR and SD outlooks. The Smolensk Union of

Zemliachestva in Petrograd (a union of the several brotherhoods of
workers from the districts in Smolensk province), for example, was SR-
dominated but had a Bolshevik as chairman. Originally moderate
socialist in outlook, the Smolensk Union became increasingly radical in
the summer, with Left SRs playing an especially important role in the
shift. Their pattern appears typical. A United Council of *Zemliachestva*
formed in Petrograd in the summer to coordinate activities of all
brotherhoods was SR-, especially Left SR-, dominated, but Bolsheviks,
Mensheviks and nonparty workers played a role as well.[14]

In addition, the industrial workers formed a host of cultural, cooperative economic and other organizations to meet their varied needs and
aspirations. The workers devoted significant energies to cultural and
educational activities. Many of the factories and unions set up workers'
clubs, which organized concerts, theatrical performances and lectures
on cultural and political issues. They also provided libraries and a wide
range of classes, from basic literacy to more advanced topics. There was
a major debate over whether these cultural activities should be focused
on *political* enlightenment and class consciousness or be more broadly
cultural, perhaps even entertaining. Some political activists denounced
the latter as frivolous wasting of time and energy, while other workers
complained of didactic performances and lectures (especially when
those seemed to be forced on them by intellectuals). What all agreed on
was that the cultural-educational activities were terribly important. In
the highly politicized context of 1917, these clubs and "enlightenment"
activities helped define and focus issues and activities of importance to
workers (and others, such as soldiers, who also sometimes attended
these meetings).

The workers' organizations also turned their attention to the health
and welfare of the workers and their families. They organized excursions
out of the city, both for enjoyment and health. Considerable attention
was given to organizing summer camps for children. This was important
given the squalor and unhealthy conditions in which many lived and
which had worsened during the war years due to overcrowding and
deteriorating public services. On June 29 Petrograd city officials stated
bluntly that "it is simply impossible to describe what is now to be
observed in the quarters of the city poor . . . The population swims in
mud and filth, insects are everywhere, and so on."[15] These living
conditions not only spawned discontent, they also helped bring forth
new kinds of social-economic demands by the workers in their dealings
with management: for paid vacations, for factory-maintained sana-
toriums and rest houses and for summer camps outside the city for

children. These and other similar demands reflected the workers' determination to use their newfound freedom and power to obtain a better life for themselves and their families.

The revolution and the strikes of spring had the effect not only of solidifying working-class identity, but also of broadening the circle of those who identified themselves as workers. Moreover, the extensive newspaper reporting about their activities, both supportive and hostile, further strengthened their group identity and forged bonds across factory lines, reinforced by the practice of raising money in factories to support strikers elsewhere. At the same time being a "worker" took on added prestige, both from their role in February and as a result of their obviously increased political influence and power. One result was that ever-larger groups identified themselves as "workers," even forming unions. This ranged from the previously unorganized lower-class elements – cab drivers, laundry workers, bath house workers, etc. – through groups such as restaurant waiters, bakers, barbers and retail clerks, to include finally lower-level white-collar workers such as office clerks and elementary school teachers, who more properly were part of the lower middle class (see pp. 111–15 on the middle classes). These occupations organized unions and sent representatives to the soviets.

The leadership for all these worker organizations came from two basic sources: from their own midst and from the socialist intelligentsia. During the long process of strikes and demonstrations stretching from the Revolution of 1905 to the February Revolution, leaders had developed among the industrial workers and these now took up the leadership of their new organizations, especially those closest to the workers in the factories, such as the factory committees and the workers' militia. These were drawn mostly from the better-educated, more assertive, more politically aware, more highly skilled and longer-experienced workers, who had developed ideas about the importance of long-term organizational efforts. Many had developed affiliations with the revolutionary parties. Originally a mixture of nonparty and party-affiliated individuals, the factory worker-activists provided the leadership in gaining immediate economic objectives and provided linkage to the political parties. As the revolution progressed a dual development occurred among these worker-leaders: they were forced to identify more strongly with one or another political party as parties took on a more important role in public life, and they became increasingly radical because of the refusal of the Provisional Government and moderate socialists to support their agenda, while the radical left did so. They both influenced and were influenced by the socialist parties.

The other source of leadership was the socialist intelligentsia, which saw this revolution as their opportunity to provide leadership in creating the new society to emerge from the revolution; for many it was the opportunity to impose their long-held vision of a socialist society. They were most important where larger geographic structures were formed beyond the factory, such as the district and city soviets and the trade unions. The linkage of the factory activists and the socialist party intelligentsia was key to the direction of the revolution. At the same time this linkage encouraged a growing bureaucratization of the worker organizations: by summer the Petrograd metalworkers' union had almost a hundred full-time officials.[16]

Initially the factory committees, district soviets and trade unions had mostly moderate socialist leadership and supported the Revolutionary Defensist position. However, growing worker fears that their gains were threatened and that the revolution would not fully realize their aspirations pushed them leftward. The factory committees were early bellwethers of political change. This was dictated by the immediacy of their contact with their constituents and their responsiveness to them and to general factory meetings where all workers could participate directly. The factory committees became an early stronghold of worker radicalism and of Bolshevik, Menshevik–Internationalist and Left SR influence. Already by June the First Conference of Petrograd Factory Committees voted for the Bolshevik-sponsored resolution rather than the Menshevik one.[b] The Petrograd district soviets began to shift leftwards one by one in the summer and fall. The trade unions remained under Menshevik leadership longer, but already by summer that was challenged. For example, a leftist alliance led by the Bolsheviks but including Menshevik–Internationalists, Left SRs and others controlled the Petrograd Council of Trade Unions. The militias/Red Guards were always more radical than the Revolutionary Defensist leadership, and even than most of the workers.

Many writers on the revolution have portrayed the workers as a passive and undifferentiated mass easily manipulated by radicals and the Bolsheviks. They were far from that. They took an active role in the revolution through factory meetings and committees, through their various organizations, through their support for one party or another and through the informal street and factory gate meetings that were common. Their participation in the various great demonstrations of

[b] In voting in soviets, factory committees and similar organizations, the practice was for various parties to put forth competing resolutions on the issue under debate. Normally the Revolutionary Defensist-sponsored resolutions won. Thus for the Bolshevik-sponsored resolution to win, here or elsewhere, signaled shifting political sentiments, perhaps a new majority in the organization, and usually led to reorganization of the leadership to reflect that.

1917, February and later, was a reflection of a decision that this advanced their interests, not a simple manipulation by political parties: they *chose* to participate. And, it must be recalled, workers had a long tradition of self-organization and of creating leaders from among themselves to draw upon, even as they also sought assistance and leadership from the socialist intellectuals and parties for larger, city-wide and national, organization as well as for sophisticated explanations of events.

At the same time the role of the political parties cannot be dismissed entirely. Factory-level party activists blended their worker and party identities and helped shape the policies of workers' organizations. Workers and socialist intellectuals reinforced in each other certain tendencies: the stress on class solidarity and struggle, an antibourgeois rhetoric, identification of class enemies and a belief that the economic system was illegitimate. The language of both had a strong moral element, especially in condemnation of privileged elements and the existing capitalist order. They also shared a special language of social-economic struggle (class, economic exploitation), symbols (red flags), a tradition of struggle against the old regime, and holidays (Women's Day, May Day, commemoration of Bloody Sunday). The socialist parties' newspapers, orators and debates informed the workers and helped shape their view of events and even of themselves as a class. Younger workers and more skilled workers were better educated and had a sense of personal dignity and class importance, and they took ideas from the ideological smorgasbord available to them according to how well they explained reality and pointed to a path toward fulfillment of their aspirations. The relationship of workers and political parties was extremely complex and by no means a one-way street, much less simple manipulation or even just one of leaders and followers.

The workers, industrial and other, saw the revolution as the beginning of fundamental changes in their lives, including important changes in the social and political structure of Russia. They were determined to have their aspirations fulfilled. Initially the programs of the moderate socialists appealed to the workers and it seemed that their aspirations could be met within the framework of the February System. However, as 1917 progressed that seemed less and less likely. Unsolved problems and deteriorating conditions in the summer pushed the workers toward the radical socialists and prepared the ground for a new, radical stage of the revolution. That happened because the workers saw the Bolsheviks, Left SRs and other radicals espousing the same positions they identified as supporting their own aspirations, not because they were some kind of inert, passive lump molded by outside political agitators. This conjuncture of interests grew along with the crises of summer and fall. Russia in

1917 was a marketplace of competing ideas, competing explanations of reality and of proposals for action, and the workers turned increasingly to those offered by the radicals. Moreover, both workers and radical socialist intellectuals realized the importance of the political arena and of control of the government for social and economic policies – hence the appeal of the idea of Soviet power.

The growing radicalism of workers coincided with the fading of the optimism of the first weeks of the revolution. The gains of March were eroded; inflation took off again; the war continued, as did their poverty. There was a growing sense of class confrontation between workers and management, as well as a belief that there was some sort of bourgeois conspiracy to suppress them and their revolution (see chapter 7 about conspiracy mentality in 1917). This was sharpened by the rhetoric of the revolutionary parties, with its Marxist categories and class conflict, which the workers found quite congenial and easy to accept. It fit their own experiences. Moreover, the workers now had institutional structures through which to wage their struggle for a better life. This growing radicalism among the workers and in the representative institutions closest to them created a tension between the higher Soviet leadership and the workers in whose name they claimed to speak. It also explains why the top Soviet leadership was continually under pressure from below during 1917. Indeed, from the very beginning a peculiar dualism existed in which the Tsereteli-led Revolutionary Defensist bloc of the Petrograd Soviet was locked in conflict with political forces to its right on the governmental level, while struggling with forces to its left at the popular level – and winning the former while losing the latter struggle. A similar problem affected the moderate socialists in provincial cities, who found themselves under pressure from the left even as they established control over local city governments.

The soldiers and sailors

The soldiers and sailors were, along with the industrial workers, perhaps the group whose aspirations bore most directly on the fate of the revolution. This was true especially of the city garrisons, which were able to influence political developments directly. The Petrograd garrison soldiers were proclaimed the heroes of the revolution, its guardians, and took that identity seriously. In Petrograd, the nerve center of the revolution, the garrison held about 180,000 men, with another 152,000 in the surrounding suburbs. Armed and organized by the military structure, they were a potent element in the life of the capital. Moreover, almost all cities and towns of European Russia had garrisons, often very large ones, which influenced local politics. Between two and two and half million men filled the rear garrisons in 1917. The impact on politics of the seven million front-line soldiers was slower and less direct, but their aspirations and actions nonetheless had a profound influence on the revolution.

The response of the soldiers focused on three sets of aspirations: service conditions, peace, and general social, economic and political issues. First, and immediately, they insisted on a change in the nature of military service. Even more than the workers, their aspirations reflected the extent to which the revolution was a demand to be recognized as human beings and treated with dignity. This in turn reflected a deeper social tension between the educated classes – noble and non-noble – who made up most of the officer corps, and the peasants and urban lower classes who made up the common soldiers. Second, and once the revolution in terms of service was secured, their chief aspiration was peace, an end to the war which consumed their lives. At the same time, however, the soldiers remained committed to the *idea* of defense of the country. Other aspirations, such as land distribution and political questions, followed these two in terms of immediate impact on soldier actions.

The initial expression of soldier aspirations was Order No. 1. The Military Commission of the Duma Committee, concerned with defending Petrograd against an assumed attack from the front by Nicholas II, attempted on February 28 to get the Petrograd soldiers to return to their barracks and to resubmit to their officers and traditional military discipline. The soldiers, having revolted against the harsh disciplinary and hierarchical system of the old army, refused to accept its re-imposition. Calls for election of officers and of unit committees were already circulating among them. Rumors that the Military Commission was planning to disarm the soldiers angered and alarmed the latter. When the Military Commission and the Duma Committee rejected soldiers' demands to issue orders restructuring military service practices, furious soldiers responded that in that case "so much the better – we will write them ourselves."[17]

Order No. 1 was the result. On the evening of March 1 soldiers literally took over the Petrograd Soviet meeting to press this issue. In quick debate they resolved the main points of the soldiers' demands and, under the leadership of a multiparty group of soldier socialist intellectuals, fashioned them into a coherent document. At the soldiers' insistence it was labeled an "order," which had more force with them than a mere resolution. It was quickly printed and spread throughout the city that night in leaflets, published in *Izvestiia* the next day and then disseminated through the entire army. Addressed "To the garrison of the Petrograd Military District, to all soldiers [and sailors] of the guard, army, artillery and fleet for immediate and exact execution, and to the workers of Petrograd for their information,"[18] it proved to be one of the most important documents of the revolution. It set in motion a vast upheaval in military relationships, which in turn had enormous implications for political power in the following months and for the fate of the Russian army.

Three major changes especially emerged from it. First, it ordered the immediate formation of "committees from the elected representatives of the lower ranks." Quickly the committee system took root with a network of committees throughout the entire army, paralleling the military command structure, from the smallest unit through regiments and armies to whole fronts. These gave soldiers a vehicle for challenging officer authority, changing the military system, and looking after their own interests and fulfilling their aspirations. Second, the relationship between officers and men was fundamentally altered. The order forbade the use of coarse and derogatory language by officers toward soldiers ("Rudeness toward soldiers . . . is prohibited") and the use of honorifics for officers. Both were standard in the Russian army. Standing at attention and saluting when not on duty were abolished. It stipulated that, while soldiers "must observe the strictest military discipline" in performance of duties, when off duty in their "political, general civic and private life" soldiers were to enjoy the full "rights that all citizens enjoy." These changes showed a new sense of dignity and assertiveness on the part of the soldiers and symbolized a whole host of service conditions which the soldiers were in effect saying were abolished. Third, the order solidified the loyalty of the soldiers to the Soviet. It provided that, "in all its political actions, the military branch is subordinated to the Soviet" and that orders of the Duma Committee were to be "executed only in such cases as do not conflict with orders and resolutions of the Soviet." This set the pattern of primary loyalty to the Soviet and only conditional support for the government. Social-political affinities would have brought the soldiers under Soviet influence in time, but Order No. 1 hastened the process. As a result the soviets now held, in fact if not in theory, the preponderance of armed coercion in Petrograd and soon in the country.

News of the February Revolution and of Order No. 1 spread simultaneously to other garrisons and to the front during the first days of March. Soldiers everywhere insisted on applying the order. Looking to protect their interests and to throw off a hated military system, the soldiers simply instituted it in all three of its main points: committees, changed relationship of officers and men, and loyalty to the soviets. The government tried to insist that it applied only to Petrograd, but was unsuccessful. The army was thoroughly revolutionized and the old relationships and order were never reestablished, despite numerous efforts to undo the changes.

Once the service conditions were altered, soldiers could then vent their feelings about the war and their aspirations for peace. They desperately wanted an end to the slaughter which had taken so many of their comrades and threatened them as well. Yet, they strongly supported the need to maintain the front and to defend Russia and the revolution. The soldiers at the front initially were hesitant to speak of peace, but as the Soviet discussion of how to end the war expanded in late March and early April the soldiers quickly took up the question also. It was as if they somehow needed a kind of authorization that it was acceptable openly to discuss peace, that it was not treasonous or a betrayal of their duty. Front and garrison soldier delegates to the All-Russia Conference of Soviets (March 29–April 3) were given a thorough explanation of Soviet policies, which they then carried back with them. As a result the front soldiers became more aware of the distinctions between the Provisional Government and the Soviet, both institutionally and in policies. The result was a quick and solid swing of the soldiers' committees to support of the Soviet's peace policy as embodied in Revolutionary Defensism. Soldier resolutions, front and garrison, soon began to include demands for an end to the war, usually through the Revolutionary Defensist slogan of "peace without annexations or indemnities."

Having begun to talk of the end of the war, the soldiers quickly translated that into a peculiar approach to all military orders and potential military actions. Soldiers felt that with the Soviet peace plan only defensive measures were necessary and offensive ones unnecessary. Refusals to execute orders for offensive operations, on the basis that "we don't need hilltop X," became common. This was compounded by a mistrust of officers and a fear that they might be withholding important information, or tricking them into improper military action. Many soldiers felt that officers might be holding back information, perhaps about either a planned land distribution (rumors of which circulated) or about plans to end the war. The front soldiers took the pieces of information available to them – through rumors, newspapers, comrades who had been to nearby cities – and tried to sort out what the revolution meant for them. To help them decipher it they often turned to a junior officer whom they trusted to some extent. One such was Fedor Stepun, a socialist intellectual then serving as an army officer:

"How is it, your Honor, now that we have freedom? In Piter [Petrograd] supposedly an order came out making peace, since we don't need anything that belongs to somebody else. Peace – that means going home to our wives and kids. But his Excellency [sarcastic reference to the commander] says: 'Nothing doing: freedom is for those alive after the war. For the time being you'll have to defend the fatherland.' But your Honor, we suspect that our colonel is a rebel against the new regime and is trying to bully us, because he knows the new law is to go into effect that removes us from the front."

"That's the truth," sounded a nearby resolute voice.

Then from the thick of the crowd came even more agitated and embittered voices: "What's the use of invading Galicia anyway, when back home they're going to divide up the land?!" "What the devil do we need another hilltop for, when we can make peace at the bottom?" "Yes, the commander gets a St. George's [Cross] for taking the hilltop, but for that we'll be pushing up daisies!"[19]

Increasingly, as the year progressed the soldiers turned to spokesmen from the socialist, especially radical, parties for these explanations.

There developed a curious situation in which the soldiers accepted, at least in principle, the need to continue to maintain the front and defend the country, but were reluctant to translate that into active fighting. The front soldiers did not want to go into action and rear garrison soldiers did not want to move to the front, and neither wanted to undertake the training activities that prepared them for fighting. Yet, neither did the soldiers abandon the front or garrisons in particularly large numbers (later claims of desertion rates were greatly exaggerated). Tsereteli's Revolutionary Defensism, with its combination of defense and peace efforts, coincided with soldier sentiment and solidified the latter's support for the Soviet leaders. For the soldiers Revolutionary Defensism implied a passive defense, and when the Soviet leaders later tried to interpret it to include offensive actions, the soldiers felt betrayed and abandoned them for the Left SRs and Bolsheviks.

Although service conditions and peace were uppermost, soldiers had other aspirations as well. They shared the peasantry's concerns – most were peasant by origins – and land distribution was a major demand. The government's failure to move quickly on it agitated them. Moreover, they were concerned about the well-being of their families – many soldiers went home for a short time in the spring or summer to check on families and perhaps even help out with crops. While at home they often helped radicalize local village politics. They also expressed demands for higher support payments to their families, guarantees about support if disabled, improvements in barracks conditions and other concerns unique to military men. Front soldiers demanded better and more adequate food and clothing. In rear garrisons they asserted their

Plate 11 Soldiers parading with the slogan, "Nicholas the Bloody into the Peter-Paul Fortress," a prison in Petrograd where many revolutionaries had been imprisoned. Courtesy of Jonathan Sanders.

"rights" as citizens: to go about town freely, to join political parties and other organizations, to attend meetings and participate in demonstrations, to use public transportation (previously denied them in some cities). The "over 40s" demanded to be discharged. Soldier resolutions also expressed the political concerns of the time that were found in workers' and peasants' resolutions: the convening of the Constituent Assembly, for the institution of a republic, civil rights for all and the end of discriminations based on religion or nationality, and support for the soviets. Later in the year resolutions expressed opposition to coalition government and called for all power to the soviets. In some units and garrisons nationality issues became important, centered on demands to reorganize as nationality-based units.[20]

The soldiers, like the workers, developed organizations to help them achieve their aspirations and to represent them in confrontations with their superiors, the officers. The most important of these were the soldiers' committees, which undertook a number of functions. They provided an alternative channel of information for the soldiers, separate from that of the chain of military command, which they did not trust. At the smaller unit level they became the primary political policy body for the unit, interpreting events for the soldiers, passing resolutions and even carrying on educational activities. They transmitted Soviet resolutions to the men and the soldiers' sentiments to the Petrograd or local soviet. They sent delegations to Petrograd or other major cities to gather information. They supervised leave time, food, financial and supply functions, sanitation and other daily concerns of the unit. They mediated disputes between officers and men, including the removal of unpopular officers and the selection of new commanders. On certain issues they cooperated with commanders to keep the units battle-ready, but in other cases they became the active agents through which soldiers challenged the authority of their officers. They played a key role in the refusal of some regiments to participate in the major military offensive in June. They were sometimes a vehicle through which imaginative commanders could get essential military tasks performed, but most of all they were a vehicle for soldiers to assert themselves and to control both their own lives and those of the officers.[21]

At the upper levels – division, army, front – the committees were more strictly political vehicles and often came to work more closely with the command structure, which in turn leaned on them and often gave them access to staff resources and equipment. The committee leaders at the upper levels, the "committeemen," were primarily socialist intellectuals in uniform. Better-educated men – doctors, doctor's assistants, clerks, specialists and technicians – came to dominate the higher-level committees. These committeemen in turn quickly became oriented toward the Revolutionary Defensism of the Tsereteli leadership of the Petrograd Soviet, thus creating the same moderate socialist leadership that led the urban soviets. The upper-level committees became the army equivalent of soviets, holding a "dual authority" relationship with commanders similar to that which the Petrograd Soviet had with the Provisional Government. With the passage of time and the failure of the government to find a way out of the war, however, both front and garrison committees elected more radical, especially Left SR and Bolshevik, leadership.

The other important institutions for expression of the soldiers' aspirations were the urban soviets. Most cities and many towns had army garrisons. These, as in Petrograd, quickly joined the soviet movement. Most cities followed the Petrograd model, which was a joint soviet with workers' and soldiers' sections. The sections met separately to discuss items of particular concern to one constituency and jointly for other purposes. In some places, such as Moscow, separate soldiers' soviets existed until after the October Revolution. SRs dominated the soldiers' soviets or sections, reflecting the peasant background of most soldiers.

These soviets provided a means for unifying the garrison units into city-wide organizations, and through them the soldiers were able to play a much more active political role than they could through the unit committees.

The troubled relationship between officers and soldiers, both at the front and in rear garrisons, was a key issue of the revolution. Soldiers saw the officers as potential counterrevolutionaries who wanted to restore the old order in the army and perhaps in the country (the latter for most officers was untrue). The soldiers came primarily from the peasants with most of the rest coming from workers and other lower-class urban groups, while the officers, although diverse, came primarily from the educated strata of society, be that noble, middle class or intelligentsia. The class distinctions between officers and men reinforced hostilities. Soldier distrust of officers as representing different social and therefore political interests from their own and as being "counterrevolutionary" was in some ways natural. In this world of class identity a single angry soldier could turn a whole unit mutinous and even violent toward officers. As an officer of the Pavlovsky Guard Regiment wrote, "Between us and them is an impassable gulf. No matter how well they get on with individual officers, in their eyes we are all *barins* [lords] . . . In their eyes what has occurred is not a political but a social revolution, which in their opinion they have won and we have lost."[22] Socialist agitation reinforced this perception.

Social-based tensions were aggravated by the changed power relationships within the army. Some officers, especially ones who were vocal in their hostility toward the new regime or had a history of especially abusive treatment of soldiers, were "arrested" or expelled from their units. The remaining officers, in addition to the fundamental problem of adjusting to a radically different system of relationships and command, were subjected to open hostility, supervision of their activities, commands being overridden by committees and even searches and other humiliating treatment. They had to tolerate sloppy behavior and careless performance of duties, even abandonment of posts. In addition they now found it necessary to cater to soldiers' whims, to spend hours in "persuasion" to get them to do things they formerly did routinely on order. This applied to minor daily tasks and to broad operational issues alike. As General Dragomirov told a meeting of front commanders and Provisional Government and Petrograd Soviet members on May 4, orders that used to be immediately obeyed "now demand lengthy argument; if a battery is to be moved to a different sector, there is immediate discontent . . . Regiments refuse to relieve their comrades in the firing line under various excuses . . . We are compelled to ask the

Plate 12 Meeting at the front. Such meetings were common features of 1917. This appears to be at the time of preparation for the June offensive. National Archives and Records Administration.

Committees of various regiments to argue the issue out."[23] Some officers soon accepted the committees as necessary evils in maintaining any degree of functioning in the army and as a buffer between officers and men, but most had a difficult task. In one sense the rise of committee authority and the reduced authority of officers were the soldiers' version of workers' supervision, of institutionalized checking on necessary but distrusted superiors.

The changed military relationship was reflected also in the officers' loss of ability to punish soldiers. On March 12 the Provisional Government outlawed capital punishment, thus removing the most awesome weapon officers had to compel obedience to orders. The officers soon lost most of the rest of their punitive authority as soldiers' committees took over much of the responsibility for disciplinary actions. The result was to leave officers with virtually no means of coercing soldier obedience or performance of duties, whether in minor matters or such major ones as going into battle. One commander, reporting refusal of soldiers to perform work duties in April, commented that "Under the old regime we could have whipped them, but now we have no means of forcing them."[24] The soldiers immediately understood this and its implications. This paralleled the Provisional Government's loss of coercive power to enforce its laws. It is hardly surprising that the restoration of the death penalty in the army became a rallying cry for conservative officers and partisans of "order" in the summer, and was bitterly opposed by soldiers.

Special mention should be made of the sailors, those of Kronstadt and the Baltic Fleet in particular. The February Revolution in the Baltic Fleet was particularly violent. About seventy-five officers were killed, including forty or more at fleet headquarters at Helsinki (Helsingfors) and twenty-four at Kronstadt (the naval fortress offshore from Petrograd). Among the dead were the Baltic Fleet commander, Vice-Admiral A. I. Nepinin and the governor-general of Kronstadt, Admiral R. N. Viren. About twenty noncommissioned officers also died, plus fifty or so civilians, police and sailors.[25] The sailors shared the basic aspirations of the soldiers for improved conditions of service, dignity, greater control of their lives and an end to the war. They implemented Order No. 1 with enthusiasm and thoroughness. Sailor-created ship committees quickly sprang into existence and took effective control of the ships. Indeed, their authority was greater than that of soldiers' unit committees or the workers' factory committees. Soviets combining sailors, soldiers and workers were created at the major naval bases. In April the Baltic sailors also created a fleet-wide organization at Helsinki, Tsentrobalt (Central Committee of the Baltic Fleet), which achieved broad authority over all issues concerning the fleet. Its chairman was Pavel Dybenko, a Bolshevik sailor who was at the beginning of a meteoric rise in revolutionary politics. Bolsheviks, Left SRs and nonparty radicals dominated Tsentrobalt, as they did both the Helsinki and Kronstadt ships and garrisons (the third major Baltic base, at Tallinn [Revel], was somewhat more moderate in politics, as was the Black Sea Fleet).

The Kronstadt sailors, who quickly developed a reputation for radicalism, in particular played an important role in the revolution. Because Kronstadt was really only an island suburb of Petrograd, the Kronstadt sailors, who had long-standing and extensive contacts with the city's industrial workers, were very much involved in the politics of the capital. The Provisional Government never successfully reestablished control over Kronstadt after the bloody explosion during the February Revolution. The Kronstadt Soviet declared itself the sole authority for the island, which the Provisional Government was powerless to reverse. Bolsheviks, Left SRs and anarchists soon emerged in control of Kronstadt, which became a magnet for radicals of all stripes.

The Kronstadt sailors played a major role in the crises of summer, especially the July Days, and in the October Revolution and its aftermath, as we will see in later chapters.

The February Revolution transformed the formerly submissive soldiers and sailors into a self-conscious political force with their own aspirations and organization. The mutinying soldiers of the Petrograd and Kronstadt garrisons were quickly transformed into a major institutional force in the new political power structure. This was replicated by garrison soldiers elsewhere. They were soon reinforced by the front soldiers. The committee system, based on the military's own hierarchical structure, augmented by the urban soviets, provided the vehicle for the soldiers and sailors to assert their aspirations and become a powerful, organized force in the revolution. The political party that could maintain their support would be in a position to lead the revolution. As one participant wrote soon afterwards, "the Petrograd garrison lived at the very center of the revolutionary storms . . . Before the soldiers' very eyes . . . the political parties, [proffering] every version of political development, did battle with slogans, today alive, tomorrow [as dead as] dry autumn leaves . . . Revolutionary events held the . . . garrison in a state of endless tensions, summoned it into the streets, awarded it the enviable role of arbiter of political conflict."[26] (The attitudes and behavior of soldiers are further discussed in chapter 7 in connection with the offensive.)

The middle classes

The educated business, professional and white-collar employee elements, what might be called the middle classes, were a growing segment of Russian society on the eve of war and revolution, both numerically and in importance. They comprised half or more of the population of the cities. The very concept of a middle class was poorly developed in the Russia of 1917, however, and it was in fact a very diverse element which had failed to develop a strong class identity or action. (See discussion in chapter 1.) Nonetheless, its members had aspirations and played important roles in 1917. It might be broken into three broad groups for purposes of discussion: (1) the business and industrial elite (industrialists, bankers, high-level managers and specialists, etc.), (2) the professional, intellectual, student and middle managerial strata and (3) the urban lower-middle strata of artisans, shopkeepers, shop employees, and lower clerical, technical and other white-collar employees.[27]

The middle classes, especially the upper and middle levels, found many of their basic aspirations fulfilled by the February Revolution:

overthrow of autocracy, beginnings of parliamentary and democratic government, greater personal freedom and civil rights, cautious social reforms. Moreover, they tended to be staunchly patriotic and supportive of the war effort. Indeed, it was primarily middle-class elements who came into the streets in large numbers in support of Miliukov and his foreign policy during the April Crisis. It was this population which most enthusiastically supported the Provisional Government.

At the same time, certain features of the new order alarmed them. One was the breakdown of public order and safety: crime increased and the new city militia (police) proved ineffective. The continuation of street demonstrations and of industrial strikes fed anxieties that the revolution was not progressing as it should. Most of the middle class was not socialist and the continued existence and influence of the soviets troubled them, especially the upper portions. They felt that political authority belonged to the government and that organizations such as the soviets should not have the kind of political role they were playing. Much of the middle class adhered to the "above classes" ideology of the Kadets, and the strident class conflict rhetoric of the socialist parties upset them. Moreover, the soviets' class-based claims implied the middle class's own exclusion from a share of political power if "Soviet power," power by the lower classes exclusively, was taken to its logical conclusion. What the middle classes had seen at first as a start toward a parliamentary, constitutional order, led by the educated classes such as themselves, by late spring appeared less certain to be the actual outcome of the revolution. The different parts of the middle classes responded differently to this development.

The business elite initially was cautiously optimistic about the new regime. Three industrialists – Guchkov, Konovalov and Tereshchenko – joined the new Provisional Government and others assumed high appointed offices. Business leaders such as Konovalov believed that entrepreneurs could play a progressive leadership role in the new Russia. This would require sacrifices for the national good, especially through concessions to labor, to keep orderly industrial production running. It also assumed cooperation from labor and the development of a "politically mature" labor movement also willing to sacrifice for the national good. This vision was not shared by all, yet the optimism of the first month or two of the revolution muted direct opposition to it from industrialists as well as labor.

These optimistic visions soon foundered, and not only from growing conflict with workers. The formation of the coalition government in May brought in socialist ministers who engaged in vigorously anti-capitalist rhetoric and actions, such as hostility to private traders in the grain collection process and a tendency toward increased state regulation in industry and trade. The Petrograd Soviet was strongly anti-business and its growing influence caused the upper middle class to despair. The business elite gave up on the Provisional Government by mid-summer, looking for some type of government which could restore "order." Some of them turned toward the idea of a military dictatorship and others gave money for patriotic or conservative propaganda. Part of their problem was that the business and industrial elite, divided by regional, religious and business concerns, did not represent a cohesive group. Once the general optimism of March passed it was unable to forge any kind of organizational unity or agree upon a line of response to the problems of 1917, including how to respond to the newly powerful workers. These divisions grew as the year progressed. Employers' associations – the Moscow Society of Industrialists, the All-Russia Society of Leatherworking Manufacturers, the Association of Textile Manufacturers and others – often tried to work together in dealing with both the workers' demands and the government, but these had only limited success or even cohesion. Indeed, overall the business and industrial elite proved unexpectedly uninfluential in the events of 1917. Their main contribution may well have been as a target for verbal attacks on "capitalists" and "the bourgeoisie" by socialists and workers.

The professional and intellectual strata and the middle managers played a greater role. They also were a diverse grouping, ranging from relatively high-status professionals to rather low-status individuals within each profession. Some were conservative while others were part of the socialist intelligentsia. Despite such differences, the professionals provided the core of support for the Provisional Government. Not only were many of the ministers of the new government from the professions – lawyers, doctors, professors – but they appointed large numbers of professionals as assistant ministers and to staff the administration both in the center and in the provinces. Moreover, the socialist-oriented wing of the professions played a leading role in the soviets, in local government and, after the formation of the coalition government in May, in the central government structures. In army uniform they provided the leadership of the higher army committees via socialist intellectuals. The professional middle classes, socialists and liberals, dominated local city councils and were influential in smaller towns and large villages through rural teachers, doctors, agronomists and other professionals. Indeed, one might argue that the professional middle classes played the leading role in politics in 1917, dominating both government and soviets, centrally and locally. They were the mainstay of the centrist coalition of liberals and moderate socialists who comprised the February System. At the same time, however, professionals and intellectuals were sharply divided along political – socialist versus nonsocialist – lines. They also felt that they had little in common with the commercial middle class and tended to be hostile toward both the industrial elite and middle managers. Few of them conceived of their newfound public roles as reflecting the interests of a middle class.

The third part of the middle classes was the lower middle strata: artisans, lower-status white-collar clerks (government, commercial and industrial), many technical employees, retail shop employees, pharmacy workers and others, plus some small merchants and traders. They saw the revolution as opening up not only a better future for Russia, but for themselves as a group. They shared in the urge toward self-organization and formed dozens and dozens of unions and professional organizations to represent their interests. They had suffered significant economic hardship and were eager to improve their economic position. Many of their early demands were similar to those of the workers in that they included higher wages, an eight-hour day and greater dignity on the job. Striking waiters demanded an end to tipping as undignified, and striking retail shop clerks in May insisted that they no longer be required to stand outside the store and entice customers in. Their early efforts were relatively successful in gaining benefits for their members, and they were generally supportive of the Provisional Government as the embodiment of the new democratic age. However, they were soon caught in an economic squeeze as inflation outstripped salary gains and as employers resisted new salary concessions. Many turned toward the socialist parties, some identifying themselves as members of the working class.

The lower middle-class employees also struggled to take a greater share of power within their various institutional settings – office, store, professional unions – from their higher-status professional or bureaucratic superiors. This involved a drive for democratization which eventually brought them to a close identification with many of the demands of industrial labor and the socialist parties. At the congress of post and telegraph workers in May, speakers called for either elected managers and section chiefs or the transfer of administrative authority to elected collective management. The congress declaration called for abolition of all hierarchical ranks and occupation distinctions among higher and lower employees. The Fifth All-Russia Congress of Commercial and Industrial Employees in Moscow in July included in their resolution the assertion that employees were part of the proletariat within the capitalist structure.[28] Salaried employees formed unions and asserted a version of "workers' supervision" within their offices over personnel matters, hours of operation, work schedules and similar issues. Medical assistants and nurses contested authority and status with doctors.

As 1917 progressed the professional and lower middle classes split apart politically. The nonsocialist elements turned toward a more conservative stance and into supporters of demands for "order," while the socialist-oriented intellectuals and much of the lower middle class turned toward the soviets and even the radicals. The evolution of much of the urban lower middle strata toward a self-identity as "workers," and their acceptance of socialism politically, was one of the major social trends of the revolution. Given their precarious economic position, low social status and the new prestige of being "workers," as well as the power of the soviets, it is not surprising that many artisanal and small shop workers – bakers, tailors and others – stressed working-class identity, formed unions and sought representation in the local soviet. More striking is that many government and commercial white-collar employees did so as well, forming unions and asserting their worker status. As Michael Hickey points out, writing of Smolensk, "the proximity for artisans, workers and employees in their daily lives, and their common struggle with bad housing, filthy water, food shortages and innumerable other hardships also helped forge a sense of solidarity, which they expressed in terms of class."[29]

The movement of the lower middle strata toward a "worker" identity not only strengthened the socialist parties' electoral hold in the cities, but destroyed any prospect for a significant specifically middle-class political movement. It damaged the Kadets and other liberals in the summer elections to the city councils and dimmed their prospects for the Constituent Assembly elections. Potential leaders of the revolution, the middle classes fractured and failed to play that role. Instead, socialist and more liberal professional and lower middle-class individuals played leadership roles on behalf of other classes, workers and soldiers especially. Indeed, most of the radical socialist leadership had social origins in the professional and lower middle class, but achieved power in 1917 by rejecting that identity.

Women

World War I and the revolution presented women with new opportunities and perhaps even greater problems and stresses. They responded in different ways, depending on personal circumstances, social-economic status, political orientation, and/or individual personalities. Women were, as we noted earlier, both very diverse and strongly influenced by nongender identities, the same political, social, economic,

ethnic and other attributes that affected men. Russian women responded to the revolution in a variety of ways, heavily influenced by
their social-economic status and/or political orientation. For most
women in 1917 their other, nongender identities were sufficiently
important as mobilizing factors that it is difficult to generalize about
women's aspirations in the way one can about workers, soldiers or
peasants. In this respect they are similar to the minority nationalities
(chapter 6). Nonetheless the war and revolution affected them as
women and they reacted to both in certain gender-specific ways.

The war had a mixed social and economic impact on women. It took
about one-third of the male population of working age away from
homes and jobs. This opened up new job and civic opportunities, but
also new responsibilities and dangers, for women. For some women,
especially those of the middle and upper classes, the war opened
opportunities for adventure and civic activism, such as serving as
nurses near the front or staffing first-aid and canteen stations. This
even led Nicholas II to create a new service award specifically for
women, the St. Olga's medal. As the war took away men to the army it
created new job and better wage opportunities for women in fields that
had previously been closed or restricted. For many women, however, it
was a new hardship. Many of the women who filled these jobs were
forced to do so because their husbands had been called to the army,
and sometimes killed, and they now bore the burden of feeding their
families. The small allowances paid to soldiers' wives and widows
hardly compensated for the economic loss of the main family bread-
winner. Their problem was compounded by the fact that, even when
women managed to obtain a job roughly equivalent to that of their
husbands or fathers, women were paid a much lower wage. Urban
women also bore the brunt of housing shortages, inflation and declining
medical and public services, while rural women had to take over the
heavy farm work formerly done by men. Moreover, for women of all
classes, even those who were economically secure, the war forced them
to take on responsibilities and decision making that they had never
expected, desired or been prepared for. One feminist journal writer
asked "How many hapless mothers are there today who until now have
been living under the tutelage of a husband but are now obliged to
struggle independently for the survival of their children? With horror
they realize that they are not capable of doing that because they lack the
experience and the skills, so they let their hands sink down, and the
family will perish."[30]

The revolution opened even wider the crack in the door that the war
had provided for women, in terms of both opportunities and hardships.

The greatest impact, and the place where gender-based aspirations and new areas of opportunity can be most clearly seen, was among educated middle- and upper-class women. From them had arisen earlier both a Russian feminist movement and women activists in the various political parties. Both the liberal and socialist parties had long stressed the importance of women's rights and had enlisted many educated Russian women in their ranks. There was, however, a long history of dispute between feminists and socialist women, and the two groups responded differently to the new opportunities presented by the February Revolution.

The feminist agenda represents one of the most clear-cut gender-specific responses to the revolution, and an area of definite gains. A feminist movement emerged in late nineteenth- and early twentieth-century Russia which stressed the particular needs and aspirations of women within whatever political and economic system existed. It drew on Western feminists for inspiration and like them put great stress on equal legal rights, access to education and professions, and after 1905 on obtaining the franchise – the right to vote. Many feminists identified with the liberal political parties, especially the Kadets.

The February Revolution and the freedoms it brought invigorated the feminist movement. Feminists immediately took advantage of it to expand organizational activities and to lobby for the vote and other rights. When the initial declaration by the Provisional Government about "universal" elections to the Constituent Assembly did not specifically include women, feminist organizations reacted promptly. The League for Women's Equal Rights organized a great demonstration on March 19 in which about 40,000 women marched to the Tauride Palace to demand the vote. Although Prince Lvov promised them support, many men opposed extending the franchise. This included many socialists who feared that women, especially peasants, would vote for restoring the monarchy. Some, like Alexander Kerensky, asserted that the question would have to be decided at the Constituent Assembly, which would have excluded women from participating in Russia's most important election. Such opposition failed. Under continued pressure from feminists the Provisional Government on July 20 granted women the right to vote. Moreover, during the summer feminists successfully pressed the government for improved access to higher education and the professions (especially the right to practice law), equal opportunities and pay in the civil service, and other rights. These activities were the purest expression of specifically women's aspirations and activism in 1917.[31]

At the same time feminists became involved in other political issues

Plate 13 Part of a demonstration for women's rights. The banner proclaims "If woman is unfree [literally, a slave] there can be no freedom. Long live equal rights for women." Courtesy of Jonathan Sanders.

and became more closely tied to the Kadet Party and the policies of the Provisional Government, including support for the war. This reflected their generally middle- and upper-class social status. Indeed, three of the most prominent women among the Kadet leadership were also leaders in the feminist movement: Ariadna Tyrkova (the only woman member of the party's central committee at the time of the February Revolution), Anna Miliukova (the wife of Paul Miliukov, the Kadet leader) and Countess Sofia Panina (deputy minister of education in the Provisional Government, the highest-ranking woman government official).

Educated women in the socialist parties, however, rejected feminism. These parties had long argued that women's interests were more strongly defined by class than by gender and that they had more in common with men of their own class than with women of other classes. Although the socialist parties' programs called for universal suffrage, for equal civil, educational, employment and other rights, and for specific programs to provide maternity leave and other needs of women in the workplace, the emphasis was on class goals. Socialist leaders were concerned with women as low-paid workers rather than as people with special gender concerns. Issues of specific interest to women, they argued, would be resolved through a sweeping revolution which would transform fundamental legal, economic and social structures, including property ownership, marriage, family life, living arrangements, the economic relations between men and women, and other facts of women's lives.[32] The socialists therefore rejected a separate feminist agenda as a distraction from the main struggle.

The socialist parties were in fact somewhat ambivalent in their attitude toward women, whom they tended to categorize as backward, unreliable and conservative. Nonetheless, they undertook to build support among women, especially urban workers. This was both a matter of principle and a realization that women would have the right to vote not only in general elections, but also in working-class organizations, helping elect factory committees, soviet delegates and trade union representatives. Therefore their support was important in the struggle among the socialist parties for dominance within those institutions. During the war the number of women in the factories increased from 26 percent to 43 percent of the nationwide industrial work force and from about a quarter to about a third in Petrograd.[33]

The Bolsheviks, consistent with their general campaigning effort in 1917, put the most effort into building a women's program and support among women. In March, under pressure from women activists, they recreated the "Bureau of Women Workers" within the party to agitate among women. Soon afterwards they authorized revival of the newspaper *Rabotnitsa* (*Woman Worker*). This was a "lively, engaging, tabloid-sized magazine containing poetry, fiction, news stories on conditions in the factories, articles on the history of the revolutionary movement and editorials on political events."[34] It published articles on child care, maternity insurance, equal rights, equal pay and other issues of particular interest to women workers as well as articles about general political and economic issues. A group Barbara Clements has called "Bolshevik feminists" conducted an extensive campaign utilizing newspaper articles, pamphlets and speeches focused on the issues and needs of special concern to women, but at the same time explaining in simple terms how the issues of concern to women – both general class issues as well as gender-specific ones – could not be solved by the Provisional Government but only by a radical socialist revolution. They stressed the importance of solidarity of women with men against the war and on other issues. The Bolsheviks loudly supported the great strike of laundresses and the demands of the *soldatki*, the soldiers' wives, for a higher monetary allotment. At the same time they vigorously attacked the feminist movement as "bourgeois." Other parties courted women also. The Mensheviks also published a special newspaper, *Women's Voice*, but appear not to have been as active in this area as the Bolsheviks. The SRs only belatedly devoted special attention to women.

The Bolsheviks, despite the efforts of their women leaders, nonetheless retained an ambivalence toward women, which probably was typical of the other socialist parties as well. While allowing *Rabotnitsa* and agitational work among women, they (including most female leaders) constantly emphasized that women could meet their aspirations only through the general social revolution. They vigilantly guarded against efforts by some women, such as Alexandra Kollontai, to set up special women's organizations within the party. Although they allowed an initiative group to work on participation in a Conference of Working Women, when it finally met November 12 (after the Bolsheviks had taken power), the party leaders beat back an effort to create special women's organizations and rejected arguments that women needed to be elected to the Constitutional Assembly to defend their particular interests. Klavdiia Nikolaeva, speaking for the Bolsheviks, warned that "we, conscious women workers, know that we have no special women's interests, there should be no special women's organizations."[35]

Nonetheless, women played an active public role. All the major parties had prominent women members – Nadezhda Krupskaia, Alexandra Kollontai, Nadezhda Stasova and others for the Bolsheviks, Maria Spiridonova for the Left SRs and Ekaterina Breshko-Breshkovskaia for the right SRs, Eva Broido among the Mensheviks and Tyrkova, Miliukova and Panina among the Kadets. These prominent women and other women activists engaged in a wide range of political roles: public orators, agitators, party organizers, union activists, writers, delegates to city councils and soviets, etc. Nonetheless, men filled almost all the leadership positions at all levels. Women tended to play secretarial and administrative support rather than policy roles, or to be assigned responsibilities for issues traditionally considered "women's" such as education, family and health. Indeed, most of the prominent Bolshevik women in Petrograd were assigned such roles. In contrast, Maria Spiridonova of the Left SRs broke that pattern and not only concerned herself with the same political issues as male politicians, but emerged as a top Left SR leader. Similar patterns could be found in the provinces and at the middle and lower levels of party activism.[36] Outside of the political parties, many educated women took active, even leadership, roles in the numerous new or expanded cultural, educational, economic and civic organizations of 1917.

While the revolution clearly stimulated and opened opportunities for

educated women, whether feminist or revolutionary socialist, the response of the great bulk of women was different. For peasant women
the revolution did not open up any kind of "women's question." Their
concerns were basically the same as the menfolk – land and peace. In
theory the revolution might have challenged the often harsh patriarchy
of the village, but it did not in 1917. Some did take advantage of the
combination of revolutionary, social and political flux and the loss of
husbands to the army to assert a louder voice in village affairs because
of their role as family heads, but these were exceptions. Mostly
illiterate, living in grinding poverty and age-old patterns of village life,
peasant women did not see the revolution as a vehicle for changing the
role of women or the rules and structures of village life as it affected
them as women. Instead of gender opportunities the revolution
brought them economic problems and general uncertainty, and peasant
women responded by sticking tightly to the traditional village values,
family and social structure as a source of protection against growing
insecurity.[37] The year 1917 had little direct effect on peasant women as
women.

Urban working-class women took a more active role in 1917 than did
their peasant sisters, but less than middle- and upper-class women.
They had already been activated by the food and goods riots that had
broken out sporadically in Russian cities and towns in 1915–16, and
played a central role in the beginning of the popular revolt in February
1917. After the collapse of the monarchy they shared the general
euphoria about a better future and rejoiced in the opportunities apparently opened up for them. Some took an active role in public life, joining
trade unions, as deputies to soviets and factory committees, and in other
ways. They were, however, a distinct minority and usually in subordi-
nate and gender-specific roles (as, for example, forming medical and
canteen auxiliaries for Red Guard units). Men dominated the working-
class institutions, especially leadership positions, although occasionally
women emerged in prominent roles. Even in predominantly female
factories the union and factory committee leaders were usually men.
Women often complained that at factory meetings they were either
blocked from speaking or not listened to.

Women workers did take advantage of the new conditions to strike for
improvement of their lot. The prolonged strike of laundry workers in
Petrograd was perhaps the most successful example of organized assertiveness by a large group of working-class women after February. Even it
underscores the problematic nature of discussing women's aspirations,
however, for it was their class role as woefully exploited workers that
drove them rather than an identity as women. It garnered political

support and monetary donations from other unions and the socialist parties on the grounds of its importance to the working-class struggles. Indeed, Koenker and Rosenberg conclude from their study of strikes in 1917 that strikes in which the workers were predominantly women were more likely to be defensive and "that women did not appear in the forefront of strikes, and that when they struck, they did so reluctantly."[38]

For working-class women the overwhelming reality was concern with their precarious economic situation, which absorbed their energies. "Most working women," as Barbara Evans Clements has pointed out, "made their way through 1917 buffeted by vague hopes, real fears, overwork, hardship, and extreme confusion."[39] Their economic fears were heightened by the fact that male workers, when faced with factory layoffs, sometimes suggested that women go first since their families would still have the husband's wages or because they were recent wartime hires. Factory women's participation in 1917 emerged most clearly in traditionally feminine concerns. Even their most famous revolutionary role, as initiators of the February demonstrations that brought down the regime, was focused on protest over traditional women's areas of concern and responsibility: bread and the need to queue for food for their families. Significantly, women were also prominent in other food-related disorders in 1917 in Petrograd and elsewhere. How important bread and prices were in women's activities is also illustrated by the public meeting that the editors of *Rabotnitsa* (*Woman Worker*) organized at the Cinizelli Circus on the theme of "The War and High Prices." About 10,000 attended with the crowd overflowing into the street, where a second meeting took place.[40]

The *soldatki*, the soldiers' wives, were a special case of women organizing to assert themselves and to press their insistence that the revolution address their needs. The *soldatki* received a government allocation for themselves and their children, while war widows received a small pension. This, however, was grossly inadequate, especially with wartime inflation. Moreover, they were a restive element, strongly assertive of their special situation as wives of men suffering at the front. They were active in food and goods riots before and after the February Revolution. In March they quickly organized, a process facilitated by their organization by the old government into "guardianship" (payment) districts. On March 29 about 2,000 delegates from seventeen guardianship districts in Petrograd met and petitioned both the Provisional Government and the Petrograd Soviet to increase their allotment to 20 rubles per month per military dependent, adult or child. A meeting of April 3 called on all *soldatki* to gather at the Kazan Cathedral

Plate 14 Soldiers' wives' demonstration on April 9 on Nevsky Prospect, with
military servicemen carrying the banners in front. The banner greets the
Petrograd Soviet and calls for an increase in their allowance. Note that their
demand is directed to the Soviet, not the Provisional Government. Prints and
Photographs Division, Library of Congress.

for a great march through the city and then to the Tauride Palace, where
they would present their list of demands to the Soviet. On April 11
about 15,000 women did so. In mid-April a meeting of *soldatki* at the
Tauride Palace formed a citywide committee of *soldatki* representatives
and in June they formed a Union of Soldiers' Wives.[41] This happened
elsewhere also: in Tula soldiers' wives created a formal organization
whose chair and vice-chair later joined the Bolshevik Party.

The *soldatki* could be a vocal, aggressive element. A meeting of
women in the harbor region of Petrograd, convened by "a group of
SDs," attracted a large crowd of women factory workers, laundry
workers, domestic servants and *soldatki*. The latter set up a cry demanding an increase in their allotment, preventing other business from
taking place and prompting complaints from other groups of women
there. The *soldatki* did not yield, however, protesting that "Everyone
speaks of the women workers, the domestic servants and the laundry
workers, but about soldiers' wives not a word." Only after passage of a
resolution calling on the Petrograd Soviet to address the allotment issue
did they quiet down and let the meeting get on to other issues.[42] This

incident revealed the extent to which the *soldatki* believed that they were an especially deprived and suffering group, and that they deserved special consideration because of the sacrifices of their menfolk at the front for national defense. The *soldatki* were both an organized women's interest group and an important part of the street crowds during demonstrations in 1917.

There was yet one other way some women asserted themselves in 1917, and that was through military service in the specially formed women's battalions in the army. The first such unit, conceived of as a means to shame the men into performance of their military duties, was formed in May 1917. Proposed by Maria Bochkareva, a woman of peasant origins who had managed to serve in the regular army, it was supported by Kerensky (then minister of war), General A. A. Brusilov (commander-in-chief) and many conservatives. Bochkareva's "Women's Battalion of Death" received extensive publicity, both in Russia and from Western feminists. It was not merely a decorative device, however, and acquitted itself well in hard fighting during the June offensive. Other women's battalions formed in Petrograd, Moscow and elsewhere during the summer, drawing on a wide range of women, from aristocrats to middle class to peasants. It was a detachment of one of these later battalions that accidentally found itself among the last defenders of the Provisional Government at the Winter Palace during the October Revolution. Perhaps as many as 5,000 women joined these battalions, although only about 300, from Bochkareva's unit, saw combat.[43]

Indeed, the primary importance of the women's battalions proved to be symbolic and political rather than military. They were supported by pro-war political forces, who admired their patriotism and hoped they would shame the men and thereby motivate Russia's demoralized armies. Antiwar socialists strongly opposed them for those very same reasons. War-weary male soldiers were not energized, however, and sometimes attacked the women's units because they represented an effort to continue the fighting. Feminists, both inside and outside Russia, saw in them an assertion of equal rights; the British feminist Emmeline Pankhurst wrote glowing reports home about them during her visit to Russia. Russian feminist leaders toyed with a proposal to conscript large numbers of women into the army to fill the noncombatant roles. It is not at all clear, however, that feminist equality was a major motivating force for the women who joined. Patriotism, adventure and other issues were important also, perhaps more so. Here as in so many instances it is impossible to separate clearly the various identities and aspirations that moved people. For the vast majority of the women of Russia, in any case, the right to serve in the army, much less a desire to do so, was much less a concern than either the pressing economic problems or even the general civil rights of the feminist movement.

However difficult it is to distinguish specifically women's issues in 1917 – aside from the feminist campaign for the vote and equal rights – from broader issues affecting all members of society or a specific social class, in the end the revolution did change the position of women dramatically and permanently. This change came primarily in the political and civic realm and represented a victory for the feminists' agenda. The obtaining of the franchise – the first among any of the belligerents and of any of the great powers – was permanent. Moreover, in 1917 women entered public and political life in unprecedented numbers and ways. They voted in general elections and participated in selection of factory committees, soviets and trade union leadership. Some served as deputies in these and in city councils. Thousands became involved in the enormous variety of economic, social and cultural organizations that sprang up across Russia in the revolutionary year. This expanded civic involvement survived the civil war and the new Soviet state after 1917 confirmed and continued their enlarged role in public life. Improved access to professions and job opportunities also proved permanent. Although expanded women's rights was not one of the issues shaping the political outcome of the revolution, in a sense women, or feminists at least, were more successful than perhaps any other constituency in terms of permanent gains and fulfillment of aspirations. These gains did not change the deeply patriarchal nature of Russian society – the fundamental assumption that men provided political and other leadership was not seriously questioned by any political or social group – but they were significant gains nonetheless. This contains a certain irony in that most feminist leaders were middle and upper class, closely identified with the Kadet Party, and were either suppressed or forced to flee the country after 1917.

Freed from the controls imposed by tsarist government, the population of the Russian Empire created a remarkable range of organizations to express their interests and advance their aspirations. So many new organizations came into being that the manufacturers of rubber stamps and printers of name cards and letterhead stationary enjoyed a booming business servicing the new freedom of organization.[44] Aside from major organizations such as those described above and in the next two chapters, thousands of others were created. House owners' and apartment residents' associations, cultural and literacy clubs, professional associations and others organized and demanded acknowledgment of their interests. Typical were the new scientific societies formed after the February Revolution, often with broad social as well as professional agendas. Some were based on a belief that science and scientific education was essential to creating a free and democratic Russia. One such was the Free Association for the Development and Advancement of the Positive Sciences, founded in 1917. It held a series of well-attended public meetings, with audiences including such diverse political figures as Kerensky, Miliukov and Sukhanov.[45]

Indicative of the new spirit were public activism and organizations among two large elements in society, youth and the Orthodox Church. Young people founded clubs and political associations to meet their educational needs, for social and civic activities, and, in the case of working-class youth, to protect their special interests within factories where they campaigned for less discriminatory pay scales. In Petrograd a youth organization oriented toward economic issues, Labor and Light, enrolled huge numbers in the spring. Some youth organizations were created by or in cooperation with local political party circles. Youth groups were subject to the same political dynamics as other groups and moved left politically. Labor and Light lost out to a more militant organization, the Socialist League of Young Workers, which in the fall aligned itself with the Bolsheviks.

The new activism manifested itself even within the Orthodox Church. Contrary to what one might expect, the Orthodox Church did not play a significant role in the revolution in terms of defining ideological positions or sides in the political struggles. Instead, its attention turned toward internal reform. In one sense, this was part of the broader democratization of society and the challenge to authority that characterized the revolution in general. Central to the debates that followed was the question of the relative authority of the church hierarchy, the parish clergy, and the laity. On March 7 the "All-Russia Union of Democratic Orthodox Clergy and Laity" formed in Petrograd and quickly became an important voice for sweeping reforms in the church. It gained the support of V. N. Lvov, the procurator of the Holy Synod (chief administrator of the Orthodox Church) in the Provisional Government. Diocesan congresses and councils of clergy and laity – including women – met and decided on a range of issues, among them removal of some bishops and placing limits on bishops' authority. Some of the top clergy, especially those closely identified with Rasputin or considered archreactionaries, were forced out, while unpopular clergy were driven from other posts right down to parish priests. These reform efforts culminated in an All-Russian Sobor (Assembly) in August based on a free and secret ballot. The Sobor was to resolve authoritatively the church reform issues (a sort of parallel to the Constituent Assembly in the political world) and, hopefully, reinvigorate the church in the new revolutionary context.[46] The religious element in the revolution was not so much an active political role by the church as a tendency by many to use religious concepts and terminology to describe it; in the optimistic early period, which coincided with the Easter season, some used the phrase "Russia has arisen," a paraphrase of the traditional Easter greeting, "Christ has arisen."

Civic identity was complex: people had multiple identities based on occupation, income, nationality, religion, gender, political affiliation and other characteristics. These often divided people otherwise closely identified. In Smolensk, for example, there was significant conflict among doctors, dentists, *feldshers* (medical assistants), nurses and other health care providers about inclusion or exclusion of lower-status professions from within an organization of higher-status ones.[47] Such sorting out of identities underscored divisions in society and undermined liberal hopes for a political consensus based on broad national common interests.

These small group identities did not, however, prevent large segments of society from perceiving events from the perspective of broad class or other interests, nor the conflict that followed. Despite the multitude of organizations and interest groups, it is clear that most of the population also coalesced into large social groupings such as those discussed in this chapter, with shared general aspirations which they organized to fulfill. With proper caution, generalizations about them are possible and indeed are essential to any meaningful discussion of the revolution. All small group identities existed alongside and usually within a very important general division of society into two broad social-political categories that were seen as inherently antagonistic. These were variously expressed as *nizy* (lower classes) versus *verkhi* (upper classes), "democratic" versus "privileged," "workers" against "bourgeoisie" and soldiers versus officers. These distinctions were widely used in 1917 in the press, speeches, and resolutions, reflecting one way people saw society and their place and interests within it. The continued public use of these categories – in speeches, newspapers and conversations – in turn helped shape social identities. They not only represented real social-economic divisions, but also took on important political implications as the revolution became an intense struggle for control of government, with full awareness that government did not merely represent the "public interest" but often advanced the interests of one group or another.

Popular aspirations came together with politics in 1917 because people were immersed in politics as a way to fulfill their aspirations. The February Revolution brought not merely the overthrow of the monarchy, but a new type of politics characterized by mass politics, the idea of popular sovereignty, and elections. Elections were a continual and varied process. People participated in local government elections and in elections for a wide range of committees, councils, soviets, associations, and other public and private organizations via their various capacities as workers, soldiers, peasants, women, nationalities, trade union members, professionals, householders, etc., across the entire enormous country. These elections were accompanied by debates, discussions, speeches, flyers, posters, and other features of electoral campaigns that drew people into political life. For those hundreds of thousands of the new "free citizens" of "democratic Russia" who were elected, it brought an even deeper involvement in public life. As Peter Holquist has noted, "The true measure of the revolutionary trans-formation in 1917 was to be found in the massive participation of citizens in this new political universe."[48]

5   The peasants and the purposes of revolution

The peasants identified revolution with obtaining land. Land was the first principle. Second was the closely related goal of gaining control over their lives and creating a new economic, political and even moral relationship in the countryside, one that fit more closely with the peasant view of the world. The February Revolution and the collapse of authority that followed it created an opportunity for the peasants to fulfill these ancient aspirations. The revolution removed or seriously weakened the traditional coercive vehicles – police, courts, army – by which state and landlords controlled peasant actions and enforced the old relationships in the countryside. The peasants quickly grasped the fact that, with the weakness of the state and of landowners, they could now act with little fear of the customary retribution. The thousands of scattered villages moved to fulfill their vision of the right order of things and, instead of the usual failure, the cumulative result produced a sweeping agrarian revolution. They were supported by peasants and former peasants in the army and cities – banners inscribed "Land and Liberty," the succinct old slogan of peasant demands, were in almost every popular demonstration in 1917, in Petrograd and across the country.[a]

The village organizes

News of the revolution trickled into the peasant villages during March. The peasants moved cautiously at first, remembering the repressions that had followed the Revolution of 1905 and watching to see if the

---

[a] The following discussion will focus on the Russo-Ukrainian heartland and peasantry. Not only did they make up over two-thirds of the total population, but were the most important peasants in terms of the impact of their actions on national politics. The remaining peasants represented diverse small rural social systems scattered mostly around the outer edges of the empire and had relatively little effect on the national debate about land or on the great peasant revolution; to deal with each of them would be extremely complex and would require much more space than we have. However, many of the basic features discussed here do apply to them also.

revolution in the cities would last and for indications of how the wind was blowing. Moreover, they were willing to give the new government an opportunity to address their main concerns. At first they were optimistic. From their point of view the issue was, after all, simple: revolution meant that the land would become theirs and that they would assume greater control over their own affairs. This was the purpose of revolution. They would judge the new government and its actions accordingly.

While waiting for the government to act on land distribution the peasants asserted ever more strongly their control over their lives and affairs. For the peasants this meant first of all the village assembly, where they gathered to discuss this revolution as they did the other important events of their public lives. Traditionally the heads of households, and hence primarily the older males, dominated the assemblies and village decision making. In a major social revolution that spread over 1917 the assembly was expanded and democratized as all adult male peasants of the village began to participate, including younger male members of households and landless laborers. Younger men, often with experience in the broader world outside the village through army service or work in the cities, took an increasing role. In this process a new village leadership emerged which was younger, less cautious, more open to new ideas and to revolutionary activism. The situation varied from village to village, and often the old village elder (*starosta*) retained an influential role if he had the trust of his fellows, but overall a transformation of village decision making and leadership began. Returning soldiers were especially assertive of their right to a voice. In some places even women participated (because of the war women represented two-thirds to three-fourths of the rural work force).

The peasants quickly institutionalized the new order in the village through the election of village committees (sometimes, especially near cities, these were called soviets). The villagers, acting through these committees and buttressed by periodic meetings of the village assembly, took control of local life, diminishing or ending the role of representatives of the government or of other outside elements. These committees discussed and increasingly acted on the whole range of issues which concerned the peasants: land distribution, rents, wages for rural laborers, relations with landlords, access to woods and meadows, public order and others. They also met and determined the course of action in the more violent deeds undertaken by the villagers collectively, such as land seizure or estate destruction. The peasantry showed the same urge to self-organization and self-assertion as the urban population, creating a variety of special committees and organizations in the villages to implement their desires.

Encouraged by initial successes in asserting themselves at the village communal level, the peasants soon moved to expand their new self-determination by creating committees at the next larger level of geographical-political organization, the *volost*, or rural district.[b] Formed by representatives from the villages in late March and April, these district committees took over local governmental functions from the old authorities. This, however, was the geographic extent of peasant self-government, and the drive to create their own institutions rarely went beyond this level to larger territorial bodies. Peasant organization was based on the village. It could spread to the group of villages that made up the small rural district (*volost*), but rarely beyond that. Larger geographic organizations were beyond the peasant approach to managing life and fell to outside organizers, the government and the political parties. The district (*volost*) therefore became the main point of contact, and conflict, between peasants and higher political authority.

Even this degree of peasant self-activity disturbed the government, however, for the latter was concerned with ensuring both a steady flow of food to the cities and army and an orderly agrarian reform. Therefore the government moved fairly quickly to create new temporary rural government institutions. On March 5 the new government formally abolished the old provincial governors' offices and appointed province and *uezd* commissars to take their place temporarily. Most of these were local zemstvo chairmen, who in most cases were local noble landowners presumed to be civic minded and perhaps reform oriented. On March 20 the Provisional Government authorized its provincial commissars to set up special district (*volost*) committees composed of peasants, nobles and other social groups of the countryside (teachers, agronomists, doctors and others of the "rural intelligentsia," and merchants and artisans of the villages and small towns). These would take responsibility for governing locally until new regular institutions could be created.[1]

The government's effort to create a new rural order had mixed results. It was not particularly successful at the district (*volost*) or village level. The initial tendency to appoint local notables or intellectuals, even if of a liberal reputation, as local administrators alienated the peasants.

---

[b] The main Russian geographic political subdivisions were, in descending order of size, the *guberniia* (province), the *uezd*, the *volost* and the village/commune. The commune was the village as a political and economic entity (most peasant land was held collectively by the commune, not privately) and an agency for self-governance. The term district is often used in English writings for both *uezd* and *volost*; I will use it primarily for *volost* and in some cases simply to mean a smaller rural administrative unit where exactitude is not essential. Where precision is necessary the Russian *volost* and *uezd* will be used.

The government's need to appoint officials to get an administrative system set up quickly conflicted with the peasants' urge for their own chosen self-government. Indeed, the peasants quickly became reluctant to have any segment of educated society speak for them or over them. By late spring a report reviewing the first three months of the revolution in the countryside stated that "the peasants avoid electing representatives of the intelligentsia – this has been particularly noticeable lately. As time went on, they became more and more convinced that the intelligentsia has no place among them; that they must manage their own affairs without interference."[2] At the district and village level the self-formed peasant committees increasingly predominated and the government-sanctioned multiclass institutions lost out to them. The peasants were taking control of their world and their lives.

The government had somewhat more success in the towns and cities of the provinces, where a larger intellectual and middle-class element existed and the political parties could play more of a role. Here the main government institutions were found. At these levels the peasant had much less influence, even over the institutions claiming to speak in his name such as provincial congresses of peasants' deputies and governmentally organized land and food supply committees. An important division in attitudes developed between the peasant-dominated village and district (*volost*) organizations on the one hand, and the townsmen-dominated *uezd* and province institutions on the other.

These differing attitudes and the conflict that resulted grew in part out of differing views of the peasant as a citizen with a role in shaping the new Russia. The peasants saw themselves, as they often put it in letters to the government and newspapers, as "free and law-abiding citizens."[3] In contrast, the new state leadership and the intelligentsia, centrally and locally, saw the peasants as the "dark people." This term summarized the widely held traditional elite and intelligentsia view of the peasants as ignorant, backward, uncultured, and perhaps morally deficient as well, and who needed extensive tutelage before they could become genuine citizens of the new free Russian republic and full participants in creating the new society. To this end the state and local elites organized meetings and festivals in the villages to celebrate the revolution and at which the peasants' new obligations were explained in speeches and sermons (often, symbolically, held at the village school and village church). These differed dramatically from traditional peasant notions of festivals and celebrations with their drinking, dancing, games and revelry. From the elite's view, peasants needed "enlightenment" and to acquire certain habits in order to become full and deserving citizens of the new Russia. These, to be acquired under intelligentsia and government tutelage, included to keep order, respect property rights, obtain education, reduce drinking, learn their duty to the nation (defined as paying taxes, providing foodstuffs and supporting the war), and generally acquire "culture." Peasants, on the other hand, saw themselves as already fully equal citizens with the right to participate in shaping the new order and state, even though they also accepted the need for "enlightenment" and often used the elite's negative terminology for themselves, such as "dark people." They often used such negative terms resourcefully, however – for example, to explain away blatantly illegal acts such as land seizures. They frequently used humble, deferential, traditional terminology to speak to the government and soviets while, with a new assertiveness, demanding land, calling for return of sons and husbands from the front, or making other revolutionary claims. The elite (especially urban) and peasants held polar opposite views of the peasantry's role, which exacerbated both peasant–elite and peasant–state conflict in 1917, starting with local governance but extending far beyond that.

The struggle over food supply

The problem of food supplies for the cities and army quickly revealed the discrepancy between peasant aspirations and government concerns, and led to conflict. The government's immediate concern was the food supply for the army and the cities. It considered land distribution and other agrarian reform issues important, but felt that they could be postponed; they took second place in its priorities to the food issue. For the peasants, in contrast, land and other immediate economic issues were not only paramount, but pressing. This urgency reflected not only belief differences, but also that the peasants were acutely attuned to seasonal time pressures for planting and harvesting. Conflict was inevitable and swift in coming. The government, having inherited from the old regime a serious shortfall in food delivery, moved quickly to set up a food procurement system. In doing so, it reflected a broad consensus among both government bureaucrats and liberal and socialist intellectuals about the importance of greater government supervision of the economy, especially foodstuffs, that had developed during the war.[4] As early as March 9 it formed a State Committee on Food Supply, followed on March 25 by the establishment of a state grain monopoly with fixed prices. The new regulations provided for a hierarchy of provincial and district food supply committees as well, representing a variety of urban and rural groups.[5] The peasants generally distrusted these primarily town committees, seeing them – correctly – as dominated by land-owners, townsmen, merchants and government officials. They recognized that these committees' primary goal was other than the peasants' interests.

Peasants resented and resisted the government controls and requisitioning. The whole grain-requisitioning process, besides controls and regulations that the peasants considered improper, assumed that the currency in which they would be paid was stable (it was not) and that consumer goods would be forthcoming at equivalent prices (they were not). Indeed, part of the problem and a source of peasant discontent was that the "articles of prime necessity" (essential consumer goods and farm items needed by the peasants), promised at set or low prices as part of the state monopoly and fixed prices on grain, were not forthcoming in adequate quantity because industry was oriented so completely toward war production. Angered by government policies, low grain prices, high costs and shortage of manufactured goods, in addition to their concern over the relatively poor spring harvest in 1917, the peasants resisted parting with their grain. Well practiced over the centuries in evading decrees from above, they now did so again.

Government collection policies and peasant resistance soon led to conflicts between peasants and food supply agents. In some cases the latter tried to use military units to force the peasants to deliver, but these were rarely successful and only fueled resentments. At one village in Samara province, for example, when the supply officials and soldiers arrived the church bells were rung, the peasants assembled, men, women and children, and shouted that the grain would be taken "only over our dead bodies." The officials left without grain.[6] Sometimes supply officials were beaten or even killed. In the end the government was forced repeatedly to raise the prices paid and to countenance evasions, while the cities expanded rationing and suffered repeated scares about food shortages. Some cities (and even individual factories) in the grain-consuming provinces of the north began to send out special purchasing agents to the grain-producing provinces to buy and transport back foodstuffs.

Despite these failures the government, especially as the influence of the socialists increased after May, was unwilling to turn from greater state control to relying more on market incentives for the peasants. They feared that this would strengthen the larger peasant producers and large estates. The SRs, whose support was essential to any government after May, were committed to destroying those larger landholdings through a land distribution program. Those larger holdings, however, produced a disproportionate part of the grain offered for sale on the market. Therefore land distribution, whether by the government or through peasant land seizures (see pp. 136–41), by reducing the holdings of larger farmers and estates also reduced the amount of grain available for transfer by any mechanism to the nonagricultural sectors. The result of government grain policies and peasant attitudes was the collapse of the system for marketing agricultural goods, which had major ramifications for the entire society. As John Keep has noted, "this was as important in the short term as expropriation of the landowners was in the long term . . .; the peasants' refusal to hand over their produce to official purchasing organizations helped to disrupt the economy. By curtailing food supplies to the towns and to the army it aggravated the social crisis and indirectly helped to bring down the Provisional Government."[7] It also stimulated peasant violence.

Land redistribution and land seizure

Throughout all the controversies over governance, food procurement and other issues, the peasants kept their attention focused on their main concern – the land and its redistribution. The peasantry believed that the land belonged by moral right to those who worked it, i.e., themselves. The purpose of revolution was to take land owned by private landlords, the state, church and other outsiders and distribute it among the peasants. The rhetoric of the socialist parties supported these attitudes.

Yet the government found it difficult to develop a satisfactory land distribution policy, even after the socialists joined it. There was a general consensus that some sort of land distribution would be a part of the revolution, but little agreement beyond that. First of all there was an absolute difference of opinion between the nonsocialist parties (the Kadets in effect) and the socialist parties over compensation to landowners for expropriated land, over communal versus private holdings, and other issues. In addition the socialists, even the so-called peasants' party, the Socialist Revolutionaries, were themselves seriously divided over what specifically to do and how to go about it. This made it extremely difficult to reach any kind of political agreement about land distribution, while making it easy to delay action, citing the authority of the Constituent Assembly on so important a matter. Indeed, as long as the political parties clung to the idea of coalition government, agreement and thus land reform were impossible.

Despite these sources of friction the Provisional Government quickly turned to the matter of land reform, which was too important to ignore. To work on the land reform question it set up a committee, the Main

Land Committee, which soon created a hierarchy of local committees and special commissions. At the top the Main Land Committee and its commissions became mired in long policy disputes and the sheer complexity of the issue. At the lowest, district level the committees tended to be taken over by the peasants and used by them to advance their claims to land. The creation of the coalition cabinet on May 4 brought the SRs into the government and Victor Chernov, the most prestigious leader of the SRs, to the Ministry of Agriculture. Many expected that "the village minister," as he was sometimes called, would move quickly to implement land reform. In this Chernov proved a disappointment. He met fierce opposition within both the government and his own party which he could not overcome, while at the same time he squandered his energies on a wide range of political and polemical battles. The end result was that, although the government repeatedly assured the peasants that there would be a general land distribution, it failed to develop, much less implement, one.

The peasant response to government procrastination varied. Most peasants waited reasonably patiently for the land distribution, even as they took control over other aspects of their lives through village committees, domination of local land committees, reaction to requisitions and in other ways. Not all waited patiently, however. Some moved quickly, even violently, to gain full control of the land, and these actions gave the rural revolution its special flavor. The rural community worked to a seasonal rhythm of planting and harvesting and this, plus the impatient demand for action which characterized all of Russia during 1917, pushed peasants to take the land issue into their own hands. Their ability to do so was facilitated by three facts: the peasants now controlled the local rural government apparatus, the new regime did not have at its disposal the means of armed coercion which could force the peasants to wait or do other than as they wished, and the mature male landowners who might have more effectively opposed them locally were largely away serving in the army or public offices. The peasants thus were free to carry out their own land revolution, in which violence in various forms played a role.

There were many types of peasant direct action in 1917, which varied by region and local agricultural characteristics.[8] About a third of all actions involved the seizure of crop land and its redistribution among the peasants, and well over half involved seizure of land in general (including pastures, meadows and woodlands).[9] For croplands, the critical time for the peasant was planting time, and thus seizure of land tended to be concentrated in the periods just before the spring and fall sowing and just before the summer harvest. About 80 percent of those in Saratov and Penza provinces – two important and restive agricultural areas – occurred at these times.[10] Often land seizure led to confiscation of tools, implements, draft animals and even buildings, as these were seen as directly tied to use of the land. Once begun, land seizure built on its own momentum: in Sychevka district of Smolensk province, the Subbotino subdistrict peasant executive committee began the seizure of "excess" gentry land as early as April 27, starting a process of seizures throughout the whole district. In June a Subbotino peasants' meeting escalated the process by ordering the confiscation of all meadowland of private landowners of any kind. By August, especially after the government tried to rein in land seizures, the process became more pervasive and more violent.[11]

Land seizures often took the guise of putting idle land to cultivation. During the war considerable private land had fallen idle. The government, concerned with the spring sowing, moved to maximize the sown acreage. A law of April 11 provided that, if a landowner refused to sow land, it "shall be placed at the disposal" of the local food supply committees and rented "for a fair price to local landowners [including peasants]."[12] The peasants quickly took advantage of the law, using it as a justification for appropriating private estate lands. Sometimes they also took over agricultural equipment, livestock, pastures and other assets, either on the basis that they too were underutilized or else were necessary for working the land which had been seized. Another decree on July 16 sanctioned the taking over of idle land in preparation for the harvest and hay gathering as well as readying land for the fall planting. Although the decree admonished the peasants against illegal action, they simply saw it both as vindication of their prior actions and justification for more seizures.

Moreover, the peasants were sometimes enterprising in getting at the land by ensuring that it was "idle" or the harvesting of it in doubt. They often took advantage of the landowners' need for hired peasant labor or renting out of land by demanding higher wages or lower rents; where landlords resisted the peasants sometimes refused them labor and then appropriated the land on the claim that it was idle. Where prisoners of war or refugees were being used to work estate land, the peasants sometimes forcibly blocked this. One district committee sent a local landowner, Prince Golytsin, a command that "by 10 a.m. on 10 April you are required to send to the district office all prisoners of war employed in agricultural work, since they are needed by the citizens of this district," and threatened use of force if he did not comply.[13] Once deprived of labor the estates could then be declared idle and taken over by the peasants via the committees. At the same time the peasants often got the prisoners as laborers for their own use, thus benefiting doubly. The peasants were able, moreover, to wrap these seizures in the mantle of patriotic duty of ensuring maximum utilization of the land, as well as claiming that they were carrying out government policy.

When seizing land the peasants generally acted together as a village, often after a meeting of the village assembly decided on the action. The villagers often required that all peasants join so that responsibility was shared by all. At the appointed time they would assemble in the village with the carts necessary to carry off the plunder and march on the estate. Frequently a written "order" was given to the landlord or his manager, spelling out in detail what lands were to be taken and what left to the landlord for his personal use (usually a "share" based on what he could personally farm with his own family's labor). When other property was taken this sometimes was accompanied by a detailed written inventory. The owner or manager, if he had not fled, might be forced to sign a document handing over land and goods to the village or district committee. Grains and other stored materials were hauled off. Usable tools and equipment were taken, while more complex machinery, which the peasants could not use, was often destroyed. Similarly, livestock was often taken. These items were apportioned among the villagers. The same practice applied when the peasants took over pastures, meadows, woodlands and other valuable land. For the most part these seizures were not accompanied by physical attacks on landowners, especially during the first half of the year.

A graphic description of an actual seizure which incorporates many of the main features of peasant seizure – including both its highly organized manner and how much chance played a role in the process – comes from a contemporary newspaper account by the victim:

At mid-day the village assembly met to decide the fate of our property, which was large and well equipped. The question to be decided was posed with stark simplicity; should they burn the house or not? At first they decided just to take all our belongings and to leave the building. But this decision did not satisfy some of those present, and another resolution was passed; to burn everything except the house, which was to be kept as a school. At once the whole crowd moved off to the estate, took the keys from the manager, and commandeered all the cattle, farm machinery, carriages, stores etc. For two days they carried off whatever they could. Then they split into groups of twenty, divided up the loot into heaps, one for each group, and cast lots which group should get which. In the middle of this redistribution a sailor appeared, a local lad who had been on active service. He insisted that they should burn down the house as well. The peasants got clever. They went off to inspect the house a second time. One of them said: "What sort of a school would this make? Our children would get lost in it." Thereupon they decided to burn it down [the next day]. They went home quietly leaving a guard of twenty men, who had a regular feast: they heated the oven, butchered a sheep, some geese, ducks and hens, and ate their fill until dawn . . . Thus the night passed. The whole village assembled and once again the axes began to strike . . . They chopped out the windows, doors and floors, smashed the mirrors and divided up the pieces, and so on. At three o'clock in the afternoon they set light to the house from all sides.[14]

The burning of the building was not entirely irrational (or because of its unsuitability as a school). Historians studying peasant revolt in Russia and elsewhere have stressed both the rational and the symbolic elements in peasant destruction of landlord property. Burning estate houses and property records reflected a hard practicality about driving the nobles away. There was a long-held peasant belief, reflected in various sayings, that if the bird's nest (the manor house) is destroyed the bird (landowner) will have to fly away. Now, more than ever, this seemed a realistic hope. At the same time the destruction of estate owners' furniture, art, books, pianos, ornamental gardens, fountains and other evidence of a privileged and alien lifestyle provided the symbolic destruction of the elite oppressor. This destruction probably also reflected hatred toward the wealthy and revenge for past wrongs. From the peasants' viewpoint, it was all rational.[15]

Beyond such seizures and estate destruction, the peasants had many ways to harass estate owners and independent peasant farmers. Farm employees were driven away. Searches were mounted by villagers on various pretexts and sometimes they forcibly inventoried estate property; the effect on the owners must have been unnerving. Peasants sometimes simply swapped their own poorer-quality livestock for the better-quality animals of the landowner. They also took goods – livestock, land, grain, equipment – and offered a payment so low as to be deliberately insulting (yet also providing a kind of bogus legality). They encroached on private land by putting their livestock on private pastures, cutting timber and similar means. Often peasants simply began using land, ignoring landowners' protests. Each success, of course, encouraged further encroachment. All of these kinds of actions drove home to the landowner how powerless he was (or she was – peasants seem to have been opportunistic in taking advantage of women landowners or wives whose husbands were away in the army). The peasants, of course, were not unaware that their actions might frighten landowners into abandoning their houses for the safety of the city, which then laid the estate lands even more open to appropriation. Appeals to local authorities were usually unsuccessful, if indeed the latter had not been involved in the infraction. Higher government officials were more sympathetic, but powerless to prevent these actions.

Physical violence increased as the year progressed, the result of growing frustration with the pace of government reform, increased peasant confidence that they could act with impunity, and increased "outside" involvement from returning soldiers and political agitators. Violent acts and land seizures tended to be sporadic and to be clustered by place and time. A region might have several incidents one month and none the next. Attacks seem to have been somewhat contagious, with one act sparking others nearby. In Tambov province in August a mob of peasants raided the estate of Prince Boris Vyazemsky and "arrested" him; he was then killed at a nearby railway station by soldiers from a troop train. A rash of attacks on nearby estates followed: fifty-seven on gentry estates and thirteen on enclosed peasant private farms.[16] Deaths were unusual, however, even in estate seizures. Few landowners were killed and, as John Channon has noted, "In general, the revolution witnessed the relatively bloodless expulsion of all types of land-owners."[17] Many of the deaths that did occur were the work of bands of robbers or groups of soldiers.

At the same time, however, it should be remembered that not all property was attacked or owners harassed in 1917, even in areas of the greatest unrest. Many landowners continued to live somewhat as before, with small adjustments, while waiting for times to change and security to return. S. P. Rudnev, a Simbirsk (Volga region) gentry landowner with good relations with the local peasants, recalled that the summer and autumn of 1917 passed pretty much as always: "the men went drinking and hunting; guests from Simbirsk came to stay, we went . . . for picnics and mushroom-picking . . . Austrian prisoners of war worked our estate."[18] Still, in between unfortunates like Vyazemsky and people such as Rudnev, most rural landowners had good reason to worry about their futures. From their perspective the whole of Russian society seemed to be spinning out of control.

Peasant actions of all kinds, especially violence and land seizure, brought them into conflict with the government, which was concerned to limit land seizure, control the grain trade, regulate peasant behavior, and maintain order in the countryside. It issued numerous appeals to the peasants for order. For example, on July 17 Irakli Tsereteli, a leader of the moderate socialists and newly appointed as minister of the interior, issued a circular which began by noting that "Information has come from many localities that the population permits seizures, plowing and sowing of fields that are not theirs, removal of workers, and the making of unreasonably high economic demands on agricultural hold-ings. Pedigreed livestock is being destroyed, farm implements are pillaged. Model holdings are being ruined. Private forests are being felled." He then went on to stress that only the food supply committees had the right to "take upon themselves the regulation of sowing and harvesting of fields," and stated that energetic measures would be taken "to put a stop to all arbitrary actions in the field of land relations."[19] This and similar orders failed to have an effect. Indeed, the peasants' response was to criticize the government. On July 24 the administrative board of Balashov district in Saratov province sent a telegram to Kerensky, Tsereteli and Chernov, the three most prominent socialists in the government, warning "Comrades! You are far removed from the temper of the villages!"[20]

The moral revolution and reassertion of communalism

The peasant revolution was not merely economic, nor was it just a lust for land. It also had a moral and cultural dimension as the peasants moved to restructure the order of things in the countryside. The attack on landlord estates also reflected the peasants' strongly held view that morally the land belonged to those who worked it and that in the right order of things each family would have use of only what it could work by its own labor. Expropriated landowners were, in fact, often left a piece of land to work themselves. In the Russian and Ukrainian heartland where most peasants lived, the revolution had a clearly egalitarian emphasis and a strongly communal bias. This worked to reconstruct the countryside in ways that were as much cultural as economic.

The strong sense of the right order of life and renewed communalism was demonstrated especially clearly when villagers forced back into the communal pool of land the farmsteads of the "separators," those peasants who had separated from the communal system and consolidated their land into separate private holdings during the "Stolypin reforms" of the previous decade. The separators' holdings often were no larger than the allotments of the communal peasants and thus there was little or no economic advantage for the villagers, but there was important moral and cultural symbolism. The peasants pressured the separators and independent farmers by threats of force, physical attacks, theft of property, public humiliations, barring them from use of common facilities such as roads and water, and in other ways. They used violence against them as readily as against noble landlords, perhaps more so. At a village in Simbirsk province, the wives of three men who held enclosed farms but were now at the front were beaten by villagers and then forced to sign documents transferring their land to the village collective holdings.[21] In another village, in an unusually brutal case, the peasants went as a group to the separator with the largest holding, dragged him to a village meeting, tied him to a stake and beat him to death in front of the other separators, who then were made to sign a resolution calling for the abolition of all enclosed separate holdings.[22]

In general communal practices underwent a revival in areas where they had become relatively weak as well as in areas where they remained strong before 1917, a process that continued through the following civil war years. Economic as well as moral forces pushed in this direction. The communal holding of property provided a ready mechanism for distribution and incorporation into the general village economy of land and property being acquired by seizure of estates and the coming land distribution. Thus it acquired a new vitality. Indeed, some separators voluntarily merged their holdings back into the communes so that they could get their share of the new land being apportioned out. This was especially appealing if their individual holdings were no larger than those of their communal neighbors, as was often the case. So striking was the peasant revival of communal practice that in the coming years separate holdings largely disappeared.[23]

It appears that the agrarian revolution had a somewhat equalizing impact in the village. Although seized land was distributed in various ways, any improvement in village holdings frequently benefited poorer peasants. They often demanded a larger share of appropriated land as "right" or pressed a special claim on commandeered horses and equipment. At the same time larger peasant holdings shrank as they were often compelled to relinquish a part of their land when forced back into the commune. In addition, to the extent that peasants were successful in forcing up agricultural wage rates this also benefited the poorer members of the community. This equalizing reinforced the "moral revolution."

The peasant and politics

The peasant revolution, while focused on land and relations within the village, was not divorced from the larger world. The peasants realized that events in the cities, especially the capital, affected their lives. They also were interested in national issues such as the war, democratizing society, the Constituent Assembly, access to education and others. The rural population became newly politically active though frequent village assemblies and through elections and electoral assemblies for local and regional councils, soviets, and other bodies. Beyond elections, discussion of public issues and the need to respond to government actions such as food collection drew them more and more into political life. Peasant villages sometimes sent delegations to the major cities, especially Petrograd and Moscow, to learn more about what was happening and even to get "instructions." Moreover, the cities did not leave them alone. Besides government intrusions, politicized soldiers and urban workers returned to their native villages, bringing with them the political issues and debates of the towns. Many *zemliachestva*, the brotherhoods of urban workers or garrison soldiers from a given rural district (see chapter 4), sent emissaries back to their home regions to explain political events in Petrograd and Moscow as well as to assess the mood of the villages. The SRs, especially Left SRs, and the Bolsheviks worked to influence these *zemliachestva* and through them the messages carried to the villages. Trade unions, factory committees, garrison committees and other urban organizations also sent emissaries to the villages. These often had an undercurrent of the urban prejudice that peasants might become a source of counterrevolution unless taught otherwise. Sometimes the peasants welcomed these arrivals and avidly listened to the news they brought, but sometimes treated them with suspicion.

The political parties, especially the SRs, immediately gave attention to organizing the peasants. The SRs were in a favorable position, being by tradition the peasant-oriented party and including much of the rural intelligentsia – teachers and others – among their adherents. Indeed, many of the village resolutions reflected the phraseology of the SR Party program and the helping hand of local SR intellectuals in drafting them. The SRs were very active in organizing regional and provincial peasant congresses. These tended to adopt resolutions based on the SR program and calling for land redistribution, which fit well with the peasants' own chief concern and sometimes stimulated land seizures. The congresses tended to be a combination of peasants and SR-oriented intellectuals, but with the latter in the leadership role; the executive committees elected at them were composed mostly of town intellectuals. This latter feature often caused resentment among the peasants.[24] Moreover, as local intellectuals, mostly SRs, took over local government posts in 1917 they often came into conflict with the peasants over land seizure, grain allocations and other issues. Despite such friction, the SRs positioned themselves as the peasant party and the peasants rewarded the SR Party by voting for them in the elections of 1917. When the peasants turned politically more radical they mostly shifted their support toward the left wing of the party, the Left SRs.

The problem for the SRs, right or left, was how to organize their peasant supporters into effective political power in the conditions of 1917. It proved incredibly difficult to organize and mobilize a scattered rural population and to have it play a direct role in the politics of 1917 the way the workers and soldiers did. This reflected the difference between political power in a settled electoral situation where peasant numbers would prevail, as against a turbulent situation such as 1917 where ability to mobilize large numbers of people in demonstrations and bring pressure to bear directly on the government was more important. And it certainly reflected the extent to which the peasants often were satisfied to go their own way quite detached from, even hostile to, the cities, parties and their activities. As a result the peasant soviets and congresses never wielded the power of their urban, worker and soldier counterparts. The SR leaders organized an All-Russia Congress of Peasants' Deputies in May in Petrograd, with a permanent Executive Committee. It, however, never exercised influence approaching that of the Petrograd Soviet or even the Central Executive Committee of the All-Russia Congress of Soviets. Indeed, even the SR leaders put their energies primarily into the Petrograd Soviet and the Central Executive Committee, the main political arenas. At the same time efforts to create a bottom-up peasants' organization, the All-Russia Peasants' Union, failed, in part because of opposition from SR Party leaders.[25]

The connection of the political parties to the peasant revolution is difficult to assess precisely. Clearly the peasants moved to achieve ancient aspirations that long predated the revolutionary movement, and usually did so in ways equally traditional. They did not need political mentors for what they did and often specifically excluded outsiders of any kind. Yet at the same time they had a long connection to the radical intelligentsia, and peasants in villages near large cities or railroad lines certainly were exposed to radical ideas. Even so, causal relationships between peasant actions and the activities of political parties are difficult to establish with any clarity. For the peasants, congress resolutions were useful in that they contained and publicized certain phrases that the peasants could exploit in carrying out their own rural revolution, but did they significantly influence that revolution? Even more difficult to assess is the extent to which SR or other party programs directly influenced the actions of the peasants. Party programs and resolutions could speak to general political and economic issues with which the peasants might agree, and by calling for land distribution they may even have encouraged land seizure. The peasants, however, had their own vision of the new society and the peasant revolution remained a fundamentally local affair, largely detached from the urban revolution except as government policies (such as grain requisitioning or attempts to impose appointed officials) intruded. It is not a given that they needed party slogans or congress resolutions. Even the Bolshevik decree on land distribution in October only legalized and speeded up what the peasants were doing anyway.

The great peasant rebellion gained momentum steadily in 1917. Revolution meant land and control of their own lives. The peasants, taking advantage of government weakness, moved to achieve both. By late summer, if not earlier, the government essentially lost control of the countryside. The peasants set up their own local authority largely excluding outsiders. They supported those government laws and institutions which furthered their aspirations, interpreted others to make them appear to do so, and ignored or openly opposed those which did not. They used local land committees and other organs to establish effective control over the land, either by seizure or other means, and reordered economic and political relations in the countryside. The government on the other hand lacked the administrative apparatus and the means of physical coercion necessary to oppose unlawful seizures or to stem the tide of peasant revolt. Some efforts were made to use army troops to stop disorders or force grain deliveries, but these were generally unsuccessful and only demonstrated the government's weakness, while breeding peasant resentment. Indeed, the central and local political leaders could never really agree on measures for order in the countryside. They wished the peasants would be more observant of legal norms and orderly procedures, but many agreed with the basic assumptions and objectives of the peasants and were, therefore, inclined to overlook infringements of the law. At the same time failure to implement land reforms pushed the peasants increasingly to take matters into their own hands and set the stage for the Bolshevik land decree during the October Revolution. Peasants were not anarchistic, however, as they so often have been misrepresented. Theirs was a more complex view of the state that insisted on decentralized, local decision making and peasant autonomy, but also assumed the existence of a strong central leader, a "master's hand." The peasantry saw 1917 as an opportunity to reshape the state as well as local affairs more to their advantage. Like every other group, they wanted to use the state to fulfill their aspirations, foremost the old slogan of "land and liberty" and the new slogans such as "down with the war."

6   The nationalities: identity and opportunity

The revolution opened up remarkable opportunities for the non-Russian peoples of the empire, who made up approximately half of the total population. First, it created the same opportunities for fulfilling general social, economic and democratic aspirations that it did for the Russian population. Second, by abolishing censorship, it allowed nationalist spokesmen an opportunity to organize, propagandize and attempt to mobilize the population along lines of national identity. Third, by loosening the control of the central government it allowed local nationality leaders to assert their claims to authority. As a result a wide variety of nationality movements burst forth, ranging from modest claims for cultural autonomy and respect for religious and ethnic differences to demands for national-territorial autonomy within a federal republic and even calls for complete independence. The demand for national-territorial autonomy was especially prevalent among the larger nationalities, while smaller groups looked to cultural autonomy. Calls for complete independence, few at first, increased as 1917 wore on. The rise of assertive nationalism contributed to the general sense of instability and governmental weakness that became part of the political milieu of 1917. Moreover, it was the more powerful for being not merely a phenomenon of the Russian Revolution, but an outgrowth of the larger late nineteenth- and early twentieth-century Europe-wide rise of nationalism and demand for self-determination. This chapter will focus on the aspirations of national and ethnic minority peoples in their identities as nationalities, and the political movements that emerged to give voice to their national aspirations. At the same time it will examine to what extent social, political and other identities competed with and may have influenced actions as much or more than national identity.

The "nationality question"

The "nationality question," as it was called, was complex. The term encompassed a large and diverse population: more than 100 different

146

Map 3 European Russia: major nationalities

ethnicities (including about twenty major nationalities) of widely differing size, culture, language, beliefs and economic development.[a] Moreover, the sense of nationality varied widely. At one extreme were
individuals, especially urban and educated, who were basically Russified
and had left their ethnic origins largely behind, or who for ideological
reasons (Marxism especially) rejected nationalism. In contrast were
those, also largely urban and educated, who were strongly nationalist
and demanded autonomy or independence. Yet a third extreme variant,
perhaps largest of all, were rural populations who identified with their
local region or clan and had only a weak sense of being "Ukrainian,"
"Kazakh" or other nationality (although they were perhaps distinctly
aware of not being Russian). In between stood people of every gradation
of national identity. Moreover, some ethnic groups had a strong sense of
national identity while others had little. This had political implications.
There were important differences, as far as political mobilization was
concerned, among simple ethnic identity (a fundamental identity as
Chechen or Latvian based on local custom, language and daily culture),

[a] These peoples had been incorporated into the Russian Empire as it expanded. They
mostly were living in their ancestral homelands; "ethnic" in Russia did not have the now
common Western, especially American, connotation of recent immigrants to a country.

national consciousness (a more complex political concept deliberately fostered by national elites and patriots) and nationalism (an ideology arguing for the establishment of some kind of nationality-based state).[1]

The problem becomes more difficult when one tries to assess the importance of ethnicity in influencing actions. Individuals usually had multiple identities and aspirations: a Ukrainian peasant could identify with the grievances of all peasants against landlords, but could also support Ukrainian cultural or political movements. Did he, however, feel any kinship with Ukrainian landlords or urban intellectuals, or were they seen as part of the hostile outside world? Did the fact that many landlords were Russian or Polish and that urban merchant creditors were likely Jewish stimulate Ukrainian national identity? How did these variables influence Ukrainian peasant actions? Similarly, a Tatar factory worker in Kazan could respond to the issues of 1917 as a worker, as an ethnic Tatar, or as a Muslim, not to mention other possible identities arising from former peasant status, gender or political beliefs. When confronted with a need to choose among parties and programs, which identity prevailed? Moreover, the identity that came to the fore at a particular time could change with circumstances.

Nationality-based politics often tended in 1917 to blend with socialism and the nearly universal call for major social change. The most successful ethnic-based parties usually were also socialist in doctrine. Some combined Marxist doctrines with a nationalist orientation, while others shared the peasant orientation of the SR Party and combined national identity with peasant concerns, especially land distribution. Thus it is difficult to distinguish to what extent their appeal rested on nationality or social-economic grounds – was a Ukrainian peasant who supported the Ukrainian SRs supporting that party's call for land distribution or expressing national identity? It appears that in most cases in 1917 social concerns eclipsed national content: nationalist parties without strong social reform platforms usually did poorly, while nonnationalist "all-Russia" socialist parties often did well even in minority areas. Together socialism and nationality were a potent political mixture. If skillfully developed by local elites the combination offered both local power and a chance to advance national autonomy, whether cultural or territorial.

For almost all nationality spokesmen and movements in 1917, at least until the October Revolution or even until the Constituent Assembly in January 1918, the objective was some kind of autonomy within a federal state. "A Free Estonia [or Ukraine or other] in a Free Russia" was a common slogan. At first glance seemingly contradictory, such calls spoke to the special situation of the Russian state in 1917. It meant a demand for the reorganization of the state as a federal republic in which administrative boundaries would be drawn along nationality lines and that these regions would have significant autonomy, with a special emphasis on expanded use of the local language and cultural development. It reflected an assumption that this was possible now that a democratic – free – Russia had replaced the tsarist regime. A "free Estonia" was not a call for full sovereignty or independence, but rather for extensive local autonomy and self-governance along ethnic lines within a radically decentralized, democratic federal Russian state. It also reflected the prevalent idea of the importance for small nationalities to exist, for safety and prosperity, within larger political states; the multinational state was then a more widely accepted idea, especially in Eastern Europe, than it is in our time. Even demands for a nationality's political assembly to possess "all authority" in the region usually meant only within the framework of a federal state, not complete independence. Full independence was not seen as essential to the goals of most national movements in Russia in 1917, and to a certain degree was even seen as dangerous in a world of great powers.

The Provisional Government and the political elite in Petrograd and Moscow were not, however, sympathetic to even these limited nationality movements and demands for autonomy. Both the socialist and liberal political parties of Russia had opposed tsarist Russification policies and supported the civil and cultural rights of the minority peoples. At the same time most political leaders at the center – Russians especially but also many of other ethnic origins – insisted upon maintaining the integrity and unity of the state. The Kadets were especially emphatic about preserving the authority of the state and opposed federalism. The SRs were more ambivalent. Their original program clearly stated the right of self-determination. During the war, however, the SR Party, especially its right wing, had become increasingly nationalist. While still accepting federalism and self-determination in theory, they no longer supported it in fact and retreated to the argument that any fundamental restructuring of relationships to allow autonomy could be done only via the Constituent Assembly. Only it had the right to determine fundamental political and constitutional issues for all of Russia, including the minority areas. This set up potential friction with large parts of the party, such as the Ukrainian SRs. The Mensheviks similarly supported self-determination in theory and even reaffirmed it at their party conference in May, but were uncomfortable with it as members of the governing coalition and preferred to defer to the Constituent Assembly. The resolution on the nationality question passed by the Menshevik–SR dominated First All-Russia Congress of

Soviets in June, while accepting the abstract right of self-determination of peoples, opposed any efforts at territorial autonomy or separation before the Constituent Assembly.

Moreover, Petrograd authorities failed to recognize the seriousness of the issue. They tended to dismiss nationality grievances, believing that they would be unimportant in the new free Russia. Through civil rights, toleration, democracy and elected local and national governments, the "nationality question" would fade away. Telling was the later comment of Irakli Tsereteli about the demands from the Ukrainian Central Rada (the main institution asserting Ukrainian national demands – see pp. 152–57) in June. He wrote that he and his colleagues failed to respond adequately because they did not recognize the importance of the nationality issue, because they misunderstood the Rada's position and because their attention was "absorbed by the stormy events" wracking national life. "Reviewing the Russian democratic press [i.e., the Petrograd socialist newspapers] of that time one is astonished at how little reflection is found there of the transformation of the Rada from an intelligentsia organization into a kind of national parliament of Ukraine."[2] A similar inattention applied to developments among most other nationalities as well. Much harsher was the statement by Alexander Kerensky, by then head of government, at the August 12 opening of the Moscow State Conference. He threatened military action against Finnish separatists and spoke of Ukrainian demands for autonomy as Judas-like acts: "And who gave thee thirty pieces of silver?" His comments received "Boisterous applause."[3] Such attitudes angered non-Russian nationalists and convinced some that the new government differed little from the old one in its attitudes toward the national minorities. The Petrograd leaders, pressed by one crisis after another, simply did not consider the "nationality question" to be especially important until it was forced on them in mid-summer and fall, and even then were often unsympathetic.

Only in late September did the Provisional Government, already badly weakened, make any concessions to the growing demands for nationality autonomy. The "Third Coalition" cabinet formed on September 25 included in its program a statement recognizing the right of self-determination, "but only on such principles as the Constituent Assembly shall determine." It promised to issue laws giving minorities "the right to use their native languages in schools" and elsewhere,[4] months after this had become a staple of demands from minority spokesmen. Moreover, by this time more aggressive nationality-based organs, such as the Finnish parliament and the Rada in Ukraine, had already proclaimed that the right to determine their future rested with the local population alone. That put them on a collision course with the government's insistence on the rights of the Constituent Assembly.

In contrast to the Kadets, Mensheviks, and most SRs (all of which parties were in the government and had responsibility for the preservation of the state), the Bolshevik Party in 1917 created an accommodating image on the nationalities question. Lenin had long argued that, while nationalism was ultimately detrimental to the interests of the working class, whether it was progressive or regressive depended on specific circumstances. For some peoples, he argued, national independence or autonomy was a prelude to socialist internationalism: let people who had never enjoyed independence have it and thus learn the superior benefits of socialist universalism. The right of independence did not, however, mean that it was wise or even permitted in all circumstances. In 1917 Lenin adapted these ideas to the reality of the situation in Russia, where nationalist sentiments were growing. He defended the right of national self-determination – whether independence or autonomy – and repeatedly attacked the Provisional Government on behalf of Finnish, Ukrainian and other movements. The Bolshevik Party conference in April, at Lenin's strong insistence and over the opposition of some party leaders, affirmed the right to secede, criticizing the government's opposition to Finnish demands for autonomy as a continuation of tsarist policies. At the same time, however, it stated that demands for secession must always be considered from a class perspective on a case-by-case basis.[5] Lenin's nationality program facilitated periodic cooperation with some nationalist-oriented parties and helped win popular support in some regions. His program rested on both practical acceptance of the force of nationality and federalism in 1917 and a confidence that ultimately the success of Bolshevik socialism would render nationalism meaningless. First, however, the Bolsheviks had to win and retain power, and that meant temporary compromises even by those Bolsheviks less tolerant than Lenin on this question. Nonetheless, local Bolsheviks often opposed autonomy for their regions in defiance of central party policy.[6]

As on many other issues, support for nationalist movements was not merely a Bolshevik position but a posture of the radical left bloc. The radical left in general, including Left SRs, was more supportive of national autonomy demands than were the moderate socialists, much less the liberals. This led to working alliances by the radical left bloc generally with nationality movements. For example, some army units on the Romanian Front that reorganized into Ukrainian regiments allied in congresses and resolutions with the Bolsheviks and Left SRs rather than with the moderate socialists. Radical left calls for immediate peace, land reforms and self-determination also resonated well with many nationality organizations and provided the basis for cooperation against the Provisional Government.

Whatever specific party or bloc programs might be, in general, Russian and minority nationality spokesmen saw the revolution, and especially what freedoms it entailed, differently. Most Russian political leaders stressed that democracy and freedom could be guaranteed only by preserving intact the Russian state, perhaps even a centralized one. They often spoke in patronizing terms of what they, Russians, had done for the minorities. Minority nationalists, on the other hand, saw the democratic promise of the revolution being fulfilled only through some major restructuring of the state toward autonomy and federalism, and as meaning even independence if that is what a people wanted. Without that, they argued, freedom and democracy, much less the Petrograd Soviet's vaunted slogan of self-determination of peoples, had no meaning.

Indeed, whatever the opinion in the center, in many areas nationalist identity became increasingly assertive and well organized as 1917 progressed. There was a sense in some regions that the new government might be different from the imperial government on most issues, but that it still represented Russian, "Muscovite" domination and was hostile to "our" aspirations. Among the larger nationalities along the western and southern borders growing nationalist movements threatened the traditional definition of the Russian state. They also undermined the authority of the Provisional Government and contributed to the growing popular sense of political disintegration. We can look at a few of these nationality regions to illustrate both the general rise of national assertiveness and the differences in the way it expressed itself among major nationalities. Developments in Ukraine and the Baltic region were especially important politically and we will turn to them first. We will then review developments in the Caucasus and Muslim areas, which had less direct impact on national politics in 1917 but which illustrate important facets of the "nationality question" in the revolution. No attempt will be made to cover all nationality groups equally or even at all; rather, some will be examined in order to illustrate the main features of the nationality question in the Russian Revolution of 1917.

Ukraine

Developments in Ukraine were especially important. Its territorial size, population (at approximately 22 percent of the empire's population, by far and away the largest national minority, second in size only to Russians), economic importance (grain, industry, coal and iron) and strategic geographic location made it a key area. Moreover, many of the main issues in the nationality question can be readily examined by exploring the Ukrainian situation.

A nationalist movement emerged among the small class of Ukrainian intellectuals in the nineteenth century, but met vigorous repression from the tsarist authorities. At the beginning of 1917 the Ukrainian national movement was weak and fragmented, ranging from those for whom national identity was of central importance to those for whom it was secondary to social and class concerns, from groups advocating independence to those stressing relatively minor concessions to Ukrainian language and cultural usage. The February Revolution opened the door for all Ukrainian spokesmen to agitate on behalf of their views, and many organizations quickly emerged. The most important of these was the Ukrainian Central Rada (Council), formed on March 4 by Ukrainian intellectuals in Kiev to articulate Ukrainian national aspirations. The Rada quickly came to be dominated by three political parties: the Ukrainian Social Democrats, the Ukrainian SRs and the Socialist-Federalists. The first two were avowedly socialist and the latter basically liberal with mild socialist leanings. The Rada thus represented a peculiarly Ukrainian version of the moderate socialist –left liberal alliance seen in Petrograd and elsewhere, with a nationalist coloration. It represented a fusion of nationalism and moderate socialism and became the dominant institution of Ukrainian national politics in 1917. Its program was summarized by the banner which festooned its meeting hall: "Long live autonomous Ukraine in a Federated Russia."[7]

To broaden its base of support, in early April the Rada summoned a Ukrainian National Congress representing a wide range of cultural, political, professional and other organizations. The congress called for an autonomous Ukraine within a democratic federal Russian republic and commissioned the Rada to work with other nationalities of the Russian Empire that were demanding territorial autonomy. Other assemblies and organizations, including the major Ukrainian political parties, a Ukrainian Military Congress claiming to represent Ukrainian soldiers and sailors, and an All-Ukrainian Peasants' Congress, passed similar resolutions on Ukrainian autonomy. These many resolutions incorporated several basic themes: territorial-national autonomy for Ukraine within a new federal state; recognition of the Central Rada as the governmental authority in Ukraine; use of Ukrainian language in schools, courts and other institutions; staffing of key governmental posts by ethnic Ukrainians; organization of Ukrainian military units; and convening of an all-Ukrainian constituent assembly.[8]

Bolstered by these expressions of support, in May the Rada leaders sent a delegation to Petrograd to obtain the government's approval (and Soviet support) for Ukrainian autonomy and recognition of the Rada's role. Both Petrograd institutions gave the Ukrainians a cool reception. The Ukrainian delegation had difficulty setting up a meeting with the Soviet's Executive Committee. The Provisional Government shunted their demands off to a special juridical commission and refused to recognize the authority of the Central Rada to speak for Ukraine. The Central Rada took up the challenge and on June 10 issued its first "Universal," proclaiming "Let Ukraine be free!" "Without separating from all of Russia, without breaking with the Russian state, let the Ukrainian people have the right to manage its own life on its own soil."[9] While not a declaration of independence, the announced intent to "build our own life" and a Ukrainian governmental structure brought cries of outrage from the Petrograd press. Petrograd newspapers, including *Izvestiia*, the Soviet newspaper, criticized the Ukrainians. The Kadets' Petrograd newspaper even saw in it "Yet another link in the German plan to dismember Russia."[10] Nonetheless the Rada pushed ahead, establishing a General Secretariat to function as an executive body, a government in effect.

Alarmed – the major Russian military offensive of 1917 was underway – the Provisional Government sent a delegation to Kiev which included its two most influential members, Kerensky and Tsereteli, as well as Foreign Minister Tereshchenko, a Ukrainian. They reached an agreement that gave the Rada and General Secretariat extensive authority in administering Ukraine and made concessions on other issues, while leaving final decisions on Ukrainian status to the Constituent Assembly. Released on July 2, on the eve of the riots in Petrograd called the "July Days," the agreement prompted the resignation of the Kadet ministers and the collapse of the government, which is often erroneously attributed to the July Days. (On the June military offensive and the July Days, see chapter 7.)

After July, relations between the Rada and Provisional Government continued to deteriorate. Despite internal disagreements on how hard and how far to press, the Rada pushed ever more vigorously for recognition of its authority while the Provisional Government resisted or made grudging concessions. Throughout 1917, however, the Rada, even as it escalated demands, remained committed to autonomy within a federal Russian state. How decentralized that might be, however, was reflected in an angry speech at the Third All-Ukrainian Military Congress in mid-October by the Ukrainian Social Democrat and Rada leader, Volodymyr Vynnychenko, who in March had been only moderately nationalist: "The secretaries general [executive of the Rada] must declare categorically that they are not officials of the Provisional Government . . . [and] in no way responsible" to the Provisional Government. "The secretaries general must further declare that the full unrestricted will of a given people can be manifested only at its own constituent assembly. And if that is sovereignty, then we welcome it. The General Secretariat shall insist that all authority in Ukraine pass into its hands."[11] Even though Vynnychenko concluded that he was confident that a federation of free states would be created, it was unlikely that any Russian central government would agree to such far-reaching autonomy.

At the same time that the Rada was asserting expanded authority, there were forces inside Ukraine inhibiting the drive for national self-assertion and autonomy. One was the significant non-Ukrainian population – 20–25 percent – which dominated the cities and government, the professions and commerce. Russians and Jews were the most important in a non-Ukrainian minority population that included Poles, Germans, Tatars, Greeks and others. They were concentrated in the cities, while Ukrainians were primarily rural and peasant. In Kiev, the presumed capital of Ukraine and where most of the Ukrainian congresses and organizations met, Ukrainians made up only 16.4 percent of the civilian population in 1917. Of the ten largest cities of Ukraine, only one had a Ukrainian majority, and in six of the ten Ukrainians were only the third largest group (after Russians and Jews).[12] These urban, non-Ukrainian elements also were more likely to be literate, well educated and politically engaged than were the predominantly rural Ukrainian population.

This demography deprived the Ukrainian nationalists of control of the cities, the natural places for a nationality political movement to operate. Concentrated in the cities, the non-Ukrainians were influential beyond their overall numbers and in a position to challenge Ukrainian political nationalism. The Russian population especially opposed the ambitions of the Ukrainian Rada and rejected calls for territorial autonomy and federalism. Moreover, most Russians, in Ukraine and Russia, did not consider Ukrainians as a separate "nationality" in the same sense as Poles or Finns, but rather to be mere dialect speakers for whom they used the then-common term "Little Russians." They were even less willing to concede autonomy to them than to others. Most Jews, Poles, Tatars and other minorities also were hostile or indifferent to Ukrainian nationalist appeals, although they approached the issue differently. They tended to stress the importance of civil rights and toleration for individual and group culture, religion and language. Most believed these could better be achieved within a unitary Russian state than within an autonomous, much less independent Ukrainian state bent on Ukrainianizing society. Despite repeated assurances from Ukrainian leaders that the rights of minorities would be respected, and despite the setting aside of seats for them in the Rada, they remained generally unsupportive of Ukrainian autonomy.

The lack of influence in the cities translated into lack of power in the most important political assemblies. The industrial workers of the eastern cities and the coal and iron miners of southern Ukraine were predominantly Russians or Russianized Ukrainians, and Ukrainian parties made a poor showing among them. Thus Ukrainian nationalists were unable to draw on the support of one of the most assertive, strategically located, best organized and most easily mobilized social groups. Instead Russian and other non-Ukrainian socialists dominated the workers' soviets, with avowedly Ukrainian parties weakly represented. Among garrison soldiers the situation was more complex, but again Russians predominated, including in the soviets. Moreover, the urban soviets – the most important institutions in Ukrainian cities just as elsewhere – were concerned primarily with social and economic issues and the war and tended to be either opposed or indifferent to Ukrainian nationalist concerns. Nor did nationalists do well in general city elections: in the July elections for the Kiev city council Ukrainian parties won only 20 percent of the vote.[13]

The other problem for Ukrainian nationalists was how to mobilize the peasantry. It is abundantly clear that the Ukrainian peasants generally supported the Ukrainian political parties. In elections, especially for the Constituent Assembly, they voted overwhelmingly for Ukrainian parties. In all probability they did so on the reasonable assumption that those who spoke their local language were more likely to defend their interests. Moreover, in 1917 class and ethnic identity came together for most Ukrainians. Ukrainians were overwhelmingly peasants, while landlords, government officials and merchants were predominantly Russians, Poles and Jews; nationality identity coincided with social-economic interests and cultural differences. Since the Rada and most successful Ukrainian parties were also socialist and supported land distribution, peasants found it easy to support them on both ethnic and social-economic grounds.

Peasant support did not, however, automatically translate into an effective national movement. Ukrainian peasants, whatever resentments they had against outsiders, often had more of a local than a general

Ukrainian self-identity. Many identified themselves in regional terms rather than as Ukrainian, and had little sense that their future well being was linked to being "Ukrainian." There is little evidence that they felt that fulfilling their aspirations required Ukrainian statehood, whether autonomy or independence. This and their scattered distribution in villages across a large landscape made it difficult for would-be political leaders to mobilize them. Still, Ukrainian identity and social-economic aims coincided to a remarkable degree, which makes it difficult to distinguish how important national sentiments were as compared to social or economic issues. Which animated a Ukrainian peasant the more, and when, is hard to separate.

Despite the problems of national identity and mobilization, the Rada emerged by the fall as the recognized spokesman for specifically Ukrainian aspirations, combining national identity with a generally socialist program of agrarian and social reform. It was successful in getting the Provisional Government to accept the formation of specifically Ukrainian regiments within the army. Moreover, it moved toward asserting first sovereignty and then near independence after the Bolshevik assumption of power in October, and finally full independence after the dispersal of the Constituent Assembly in January 1918 fragmented what unity remained in the Russian state.

The Baltic region: Finland, Latvia and Estonia[b]

The Baltic region produced the only new independent states, besides Poland, to survive the turmoil of war, revolution and civil war, although in 1917 they experienced quite different nationality movements. Finland represented perhaps the best-defined nationality movement in 1917, but one also accompanied by sharp class conflict. Finland enjoyed a special autonomous and constitutional status after its annexation by Russia in 1809, with its own legislature, laws, bureaucracy, currency, frontiers and other features of extensive autonomy. The Russian emperor ruled as grand duke of Finland. Despite divisions between the Finnish-speaking majority and the politically dominant Swedish-speaking minority, Finland developed a strong national identity during the nineteenth century. This national identity was maintained despite growing social antagonisms which came with the growth of a Finnish

---

[b] Poland, Lithuania and Belorussia (now Belarus) are not discussed here. Poland was under German occupation, and the Provisional Government immediately recognized its right to post-war independence (which weakened its argument with other nationality groups that only the Constituent Assembly could make territorial decisions). Lithuania was also under German occupation. Belorussia had a very weak sense of nationhood or even ethnic identity, among an overwhelmingly peasant people.

industrial working class who embraced revolutionary social democracy. Russian imperial government restrictions on Finland's autonomy around the turn of the century only intensified nationalist sentiments among both Finnish and Swedish speakers.

The February Revolution sparked a controversy between the Provisional Government and Finland. After the February Revolution the Provisional Government immediately restored traditional Finnish rights and autonomy, but put itself in the emperor's place as supreme political authority for Finland. Finland's political parties, socialist and non-socialist, challenged the latter move, claiming that the fall of the monarch severed the connection of Finland to Russia and made the Finnish government the supreme authority in Finland. Although most political leaders accepted the new Russian government's temporary right to direct foreign and military affairs, many also spoke of independence as a given and certainly as Finland's decision. Russian government and Soviet leaders rejected the Finnish formulation and responded that only the All-Russia Constituent Assembly could determine Finland's ultimate political status. Some even threatened to use force to prevent Finnish independence. After Kerensky gave a strong warning to the Finns, the moderate socialist newspaper, *Den'*, applauded him, disdainfully asking "what kind of intoxication has seized these quiet, reserved people."[14] Nevertheless, the Finns persevered. By this time the idea that political legitimacy derived from the people of Finland had taken deep root. On July 5 the socialist-led parliament of Finland issued a law defining Finland's sovereignty. In response the Provisional Government successfully forced the dissolution of the parliament and scheduled new elections for September. All major Finnish parties, both Finnish- and Swedish-speaking, socialist and nonsocialist, campaigned in support of full political rights for Finland. In Russia only the Bolshevik Party fully supported them. The Finnish controversy became one of the issues roiling the political waters in Petrograd, contributing to the growing sense of disintegration during the summer and fall.

At the same time, a deep social cleavage divided Finland, which the full freedom of organizations and speech brought by the revolution allowed to developed into sharp social-political conflict. Finnish industrial workers pushed for fulfillment of economic aspirations similar to those of the working class in general, and met the same responses as in Russia. In the summer they became more militant, including formation of armed worker Red Guard units (the very term had originated in Finland during the Revolution of 1905). Meanwhile more conservative elements, drawing support from the urban middle class and rural peasants, also prepared for a social conflict, including formation of their own armed forces, the Home Guards. To further complicate matters, radicalized Russian soldiers and sailors of the Helsinki garrison demanded an end to the war and sweeping social reforms, and supported the authority of the Helsinki Soviet against both the Finnish parliament and the Provisional Government.

The September elections in Finland returned a nonsocialist and prosovereignty majority in parliament. By the time it convened on October 19, Russia was in deep crisis. The parliament moved to assert Finnish sovereignty. On December 6, after the October Revolution, it declared Finland independent, which the Soviet government recognized on January 4. Finland's unified nationalist sentiment led to independence, but its sharp internal social tensions quickly led to a Finnish civil war.[15]

Latvia and Estonia represent other variations on the nationality issue. Both peoples lacked historic traditions as nation-states and within the Russian state were divided among multiple administrative districts, although the terms Estonian and Latvian were used extensively for both organizations and individuals. Both were traditionally peasant populations with strong regional identities, but had recently developed an extensive urban population, both middle class and industrial working class. Nobles of German descent held large tracts of land and a large landless peasant population existed along with a significant population of peasant smallholders. Baltic Germans had long dominated the area and any ethnic animosities by Estonians and Latvians were directed more against them than toward Russians. A growing sense of national consciousness emerged prior to 1917.[16]

Estonia and Latvia were the only instances of the Provisional Government restructuring provincial administration along ethnic lines (old provincial boundaries in the area ignored nationality). Estonian nationalists (primarily middle- and professional-class liberals) visited Petrograd within a week of the formation of the Provisional Government and successfully got the government to establish for the first time a specifically Estonian administrative territory drawn along ethnic lines. After pressure from Latvians a similar act in July united most ethnic Latvians still under Russian control (large parts were under German military occupation) into a single administrative district, called Latvia for the first time. These two government actions appear to have been based more on concerns about effective local administration than on any kind of nationality policy. They also reflected Prince Lvov's interest in extending local self-governing institutions to areas where they had been weak or nonexistent. These consolidations along ethnic lines may also have reflected the anti-German sentiment of the Provisional Government, for the major losers in the regional reorganization were the traditionally dominant Baltic German nobility.

Estonian provincial self-administration in 1917 was vested primarily in an elected assembly, the Maapäev, elected in April and fairly evenly split between socialist and nonsocialist parties. The formation of the Estonian Social Democratic Union in June, with a strong emphasis on Estonian self-determination and significant popular support, meant that many of the socialists supported Estonian national demands. Relations between the Maapäev and the Provisional Government quickly deteriorated as the former advanced a broad interpretation of its powers and autonomy, which the Provisional Government and local bureaucrats resisted. Increased educational opportunities in their own language and use of Estonian as the administrative language were especially important to Estonians, but Russian central authorities dragged their feet, causing resentment toward the Provisional Government. The Maapäev used Estonian as the language of business and also supported formation of Estonian military units composed of those Estonians serving in the Russian army. They made other demands common to the various national autonomy movements, similar to the ones we have seen with the Ukrainian Rada. On September 25 the Maapäev called for an autonomous Estonia inside a democratic federal Russia.

Much like the Rada's situation in Ukraine, the Maapäev was challenged inside Estonia by the city soviets of workers' and soldiers' deputies, especially in Tallinn (Revel), which mostly represented Russians and other non-Estonians and used Russian to conduct business. The city soviets also were more radical politically, with the Bolsheviks and leftist SRs doing well. The political situation remained fluid into the fall, with popular support divided nearly equally between socialist and nonsocialist parties, with the Bolsheviks the largest but by no means only party among the socialists.

The Latvian situation unfolded rather differently. While Latvian nationalists soon pressed for recognition of an autonomous Latvia within a Russian federation, they – liberals and moderate socialists – found themselves in losing competition with the Bolshevik-dominated Latvian Social Democratic Party. The latter by early summer became the majority party in unoccupied Latvia. As Ronald Suny has noted, in Latvia as in Georgia, Marxism took hold in part because its social and political critique paralleled ethnic lines. In Latvia Germans were the dominant social and economic group, supplemented by Jews, Russians and Poles, while the Latvians made up the working and peasant lower classes and part of the middle class.[17] Latvia was one of the more

Plate 15 Estonian soldiers demanding the formation of separate Estonian military units. The banner reads: "Long live an autonomous Estonia in a free Russia." *Eesti Vabadussoda, 1918–1920* (Tallinn, 1937).

industrialized regions of the empire and had a militant labor force, while much of the peasantry was landless. The Bolsheviks managed to articulate a radical program of land, workplace, and cultural reforms that spoke to both the ethnic and social grievances of Latvian landless peasants and industrial workers, much as the Mensheviks did for Georgians (see pp. 165–66). As Latvia had been divided by the military front since 1915 and Riga was captured by the Germans in September 1917, Bolshevik calls for peace also resonated especially well. In May the Latvian SDs (Bolsheviks) won the support of the special Latvian Rifle brigades (along with a Polish division the only nationality-based units of the imperial army in the war). By summer they effectively controlled the key institutions – government, soviets, military – of unoccupied Latvia. Latvia quickly supported the Soviet government after the October Revolution and the Latvian Riflemen became one of the most dependable army units for the new Soviet regime.

In both Estonia and Latvia, then, strong nationalist movements developed rather quickly and demanded the creation of separate administrative entities based on ethnic lines. As in Ukraine, nationalists focused on the call for autonomy within a federal state. In both, however, workers and peasants appear to have been concerned primarily with economic issues and to have supported parties with strong social platforms. How important nationality issues were is hard to gauge as all successful parties, including the Bolsheviks, used the Estonian or Latvian language and incorporated both a stress on language use and local autonomy into their platforms. The Bolsheviks, with their combination of radical social policies and support for self-determination, gained broad support in the countryside as well as in the cities of the Baltic region, especially Latvia. Because of close geographic proximity to Petrograd, this had implications for politics there, especially in October and after. At the same time national identity grew perceptibly in both regions in 1917, preparing the way for independence soon after.

Muslim areas and Transcaucasia

The Muslim and Turkic regions (90 percent of Russia's Muslims were ethnically Turkic) represent an important example of the complexity of nationality as an identifier, especially when issues of religion and territory are mixed in. Most of the Muslim population was distributed in three major blocks: the Central Asians (modern Tadzhiks, Turkmen, Kirghiz, Uzbeks, Kazakhs); the Azeri Turk (Azerbaijani[c]) population of Transcaucasia; and the Tatars of the Volga River, Ural Mountains and Crimean regions. The first two groups lived in reasonably compact population regions, but the third was more scattered geographically and more interspersed with Russians. Muslims were a population united by a common religion but divided in many ways: by spoken language, history, geography, social-cultural characteristics, social-economic class, ethnicity and a sense of being different peoples. In many areas, especially Central Asia, identities were not well fixed in modern nationality terms, and many names were in use for various groups (Sarts, for example) that are no longer used. Moreover, many specific local issues drove the revolution in the different Muslim areas.[18]

Muslims shared the initial universal support for the February Revolution, the Provisional Government and the promise of democracy and a constituent assembly. The government's early removal of all civil restrictions based on religion or nationality was doubly important to them. They also participated in the post-February enthusiasm for creating organizations to express their political, cultural, economic and other aspirations. Muslims shared certain concerns of the other large non-

---

[c] What term to use for this population is itself indicative of the problem of national identity during this era. The term Azerbaijani is an anachronism for 1917, when Azerbaijan was a territory (and later, in 1918, a state), but the population was referred to by a variety of terms – Turks, Azeri Turks, Tatars, other. Henceforth I will use Azerbaijani for convenience, realizing that such an identity was just beginning to form.

Russian nationalities having to do with cultural autonomy, control of schools, formation of nationality-based military units and use of local languages in administration, courts and education. At the same time revolutionary upheaval in Muslim areas had its own special features. The revolution raised fundamental questions about the relative importance of their religious and national identities, and which would take precedence. It also sparked internal conflict over cultural authority in the community and which competing Muslim visions of the new order would dominate.

One central political dispute was what kind of autonomy they should have in the new Russia. Nationalists argued for a federal state based along ethnic/nationality territorial lines. Pan-Islamists argued for an extra-territorial, religiously–culturally based autonomy uniting all Muslims within a unitary Russian state. The national-territorial advocates quickly gained the upper hand among the Azerbaijani and Central Asian Muslim political leaders, while the Tatars, who were geographically scattered, supported pan-Islamic unity and extra-territorial cultural autonomy. At the All-Russia Congress of Muslims in May the advocates of territorial federalism won easily. The resolution followed the proposal of Mehmed Emin Resulzade, an Azerbaijani, for "national Turkic autonomous local statehood . . . I recommend the creation of autonomous Azerbaijan, Daghestan, Turkestan, Kazakhstan, etc., since all these peoples have their specific local particularities . . . Each of these autonomous states should govern its local affairs." At the same time he also proposed an All-Russia Muslim Council for coordination of religious and cultural development of all Muslims.[19]

Meanwhile a struggle developed within the Muslim community over cultural and moral authority, with major implications for political power in the region. This is well illustrated by events in Russian Turkestan and its administrative capital, Tashkent.[20] In Tashkent both a (Public) Executive Committee and a Soviet of Soldiers' and Workers' Deputies were quickly formed after the February Revolution. These, however, represented primarily the Russian population of Tashkent (perhaps 20 percent of the city and 2 percent of Turkestan), and largely excluded the native Muslim population. As a result local Muslim leaders founded a Muslim Council to administer affairs of the Muslim "old city" as their counterpart to the Russian political organs. Both the Muslim Council and the First Turkestan Muslim Congress, which met in Tashkent on April 16–22, were dominated by the Jadid movement. The Jadids saw themselves as leaders of a modernizing movement within Muslim society, attuned to new technologies and economic systems, functional literacy and active participation in the broader Russian polity. The revolution seemed to offer them new opportunities. They were challenged, however, by the Ulāma, which represented the traditional cultural elite and religious leadership. The revolution and the Jadids threatened the Ulāma's preeminence if allowed to introduce rapid social and cultural change. The Ulāma therefore tried to use the revolution's weakening of the central government's power to broaden local – their – authority, especially that of the religious courts.

Two parallel, but occasionally intersecting political competitions were fought out in Tashkent and Turkestan. The Ulāma and the Jadids struggled for dominance among the Muslim population of Turkestan, while political struggles in the Russian community roughly followed the lines described in chapters 3 and 4. The Ulāma entered the political arena in the city council elections in July, stressing traditional cultural values, and won a majority.[d] Ulāma leaders then formed an alliance with Russian conservatives – Muslim leaders still conceded to Russians a special role in political governance – to give the city what may be the only conservative local government elected in the country in 1917. The Jadid, in response to the Ulāma's success, turned increasingly to ethnic nationalism to find a base of support. The Russian socialists in Tashkent, based in the Tashkent Soviet, turned increasingly radical, leading to an unsuccessful attempt to seize power in September.

The general social and economic conflicts of 1917 affected Muslim society also. The fact that Muslims tended to be at the bottom of the social-economic order in cities where ethnic populations intermingled made radical social reform appealing to many, as well as reinforcing ethnic identity. In Baku and some other cities Muslim workers focused initially on economic and workplace issues, just as did other workers. Although land issues were not as explosive as in Russia and Ukraine, support for sweeping agrarian reform also was widespread. These economic issues gave rise to socialist movements of significant popular appeal, especially when they managed to combine Muslim, ethnic and socialist identities (the Musavat in Azerbaijan, for example).

The result was an extremely complex situation in predominantly Muslim areas, with simultaneous conflicts between different Muslim ethnic groups (Tatars, Uzbeks, etc.) over federalism, within the local Muslim population on cultural and social issues, within the local Russian population on political and social-economic issues, between Russians and "natives" and between Muslims and other religious/ethnic groups (such as between Azerbaijanis and Armenians in Baku), and

---

[d] The Ulāma emphasis on tradition included opposition to women having the right to vote, at the same time as the Provisional Government was finally confirming that women would have the franchise (July 20).

along economic class lines that cut across ethnic or religious lines. "Moscow" Bolsheviks and Kadets, "local" Bolsheviks and Kadets, Jadids, Ulāmas, Russian settlers, native populations – all fought a multi-sided contest for power. In this process a variety of temporary alliances might be formed in the struggle for local influence. All generalizations about people acting on the basis of class, ethnicity or religion become difficult, especially about their turning those identities into political action. Some Muslims joined local branches of the national political parties – Kadet, Bolshevik, SR, Menshevik – but most identified with Muslim or nationality-based parties of various social and political orientations. A unified Islamic movement failed to develop.

Despite internal divisions, the Muslim/Turkic parties were generally supportive of the Provisional Government in the spring, but became more hostile to it during the summer. Some of the alienation grew out of the same factors as for the rest of the population, such as opposition to the war and economic problems. At the same time there were special nationality factors. One was the Provisional Government's refusal to yield on the principle of a unitary state and its refusal to endorse the concept of a federal republic on nationality lines. This was compounded by the Petrograd leaders' rejection of an overture from Muslim leaders in July to support the government in return for ministerial posts in the central government. By fall some Muslim leaders found Lenin's theory of self-determination more attractive than the stance of the Provisional Government or other parties, and this provided the basis for coopera-tion. For example, the Musavat, the most important party of the Azerbaijan Muslims of Transcaucasia, became increasingly critical of the Provisional Government and began to cooperate with the Bolsheviks in Baku. The Provisional Government's belated declaration in Sep-tember that the "Recognition of the right to self-determination will be established on foundations which will be laid by a constituent assembly" was too little, too late.[21]

Georgians and Armenians, who shared Transcaucasia with the Azer-baijanis as well as many small nationality groups, represented yet other facets of the nationality question. Georgia and Armenia were areas where ethnicity and religion coincided, and each had a long history. By 1917 each had a dominant political party which expressed national aspirations. In both, national identity was important but did not lead to significant movements for autonomy until very late in the year. Armenian national sentiment was profoundly affected by the fact that Armenians were dispersed across three states – Russia, Turkey and Persia – and by memories of recent Turkish massacres of Armenians and the continuing need to defend themselves against the Turks. The collapse of Russian authority after February therefore meant a double threat, from the Turkish army with which Russia was at war, and from the neighboring Azerbaijanis. This helped rally Armenians behind the Dashnaktsutiun party, which combined nationalism with vaguely socialist tendencies. At the same time, however, the Armenian dependence on Russian protection against Turkey meant that it wholeheartedly supported the central Russian government and that autonomy sentiments were muted.

Georgia before 1917 already had developed a dominant political party, the Mensheviks, who had established themselves despite the fact that Georgians were primarily a rural population. In Georgia, and especially the capital of Tbilisi (Tiflis), the merchant class was primarily Armenian while Russians dominated the political administration. As a movement which was both antibourgeois and anti-tsarist, Menshevism tacitly allowed Georgian identity to stand in contrast to Armenians (the bourgeoisie) and Russians (tsarist officials), without being explicitly nationalist. There were strong similarities to the reasons for Bolshevik success in Latvia. The Mensheviks stressed Georgia's continuing place within the new Russian republic. Autonomy and federalism had only weak appeal. Thus Georgians, along with Latvians (where Bolsheviks dominated), were represented by perhaps the least nationalist, but most avowedly socialist, political parties of any large minority nationality.

Tbilisi (Tiflis), the capital of Georgia and also of Russian administration in Transcaucasia, shows unusually clearly how class, nationality and political lines intersected. The pre-revolutionary city council was primarily Armenian, reflecting voting restrictions based on wealth and Armenian prominence in the commerce of the city. The new democratic elections brought Georgian control. The real power after February, however, rested with the Tbilisi Soviet of Workers' Deputies, which was Menshevik-dominated. The main threat to that dominance came from the huge military garrison, which was primarily Russian and elected SR leaders. They usually allied with the Mensheviks to form the same moderate socialist bloc we have met elsewhere, but which here represented two ethnic groups as well. Despite efforts by local political leaders to dampen nationality conflict, the situation was such that, as Ron Suny notes, "Every issue which arose in 1917 – the introduction of the eight-hour day, the question of the war, the coalition government, Georgian national autonomy, or Soviet power – was debated and decided by balancing and satisfying the competing interests and suspicions" of Georgian workers, Armenian middle class and Russian soldiers.[22]

Revolution on the Jewish street

Russia's Jews greeted the overthrow of tsarism enthusiastically. Jews had been especially subjected to official discrimination as well as anti-Semitic riots – pogroms – in late imperial Russia. They more than any group benefited directly and immediately from the abolition of laws discriminating against people on religious or nationality grounds. The end of the restrictions on Jews led to a remarkable outpouring of activity: publication of newspapers and books in Hebrew and Yiddish, Jewish musical societies, Yiddish and Hebrew theatrical performances, expansion of religious schools, establishment of self-governing councils and so forth. At the same time individuals obtained the freedom to pursue previously restricted professional and educational opportunities and to hold important public positions. Jews participated in a way never before possible in the vast array of new civic, social, economic and political organizations created out of the revolution. Jews, as Michael Hickey has noted, "rushed to organize both as citizens and Jews."[23] At the same time the revolution forced Jews to debate their identity as a people, perhaps a nationality, and how they as an identifiable group should respond to the revolution.

The revolution raised many of the same issues – national autonomy, forms of self-governance, language use, schooling, etc. – for Jews that it did for other nationalities. At the same time, however, Jews faced unique issues. Chief among these was that Jews were scattered geographically rather than occupying a traditional homeland in which they were the majority. There were about three and half million Jews in Russian territory in 1917, concentrated especially in the western regions – Belorussia and Ukraine – that were in the Pale of Settlement to which most Jews had been confined by tsarist policy. Another two million Jews were in areas of the former Russian Empire under German occupation, especially Poland and Lithuania. This made them one of the largest officially recognized population groups in the empire, but a scattered one. Given their dispersed settlement, it not surprising that many Jewish leaders argued for some form of national-cultural autonomy (in this they resembled the Tatars) rather than national-territorial autonomy as most large minorities did. National-cultural autonomy assumed that the Jews were a nationality who should have some kind of regional and nation-wide assemblies within a federal Russian state to speak for all Jews no matter where they lived, as well as communal self-governance for their communities – for "Jewish Street" – within the cities and towns where they resided. A second special Jewish issue was the Zionist call for immigration to set up a Jewish homeland in Palestine.

The Jewish political response to the revolution was something of a paradox. Jews were now able to organize and propagandize on behalf of their group interests. This revealed how fractured Jewish society was, along religious, social, economic and political lines. Such a large number of Jewish parties and movements emerged that they failed to create a unified political movement able to have much influence on the course of the revolution or Jewish interests therein. Many Jews supported the all-Russia political parties – Kadets, Mensheviks, SRs – while others supported specifically Jewish parties. The Jewish National Group, for example, were liberals close to the Kadets in outlook but with a special concern for issues of Jewish religion, culture and language. Jewish socialist parties combined class struggle and religious–cultural issues. The most important was the Bund (Jewish Labor Union), a Marxist party ideologically close to the Mensheviks and part of the Revolutionary Defensist bloc. Other parties – SERP (which was close to the SRs), Poale-Zion, Zionist-Socialists – combined various forms of socialism with claims for Jewish uniqueness and focus on specifically Jewish issues. Some Orthodox Jewish movements, such as the Unity of Israel and the Tradition and Freedom Parties, focused primarily on religiously based issues and attempted to cut across political and class lines. Ironically, the largest vote-getters in the elections during the second half of 1917 were the Zionists, who were relatively unengaged in Russian politics but focused instead on creation of a Jewish homeland in Palestine. Jewish politics fractured along numerous fault lines: anti-Zionists battled Zionists, socialists against liberals, workers and artisans against "bourgeoisie," advocates of Hebrew fought supporters of Yiddish, assimilationists versus those who sought to maintain distinctive Jewish life and culture, and in other ways.

Because of this political splintering, specifically Jewish political influence was reduced, even in those cities of Ukraine and Belorussia where Jews were a large part of the population. Not uncommonly about four Jewish socialist parties, one or two liberal parties and two to four religiously oriented parties competed for the Jewish vote, along with the all-Russia parties such as the Mensheviks, SRs and Kadets (Bolsheviks fared badly in Jewish communities). Jewish political weakness was reinforced by the problems of mobilizing a politically passive and culturally conservative population, the dispersed nature of Jewish settlement and their status as a minority everywhere without claim to a territory as "our land" in the way other large minorities did. Only in Ukraine, where they made up about 9 percent of the population (and where over half the Jewish population of 1917 Russia lived), did Jews as a nationality manage to wield some political authority. The Ukrainian

Central Rada, sensitive to the problem of the large non-Ukrainian population of the cities, set aside offices especially to represent the Jewish, Polish and Russian minorities. Nonetheless Jews, whether Russified or traditional, felt threatened by Ukrainian nationalism and by being politically cut off from the rest of the Jewish population by new national frontiers. Indeed, popular anti-Semitic riots broke out in the fall, while relations with the Rada deteriorated when Jewish deputies voted against Ukrainian independence. Later, during the civil war, the Jewish population of Ukraine suffered grievously from anti-Jewish depredations.

While Jews as an organized political force were not particularly successful, individual Jews reached levels of political authority never dreamed of under tsarism. A few Jews served as assistant ministers of the Provisional Government and on its important commissions, and a Jew, Osip Minor, a SR, served as mayor of Moscow. Locally Jews served on the Public Committees set up after the February Revolution and in the city councils elected in the summer. They were even more influential in the soviets. Large numbers of Jews served in the soviets of all major cities, and about 20 percent of the Executive Committee of the Petrograd Soviet in the spring was Jewish, many of them assimilated intellectuals. Jewish socialist parties such as the Bund and SERP shared power in the soviets as junior partners in the moderate socialist bloc. Abram Gots, a SR, became vice-chairman of the Petrograd Soviet during the Revolutionary Defensist leadership. Ironically, the most powerful position held by a Jew was by a man who rejected Jewish national identity in favor of assimilation and purely secular politics: Leon Trotsky as the Bolshevik chairman of the Petrograd Soviet in September–October. The revolution brought Jews as individuals a level of freedom and opportunity in public life that they had never before had in Russia.

Trotsky's role in the Bolshevik Party reflects another paradox of Jews in political life in 1917. The Bolshevik Party had a number of assimilated Jews among its top leadership: Trotsky, Grigorii Zinoviev, Iakov Sverdlov and Karl Radek among others. However, the Bolsheviks had long rejected the idea of Jews as a nationality, condemning the idea as "reactionary." One result was that in 1917 none of the Jewish parties supported the Bolsheviks and Bolsheviks did poorly among Jews during elections. As the moderate socialist parties lost support in the fall Jewish workers and artisans tended to turn toward Zionism rather than to the radical left. Thus after the Bolsheviks took power in October Jewish parties found themselves in a difficult position vis-à-vis a regime that opposed anti-Semitism on principle but regarded Jewish identity as either unimportant or something to be overcome in the march to socialism.

In summary, several conclusions can be drawn about the revolution in the nationality areas and its relation to the larger revolution. The "nationality question" developed in different ways and at different tempos across the huge expanse of Russia and among its many nationalities and ethnic groups. Some populations asserted strong nationalist sentiments, while others were largely indifferent. The intertwining of national or ethnic identity with social, economic and even cultural issues is difficult if not impossible to separate and the most successful political parties usually incorporated both national identity and socialism (extensive social and economic reform). For some groups class and nationality tended to coincide, while other nationalities were socially more diverse. Urban intellectuals were the most concerned with nationality issues, but urban working class and rural populations often supported them if they also addressed their class/economic concerns. The main emphasis, at least until October was upon self-determination and some form of autonomy – political or cultural – within a federal Russian state, with most preferring a nationality-territorial basis for federalism. The resistance to federalism by the Provisional Government undermined its support and authority, even as nationality-based political organizations (the Ukrainian Rada and others) came to assert and exercise ever more authority locally. The weakness of the central government in turn encouraged more assertive nationalist movements. Even so independence became a major force only after the October Revolution shattered national unity and after the closing of the Constituent Assembly by the Bolsheviks in January 1918 reduced prospects for resolving national aspirations through a constitutional order within a multiethnic, probably federal Russian state (see chapter 10).

It should also be noted that, while the nationality groups were the main source of demands for federalism and autonomy, they were not the only ones. The demand for national autonomy also fit with one of the widespread, if vague, sentiments of 1917 – movement away from the tradition of highly centralized government of the tsarist era toward greater local self-government and control over affairs. This even affected some ethnically Russian groups with a strong sense of special identity. In the Don territory strong regionalist sentiments emerged among the Don Cossacks based on a feeling of being a unique people with special interests to defend.

The Don Cossacks struggled to find an identity within the new system now that the old tsarist legal categories that had defined them were gone. How were they to distinguish themselves from the general (mostly peasant) population of the region, and especially how to establish a separate, Cossack, political structure within a regional one that included all of the population, including non-Cossacks? They successfully pressured the Provisional Government to agree to broad Cossack autonomy in managing their affairs under elected leaders. A Don Cossack government emerged as an institution claiming to represent Don Cossacks as a distinct population. In doing so, some Cossacks began a shift away from seeing themselves as a legal estate to seeing Cossacks as an ethnic or nationality group. This despite the fact that simultaneously their leaders and many Provisional Government leaders and conservatives saw them as a bastion of Russian state interests.[24] A similar sentiment emerged among the Terek Cossacks. A small but vocal movement for Siberian regional autonomy appeared, centered in Tomsk, among the ethnically Russian population.[25] Ultimately nationality and regionalist movements, of whatever kind, were a major destabilizing factor in the life of Russia in 1917 and added to the growing sense of chaos and national collapse that became so strong in the summer and fall.

7   The summer of discontents

The new Revolutionary Defensist–left liberal political leadership that controlled the Petrograd Soviet and the Provisional Government after April found it impossible to meet the many aspirations of the population, and the general optimism of spring gave way to a summer of discontents. First and especially pressing was the "peace offensive," which started amidst great hopes but failed during the summer. Moreover, problems with it contributed to the decision to launch a military offensive on June 18, which was massively unpopular and turned out to be both a military and a political disaster. July began with the second major political crisis of the revolution, the July Days, and August ended with the third, the Kornilov Affair (counting the April Crisis and the collapse of the initial Provisional Government as the first major crisis). Government instability became chronic. Along with those political crises a cauldron of discontents bubbled away. The question of land distribution remained a major source of dissatisfaction, among both peasants and soldiers. A general economic disintegration coupled with inflation made workers fear the loss of gains made thus far and fueled industrial conflict. Apprehensions grew about adequate food provisions for the cities and the army. Separatist movements in some of the national minority regions gained momentum. Fear of crime and demonstrations by all sorts of groups added to the discontents of the summer.

Peace offensive, war offensive

Walking home through quiet streets the night of May 5 after the announcement of the coalition government, N. N. Sukhanov encountered a "lanky figure" staggering toward him, "waving his arms and chanting in *basso profundo*, like an archdeacon: 'Let us pra-a-y to the Lord, for pea-a-a-ce for the wo-o-rld, without annexations or inde-e-emnities!' "[1] To obtain that peace and make the coalition work, government and Soviet leaders initiated a two-pronged peace offensive. The Soviet leadership undertook to work with the socialist parties of Europe to generate popular opinion in favor of a negotiated peace and to organize a great international socialist conference to pressure European governments to accept the Russian peace program. Simultaneously the Provisional Government attempted to get the Allies to agree to revise Allied war aims to repudiate the territorial and other claims found in the "secret treaties" made by the warring powers; there could not be serious peace talks as long as both sides pressed claims against the other. The peace effort was to be, then, a double effort, government and Soviet, each working with their Western counterparts to move toward a negotiated general peace as a way out of the war.[2]

The situation in Europe in the spring of 1917 seemed to the Soviet leaders to justify great optimism. The tremendous strains of the war led in April–May to a great Europe-wide wave of war-weariness and antiwar sentiment, even army mutinies. From one perspective events in Russia were the most dramatic part of a broad political upheaval across Europe in the spring of 1917. The Soviet leaders hoped that these discontents would provide the basis for Europe-wide popular support for a negotiated general peace. Moreover, many Russian socialists saw the Russian Revolution as a flame that would illuminate Europe, bringing not only peace but also achievement of socialist ideals, whether revolutionary or evolutionary. Tsereteli told the All-Russia Conference of Soviets on March 29 that he believed the Russian Revolution and its foreign policy were "a turning point not only for Russia, but also a torch thrust over Europe, and that those ideals that now barely flicker there will soon glow as brightly [across Europe] as they have illuminated all of our internal life."[3] Indeed, the inspiration of the Russian Revolution did combine with the general war-weariness to reinvigorate the European left and antiwar sentiment.

The Soviet leadership focused on convening an international socialist conference to meet in neutral Stockholm in June. They believed that if they could bring the socialist parties of the warring camps together this would be a first step toward breaking through wartime hostilities. The socialist parties would then pressure their various governments to agree on a negotiated peace based on the Soviet formula of "peace without annexation or indemnities, self-determination of peoples." To generate support the Soviet sent delegates to France, Britain and Italy to encourage the socialist parties to join the effort, while Allied socialists came to Russia both to discuss the conference and to stimulate the Russian war effort. On May 15 the French Socialist Party voted to attend the Stockholm conference, while the British Labour Party seemed to be moving in the same direction. The radical left wings of the Western socialist parties fully supported participation.

Meanwhile, the Russian government attempted to get the Allied governments to revise war aims as a step toward peace negotiations. The key person was the new foreign minister, Michael Tereshchenko, only twenty-nine at the time.[a] Tereshchenko and the government leaders accepted the idea of revising war aims because they believed the only way to prevent the disintegration of the army was to assure the soldiers that they were continuing the war only for democratic and defensive purposes. Nekrasov told the Kadet Party congress on May 9 that his support for the peace effort was decided by the reports of army delegates, stating "if you want the army to march into battle, if you want to see the old discipline and unity restored to it, then give it something to fight for which it can understand and can see and can really defend."[4] This was critical because the belief was spreading among the troops – encouraged by leftist agitation – that French and British territorial ambitions were prolonging the war. If the Allies would announce their adherence to the Soviet no-annexations formula it would, they hoped, convince the country that they were making real progress toward peace, keep the restive masses aligned behind the Revolutionary Defensist leadership and give the government time to deal with its many serious problems. If Germany also agreed that would lead to peace negotiations, but if Germany declined that (it was hoped) would convince Russian soldiers of the need to continue fighting. Revision of war aims thus became a kind of panacea for all problems, foreign and domestic.

The Allies, although concerned about the Russian army's fighting ability, refused to agree to a conference to revise war aims. Indeed, the Allied governments took a diametrically opposite stance: they felt that talk of war aims and peace negotiations would undermine fighting morale, not strengthen it. On May 19 the French government announced that it would refuse passports to French citizens to attend the conference in Stockholm. The Italians soon followed suit and the United States had already announced opposition. Only the British government, for the moment, hesitated before finally announcing its opposition. By June even many Western socialists were having second thoughts. The peace offensive was imperiled, and with it the political dominance of the Revolutionary Defensists. They desperately needed a breakthrough.

[a] The leaders of the Provisional Government and the Soviet were, for the most part, rather young men. Kerensky was thirty-five at the time of the February Revolution and thirty-six when he became head of the government in July. Tsereteli was also thirty-five when he returned to Petrograd and took leadership of the Soviet. Miliukov and Lvov were "elders" at fifty-seven and fifty-five respectively. Among Bolsheviks, Lenin at forty-seven was considered an elder; Trotsky turned thirty-eight during the October Revolution.

The Revolutionary Defensist leaders turned toward the idea of a military offensive to break the stalemate in the peace offensive. The Russian army and front had been relatively quiescent since the February Revolution. Now the idea of an offensive action by the Russian army took shape against the background of the difficulties of the 'peace offensive' and growing concerns about internal disorders. Not surprisingly, it found its most fervent support among army officers, conservatives and liberals. Most Russian army commanders supported it in the belief that continued inactivity was destroying the army, whereas a resumption of active operations would encourage the reestablishment of more traditional discipline and command relationships within the army and stop its deterioration. General A. I. Denikin later wrote that they hoped that "a successful advance might lift and heal the [army's] *morale*, if not through sheer patriotism, at least through the intoxication of a great victory. Such feeling might have counteracted all international formulas sown by the enemy on the fertile soil of the Defeatist tendencies of the Socialistic Party."[5] The idea also found favor among conservative and liberal political leaders, who hoped that it would check radicalism in the country. Indeed, some suggested that a redisciplined army could be used to suppress radical activity and alter the general power relationships in Petrograd and the country. They also were responsive to pressure from the Allies, France especially, that the Russian armies become more active in order to relieve military pressures on the Western Front.

The key support, however, came from a surprising quarter – the moderate socialist leaders of the Petrograd Soviet. As early as May 2 Tsereteli made the connection between the peace effort and a strong military when he argued at a Soviet meeting: "What sort of impression would it make on the people of the world if a catastrophe at the front accompanied our appeal to them? The governments of other countries would say to their people, pointing to us: they call you to follow their examples, and this is what it leads to. They would destroy you, as they destroy themselves."[6] Soon the idea took hold that the Allied governments were ignoring the peace offensive because of the virtual truce on the Russian front and the disarray in its army. The moderate socialist newspaper, *Den'*, complained that the Allies were ceasing to take Russia seriously as a major factor in the war and that Russian peace demands were making no impression because Russia lacked the power to back them up. "Russia will be crushed, if not on the field of battle, then at the peace conference."[7] An offensive would show that Russia was still a military and diplomatic force and give weight to its words.

The logic of the connection between peace and a military offensive was dubious, for a successful offensive might have just the opposite effect, removing any French and British incentive to agree to a negotiated peace. However, from the perspective of the time, the Russian leaders seemed to have little choice. To continue the war without an active peace policy was politically impossible. The only other alternative was a separate peace with Germany, but all political factions, even the Bolsheviks, rejected that. All political leaders feared that a separate peace would result in a German victory and domination of Europe, especially in the east, leading to harsh economic and territorial terms that would make Russia virtually a German colony (in light of the peace terms Germany imposed at Brest-Litovsk a few months later, this fear was well founded). They also feared that a German victory might mean the restoration of the Romanov dynasty.

Fascination with the French Revolution as the model for revolutionary development helped make the offensive more palatable to many socialists. They recalled the great successes of the French revolutionary armies and argued that, now that the Russian soldier had a democracy to fight for, there could exist a powerful new Russian revolutionary army. The intellectuals of the Soviet and some military officers deluded themselves with a false historical analogy. Even so, the Soviet leadership was circumspect in its support of the offensive, knowing that the idea was unpopular with its soldier and worker constituents. *Delo naroda*, the SR newspaper, argued that there was no need for the "panicky fear and superstitious terror" that the word offensive caused in some circles. *Izvestiia* insisted that the issue was "not an offensive but creating *the possibility of an offensive*."[8] Vladimir Voitinsky, in a pamphlet written to explain the policies of the Soviet leadership, argued that the aggressive or defensive nature of a war depended on its aims, not its strategies, and a purely defensive war might require offensive operations.[9]

A broad spectrum from right-wing conservatives to moderate socialists came to support the offensive, for different reasons. The moderate left hoped a successful offensive would revive their peace policy and thus their political fortunes, while the right hoped it would weaken the political left generally. Both hoped that military success would halt the disintegration of the army and of society in general. Neither, apparently, gave much thought to – or simply put out of their minds – what would be the effect of a disastrous defeat. The one political grouping that opposed the offensive was the radical left, especially the Bolsheviks and Left SRs. Radical left orators and newspapers harshly attacked the idea of an offensive and the war generally. *Pravda*, for example, under the headline of "Who Needs 'War to Victory,'" published data on wartime

Plate 16 Kerensky addressing troops at the front during a tour to urge the June offensive. After becoming minister of war in May he often wore a military tunic. Courtesy of Columbia University Library Bakhmeteff Archive.

profits of some factories and concluded "This is why Messieurs capitalists and bankers, their 'executive organ' the Provisional Government and the entire bourgeois press with such insistence preach 'war to victory.'"[10] Moreover, given that the soldiers were hostile to resuming military operations with the resultant casualties and restored officer authority, the critics of the offensive were the most likely beneficiaries of it, as in fact proved to be the case.

A major effort to pump up support for an offensive, and especially the enthusiasm of the troops, began. Kerensky, now minister of war, embodied the effort. On May 14 he issued an order calling for discipline in the army and readiness to undertake military action in the name of the lofty ideals of the revolution: "not a single drop of blood will be shed for a wrong cause."[11] Kerensky followed this up with tours of the front where he harangued the troops in great open air assemblies. He usually received a tremendous immediate response – he was a spellbinding orator – but the impact evaporated when he left. Phrases such as "I summon you not to a feast but to death"[12] caught the emotion of the inspired moment, and especially moved the newspaper journalists

Map 4 Russia, May 1917: military fronts against Germany and Austria-Hungary

accompanying him, but had no appeal to the soldiers after the moment passed. The soldiers' enthusiasm vanished as quickly as it came. Kerensky's critics derisively dubbed him the "persuader-in-chief." Some military leaders tried to capitalize on Kerensky's tour to attempt to restore traditional discipline. Attempts by officers to resume training, reimpose more traditional discipline and otherwise prepare for offensive action, however, aroused the hostility and opposition of the troops.

The burden of obtaining the soldiers' support for the offensive and a return to military discipline and activity fell most of all on the army committees, which were primarily Revolutionary Defensist in outlook. After February a complex network of committees had developed in the army, from the smallest unit up through regiments, armies and fronts. In March and April the committees had focused on defending the soldiers' interests against officers and the Soviet peace program against advocates of war to victory. This was popular with their comrades. Now their task became to propagandize for the idea that the defense of the revolution required restoration of discipline and preparation for an offensive. A new revolutionary official – the army committeeman – emerged, who could advocate measures such as military discipline as *revolutionary* goals, essential to defense of the revolution.[13] The committees became vehicles for implementing government and Soviet decisions about preparation for an offensive, including discipline, training, officer authority and replacements from the rear – all of which were contrary to the soldiers' perceived self-interest and very unpopular.

In these circumstances the soldiers increasingly looked to alternative spokesmen who articulated their opposition to the offensive. Although most soldiers acquiesced, however reluctantly, to the pro-offensive arguments of the committeemen, a growing number seized on the alternative arguments put forth by the Bolsheviks and other radicals. The leftists explained that the capitalists and landowners of all countries had started the war and that it continued only in their interests; continued fighting meant that they shed their blood for the profits of foreign and Russian capitalists. In short, the argument told soldiers, the war was not really one of defense of Russia and was in no way in their interest or worth their blood and the suffering of their families. Combined with assertions about the political unreliability of officers and danger of a counterrevolution, it explained the war and the offensive in terms that made sense to war-weary soldiers. The radical left argument that repudiating the offensive was the best road to peace and that the war served only the interests of the privileged classes echoed the soldiers' own inner feelings and provided a rationale for their instinctive desire not to resume fighting.

These ideas were picked up by a variety of front agitators. The result was that, as Allan Wildman noted, "in the course of May a vulgarized 'Bolshevism' became the chief mobilizing force of the soldiers' mounting hostility to the new offensive, far outstripping the organized forces of the [Bolshevik] Party and expressing itself in a rash of major mutinies and disorders."[14] The conservative newspaper *Novoe vremia* was more accurate than it probably realized when it wrote on June 6: "Lenin! His name is legion. At all crossroads a Lenin pops up." Indicative of the power and attractiveness of these arguments and slogans was the statement of the commander of the Twelfth Army, General Radko-Dmitriev, that "a single agitator can set back on its heels an entire regiment with the propaganda of Bolshevik ideas."[15] Over and over again it took the combined efforts of Menshevik–SR committeemen, the command staff and sometimes representatives from the Soviet to combat the influence of a single radical orator. Conversely, one agitated orator could undo the careful building work of committeemen and staff. What General Radko-Dmitriev and others who complained of "Bolsheviks" missed was that these orators were effective because the antiwar and antiofficer feelings they expressed resonated so deeply among their compatriots. The officers' faulty analysis of events was not helped by a tendency to label all opponents of the offensive "Bolsheviks," regardless of their true affiliation (many were Left SR or nonparty). This probably also raised the esteem of Bolsheviks in the eyes of the soldiers.

Ironically, the High Command's determination to send reserve units to the front as replacements reinforced the growing rebelliousness of the soldiers. Soldiers from Petrograd and elsewhere, already more politicized than their trench brethren and now additionally embittered by being sent to the front, carried the political turmoil of the cities to the front. There they became agitators and leaders of opposition to discipline, officers, the offensive and Revolutionary Defensist committeemen. Their mere arrival was often a source of dismay for commanders. Reports flooded into military headquarters of the unrest caused by arrival of replacements (especially from Petrograd), rendering some regiments incapable of active operations. The desperate commander of the 61st Siberian Rifle Division wrote that "I and my officers have no recourse but to save ourselves as best we can, as five companies of Leninists have just arrived from Petrograd. A meeting was called for 1600 hours, and it has been decided to hang myself, Morozhko and Egorov."[16]

Both officers and political leaders, including the Revolutionary Defensist leadership, attributed the soldiers' opposition to the offensive to the Bolsheviks' influence, which missed the point and probably reversed the causation. Soldier opposition to the offensive – and the whole set of associated actions such as training, discipline and troop movements – were genuine reactions of the soldiers to efforts to continue the war. They had seen the horrible costs in human life first hand and had no desire to continue paying those costs with their own lives. Their opposition was real and deeply felt, not merely the result of Bolshevik manipulation and agitators, as the commanding officers and much of the Petrograd press claimed. Indeed, the pro-offensive spokesmen could not acknowledge that these soldiers' sentiments were genuine; their fundamental policies were based on the assumption of enthusiastic soldiers fired by revolutionary zeal. Blaming Bolshevik agitators and German agents was easier than admitting that their vision was wrong and that the soldiers genuinely opposed resumption of offensive actions. This prepared the ground for the alienation of soldiers from the Revolutionary Defensist committeemen, who soon found their soldiers in mutiny against them, Revolutionary Defensism, coalition politics and the whole February System. The soldiers turned to "Bolshevism" because of their opposition to the offensive rather than opposing the latter because of Bolshevik influence.

Opposition to the offensive was not limited to the soldiers, but widespread in the society. Industrial workers, whose antiwar sentiments had already found expression in April, were strongly opposed to the offensive. In Petrograd antioffensive feelings combined with a rising tide of worker and soldier discontent over economic and other issues to lead to the "June Demonstrations." Aware of popular discontent (which they and other leftists – especially the anarchists – had been busily stimulating), the Bolshevik leadership on June 8 decided to organize a mass demonstration. They worked through the 9th to organize it and on the morning of June 10 they announced it through their newspapers, for 2:00 p.m. that day. They cast the appeal in broad, simple terms: "Comrades! Those who are for the brotherhood of all peoples, those who favor an open and honest democratic policy for an end to the war, those who oppose the capitalists . . . who force the people to starve – all who are against the curtailing of soldiers' and sailors' rights and who oppose bourgeois persecution – come out and express your protest." The proposal also called for the transfer of all power to the Soviet of Workers' and Soldiers' Deputies.[17]

Word of the planned demonstration reached the Soviet leaders on the afternoon of the 9th. They moved quickly to block what they saw as a Bolshevik and anarchist challenge to the authority of the Soviet as well as a possible source of street fighting, casualties and of a counterrevolution. A constant theme of 1917 was a fear that irresponsible actions from the radical left were not themselves so much a threat but that they might provoke a possibly successful counterrevolution. The Congress of Soviets formally banned the demonstration and the Soviet leadership sent delegates to factories and barracks to try to stop participation in it. The Bolshevik Central Committee called it off at the last minute, leaving thousands of radically inclined workers and soldiers disgruntled and restive.

The Soviet leaders then decided to call a great demonstration on June 18 to show support for the policies of the Revolutionary Defensist leadership of the Soviet, including coalition government and the offensive. The Bolsheviks, Left SRs and anarchists decided to participate, but with the intention of turning the demonstration into an expression of opposition to the war and the government and a call for the transfer of all power to the Soviet. To that end they worked feverishly in factory and garrison meetings to get workers and soldiers to adopt and march under radical slogans. They were wildly successful. Nearly a half-million people marched that day, but only a minority carried banners supporting the policies of the coalition government. Instead, as rank after rank of marching factory and army units passed the reviewing stand, most marched with banners calling for an end to the war, opposing the offensive and the coalition government and, a harbinger of the shifting allegiances of the urban masses, demanding "All Power to the Soviets." The moderate socialist leaders of the Soviet suffered a crushing defeat in the bright sunlight of a clear June day in Petrograd.

Far off in Galicia that same day, the Russian offensive began, which would result in an even greater debacle. The offensive opened with the greatest artillery barrage the Russian armies had ever laid down: for the first time in the war the Russians had a clear predominance of heavy guns. So effective was this "fire of such intensity as I had never heard before," as General A. I. Denikin remembered it, that the initial infantry advances were almost unopposed.[18] Kerensky, watching the offensive begin, sent Petrograd a triumphant telegram and requested special red revolutionary banners for the participating regiments. They could not sustain the initial victories, however. Some units refused to advance farther after initial successes, while others voluntarily retreated to their original trenches without waiting for any counterattack. Some reserve units refused to move up to replace tired front regiments. Many units held meetings to discuss specific orders or even the whole principle of the offensive, and usually resolved not to obey military orders. When the German counteroffensive began, some units broke and fled, others quickly withdrew before being attacked and some reserve units refused to move forward to the aid of units under attack. Withdrawing soldiers attacked officers and representatives of the Soviet who tried to stop them. A joint telegram from the Executive Committees of the South-western Front and of the Eleventh Army and Provisional Government commissars on July 7 catalogued the disaster:

The German offensive, which began on July 6 on the front of the 11th Army, is assuming the character of a disaster which threatens a catastrophe to revolutionary Russia . . . Most of the military units are in a state of complete disorganization . . . and they no longer listen to the orders . . . even replying to them with threats and shots. Cases are on record in which an order given to proceed with all haste to such-and-such a spot, to assist comrades in distress, has been discussed for several hours at meetings, and the reinforcements were consequently delayed for twenty-four hours. These elements abandon their positions at the first shots fired by the enemy . . . long files of deserters, both armed and unarmed . . . are proceeding to the rear of the army. Frequently entire units desert in this manner.[19]

By early July the offensive was a total disaster, militarily and politically. With it were swept away the last illusions of a new revolutionary army. The Russian army, while it continued to exist physically, ceased to exist as an organization capable of fighting. Now it became a mass of angry, resentful, mutinous soldiers and a source of social and political unrest. The fact that the most reliable and best-disciplined units were the ones most heavily mauled by the offensive, while the least-disciplined and most "revolutionary" ones refused to fight and survived, only worsened the situation in the army. The disastrous offensive destroyed hopes for a successful Revolutionary Defensist peace program. It undermined the position of the centrist coalition and introduced a period of even greater political instability to go along with rising social and economic discontents. Just when Russia needed an effective government, its governments – there would be a series after the "first coalition" government collapsed on July 2 over the question of Ukrainian autonomy – became even weaker. The discontents of summer intensified.

The July Days and "Soviet power"

Unfulfilled aspirations, opposition to the war, worsening economic conditions and a foreboding sense of pending social conflict amplified the demand for "Soviet power," especially among the urban workers and garrison soldiers. On the surface this meant simply that an all-socialist government based on the Petrograd Soviet or Congress of Soviets should replace the Provisional Government. Beyond that, however, was an underlying demand for a government that unequivo-cally advanced the interests of the workers, peasants and soldiers against the "bourgeoisie" and privileged society, one that would rapidly carry out radical social and economic reform and end the war. This yearning came together in the simple slogan of "All Power to the Soviets," Soviet power.

The demand for Soviet power and the underlying frustrations of the workers and soldiers burst loose with the tumultuous disorders usually called the "July Days" or the "July Uprising." Some units of the Petrograd garrison – which consisted primarily of troops training as replacements for the front – had become increasingly discontented with the policies of the government and Soviet and bitterly opposed the offensive. Some remained restive after the June demonstrations and resisted being sent as replacement troops to the front for the offensive. One such unit was the First Machine Gun Regiment, which was quartered in the industrial Vyborg district. Their discontent coincided with growing restiveness in nearby factories. The two sets of discontents interacted with each other. On June 20, for example, twenty-five worker militiamen from the Rozenkrants Factory, where anarchist sentiment was high, appeared first at the barracks of the Moscow Guard Regiment and then at the Machine Gun Regiment, calling them to "come out." Only with difficulty were Left SR and Bolshevik leaders in the regiments, who themselves had been stoking discontents, able to hold them back. Although they sometimes restrained what they saw as rash actions, as in this instance, more often Left SR, Bolshevik and anarchist agitators stirred the discontents. Their successes in the June 18 demonstration convinced many Bolsheviks and Left SRs at the factory and army unit level and in the district and city organizations that the time was ripe for action, perhaps even a seizure of power by the Soviet. Certainly the successes of the February Revolution and the April Crisis had shown how mass street demonstrations could change policies and even governments – why not again?

On July 3 the discontents exploded. Several strikes broke out in the Vyborg district and elsewhere. The First Machine Gun Regiment, after a tumultuous meeting, resolved to stage a demonstration that day with the purpose of overthrowing the Provisional Government. They sent spokesmen to other regiments and to factories to persuade them to join in. Anarchist, Left SR and Bolshevik factory activists now took the lead in the agitation – neither the Central Committee nor the Petersburg Committee[b] of the Bolshevik Party authorized it. About 6:00–7:00 p.m. workers from several factories and soldiers of the First Machine Gun Regiment took to the streets calling for "All Power to the Soviets" and other radical slogans. Other regiments and factories soon followed them. Through the long twilight hours of Petrograd's "white nights" they moved into the city center. As Sukhanov described them, "from all sides enormous detachments of soldiers made their way toward the centre – some of them to the Tauride Palace. Some started shooting into the air . . . lorries and cars began to rush about the city. In them were civilians and soldiers with rifles at the trail and with frightened-fierce faces."[20] By midnight tens of thousands of workers and soldiers had assembled at the Tauride Palace, where they angrily demanded the transfer of all power to the Soviet. The Revolutionary Defensist leadership, however, refused, and the demonstrations broke up temporarily between 3:00 and 4:00 a.m. on the 4th.[21]

The Bolshevik leaders in Petrograd met during the night to assess what was happening and decide what to do. The top party leadership, the Central Committee, had not planned the demonstration and Lenin was vacationing in Finland. Nonetheless, because of the activities of lower-level Bolsheviks from the factory and regiment levels and even

---

[b] The Bolshevik city organization; it refused to change its name to Petrograd when the city was renamed in 1914, considering it an act of nationalist chauvinism.

some mid-level leaders from the Bolshevik Military Organization and the Petersburg Committee, who stoked discontents and encouraged the rebelliousness, the party was involved regardless of what top party leaders wished. Faced with possibly alienating their own impatient supporters, mid-level Bolshevik leaders finally gave their blessing to a new march to the Tauride Palace, and the Bolshevik Military Organization began to prepare for the next day's demonstrations. Still, however, the Central Committee hung back. Finally, faced with news from all sides that it would be impossible to stop demonstrations from resuming on the 4th, and with crowds surrounding Bolshevik headquarters demanding action, the Bolshevik Central Committee gave in during the early morning hours. They agreed to authorize and lead, in the words of the broadside issued about 4:00 a.m., "a peaceful, organized expression of the will of the workers, soldiers and peasants" for Soviet power.[22] They also sent for Lenin to return as soon as possible.

On the morning of the 4th, ignoring Soviet leadership appeals to the contrary, most factories and military units joined the demonstrations, as did sailors from the Kronstadt naval base. Armed workers' militia detachments accompanied most factory demonstrations and the soldiers and sailors marched armed. The focus was again the Tauride Palace, where the Soviet leadership sat; the demonstrators largely ignored the nearby Provisional Government, treating it as irrelevant to the decision. Again the demonstrators met the obstinate refusal of the Menshevik–SR Soviet leadership to abandon coalition and take sole power. In the turmoil that followed Kronstadt sailors seized the SR leader, Victor Chernov, and declared him a hostage. The worker who shook his fist in Chernov's face and yelled "Take power you son-of-a-bitch when it is offered to you"[23] illustrated the frustration of the crowd. Throughout the day there was extensive shooting – sometimes from uncertain sources and sometimes wild firing by panicked soldiers and sailors – with heavy casualties.

The demonstrations finally foundered during the night of July 4–5, the result of several factors coming together. First, news circulated in the city that battle-tested troops were on the way from the front to support the Soviet leaders (these soon appeared). Second, the government released documents purporting to show Bolshevik ties with Germany, which brought some previously "neutral" garrison regiments out in support of the Soviet leaders while dampening the enthusiasm of many demonstrators. These charges, printed and distributed on the 5th, produced a sensation and led to a sudden drop in the Bolsheviks' popularity. Lenin and several leading Bolsheviks fled into hiding in Finland to avoid the arrest warrants issued by the government, while some local leaders found themselves abused or even attacked by their fellow workers and soldiers. Third, the demonstrations, despite their massive size, lacked leadership and direction. The demonstrations began at the regiment and factory level and no plans had been made by anybody to orchestrate a seizure of power. Rather, they attempted to force the Petrograd Soviet leaders to take power and create a new socialist government to replace the coalition government, which had just collapsed (news of that began to spread on July 3 and was widely known by the 4th). The Revolutionary Defensist leaders of the Soviet, however, refused to do so, and thus blocked attainment of Soviet power in this manner. Even after their refusal became clear by midday on July 4, and even after Lenin's return to Petrograd about 11:00 a.m., the Bolshevik leaders hung back. Lenin in particular seemed skeptical about where the demonstrations might lead and unprepared to commit himself and his party to decisive leadership. A general disillusionment and frustration took hold of the demonstrators after they found that although they controlled the city streets they could not force their program on the Soviet leaders or produce new leaders. Finally, it is possible that the heavy casualties contributed to the end of the demonstrations. Perhaps as many as 400 people were killed in random shooting, wild firing by soldiers and sailors, and in clashes between army units opposing and supporting the government and Soviet leaders. This raised the specter of civil war.

The July Days were not, as the Bolsheviks' opponents immediately asserted (and later mythology repeated), an abortive planned Bolshevik coup. They represented a genuine outburst of popular discontent. They were a demand for a more radical and effective government – an all-socialist government – which would fulfill popular aspirations for peace, economic reform and solutions to the many problems wracking the country. The Bolsheviks were the major party supporting these demands and their harsh criticism of the government helped focus worker and soldier discontents on the demand for Soviet power as the solution to their problems. This, and the deep involvement of Bolshevik activists, forced the Bolsheviks to attempt a belated leadership role in the demonstrations. Ironically, the latter also concentrated attention on the Bolsheviks' role in fomenting the demonstrations while ignoring the very important role of the Left SRs and anarchists as well as of popular grievances. This focus on the Bolshevik leaders distorted interpretations of the July Days, both at the time and later. It allowed Provisional Government and Revolutionary Defensist leaders to avoid coming to grips with the genuineness of popular discontent and the implications of growing political support for the notion of Soviet power. As a result they

Plate 17 A bullet hole in a Petrograd tobacco store window after shooting during the July Days. The sign on the window says "no *papirosy* [a type of cigarette, especially popular with lower classes] or tobacco." Prints and Photographs Division, Library of Congress.

did not move to deal with those discontents, which helps explain the rapid revival of leftist, including Bolshevik, popularity soon thereafter, despite repressive measures against the Bolsheviks.

The aftermath of the July Days left a peculiarly confused political situation, but one that temporarily benefited the leaders of the government and the Soviet. Because the July Days coincided with the collapse of the military offensive, they were able to shift the blame for the latter onto the Bolsheviks and the July Days, which in fact had little to do with it. This allowed Kerensky, the man more than any other associated with the disastrous offensive, to avoid the immediate personal political catastrophe one might have expected. Instead, after three weeks of political confusion he became minister-president of the newly formed "second coalition" government. Kerensky and the Revolutionary Defensists could only temporarily avoid the political consequences of the disastrous offensive, however, and the popular reaction against it and them soon manifested itself both in a swift decline of Kerensky's popularity and in the rapid resurgence of the radical left. This recovery was somewhat obscured at the time by the fact that the July Days also sparked a resurgence of the political right which dominated the newspaper headlines. This political revival on the right proved as temporary and as illusory as the drop in Bolshevik support. Nonetheless, it led directly to the disastrous "Kornilov Affair" in August.

The economic crisis and conspiracy theories

An important reason for the ongoing discontent and the growing popularity of the radical left was a deepening economic crisis. The tumult of revolution added yet new stresses to the tremendous strains that the war had already put on the Russian economy. Shortages appeared everywhere, from raw materials for factories to food and other necessities. Management–labor conflict, breakdown of overused and undermaintained equipment, fuel and materials shortages, a credit squeeze, food scarcity, agrarian conflict over the land and other problems not only grew, but magnified each other. As 1917 wore on a broad, general economic collapse gathered momentum, exacerbating social and political problems.

Industrial strife became a basic feature of 1917, with overtones of class warfare and with major political implications. The new political freedoms allowed a confrontation between labor and management such as had not been possible before 1917. Workers demanded higher wages, better working conditions and a greater voice in factory affairs and, later, simply that the factories be kept open and their jobs intact. At first the industrialists granted wage increases, but by midsummer whatever wage gains the workers had made in the spring were wiped out by inflation. Industrial workers demanded new raises, but in the new post-July Days mood management increasingly refused. The hardened attitude of employers was partly a response to politics, but also reflected economic realities. Profits disappeared as not only wages but also the costs of raw materials and fuel increased dramatically: the cost of fuel doubled during the first few months after the February Revolution. Moreover, shortened work days, meetings and other new activities of the workers cut into productivity. Wages during the first four months of the revolution increased between 200 and 300 percent while productivity declined between 35 and 50 percent.[24] Caught in this squeeze, factory managers found that they could do little about increased cost of fuel, raw materials, transport and credit, and so focused their attention on the one cost within their ability to affect: the wage demands of labor. This put them on a collision course with the newly empowered workers.

Indeed, two fundamentally different ways of looking at the industrial situation emerged: factory owners and managers stressed the relationship between wages and productivity, while workers emphasized the relationship between wages and living costs.[25] This inevitably created industrial conflict. Inflation prompted workers to press for new wage increases, which management resisted as incompatible with decreasing productivity and rising production costs. Management, attempting to improve productivity and regain some control over internal workings of the factory, refused worker demands that the factories pay wages for time spent for nonworking activities such as meetings and for service in the workers' militias, as well as for "down time" caused by material shortages and other problems. Moreover, they increasingly resisted "workers' supervision" and what they saw as a whole range of efforts to whittle away their control of the factory. Many saw an irreconcilable contradiction between worker demands and keeping the factories functioning – and especially functioning profitably. Indeed, temporary and permanent shutdowns and below-capacity operation caused by the shortage of raw materials or supplies became common.

Workers responded to management claims about costs, profits, and the need to close down factories with new demands for workers' supervision. They were aware that some industries had made huge profits during the war years, profits that Bolshevik and radical propaganda now frequently touted against management. They demanded to see the books of the enterprises. When management agreed (often they did not) workers found 1916 profits, which only reinforced their belief that management was holding out on them, ignoring the fact that the economic situation, including profits and costs, had changed dramatically since February 1917. Management was frustrated at the "wrong" conclusions drawn by workers. Workers also demanded a larger voice in hiring, firing and work assignments, insisted on inspecting inventories and shipments out of the factory and took steps to protect jobs. Underlying this was a suspicion that the cutbacks were not economically necessary, but were rather an attack by management on labor (which they were in some, but not most, cases). Many saw a capitalist conspiracy to choke off the revolution. Labor and management hurled charges and countercharges in an atmosphere where neither side trusted the other and suspected the worst motives. Labor conflict escalated, the number of strikes grew rapidly, a sharper "us–them" conflict developed. The crisis in industrial relations, based on very different perceptions and self-interest by workers and industrialists, became irreconcilable.

Factory closings, and threats thereof, became a major issue, further poisoning industrial relations. Sometimes these led to violence: in Kharkov the workers at the Gerliakh and Pulst Factory "arrested" their administration, which had threatened to close the factory because of labor and supply problems, while the Gelferich–Sade Factory workers seized control on September 27 and ran the factory until October 5.[26] Both the Ministry of Trade and the Petrograd Council of Trade Unions (in August and September respectively) came to the same conclusion: by winter, if not before, half of Petrograd's industries would probably close down.[27] Cutbacks, stoppages and rumors of closures, reported in the press and by word of mouth, created an air of uncertainty and fear. From the perspective of workers, factory closures fit within a broader picture of attacks on their post-February institutions, power and sense of gaining control over their lives. They fed class antagonism and reinforced worker demands for Soviet power and workers' supervision.

Growing industrial conflict had political implications as both sides appealed for government intervention on their behalf. The workers called for the government to play a more active role economically, especially in support of their demands, while management wanted it to help keep workers in line, prevent "outrageous" demands and keep production going. The government wavered, alienating both workers and management. Both looked elsewhere for solutions. From June onwards workers turned increasingly to the slogan of "Soviet power," meaning a socialist government more attuned to fulfilling their aspirations and protecting their interests. Moreover, they turned toward more radical economic solutions, especially those associated with greater state control, even socialization, of industry. They became ever more attuned to explanations that their economic problems could not be solved within the framework of private property and the current political system. This bode ill for the moderate socialist leaders of the Petrograd Soviet, for it ran directly contrary to their insistence on coalition government with nonsocialist elements and that the Soviet *not* assume power alone. At the same time industrial entrepreneurs began to search for a "strong government" and their demands helped fuel the conservative boomlet of July and August which led to the Kornilov Affair. Both groups were abandoning the centrist coalition of the February System.

Industrial strife was only one part of the developing economic chaos. The supply problem was becoming especially perilous. Petrograd, and many other cities, stood at the end of a long and increasingly tenuous supply line, a fact that manifested itself in every kind of shortage. The food supply was especially critical. The government introduced bread rationing in Petrograd in March and reduced the allocated amount in

April. On August 10 there were only enough bread reserves in Petrograd for two days. Other foods also became scarcer and ever more items joined bread and sugar on the list of rationed goods, and sometimes were not available at all. Government attempts to fix prices and set monopolies seemed only to compound the problem. Nor was this limited to Petrograd: it began to affect other cities as well. In Baku, for example, protests against food shortages fueled demonstrations in the summer. Reduction of the grain ration there by a quarter in August sparked searches of houses by groups of workers and urban poor looking for hoarded foodstuffs. These in turn sparked ethnic conflict among Azerbaijanis, Armenians and Russians.[28] Similar shortages and attendant problems emerged in other cities as well. The food supply problem added to the general sense of insecurity and discontent, and worsened in the fall as winter loomed.[29]

The appearance of the "bagmen" in late summer of 1917 personified the developing economic chaos. They typically were individuals from the cities and the grain-poor northern provinces who went to the southern food-surplus producing regions to obtain foodstuffs, which they then transported back either for their own consumption or for distribution via legal or black-market channels. Some were representatives of various organizations carrying documents of variable legitimacy and attempting to purchase large amounts of grain for transport back to their factory, cooperative or town. Some used violence to obtain grain. In Voronezh province a band of bagmen hijacked a train to carry their grain back and were stopped only after a pitched battle with soldiers.[30] Most, however, were individuals, thousands upon thousands of widows and soldiers' wives, workers, peasants and others. Often, after long journeys, bribes and great hardship, they obtained a single sack of foodstuffs which they hauled homeward, sometimes only to have it seized at a railroad station by the militia or predators. As the military system broke down and desertion increased, armed soldier-bagmen began to appear, either with documents asserting their rights to seize foodstuffs for their units or simply as thieves. The bagmen brought disorder, violence and heightened social tensions in broad areas of the country. They were symbols both of the breakdown of the economy and of the disintegration of the state and society.

The economic crises encouraged the Provisional Government to get more deeply involved in regulating the economy. It inherited the imperial government's extensive involvement in control of the economy, including ownership of some industry, and extended it. On May 5, the new liberal–socialist coalition government announced that it would "fight resolutely and inflexibly against the economic disorganization of the country by the further systematic establishment of state supervision over the production, transportation, exchange, and distribution of commodities, and in necessary cases, resort as well to the organization of production."[31] This reflected to some degree the basic hostility of the new socialist members to private enterprise, but more fundamental was a shared view about the role of the state in supervising the economy, especially food supply. The government visualized such state supervision as politically and socially neutral, as serving *state* needs and general societal needs. They saw these as a way to regulate the economy in the general interest.

The problem was how to decide whose view of state and society's good was to prevail. This inevitably led to debates on private ownership versus socialism as the means to achieve the public interest. The Soviet leaders clearly believed, as *Izvestiia* – the official newspaper of the Petrograd Soviet – wrote on April 30, that "the time of 'free enterprise,' of a government policy of noninterference in the economy, has passed, never to return."[32] The Soviet leaders looked to the formation of governmental agencies that could regulate the nation's economy in a planned and organized manner. Industrialists were divided over state regulation. Some were not entirely opposed to state regulations, as many of them, especially in Petrograd, had profited from it. Others, especially Moscow industrialists, were more opposed to government intervention. Greater government regulation soon became reality. In June, under pressure from the Soviet, the government set up an Economic Council whose task, as described by Minister-President Kerensky, was "drawing up a plan for the gradual control of all economic-financial life."[33] To deal with economic problems the government declared several state monopolies, including a trade monopoly on fuel (coal) from the Donets Basin. The government also became deeply involved in efforts to mediate industrial disputes. Mediation and regulation activities, however, inevitably favored one social group or political viewpoint over another. Attempts at an ostensibly neutral posture aroused the fear or anger of one group or another, and in fact alienated both industrial workers and the industrialists, both the peasants and landowners. Underlying all of this was the fundamental question of whether the future society would be based on private property or on socialism, as the dominant socialist political leaders insisted, and if on socialism how soon and in what way that would be instituted. Social and political antagonisms became ever more tightly intertwined.

Throughout the summer and fall the social and economic disintegration of Russia proceeded, quite apart from such major political events as the June Demonstrations, the July Days and continual cabinet reshuffling. The breakdown of distribution systems for food and other goods rippled through the economy and through people's lives. Labor strife increased. Street demonstrations by one group or another were regular occurrences. Soldiers walked about with caps tilted or tunics unbuttoned, a deliberate flaunting of military regulations and public decorum. Public drunkenness, random firing of weapons into the air, rude behavior, unreliable train service and other signs of a breakdown of public order gave a sense of life falling apart. Unruly soldiers, both whole units and small bands of deserters, disrupted life in towns, villages and railroad stations. Peasant land seizures ebbed and flowed across the country. The emergence of separatist movements in some of the national minority regions, especially Ukraine, agitated public life. Government authority in the provinces declined, giving way to a growing localism. To add to the sense of chaos, "anarchists," real and false, undertook to "expropriate the expropriators."

A dramatic increase in crime and arbitrary violence intensified public discontent in 1917 and contributed to the rise of antigovernment attitudes on all levels and among all classes. Crime took many forms. Simple theft, robbery and pickpocketing increased dramatically. Armed robbery, previously rare, also increased in the new world of readily available arms. Some was even done in the guise of "official" searches by men dressed as soldiers or militiamen (police), which furthered distrust of government officials. Murder and other violent crimes increased. Criminals and deserters even formed their own communities in larger cities, areas which the militia hesitated to enter and from which the criminals preyed on the larger community with little fear of retribution. Lynch-law by angry mobs appeared, reflecting the breakdown of order and the frustration of the population over the growth of crime, but also adding to public insecurity. Mob action was directed against ordinary criminals such as pickpockets and thieves, but sometimes also against merchants suspected of hoarding or charging too high a price for scarce goods. In the charged atmosphere it took only a shout of "he's the one" or "I know him; he is a thief" to lead to beatings and sometimes death. The innocent sometimes suffered as well as the guilty: a refugee at the Smolensk train station was killed by a crowd after being falsely accused. Militiamen who tried to intervene to save victims were sometimes beaten themselves. Crowds often refused to turn suspects over to the militia on the grounds that the militia or courts would only release them.

Neither the militia – understaffed, undertrained, underpaid and poorly armed – nor the judicial system was able to cope with the situation to the satisfaction of the populace. A careful study of Smolensk shows a rough doubling of crime, while studies on Petrograd suggest a much larger increase, as one might expect for a large city in comparison with a smaller one.[34] Whatever the actual crime figures, public perception was of an even greater number, which created a strong sense of insecurity among the populace. Knowledge that many criminals had been released in the general opening of prisons in Petrograd and many other cities during the February Revolution added to public insecurity. At the same time military deserters and idle soldiers from the garrisons swelled the criminal ranks. By summer residents of apartment houses began to form house committees to organize the security of their buildings. Sometimes they took turns performing watch functions, and sometimes hired soldiers to guard the building and its residents. The popular impression, fed by sensationalist newspaper reports, was of a breakdown of public security and a resulting threat to life and property regardless of social class. Crime added to the other problems to create a general sense of disorder and insecurity that led *Rabochaia gazeta*, the Menshevik newspaper, to write of the appearance of "new, grievous and even terrifying signs of the beginning of a breakdown." It went on to cite reports of "lynchings, savage arbitrary dealings with those holding different views, the wanton tearing down of placards bearing slogans of confidence in the Government, . . . drunken pogroms, [and] mass rapes of women and girls."[35] Society seemed to be disintegrating.

In an effort to find an explanation for events swirling around them, many Russians in 1917 turned to various conspiracy theories. In a situation where things are breaking down, but where the reasons for that are complex or difficult to understand, and especially in circumstances of extreme economic and other distress, conspiracy theories find ready attraction. Various people had already used them to explain the problems of late imperial Russia (especially the theory of German sympathizers at court), and they flourished in the new revolutionary milieu as people sought explanations for the many crises and hardships. Some kind of sabotage by "dark forces" was a popular explanation for economic breakdowns, especially for the food supply problem. Virtually all political groups used various conspiracy theories to explain what was happening in Russia. Jews, Germans and capitalists were especially popular scapegoats. Blaming a Jewish conspiracy for problems was a long-time popular device. Socialists constantly searched for evidence of capitalist conspiracies. Germans were seen as behind all kinds of problems, from minority nationality assertiveness to military defeats or economic dislocations. The myth of Lenin as a German agent and of the Bolsheviks as surviving only because of "German gold" is only the most historically enduring of the many conspiracy theories current in 1917.[36]

It is therefore ironic that the Bolsheviks themselves made conspiracy and sabotage a central theme in their propaganda. One Bolshevik spokesman, E. Iaroslavsky, put it all together in a pamphlet in the fall of 1917 entitled "Why There Are Neither Goods in the Village Nor Bread in the Towns." "The reason lies in the intentional derangement of all economic life by the messieurs capitalists, factory owners, plant owners, landowners, bankers, and their hangers-on . . . All this is done deliberately so that the bony hand of hunger will grab the working class by the throat."[37] These anti-capitalist sentiments, extended to include the British and French allies, were folded into conspiracy theories as a way to explain the continuation of the unpopular war. Typical was a July 8 letter from a front soldier to the Petrograd Soviet which blamed the continuation of the war on "the bourgeoisie" and the government ministers and called on them to "look at the mothers who are weeping over their sons who have fallen on the field of battle for English and French capital."[38]

Conspiracy and sabotage were easier explanations for industrial layoffs, bread shortage and hunger than were discussions of complex economic issues. Moreover, they fit with political predispositions, especially of the radical socialists. If deliberate sabotage by definable groups was responsible for economic problems, then not economic programs but political will was needed to solve them. As Lars Lih has pointed out, "The sabotage outlook could easily be couched in the Marxist rhetoric of class, and this allowed the Bolsheviks to give expression to deep popular feelings of suspicion and outrage. In turn a sabotage theory was needed to support the position that class struggle was an adequate response to pressing practical problems."[39] If the source of Russia's problems was a conspiracy by capitalists, landowners and officers, then political action that deprived those groups of power could solve the problems. A radical, socialist revolution would replace the current political office holders with new ones, solving the problems.

Indeed, the new socialist rhetoric fit well with traditional lower-class perceptions about justice coming from the ousting of bad office holders and their replacement by new, honest people. From this perspective, such a replacement of office holders had taken place in February, and again in May and in July, as new leaders proved unequal to the task and were themselves replaced at popular demand. Because of disappointing results, however, the hardships of summer 1917 led to a growing clamor for an even more thorough replacement of office holders, and particularly for the removal of all nonsocialists from the government, to be replaced by an all-socialist, "Soviet" government. This was supplemented by the socialist argument that private property was responsible for oppression, poverty, war and all other problems, and that only a socialist reconstruction of the economy could solve Russia's social and economic problems. Dispossessing the privileged classes was seen as an essential part of improving government and people's lives. There was, as Mary McAuley has noted, "a powerful fusion of the older idea of the need for the common people to control their rulers with the socialist belief in the need for class power."[40] Wracked by forces they poorly understood and had negligible control over, and confronted by very real economic and political threats, the workers and soldiers increasingly saw "Soviet power" as the only way out, a sort of panacea, while the peasants turned inward to their own villages as the source of authentic authority and security.

Political crisis, polarization and the Kornilov Affair

As the fears and insecurity of summer grew, an ongoing governmental crisis accompanied a drift of politics toward the two extremes of the spectrum. July and August were months of almost continual government instability. On July 2 the Kadets resigned from the government over the Ukrainian issue and general unhappiness with the government. The July Days, with the demand that the Soviet take governmental power, began the next day. Then on July 7 Prince Lvov resigned as minister-president when the government, now overwhelmingly socialist, adopted a program statement promising more sweeping social and economic reforms than he felt it within the rights of the Provisional Government to do. This inaugurated a prolonged political crisis while Kerensky, as the newly designated minister-president, attempted to form a new government. On July 13 the continuing government ministers, in order to facilitate government reconstruction, put their posts at Kerensky's disposal.

Forming a new government proved extremely difficult. The Kadets refused to join the reconstituted government if Victor Chernov, the SR leader, was included, and also objected to some proposed policies of the socialist ministers. Chernov, because of his reputation as a "defeatist" (advocating Russia's defeat in the war as the lesser evil), his advocacy of land distribution as minister of agriculture, and his penchant for partisan polemical battles, had become the lightning rod for the frustrations, fears and hatreds of the nonsocialist parties and newspapers. Chernov resigned on July 20 in order to be free to engage in political combat with his detractors. On July 21 the frustrated Kerensky formally asked the Provisional Government to release him from his posts. The remaining government ministers, as he probably expected, refused. That night a hastily convened conference of party leaders and representatives of the Petrograd Soviet, the All-Russia Soviet of Peasants' Deputies and the Duma Committee (from the February Days) met to stave off the complete collapse of the Provisional Government.

After much finger pointing about who was responsible for the country's ills, the meeting faced the question of government authority. Nekrasov, a key liberal advocate within the government for a liberal–socialist coalition, and acting as temporary head of government until Kerensky returned, criticized the Soviet leaders for constantly undermining the government and challenged them: "Take, then, this power into your own hands and bear the responsibility for the fate of Russia. But if you lack the resoluteness to do so, leave the power to the coalition government, and then do not interfere in its work." This reference to the Soviet leaders' refusal to take power during the July Days was taken up by Miliukov: "is it [the Soviet] prepared to take the power into its own hands or [is it willing] to show confidence, without reservations and reports, in the government which will be formed by A. F. Kerensky?" Tsereteli responded in kind, demanding that the Kadets stop criticizing the government and cease boycotting it: "And since you, Pavel Nikolae- vich [Miliukov], have no hope of giving the country another government tomorrow [a sarcastic reference to Miliukov's role in the first Provisional Government], you must abandon the tactics of boycott."[41] Rhetoric could not hide, however, the fact that the Revolutionary Defensist leaders were again being challenged to have the Soviet take power – this time by the liberals' taunts rather than by the demand of crowds in the streets – and were being shown to be still unwilling to do so.

Finally, after an all-night meeting, the party representatives entrusted Kerensky with the formation of a new cabinet. With his hand thus strengthened, Kerensky managed to form a new government on July 23 which included both Kadets and Chernov. Its formation, however, reflected desperation to get some kind of government formed, not resolution of the acute disagreements among the parties. The new government proved ineffective in solving the problems of Russia or even of providing stable government during its five weeks of existence. Talk about its reconstruction, and especially what role the new army com- mander, General Kornilov, might play, began almost immediately and dominated political discussion in August.

Not only did the new government fail to represent a genuine political reconciliation, but an ominous political polarization continued. On the one hand was a resurgence of the right, which had largely disappeared as an organized political force after February. The right resurgence was diverse and poorly organized. One feature was the emergence of small groups of army officers, industrialists, conservative politicians and others who discussed the need to reverse the "rot" and who sought to find a strong man to take control and rescue Russia. The increased influence of socialists in the government, the July Days and the failure of the offensive strengthened the determination of many to find a military champion to take power. Their problem, as one leader, the industrialist A. I. Putilov, acknowledged, was that they could raise vast sums of money easily but did not know how to use it effectively. The frustration of the political right, liberals and conservatives, was expressed clearly at the "private session" of members of the State Duma on July 18 (the Duma no longer met as an official body after the February Revolution). One member, A. M. Maslennikov, assailed the left as "Those dreamers and lunatics who imagine they are the creators of world politics . . . !" The session endorsed a resolution condemning "the seizure by irresponsible elements [the soviets] of the rights of the government and the creation of dual power in the center and anarchy in the provinces," and went on to call for a strong government.[42] These sentiments were echoed in conservative and some liberal papers, which stepped up their criticism of the Soviet, the developments in the army, and especially of the Bolsheviks. Increasing numbers of educated society, alarmed at the social and political disintegration they saw around them, were receptive to calls for "order," but they were handicapped by their small numbers in the overall population.

Actions of the Provisional Government in July bolstered the general perception of a shift rightwards and reinforced the left's fear of counterrevolution and conspiracies. On July 12 the government authorized the closure of newspapers advocating disobedience of military orders or containing appeals to violence, and the main Bolshevik newspaper, *Pravda*, was shut down (although a replacement immediately appeared). It also provided for administrative arrest of "persons whose activity constitutes a particular threat to the defense and internal security of the State."[43] On the same day the government restored the death penalty in the army, a favorite demand of the generals and conservatives. The right applauded this as a necessary step toward order, while the left attacked it bitterly. It had little practical effect on military discipline, but had enormous political repercussions, giving a strong push to the political radicalization of the soldiers while fueling fears of counterrevolution. In the industrial sector a Ministry of Labor circular – the minister was the Menshevik and prominent Revolutionary Defensist, M. I. Skobelev – reaffirmed that plant owners and managers had full rights over hiring and firing of employees unless modified by prior agreement, a statement seen by many as an attack on factory committees. The government repeatedly warned against unauthorized land seizures by peasants, and hundreds of peasant rural land committee members were arrested in connection with an attempted government crackdown on agrarian disorders. In July Kerensky ordered a special military expedition to the Volga River city of Tsaritsyn to suppress the Bolshevik-led radical soviet there and the exceptionally mutinous local army garrison; the radicalness and unruliness of the "Tsaritsyn Republic," as it was dubbed, had been a national news story for some weeks. These and other efforts of the government to assert its authority and what it saw as public order in the weeks after the July Days were taken by both right and left as signs of a conservative reaction.

Particularly indicative of trends was the shift in the position of the Kadets. Dismayed by reports of scattered violence against Kadet news-papers and party members and by what Miliukov at the Ninth Party Congress in late July called "chaos in the army, chaos in foreign policy, chaos in industry and chaos in nationalist questions,"[44] they moved to the right. They now began to seek allies among socially conservative groups while despairing of cooperation with even the moderate socia-lists. Some Kadet leaders still hoped that coalition would work, but most, symbolized by Miliukov, moved toward a struggle against the socialist left. They took an active role in the Conference of Public Figures on August 8, where liberal and conservative political figures gathered to denounce the socialists for destruction of the country and to assert a nationalistic, deeply patriotic and statist position. Miliukov decried the "subordination of the great national tasks of the revolution to the visionary aspirations of socialist parties."[45] The meeting, in effect a gathering of educated and privileged society (what Kadet speakers called "healthy elements" of society), underscored the social cleavage and certainly reinforced leftist fears of a "bourgeois conspiracy." The Kadets also began to cultivate contacts with the Don Cossacks, among whom they traditionally had significant electoral support, and with officers' groups. They opened communications with Kornilov and the military high command. They strongly supported Kornilov's demands for military discipline and worked with various patriotically oriented groups supporting strong government and war to victory. At the same time, however, most of the Kadet leadership, Miliukov specifically, rejected the idea of a military coup.

The new public assertiveness by the conservative right was extensively discussed in the socialist and nonsocialist press, creating an image of July–August as a period of a shift to the right. Curiously, while the newspapers talked constantly of a rightist resurgence in their editorials and front pages, careful reading of the news articles of the inside pages suggested quite another development: a continued radicalization of the lower levels of society and political activity. The leftward drift that began in the late spring was barely disturbed by the July Days and their aftermath. Its continuation manifested itself in various ways, but perhaps most unequivocally in the electoral results of late July and August in worker and soldier organizations. Reelections at factories and regiments replaced moderate representatives to soviets, factory committees and soldiers' committees with more radical ones: Mensheviks by Bolsheviks, moderate SRs by Left SRs and Bolsheviks. Worker self-assertiveness continued, as for example in the Red Guards, which survived post-July efforts to disband them and became ever more radical, more "Bolshevik" in outlook. An antigovernment and anti-Revolutionary Defensist leadership was taking over control of the lower-level popular political institutions.

A genuine political polarization developed, with the center being squeezed between the very real growing strength of the left and the weaker but very vocal new activism of the right. The Revolutionary Defensists responded to their dilemma by lashing out against both the left and the right. Tsereteli, as minister of the interior, insisted on July 18 that the "Government cannot tolerate any further demonstrations of anarchy" such as the July Days, but also that it was "well aware of the danger with which the country is threatened by the counterrevolution which is rearing its head."[46] The growth of the radical left within the soviets and other popular organizations meant that the Revolutionary Defensist leadership was under constant attack from the left, even as it felt threatened by the resurgent right. At any time, in any organization, over any issue, Bolsheviks or Left SRs might advance a resolution that put the leadership of the Revolutionary Defensists to the test of popular support. Moreover, these resolutions and the debates accompanying them constantly raised before workers and soldiers the idea of more radical solutions to issues and helped push them leftward.

The Revolutionary Defensist leaders, fighting an ongoing defensive action on their left and now attacked from the right, became afflicted by self-doubt. In August they spoke regularly of the soviets being seriously weakened since the July Days, which was true only in that their vision of the role of the soviets was being squeezed between left and right. In fact the soviets were still the dominant source of popular political authority, in Petrograd and elsewhere, and in many ways were stronger than ever because of worker and soldier demands for Soviet power and the end of coalition. The Revolutionary Defensists, however, refused to use that popular demand to assert the Soviet's authority and carry out a sweeping social revolution.

These trends – the conservative resurgence at the level of "high politics," the growing popular radicalism, and the increased weakness of the Revolutionary Defensist alliance – set the stage for the "Kornilov Affair." This centered on the person of General Lavr Kornilov, who emerged as the potential "man on horseback," the Napoleon of the Russian Revolution. Of humble Cossack origins, Kornilov had risen in the military and had won some fame for exploits in Central Asia before the war and as a daring commander in the early stages of the war. He achieved hero status in 1916 following escape from an Austrian prisoner-of-war camp disguised as a peasant. His dramatic features – prominent high cheekbones, dark slanted eyes, black hair and moustache – combined with his exotic bodyguard of Caucasus mountaineers to provide a dashing figure. Kornilov had been appointed commander of the Petrograd garrison after the February Revolution. In that position he came into conflict with the Petrograd Soviet over control of the troops during the April Crisis and was humiliated when it countermanded his orders. Frustrated and angry, he asked to be relieved and sent to the front. He left convinced that the government could never be strong as long as the Soviet exercised the power it did. After the June offensive he became one of the most outspoken voices calling for draconian measures – including the death penalty – to restore discipline in the army. He made a strong impression on the commissar for the Southwestern Front, Boris Savinkov, a Right SR, former terrorist and confidant of Kerensky. Savinkov recommended Kornilov to Kerensky as a strong leader, but one of democratic leanings. The nonsocialist members of the government joined in pushing Kerensky to appoint Kornilov as supreme commander of the Russian army. On July 18 Kerensky appointed Kornilov to the post, also appointing Savinkov as assistant minister of war.

Kornilov immediately took an aggressive stance toward the government and Soviet. Upon his appointment Kornilov announced that he would answer only to his conscience and to "the people," and would not allow the government or soviets to interfere with military operations. This remarkably arrogant display did not bode well for his cooperation with the government and must have reinforced the uneasiness of some democratic political leaders about his suitability and intent. Moreover, Kornilov was contemptuous of the Petrograd politicians generally and the socialist ministers especially. His trips to the capital in his new capacity convinced him that political leadership was at best paralyzed and perhaps even treasonous. Once while he was speaking to the government ministers Kerensky slipped him a note warning him to be careful of what he said because not everyone present was reliable.

Kornilov apparently took this to mean that even among the government ministers there were German agents, a quite erroneous assumption since it was merely an attack on Chernov's ability to keep information to himself. The incident reinforced Kornilov's sense that drastic changes were necessary.

Kornilov quickly drew the attention of those looking to the military to provide a savior for Russia. By late summer a broad array of nonsocialist elements – political figures, industrial leaders, army officers and the increasingly fearful middle class – were convinced that the government absolutely had to be reformed and that it required more than another reshuffling of ministerial portfolios. They looked to reduce the power of the left, and of the soviets in particular. Many felt that, if the Petrograd Soviet's domination over the government were broken, they could form a strong government to arrest the breakdown of social order, restore the fighting ability of the army and lead the country through to the Constituent Assembly. The idea of a military dictator to accomplish these goals gained ground. The conservative press began to build Kornilov as a national hero and future savior of the country. At his arrival in Moscow for the State Conference in August Fedor Rodichev, a prominent Kadet, declared "Save Russia, and a grateful people will revere you."[47] For the left – moderate and radical – Kornilov became the symbol of counterrevolution.

The polarization of Russian political life, with Kornilov its focus, highlighted the Moscow State Conference of August 10–13. The Moscow State Conference was an effort by Kerensky to strengthen his government and to paper over political differences by bringing together all significant political and social groups in a great show of revolutionary unity in support of strengthening "the state." Instead, it displayed the depth of the divisions. Conservative representatives (industrialists, higher-level army officers and conservative political leaders) vented their frustrations, their criticisms of the Soviet and government, and their demand for social order and military victory. Moreover, they focused their positive attention on Kornilov and left no doubt that they gave him their full backing. The depth of the political division was revealed in the responses to speeches: the right sat still when socialists spoke but cheered lustily for Kornilov and their own speakers. When conservatives spoke, the socialists refused to applaud and remained stonily in their seats. Kerensky received only a lukewarm response to his speeches and appeals to maintain political unity, becoming hysterical in his closing speech and collapsing in his chair in such an alarming fashion that a doctor was called. As if the speeches at the conference were not enough to emphasize the divisions, the Bolsheviks boycotted it and the Moscow

Plate 18 General Kornilov being carried aloft from the train station on his arrival for the Moscow State Conference. General A. I. Denikin, *Ocherki Russkoi smuty* (Paris, 1921).

trade unions declared a strike to show their opposition to it – the conference opened in a largely closed-down city. The conference underscored both the divisions in society and the emergence of Kornilov as the darling of the right.[48]

In the days following the conference the political atmosphere turned from bad to worse as new military disasters were added to the ongoing process of economic crisis, labor strife and peasant unrest. A few days after the conference the Germans attacked the key industrial city of Riga and easily overran it as the Russian Twelfth Army broke and fled. The loss of Riga sparked a series of political charges and countercharges. For Kornilov and the right it was more evidence of how far the disintegration of the army had gone, more proof that decisive measures were needed to restore order. The soldiers' committees and leftist newspapers counter-attacked by defending soldier behavior, charging inadequate preparation by the command staff and even hinting that perhaps Riga had been deliberately betrayed as part of some right-wing plot. Other military-related disasters, such as an explosion at the Kazan munitions depot, added to the recriminations and tense atmosphere.

By mid-August Kerensky and Kornilov cautiously worked toward some kind of political understanding, urged on by Savinkov and non-socialist political leaders. This was not easy. They could agree that something needed to be done to enhance the authority of the government, reduce the power of the Soviet and "restore order," especially in the army. However, this meant very different things to the two men. Kornilov was a conservative and a believer in order and discipline, in the army and in society. He had only a very rudimentary understanding of politics and a serious misconception about the existing political parties, including a tendency to lump all leftist critics together as "Bolsheviks." Impressed by the many offers of support from prominent industrialists and politicians, Kornilov determined to press for a major reconstruction of the government, perhaps by force if need be. He aggressively pushed a series of demands in negotiations with Kerensky, carried out mainly through intermediaries, especially Savinkov. He believed it necessary to form a strong government, purged of socialists, and either led or dominated by himself. Kornilov felt, or at least hoped, that he was working with Kerensky and the "healthier" elements of the government, that he was truly rescuing it from unsavory elements and perhaps even traitors. He apparently vacillated between ideas of outright military seizure of power and of acting on behalf of the government against some Bolshevik demonstration. He was politically inexperienced and his plans probably were not fixed, but rather changed regularly under pressure from competing advisors and meetings.

Kerensky, on the other hand, was nominally a socialist, a man for whom reducing the power of the Soviet and restoring order meant something quite different. He wanted to *reduce* the Soviet's power over the government, but by no means wished to destroy the Soviet or even to damage it to such an extent as to provoke either the triumph of the conservatives or civil war. The Soviet was an integral part of the February System of politics, of which he was the prime exemplar. Its destruction likely meant his own, or at least his eclipse as a public figure and removal from power. He wished to strengthen the existing government, not destroy it. Kerensky was wary of Kornilov, but attempted to use him both to placate the right and to strengthen the government's position against the left and the Soviet.

Given differences between the two men, cooperation was possible only so long as they did not have to be too precise about what slogans calling for "order" meant and as long as they could focus on common enemies, especially "Bolsheviks." During the third week of August intermediaries made efforts to bring the two men closer, working toward an uneasy agreement amid rumors of a Bolshevik uprising – the papers were full of this – to coincide with the upcoming six-month anniversary of the February Revolution (August 27). None was in fact planned, but fear of one, plus the need to control the popular opposition that any attempt to implement their "restoration of order" and reduce Soviet authority would provoke, kept them focused on common enemies. To deal with either the demonstrations or the presumed uprising, Kerensky sought Kornilov's support to enforce martial law in Petrograd if Kerensky declared it, while Kornilov, with government blessing, moved some especially reliable troops closer to Petrograd should they be needed. However, prominent among the troops he sent was the so-called Savage Division, made up of non-Russian Caucasus mountaineers, even though he had been told not to include them. It appears that Kornilov was coming to the opinion that it was necessary to move against "Bolsheviks," by which he meant radicals generally, and that he was willing to do this even if he destroyed the current government itself in the process.

At this point V. N. Lvov (not to be confused with Prince Lvov) appeared fatefully on the main stage of Russian history. Procurator of the Holy Synod (civilian chief administrator of the Orthodox Church) in the first cabinet of the Provisional Government, he had a reputation as a meddler. He now undertook the self-appointed role of intermediary between Kerensky and Kornilov, and then apparently garbled his messages. As a result he heightened Kornilov's suspicions about Kerensky's reliability, while feeding Kerensky's anxiety that Kornilov's idea of restoration of order was a much more sweeping concept than his own, perhaps including even his own destruction. On August 27 the suspicious Kerensky sent a teletype message to Kornilov that purported to be from Lvov, asking him to confirm the message Lvov had brought.

Without asking what precisely Lvov had said, Kornilov confirmed his "urgent request" that Kerensky come to military headquarters. Believing this to be a trap and proof of a plot against him, Kerensky announced Kornilov's removal as commander-in-chief. A thunderstruck Kornilov responded in outrage at what he saw as betrayal and further proof of the government's weakness. He issued a statement denouncing Kerensky, the Soviet, and the Bolsheviks and ordered General Krymov, with the "Savage Division" and Third Cavalry Corps, to take Petrograd.[49]

Now, however, Kerensky was rescued by the very Soviet and the workers and soldiers he had intended to move against. The socialist parties, always on the lookout for counterrevolution, responded energetically, calling on the workers and soldiers to rally to defense of the revolution. Arms were distributed to the Red Guards, which now expanded dramatically, and the more revolutionary Petrograd garrison regiments were called out. Even before they had to act, however, railway workers hindered the advance of Krymov's troops, while agitators from Petrograd and local towns filtered into the soldiers' ranks to warn them that they were being used for counterrevolution. The soldiers stopped and refused to go further. General Krymov, after a tumultuous meeting with Kerensky, retired to the apartment of a friend where, after declaring that "The last card for saving the homeland has been beaten – living is not worthwhile any longer," he shot himself.[50] By August 31 Kornilov's effort collapsed and he and several associates were placed under arrest near the front military headquarters (though guarded by Kornilov's own loyal bodyguard unit).

Kornilov's movement collapsed with enormous repercussions. Kerensky's reputation was badly damaged. Although he remained minister-president until the October Revolution, he never again wielded his former personal authority. Both left and right accused him of having been involved in a conspiracy and then having betrayed his co-conspirator. He was morally compromised. The same kind of ridicule that had been heaped on Nicholas after his abdication began to attach to Kerensky. The question now was when, how, and by whom he would be replaced, not if he would be. The affair also damaged the position of the moderate socialist leaders of the Soviet; although distrustful of Kornilov they had approved his appointment as commander-in-chief, while the radical left had opposed it. The Kornilov Affair also finished off what remained of soldiers' trust in their officers and further weakened the army, an ironic result given that to restore officer authority and army discipline had been a primary aim. Even though few officers actively supported it, all were suspected of wanting to do so. Antiofficer hostility, even violence, revived, and their authority over soldiers declined even further. Discipline further deteriorated. With a strong sense of poetic justice many soldier resolutions demanded that Kornilov and other conspirators be subjected to the death penalty that they themselves had reimposed in the army.

The winners out of the Kornilov Affair were the radical left. The mobilization and arming of workers, especially Red Guards, were an important energizer. The Red Guard, for example, remained permanently larger, radicalized and better armed and organized, which was important for the role it would play in the October Revolution. Fear of "Kornilovites" similarly radicalized workers, soldiers and politics in many provincial cities. The Kornilov Affair fit perfectly into the conspiracy scenarios that were so widespread and also reinforced the suspicion that counterrevolutionaries were everywhere and ready to strike. It gave a major psychological and organizational boost to radicals of all stripes. The Bolsheviks in particular profited and their popularity soared. They had harped on the danger of a counterrevolutionary conspiracy and of Kornilov in particular, and now were shown to be prophets. But not just the Bolsheviks: the Left SRs and even Menshevik–Internationalists found that their popularity surged as well. The new popularity of the radical left quickly translated into an elected majority for a Bolshevik-led radical left coalition in the Petrograd Soviet and in many other city soviets and army committees. That, in turn, set the stage for the October Revolution.

8 "All Power to the Soviets"

The rise of the Bolsheviks and the radical left

The Bolsheviks started in the spring of 1917 as the least influential of the three major socialist parties, but grew rapidly in size and importance. By fall they had surpassed the Mensheviks and were challenging the SRs in popular support; in Petrograd and many urban centers they had surpassed both parties. The reasons are complex. One was the Bolsheviks' success in positioning themselves as the opposition to both the government and Soviet leadership, attacking their failure to deal decisively with the land issue and blaming them for the deteriorating economy, for mishandling the nationalities question and for a host of other problems. The Bolsheviks hammered the Revolutionary Defensists for failing to end the war and for their commitment to coalition government (which was increasingly unpopular with workers and soldiers). They accused them of counterrevolutionary sympathies and even, ironically as it proved, of plotting to prevent the Constituent Assembly from meeting. As the Provisional Government and Revolutionary Defensist leaders failed to solve the problems of Russia and to meet the aspirations of society, the radical left prospered. The Bolsheviks in particular became the political alternative for the disappointed and disenchanted, for those looking for new leadership.[1]

The Bolsheviks' appeal was not merely negative, however. They also drew support for the policies they advocated. They promised quick action on the problems facing Russia: immediate peace, rapid and complete land distribution, workers' supervision in industry and various other social-economic changes. They were able to champion the demands of specific groups, such as the *soldatki* for stipends and the "over 40s" for discharge from the army, in a way that the parties responsible for government or even Soviet actions could not. Moreover, they provided clear and believable, if often simplistic or even erroneous, explanations for the complex problems and uncertainties of the times. Their explanation that the problems of society grew out of hostile actions of "capitalists," "bourgeoisie" and other privileged elements was more easily grasped than was the working of complex and often impersonal forces. That some known or unknown "they" threatened the revolution was a popular belief in the unsettled world of 1917; few asserted it more forcefully or more effectively than the Bolsheviks. The lesson to be drawn, of course, was that therefore the problems of society could not be solved as long as the capitalists and bourgeoisie held any share of power.

Excluding the upper- and middle-class elements from power and the demand for radical change were both neatly summed up in the call for "All Power to the Soviets." The growing demand for a Soviet-based government paralleled a linguistic evolution of the terms "democratic" and "the democracy" into meaning the lower classes, and as being in opposition to "the bourgeoisie" and propertied society generally. By summer and early fall the idea was widespread that only a socialist, soviet-based government could be "democratic," since democracy was equated with the lower classes and excluded the "bourgeoisie" and all propertied elements. Any government containing members of the "bourgeoisie" and the Kadet party could not by this newly evolving definition of democracy and class characteristics be democratic. Only a soviet-based government could be democratic in the new socio-political vocabulary. Both the Bolsheviks and growing numbers of the population embraced the slogan of All Power to the Soviets in this political-democratic meaning, but the Revolutionary Defensist leaders stubbornly rejected it. The Bolsheviks capitalized on the growing correspondence of their views with that of the workers and soldiers by waging an energetic propaganda campaign in the press and by orators, in which they drove home their criticism of the government and Revolutionary Defensism and highlighted their own prescription for radical change. Their politics of sweeping change, of a revolutionary restructuring of society, aligned them with popular aspirations as the population turned toward more radical solutions to the mounting problems of Russia.

The party's success also grew in part out of its organization. The Bolshevik Party in 1917 was a unique combination of centralization and decentralization. A small Central Committee served as its top decision-making body. Below it were city and provincial committees, of which the most important was that in Petrograd, the Petersburg Committee. Further down were the district committees in large cities and the smaller regional organizations countrywide. At the bottom, at the grass-roots level, stood the party committees in factories and army units. The Bolsheviks also had a special Military Organization to work among the soldiers. Not being distracted by the problems of central and local governance that affected other parties, the Bolsheviks were able to devote more energy and personnel to party organizational work and to gaining new supporters among the mass organizations and committees. Moreover, the party leadership was more cohesive than the other major parties. The others suffered from numerous deep splits, most significantly the Defensist versus Internationalist division. The Bolsheviks did not have that division, Lenin having crafted the party along strictly Internationalist lines and any Defensist-oriented members having left the party already.

Not that the party was without internal divisions. Despite Lenin's traditional emphasis on leadership and discipline, the lower party organizations had considerable freedom to adapt to the demands of their worker or soldier constituencies and to changing circumstances. They sometimes challenged or ignored the policies of the top leaders. Although Lenin temporarily abandoned the slogan of "All Power to the Soviets" following the July Days, for example, most of the party, especially at the lower levels, never ceased to support it. The lower-level party organizations tended to be more radical and more activist than the upper-level organizations. This reflected the fact that the Bolshevik Party, as the party of radical extremism, attracted the most radical and impatient individuals from the factories and garrisons. The top party leadership, on the other hand, was concerned with broad strategic issues and was of necessity somewhat more cautious than the rank and file. The leadership sometimes found it difficult to keep their more impatient members in step with overall party policy and strategy, as the July Days had shown. There were important disagreements among the party leaders as well, especially over taking power in October, but the Bolsheviks were still the best organized and most cohesive, and had the most clearly authoritative central leadership of any of the revolutionary parties.

The Bolsheviks also had the advantage of a recognized leader – Lenin – with a focused drive for power and a vision of a new political system. Only gradually did even Lenin's closest associates come to realize the degree to which Lenin's thinking was evolving toward a violent seizure of power and the creation of a new type of governmental apparatus based on the soviets. This evolution had begun even before his return to Russia in April and continued and took firmer shape in the summer.[2] Although Lenin wavered in his enthusiasm for the soviets after the July Days, he soon returned to them as the basis for a new form of government, state and society. He was talking about changing not just who ran the government, but the very nature of government. "Power to the Soviets," Lenin wrote in mid-September, is usually "taken quite incorrectly to mean a 'Cabinet of the parties of the Soviet majority.'" The latter meant merely "a change of individual ministers, with the old state apparatus left intact . . . 'Power to the Soviets' means radically reshaping the entire old state apparatus . . . [The Soviets] are particularly valuable because they represent a new *type* of state apparatus."[3] Lenin and the Bolsheviks became the most vigorous advocates of "All Power to the Soviets," a slogan of great popularity among the masses, signifying not only radical social and economic reform, but a new, if ill-defined, political system. Lenin spent July–October in hiding with a warrant for his arrest still current from the July Days, but he remained the party's leader, if less dominant than if he had been on the scene. Even in his absence from the capital Lenin, "Leninists" and "Leninism" were major commodities in the political life of July–October, the symbol of radical change both for those opposed and for those in favor of it.

The Bolsheviks, however, were not the only political group advocating sweeping changes and reaping the benefits of popular dissatisfaction with government and Soviet policy. Others shared their criticism of the government and Soviet leaders, offered similar analyses of why things were wrong and held out visions of a better future. The rise of the Bolsheviks was in fact part of a broader phenomenon of the growth of the radical left (the origins of these left tendencies and the "left bloc" are discussed in chapter 3). Radical victories in soviets and workers' and soldiers' organizations in late summer and early fall usually rested on a left-bloc coalition of Bolsheviks, Left SRs, Menshevik–Internationalists and other smaller groups such as the anarchists, among whom Bolsheviks were usually but not always the predominant group. What unified this left bloc was opposition to the Revolutionary Defensist leadership of the Soviet and a call for different policies. They opposed continuation of coalition government and stressed class hostility instead of cooperation. They opposed continuing the war and demanded immediate peace. They insisted on quicker action on social and economic reforms and called for some form of Soviet power or all-socialist government. Many so-called Bolshevik resolutions were in fact joint left-bloc resolutions, and this left bloc provided the majority in many local soviets and other organizations often described as "Bolshevik" by later accounts and even by some contemporaries.

The Left SRs were the most important group, next to the Bolsheviks, in the radical left bloc. The left tendency within the SR Party emerged as a potent force on the radical left in the summer and early fall. It took clearer form as they became increasingly vocal in their opposition to the Revolutionary Defensists – and thus the right and center wings of their own party – on the above issues. Their opposition to the offensive and the reimposition of the military death penalty swung the vote of many garrison soldiers to them within the SR Party. Left SR spokesmen such as Spiridonova, Kamkov and Natanson bitterly attacked the government, Kerensky (still officially an SR), Chernov and the SR leadership for continuing to support the war, for continuing coalition with the Kadets, and for failing to deal decisively with the land question and other social issues. By fall the Left SRs became the major force in the Soldiers' Section of the Petrograd Soviet and in some other soviets as well. This plus some support in the workers' sections made them increasingly influential in the soviets generally. Their influence also grew inside the party. The leftists won 40 percent of the vote at the SR Party council of August 6–10, before the Kornilov Affair. On September 10, after Kornilov, the leftists won control of the Petrograd SR Party organization. This gave them control of its newspaper and thus of an important vehicle for putting forward their views. On September 14 they issued a manifesto in the paper demanding a general armistice, an end to coalition, workers' supervision, land to the peasants and the convocation of a new congress of soviets. The leftists were also gaining influence in the party across the country. They already controlled party organizations at the northern naval bases (Kronstadt, Helsinki, Revel), in widespread cities such as Kharkov, Kazan and Ufa, and in many army committees. Their strength continued to grow and by fall the majority of SR Party organizations were for Soviet power, despite the official position of the central party leaders.[4]

The leftists, however, hesitated to break entirely with the SR Party. They hoped that they could win control of the party and thus make their policy the program of the entire official SR Party, with all of its traditional influence and prestige. One result of staying inside the larger party, however, was that the Left SRs lacked the clear organizational identity that the Bolsheviks had. This blunted the impact of their criticisms and made it more difficult for the Left SRs to establish themselves as a clear alternative to either the Soviet leadership or the government (in both of which center and right SRs were prominent). As a result, when mass support shifted left in late summer and fall 1917 many former moderate SR supporters shifted to the Bolsheviks rather than to Left SRs within the party. For example, when the huge Obukhov Factory in Petrograd, a moderate SR stronghold through the summer, reelected its deputies to the Petrograd Soviet in September, it sent nine Bolsheviks and two anarchists, with no SRs or Mensheviks. Despite such setbacks, the emergence of the Left SRs allowed many who still clung to the traditional peasant–soldier identification with the SRs to vote for radical resolutions, including demands for Soviet power, without breaking with the party. Moreover, it provided the basis for the radical left alliance that was so critical to the movement for Soviet power, the October Revolution and the new Soviet government afterwards.

The left-wing Mensheviks were the third significant part of the left bloc. They emerged in late spring as a loosely knit group critical of the policies of Revolutionary Defensism, to which the Menshevik Party was committed under the leadership of Tsereteli and Dan. The left Mensheviks found leadership with the return in early May of prominent exiles, most importantly Iulii Martov, a founder of Menshevism. They adopted the name Menshevik–Internationalists to distinguish themselves from the Revolutionary Defensist leadership under Tsereteli, but did not leave the parent party. Like the Left SRs, they hoped to gain control of the entire party. In fact they did gain strength within the party in the late summer and fall, garnering over a third of the vote at the Menshevik Party congress in August, holding a loose majority in the Petrograd city organization and becoming the dominant faction within the party in some provincial cities (Kharkov, Tula and elsewhere). Popular support for Mensheviks of any variety was fading rapidly, however, as shown in disastrous electoral results of late summer and early fall. Moreover, the Menshevik–Internationalists were even less successful than the Left SRs in creating a separate identity and drawing to themselves the popular support deserting the center and right wings of the Menshevik Party. If many peasants and soldiers continued their traditional support for "the peasants' party" via the Left SRs, industrial workers felt no such need: they could satisfy the traditional appeal of social democracy to them as well by Bolshevism as by Menshevism of any type. Even some of the Menshevik–Internationalist leaders abandoned the party; a large group led by Iurii Larin joined the Bolsheviks in August.

The anarchists rounded out the radical left bloc. Their absence from "high politics" of the government and Soviet masks the fact that all through 1917 they were important at the lower levels of politics, and especially in the factories of Petrograd. They focused their energies at the factory level and pinned their political ambitions to the factory committees in particular. This paid dividends. By late summer and fall elections at a large factory, as Paul Avrich has noted, "might have elected a dozen Bolsheviks, two anarchists, and perhaps a few Mensheviks and SRs."[5] The anarchists were a constant source of antigovernment, anti-Revolutionary Defensist, anti-factory management rhetoric, and they articulated worker discontents while helping to reorient them toward more radical politics. The anarchists found it easy to work with the Bolsheviks in the fall, not only because they shared the Bolsheviks' hostility toward the February System, but because Lenin's own antigovernment rhetoric in 1917 convinced many anarchists that his views were coming close to their own. Indeed, their ongoing attacks on the very idea of a Constituent Assembly probably helped prepare the ground, in Petrograd at least, for popular acceptance of its dissolution by the Bolsheviks in January 1918 (it is fitting that an anarchist sailor led the detachment that dispersed the assembly). Their organizational weakness, internal divisions and their hostility to government in general, however, made it difficult for them to translate their popularity into political authority.

By August the radical left's criticism of the failure of the moderates, its advocacy of radical reform, and its calls for Soviet power began to translate into institutional power. Factories and army units continually reelected deputies to soviets, something the Bolsheviks and Left SRs pressed for in the name of accountability and democracy. As a result a combination of Bolsheviks, Left SRs and Menshevik–Internationalists took control of one after another of the Petrograd city district soviets in the summer, dominated the Petrograd trade unions and the factory committees, and gained control of some provincial city soviets and soldiers' committees. The process accelerated in September after the Kornilov Affair gave the left a gigantic boost. Especially important was the capture of the main bastion of revolutionary authority, the Petrograd Soviet. On August 31 a Bolshevik-sponsored resolution passed in the Petrograd Soviet for the first time. In response the Revolutionary Defensists put their leadership to a vote of confidence on September 9 and lost. On September 25 the Soviet elected a new radical left leadership. Leon Trotsky, who had joined the Bolshevik Party in July and swiftly became one of its most prominent leaders, became chairman of the Soviet, replacing Chkheidze. The new presidium had four Bolsheviks, two SRs and one Menshevik. Simultaneously, the Bolsheviks took over the Moscow Soviet of Workers' Deputies, thereby giving them leadership of the two most important soviets. Victories in other cities accompanied this as the radical left bloc – and sometimes the Bolsheviks alone – won reelection campaigns in factories and barracks and took over control of soviet after soviet.

General elections to city and district government councils also revealed the shifting political loyalties. The Bolsheviks received a third of the votes in elections for the Petrograd city council on August 20, despite the absence of Lenin and some other top party leaders. In Moscow, Bolsheviks gained an absolute majority in voting for city district councils in September, a dramatic rise from June when they had obtained only 11.7 percent of the vote for the city council (the SRs won 58 percent in June but only 14 percent in September). These Bolshevik successes, it should be noted, came within the context of a dramatic falling off of voting in general. In Petrograd, voting for the city council fell from 792,864 in May to 549,374 in August, while in Moscow 646,568 voted in the city council elections in June but only 385,547 voted in the district council elections in September. A similar falling off happened in many factory and other elections. This meant that in absolute numbers the Menshevik–SR drop was even worse than the percentages suggest.[6]

Through these reelections of deputies and officers the Bolsheviks and other leftists were *elected* to leadership of the Petrograd and other soviets, and also of trade unions, factory committees, army committees and some public offices. They could reasonably claim *at this time* to speak on behalf of "Soviet democracy," the worker and soldier masses of the urban soviets and their demand for Soviet power. This control of the Petrograd Soviet and some other soviets allowed the October Revolution to take place; without it that revolution is difficult to imagine. Under Bolshevik leadership the Petrograd Soviet, the most influential institution in Russia, now became the main vehicle of the drive for Soviet power, supported by other soviets and popular organizations. Indeed, as it turned out, the October Revolution would begin as a defense of the Petrograd Soviet and the idea of Soviet power.

Soviet power, however, was an ambiguous slogan, meaning different things to different people. For most it meant the Soviet in some way taking power and replacing the current "coalition" government (one including nonsocialists) with a new multiparty all-socialist government. The Menshevik–Internationalists and some others argued for a "homogenous democratic government," i.e., one that would include besides the soviets the representatives of other worker, peasant and even lower middle-class organizations such as cooperatives, democratically elected city councils, peasant organizations, etc. Many saw this as an alternative both to the old coalition government formula and to the Bolsheviks' narrower and more radical "Soviet power." It appealed to many socialists – including some Bolsheviks – who wanted to abandon governmental coalition with the liberals but who feared that a narrowly soviet-based radical government meant reckless policies, anarchy and civil war. Even some of the Revolutionary Defensists were moving toward this idea.

The crisis of coalition government

The Bolshevik and radical left rise in the soviets paralleled an ongoing government crisis that made government restructuring a pressing issue in the political life of fall 1917. The second coalition cabinet founded with such difficulty in July collapsed during the Kornilov Affair, and the parties and leaders that had championed coalition could not immediately agree on its reorganization. Therefore on September 1 the Provisional Government ministers turned the running of the government over to a Council of Five, which was immediately dubbed "The Directory" in reference to perceived parallels to the history of the French Revolution. Headed by Kerensky, it was notable for the absence of other important political leaders and was in effect his personal regime. Kerensky's personal leadership was reinforced by his assumption of the position of supreme commander of the army. He now had virtually complete responsibility and authority for running both the civil and military affairs of Russia until a new government was formed.

Forming a new government, however, again proved difficult. Chernov and the SRs insisted that the Kadets, widely held to have backed Kornilov (some did, some did not), be excluded from any new coalition government. The problem with this was that the Kadets were the only significant nonsocialist party, so there could not be a meaningful "coalition" without them. The question of coalition with the Kadets stimulated the debate among socialists over forming an all-socialist government, and if so what kind, or whether to continue with some kind of coalition – and if so what kind. To help resolve this a "Democratic Conference," a gathering of representatives of socialist parties, soviets, trade unions, cooperatives and elected popular institutions such as city councils (which were mostly socialist-controlled) met September 14–19. The Left SRs pushed hard for formation of a multiparty all-socialist government. After prolonged and acrimonious debate the conference passed muddled motions: first for the principle of coalition, then an amendment against including members of the Kadet Party, and then rejecting the whole resolution. The failure of the Democratic Conference to reach agreement allowed Tsereteli and the partisans of coalition, from their old base in the Central Executive Committee of the first All-Russia Congress of Soviets (June), to support Kerensky in forming a new Provisional Government, the "Third Coalition," on September 25. Headed by Kerensky and including Kadets, Mensheviks, SRs and other moderate socialists and liberals, it was even weaker than its predecessors, devoid of authority or significant support from any quarter. While formally a continuation of coalition, no one had much hope for it and all talk was of what would replace it.

The Democratic Conference revealed the extent to which the formerly unified ranks of the Revolutionary Defensists were in disarray. They no longer had an operable peace policy. Many of them had lost faith in coalition government, but clung to it because they feared the alternatives. The newspapers chronicled the steady erosion of their popular support, heralding an unbroken string of defeats by the radical left in factory and army committees, soviets, trade unions and other mass organizations. The SR Party was so wrapped up in internal conflict among its left, center and right wings that it was unable to wield the kind of influence that its continuing popularity among workers and soldiers as well as peasants warranted. Thus engaged, the right and center SRs were forced to follow Tsereteli and the Revolutionary Defensist leaders into yet another coalition, while the left had to cede much of their authority to Bolshevik leadership. The Mensheviks watched their own popular appeal sink to new lows. By the end of September the Revolutionary Defensist leadership had lost both its moral and main institutional authority (the Petrograd Soviet), although it still held on in the Central Executive Committee elected at the June Congress of Soviets. At the same time in the provinces many Menshevik and SR city committees were moving toward some kind of all-socialist-based political alternative to coalition and to the Provisional Government, toward local "Soviet power," despite the opposition of the Menshevik and SR leaders in Petrograd. By September, politics had undergone another realignment, this time into the supporters of continued coalition versus the advocates of an all-socialist government.

There is an appropriate symmetry to the coincidence that the "Third Coalition" government, headed by Kerensky and even weaker than its predecessors, was finally formed on September 25, the same day Trotsky became chairman of the Petrograd Soviet. The Bolshevik control of the Petrograd Soviet meant that the new government was faced with determined opposition there rather than the cooperation (even if sometimes strained) between the government and the Soviet that had been at the heart of the February System from March through August. It was the first cabinet of the Provisional Government that was formally denied the support of the Petrograd Soviet. Discussion of the government's pending demise and of how it might be replaced – by a broad socialist coalition or a radical Soviet government – or whether it might survive until the Constituent Assembly, began immediately. Moreover, the discussion went far beyond party leadership circles. It was the subject of intense debate in newspapers, in cafes, in barracks and factories, at public meetings and private clubs, on street corners and anywhere else people gathered. The question of some kind of Soviet power had existed since March, was argued ever more often and seriously as 1917 progressed and now became the chief topic of public discussion. What had changed was that, while previously the Petrograd

Soviet leaders cooperated with the Provisional Government, the new leftist Petrograd Soviet leaders refused to do so and instead intended to replace it. Thus the government's weakness, combined with the new Bolshevik leadership of the Petrograd Soviet, gave urgency to the new question being posed in the streets and in the newspapers: "What will the Bolsheviks do?"

The popular mood – hopes and fears of the fall

The discussion of Bolshevik plans and the calls for Soviet power took place within the context of the deepening social and economic crisis and the growing popular demand for change. By late summer the revolution clearly had thus far failed to meet the aspirations of the people of the former Russian Empire. Indeed, unsolved political, social and economic problems created a mood of anxiety and tensions that fed directly into the growing clamor for a radical change of government. By fall Russians realized that they were suffering through almost continuous political instability punctuated by sharp crises marked by street demonstrations and loss of life. Newspapers and street orators traded recriminations over responsibility for the collapse of the summer military offensive and for the growing social and economic disorders. Strident demands by industrialists and workers, generals and soldiers, nationalities and others filled the air. Charges and countercharges among political parties resounded from oratorical platforms and filled the newspaper editorials. A sense of general crisis pervaded life, a feeling that things could not go on as they were. The latter was similar to the feeling that had preceded the February Revolution, that life could not long continue unchanged.

The war continued to loom as a fundamental problem. It put enormous stresses on the economy, which could not be corrected as long as war continued. The desire for peace became overwhelming by fall, among both soldiers and civilians. In addition, the unruly garrisons became ever more a problem for the government and for city administrations everywhere. Finally, the war fed into a major confrontation between the government and the Petrograd garrison which helped shape the October Revolution. The spark for the confrontation came from government responses to German military advances in September that threatened both land and sea approaches to Petrograd. On October 6 the government announced plans to send much – perhaps half – of the garrison to defend the sagging approaches to Petrograd. The garrison troops reacted to this news by vehement denunciations of the government, declarations of refusal to move to the front, pledges of support for the Petrograd Soviet and calls for Soviet power. Radical political agitators quickly tied the effort to move the garrison soldiers not only to a new "Kornilovite" counterrevolution, but to a possible subversion of the forthcoming Congress of Soviets. The controversy gave the Bolsheviks and radicals a golden opportunity to extend their influence in the garrison and further undermine government authority. The German military threat to Petrograd also worsened the government's relations with the workers as the government began planning for evacuation of key industries should that become necessary. As word of this spread the radical left denounced the government for preparing to abandon Petrograd, even charging that it was a counterrevolutionary scheme to choke off radical revolution.

Growing political radicalism fed also on the worsening economic situation. An important factor in the mood of fall 1917 was the sharp increase in prices coupled with growing scarcity of food and other supplies. The situation in Petrograd was both especially bad and especially critical, given its political importance and volatility. Bread had been rationed since spring, but in mid-October incoming bread supplies fell dramatically below daily demands. Although most attention focused on bread – the staple of lower-class diets – delivery of other foodstuffs also lagged dangerously behind previous consumption levels. By October only about one-tenth of the prewar milk supply was arriving in Petrograd, although the city had grown significantly. A conference on October 15 painted a bleak picture of a city with only three to four days of food reserves and little prospect for improvement.[7] Once again long lines snaked out from food shops. Sometimes lines for food formed before midnight for the next day. Moreover, prices rose rapidly, increasing about fourfold from July to October. The specter of starvation was real, especially for the lower classes, who were least able to take advantage of the flourishing black market with its high prices.

The problem existed in other cities as well. A survey of the food situation by the Ministry of Food Supply on October 12 registered for Novgorod the bleak entry: "starvation is appearing."[8] N. Dolinsky, a food supply official, wrote in the fall issue of the journal of the Ministry of Food Supply that "tragedy has become our everyday reality." A review of newspapers from around the country, he said, revealed that "ordinary labels such as *crisis, catastrophe* and so on . . . pale before the frightful hue of reality."[9] In Baku in September food shortages combined with labor conflict to stimulate demonstrations and riots. At the Baku Soviet one speaker stated that "Daily at the [food] supply center excited crowds gather, led by a few constantly active agitators, provoking the crowds to violence."[10] Indeed, the food lines emerged as important venues for political discussions and radicalization, including even

Plate 19 A food line. Courtesy of Jonathan Sanders.

debates over whether life was better under the old regime. "Every discussion in a public place in Russia now concerns food," wrote Morgan Phillips Price on October 8 at the conclusion of a long trip along the Volga River, "It is the essence of politics."[11] Moreover, the food crisis fed the general perception of the Provisional Government as having failed and of the need for radical change.

The industrial economy also continued to deteriorate, and that in turn helped drive other discontents. Whatever economic gains workers had made in the spring had long since been wiped out by skyrocketing prices, management resistance to new salary increases and wage losses due to factory closings and shortened hours. Production fell, the result of material and fuel shortages, falling productivity, and industrial strife. Strikes became even more bitter and politically polarizing. In Baku, for example, a six-day general strike against 610 firms in September–October radicalized workers and the conference of factory committees became thoroughly Bolshevik.[12] The collapsing railroads moved less and less food and materials, compounding all other problems. In a desperate effort to improve fuel production, the government in October decided to dispatch a special military commissar with dictatorial powers to the coal-producing Donets Basin.[13] In Petrograd, management and government officials in October warned of forthcoming factory shutdowns, affecting perhaps half the city's factories, because of fuel and materials shortages. On October 9 the director of the Putilov factory, Petrograd's and the country's largest factory, reported that it had run completely out of coal and that as a result thirteen shops were completely closed and six would operate at partial capacity.[14] At the factory committee meeting the next day an anxious worker asked whether the fact that the factory was receiving one-third less fuel than it needed to operate meant that one-third of the workers would be laid off. The committee discussed various schemes for partial work and pay.[15]

Factory closings and shortened work hours threatened the workers' very livelihood and fed suspicions that owners were deliberately using reductions and closing factories to throttle the revolution. For workers, therefore, preserving factories, employment and their economic and organizational gains became the focus of a desperate struggle against employers and the Provisional Government (which they believed supported the employers). Workers pressed their representatives toward more vigorous action, both to preserve their organizations and to keep the factories working. Many called for state subsidies to, or takeovers of, declining factories to keep them running. In Petrograd rumors that some factories might be moved from the city because of the threat of a German attack fed fears. Some cities, such as Kharkov, saw even greater strife over the issue of factory closings than in Petrograd, including worker seizure of factories. As the situation worsened workers turned to more radical leadership, fueling the leftward shift of politics.

The crisis in the factories inevitably led the workers to the question of the use of state power to defend their interests. Worker conflicts with management and concern over wages, jobs and protection of their organizations led inexorably to a belief that those required a political solution. The issue before the workers by mid-October was not *whether* a socialist government, but *when* and *how*; whether to support a transfer of power at the forthcoming Second Congress of Soviets or wait until the Constituent Assembly. Either would provide a socialist government, with the radicals urging the former course and the moderate socialists the latter. In the mood of crisis that existed the former seemed preferable to ever more workers; steps were needed *now*. This was what the call for Soviet power meant – a government that would use state power in their interests, to solve their problems. Bolshevik, Left SR and other leftist political rhetoric supported workers' demands and provided an explanation of why their perceptions were correct. Some went further, arguing that only Soviet power would guarantee the convening of the Constituent Assembly, charging that otherwise Kerensky and "counterrevolution" would find a way to block it. Worker support for a socialist government – Soviet power – and Lenin's insistence on an armed seizure of power by the Bolsheviks were not the same thing, but they would unexpectedly converge in October because of Kerensky's actions on the morning of October 24 (see pp. 235–37). In contrast, the moderate socialists were losing support because in opposing Soviet power they implicitly denied the need for and legitimacy of an immediate socialist revolution.

Other problems heightened the sense of a society falling apart and in need of drastic measures. The growth of crime and public disorders described in the previous chapter intensified in the fall. The newspapers were full of reports of robberies, assaults and other violence. One Petrograd newspaper that devoted extensive coverage to crime had lamented on June 16 that over 40 cases of theft and robbery were reported in the previous twenty-four hours; now on October 4 it reported 250 during the previous twenty-four hours and on October 7 reported 310, dramatic increases.[16] These figures fit with popular perceptions, which saw an enormous crime wave that the militia (police) could not cope with. In Petrograd and Smolensk, and likely in other cities as well, quarrels among government officials over the militia led in October to discussion of possible police strikes, which certainly added to the sense of insecurity on the eve of the October Revolution. Newspaper articles and public debates about the adequacy of the militia fed a public perception of rampant crime and that the government, local and national, was unable to guarantee public safety. Crime became a political football with perceptions exceeding the considerable reality. Nonetheless, public perception was what was important, and it saw a huge crime wave that endangered life and property for all citizens. This in turn stimulated belief in government incompetence at all levels.

Nor was this the end of evidence of a society in collapse. Petty as well as serious misbehavior in public places – drunkenness, random shooting of firearms, looting, violence at train stations (usually by soldiers), a new rudeness of speech and behavior, open flaunting of the law, unruly garrison soldiers – reinforced the impression. Continued lynch-law shocked Russians and foreigners. John Reed in Petrograd in the fall saw "a crowd of several hundred people beat and trample to death a soldier caught stealing."[17] In October two shoplifters in Petrograd were killed by a crowd despite the efforts of both militia and some soldiers to prevent it, and one militiaman was beaten as well. Travel became unreliable and more dangerous because of breakdowns on the railroads and the appearance of thieves and riotous soldiers – often deserters – on trains. Hundreds of thousands of soldiers from the front and garrisons roamed the country in the fall, pillaging, disrupting trains and towns, spreading rumors and violence, and offering fresh evidence of a social and political breakdown. The stock market collapsed after the Kornilov Affair, impoverishing portions of the middle classes and creating financial chaos. The government found itself less and less able to collect taxes. Continuing agrarian unrest and violence agitated the city as well as the countryside – large parts of the urban population, and especially garrison soldiers, had close ties to the villages. From the borderlands came news of nationalist movements demanding autonomy or even independence. The litany of problems was well summed up in an article on September 20 in the Moscow newspaper of the most moderate wing of the Socialist Revolutionary Party:

Against the background of merciless foreign war and defeats of the armies of the Republic, internally the country has entered upon a period of anarchy and, virtually, a period of civil war . . .

An open revolt flares up in Tashkent, and the Government sends armies and bullets to suppress it.

A mutiny in Orel. Armies are sent.

In Rostov the town hall is dynamited.

In Tambovsk province there are agrarian pogroms; experimental fields are destroyed, also pedigreed cattle, etc.

In Novgorod–Volynsk district the zemstvo storehouses are looted.

Grain reserve stores in Perm province are looted.

Gangs of robbers appear on the roads in Pskov province.

In the Caucasus there is a slaughter in a number of places.

Along the Volga, near Kamyshin, soldiers loot trains.

In Finland the army and the fleet have disassociated themselves completely from the Provisional Government.

Russia is threatened by a railway employees' strike . . .

Unbridled, merciless anarchy is growing. Any cause is used.

Events of colossal importance take place throughout the country. The Russian state collapses.[18]

The growing fears and fading hopes of the population demanded action either by the old leadership or by a new one. This set the stage for the struggle for power in the fall and the debates over Bolshevik intentions.

The Bolshevik debate over power

What were the Bolsheviks planning to do? That was the question on everyone's lips by mid-October. They debated it in the press, on street corners and in street cars, in food lines, at factories and army barracks, in political circles, even in the government. What, especially, were they planning for the upcoming Second All-Russia Congress of Soviets, originally scheduled for October 20 but then postponed to the 25th?

Apprehensions about Bolshevik intentions came to the fore when the Bolsheviks walked out of the Provisional Council of the Republic, or "Preparliament" on October 7. The Preparliament, another effort to strengthen the shaky government by convening a gathering of leading political figures from all groups, opened with a flurry of patriotic speeches and calls for revolutionary unity and discipline. Then Trotsky demanded the floor. Denouncing the government and the Preparliament as counterrevolutionary tools, he appealed to the workers and soldiers to defend Petrograd and the revolution. "Only the people can save themselves and the country! We turn to the people! All power to the soviets! All land to the people! Long live an immediate, just, democratic peace! Long live the Constituent Assembly!"[19] The Bolshevik delegates then rose and walked out amid jeers and taunts from the rest of the assembly. Their action intensified the debate about their intentions. What were the Bolsheviks planning to do?

That very question tormented Lenin as well. He feared that they would do too little, too late. From his Finnish hiding place – an order for his arrest dating from the July Days still existed – Lenin worried over Bolshevik intentions. He had already turned away from any idea of cooperation with the Mensheviks and SRs in some kind of shared Soviet power. Lenin's hostility to the moderate socialists and his view of them as betrayers of Marxism and accomplices of the bourgeoisie and the capitalists made cooperation within the generally understood meanings of Soviet power unacceptable. Bypassing entirely the debates going on in Petrograd about what kind of broad socialist government to form, Lenin in mid-September shifted to a strident call for an immediate armed seizure of power by the Bolsheviks. For him Soviet power meant a new type of government dominated by the Bolsheviks. From Finland he wrote to the Bolshevik Central Committee that "The Bolsheviks, having obtained a majority in the Soviets of Workers' and Soldiers' Deputies in both capitals [Petrograd and Moscow], can and *must* take state power into their own hands . . . The majority of the people are *on our side*."[20] Limited in his ability to impose his will on the party from Finland, he sent message after message insisting that the time was ripe for a seizure of power and that the party must organize and prepare for it. In a letter of September 27 he wrote, in his usual polemical style with extensive use of stressed words, that there was a tendency

among the leaders of our Party which favours *waiting* for the Congress of Soviets, and is *opposed* to taking power immediately, is *opposed* to an immediate insurrection. That tendency, or opinion, must be *overcome*.

Otherwise, the Bolsheviks will cover themselves with eternal *shame* and *destroy themselves* as a party.

For to miss such a moment and to "wait" for the Congress of Soviets would be *utter idiocy,* or *sheer treachery.*[21]

Lenin realized that the fall of 1917 offered a unique opportunity for a radical restructuring of political power and for a man such as himself. He believed that not only was the situation in Russia ripe for revolution, but also that in Germany and elsewhere in Europe. Like other Russian socialists in 1917, Lenin saw the Russian Revolution as a central part of a broader, sweeping world revolution. He saw it as a fundamental turning point in both Russian and world history: "history will not forgive us," he wrote, if this opportunity to take power was missed.[22] Moreover, he realized that the Bolsheviks had to move quickly because the Menshevik and SR Parties were turning toward their left wings and moving toward the idea of an all-socialist government – the recent Democratic Conference had nearly achieved that. If a new effort were successful that would placate one of the most insistent popular demands and eliminate one of the mainstays of Bolshevik agitation. Lenin realized that even the more moderate wing of his own party supported the idea of a broad socialist government. Lenin had to move before that happened and the party found itself merely a part, perhaps even a minority part, of a broad socialist government. The seizure of power by the Bolsheviks was now his obsession.

Lenin's call divided the party leadership. A minority supported Lenin's call to arms, especially the second-level leaders in the Petersburg Committee and some district committees, but even there many doubted the feasibility of such an action. Another group, led by Grigorii Zinoviev and Lev Kamenev, two of Lenin's oldest and closest associates and most authoritative party leaders, urged caution. They argued that the party was growing stronger day by day and that it would be foolish to risk that in an ill-conceived adventure that the government might yet have the strength to suppress. Moreover, they had a different vision of the future revolutionary government, favoring a broad coalition of socialists in a democratic left government (a position Lenin had held earlier but now abandoned). They opposed any risky ventures even by the Congress of Soviets. Their status in the party and Kamenev's prominent role as a party spokesman in Petrograd – in contrast to Lenin's absence – reinforced the influence of this position.

In between Lenin's demand for a violent seizure of power by the Bolsheviks and the caution of Zinoviev and Kamenev, a third position emerged. Increasingly identified with Leon Trotsky and probably representing a majority of the party's leadership, this looked to the forthcoming Second All-Russia Congress of Soviets as the place and time for the transfer of power. The Bolsheviks and other parties supporting

Soviet power would likely have a majority at the congress, and the congress could then declare the transfer of power to itself. The government, they believed, would be helpless to resist this. The Bolsheviks would be the largest and thus most important party within the new soviet-based government. They would be its leaders, yet able to pose as the embodiment of "soviet democracy" and not as a single-party government. Moreover, they argued, the mood of the workers was such that they would "come out" for Soviet power, but not for a Bolshevik Party action. The Soviet had to be the focus of a transfer of power, of a second revolution. They correctly believed that the worker and soldier masses of Petrograd generally assumed that Soviet power meant a government of the socialist parties making up the soviets.

Despite Lenin's demands, therefore, the party's political effort focused on the forthcoming Second All-Russia Congress of Soviets as the means for a transfer of power. The Bolshevik leaders undertook to mobilize support for the selection of deputies to the congress who would support a transfer of power. The Central Committee resolved on September 24 that "it is necessary to strive to develop the activities of the Soviets and to increase their political importance until they assume the role of organs opposing bourgeois state power." It ordered party members to press for reelection of local soviets that were still controlled by moderates. It encouraged the convocation of regional soviet congresses and other activity to build support for a transfer of power at the Congress of Soviets.[23] From September 27 onward the main Bolshevik newspaper carried across the front page the headline: "Prepare for the Congress of Soviets on October 20! Convene Regional Congresses Immediately." Nor were the Bolsheviks alone in this focus: the Left SR newspaper carried a similar slogan, as well as regularly cautioning against any kind of "coming out" before the congress.

Getting the congress held and getting it to take power were sources of anxiety for the Bolsheviks and other leftists. Although the power of the soviets as institutions and the growing popularity of the Bolsheviks in them seems so great and unstoppable in retrospect, that was not at all clear at the time. The moderate socialists had agreed to convene the congress only reluctantly. The Bolsheviks and Left SRs labored under a constant fear that some kind of counterrevolution might yet block the congress, crush the revolution and snatch away their gains. They regularly warned that "counterrevolutionaries" might attempt to prevent the Congress of Soviets and appealed to workers and soldiers to be ready to defend it. Indeed, central to the campaign for Soviet power was precisely the argument that only Soviet power guaranteed the convening of the Constituent Assembly. Without remembering these fears, as well as the more general mood in October of disaffection, apprehension, desperation and growing social-political conflict, it is easy to misinterpret the mobilization of forces on the eve of the Congress of Soviets and the October Revolution itself.

Lenin did not share the Petrograd party leaders' focus on the Congress of Soviets. Frustrated and fearing that an irretrievable opportunity was slipping by, Lenin took the chance of moving from Finland to Petrograd. On October 10 he met, for the first time since July, with the Central Committee of the party. After an all-night debate the Central Committee seemingly gave in to Lenin's passionate demands for a seizure of power. It passed a resolution stating "the Central Committee recognizes that . . . [follows a long list of international and domestic developments] all this places armed uprising on the order of the day."[24] This resolution later became central to the myth of a carefully planned seizure of power carried out under Lenin's direction. It was, in fact, something different and rather more complex than that.

What did this resolution mean, or not mean? First, it is important to note that it did *not* set any timetable or plan for a seizure of power. Rather, it was a formal reversion of Bolshevik Party policy to the idea that an armed uprising was a revolutionary necessity, after the interlude since July in which they had held that a peaceful development of the revolution was possible. After cataloging the international and domestic political situation, it asserted that "therefore . . . an armed uprising is inevitable and that the time for it fully ripe," and instructed "all Party organizations to act accordingly and to discuss and resolve all practical questions (the Congress of Soviets of the Northern Region, the withdrawal of troops from Petrograd, the reaction of the people in Moscow and Minsk, etc.) from this point of view."[25] The resolution thus represented a shift in formal policy, but did not commit the party to a seizure of power *before* the Congress of Soviets or at any other specific time. Nor did it start actual preparations for a seizure of power. It was a general statement of policy for a turbulent and seemingly favorable period in the revolution, not a plan for the immediate seizure of power. At the most it was a statement of intent to overthrow the Provisional Government and replace it with a Soviet-based government when the time was right and a suitable opportunity arose, whenever that might be. This was hardly a new idea by October.

The resolution of October 10 did, however, do two things: it set off a vigorous debate within the Bolshevik Party about the meaning of the resolution and their future course of action, and it revealed the divisions in the party. A few interpreted it in a narrow sense, in Lenin's meaning, as a decision to launch an armed seizure of power as soon as possible.

"The sooner the better," argued I. Rakhia at a meeting of Petersburg Committee on October 15. Most, however, interpreted it in a broad sense, of meaning that a seizure of power would be carried out at some time, in some way, probably via the Congress of Soviets or in reaction to some government provocation. At the same meeting Andrei Bubnov, while pressing for action with the argument that "the general situation is such that an armed uprising is inevitable," admitted that "it is impossible to set a date for the insurrection, which will come of its own accord if conditions are right for it." Mikhail Kalinin expressed the uncertainty of many: he praised the Central Committee resolution of October 10, but added that "when this uprising will be possible – perhaps in a year – is uncertain."[26]

The Bolsheviks were also debating the question of power in other settings, ones where Left SRs and other radicals participated. The Congress of Soviets of the Northern Region (CSNR) meeting on October 11–13 was especially important.[27] Its organizers, mostly Bolsheviks, saw it as a vehicle for organizing the Baltic–Helsinki–Petrograd region soldiers, sailors and soviets behind the push for Soviet power and to ensure the meeting of the forthcoming Second All-Russia Congress of Soviets. Although the question of an immediate seizure of power was raised – Lenin in one of his writings specified the CSNR as a possible vehicle for seizing power – Trotsky and the CSNR leaders steered discussion toward preparations for the All-Russian Congress of Soviets and the assumption of power there. This was very different from Lenin's talk at this time about an armed attack on Petrograd using troops from the Baltic fleet and northern region as the means of seizing power.

The Bolsheviks continued to debate among themselves the degree of popular support for a seizure of power and their own preparedness. At the meeting of the Petersburg Committee on October 15 speaker after speaker reported doubts that the workers and soldiers would come out in support of an attempt to seize power, especially before the Congress of Soviets, although they would rally to defense of the Soviet and the revolution. Some, however, argued that the mood was ripe and that striking quickly was important. Still, everyone had to admit that little or nothing had been done to organize the soldier and worker supporters who would presumably carry it out, and nothing done to prepare Bolshevik cadres in key centers such as Moscow or to insure control of railroads and communications. Indeed, they had organized no central planning or directing center. The Red Guards, though militant and increasingly pro-Bolshevik, did not have any citywide central organization and the Bolsheviks had only a poor sense of their strength, mood and organization. At a key party meeting (with Lenin present) the night of October 16, one speaker noted that "If the resolution [of October 10] is an order, then it has not been fulfilled and we have done nothing about it."[28] This was six days after the October 10 resolution and fewer than four days before the congress was supposed to open – it was still scheduled for the 20th. Kamenev, who was strongly opposed to a seizure of power, argued that during the week since the resolution of October 10 "nothing was done . . . We have no apparatus for an uprising."[29]

The meeting of October 16 finally reaffirmed the resolution of October 10. This reaffirmation, mingled as it was with Lenin's idea about sending Baltic troops to attack Petrograd and seize power, led Kamenev to declare that he so disagreed that he was willing to resign from the party's Central Committee. Joined by Zinoviev, the two prominent Bolshevik leaders even took their case outside party circles, publishing their arguments against a seizure of power. This further stimulated public debate about Bolshevik intentions, as did Lenin's bitter attack on his old colleagues. As the Congress of Soviets neared the Bolshevik leadership was in disarray over how to proceed. In part by default and in part because that seemed to reflect the opinion of most party leaders, attention increasingly focused on the Congress of Soviets as the time, place and vehicle for the seizure of power, for making the new revolution called for in the Bolshevik resolution of October 10 as well as in hundreds of local workers' and soldiers' resolutions.

The debate about taking power was not limited to the Bolsheviks. They were not the only members of the leftist coalition that had been gaining power in city soviets in the fall and which would form the majority at the Congress of Soviets. The Left SRs and Menshevik–Internationalists totally opposed any action before the Congress of Soviets. Indeed, the influential Left SRs were focused on forming an exclusively socialist, but genuinely multiparty, government based on a broad spectrum of socialist parties. They had argued for such a government at the Democratic Conference and at the Preparliament, without success, and now turned to the Congress of Soviets as the vehicle for creating it. They approached late October trying simultaneously to prod their SR Party colleagues into agreeing to such a government while restraining what they feared to be Bolshevik adventurism. Left SRs were convinced that any solution to the crisis of power and to the social and economic problems and the war required an all-socialist government based on soviets. Many Menshevik–Internationalists had similar views. The Bolshevik leaders in Petrograd could not ignore the Left SRs' opinions, given their popular support in the garrison and factories. At the same time the Left SRs looked to the more cautious Bolsheviks such as Kamenev and Zinoviev and the Moscow leaders as evidence that such a course of action was possible in collaboration with the Bolsheviks. Even Trotsky's position was compatible with their approach.[30]

On the eve: the mobilization of forces

In the retrospective light of these debates and of the events of the next week that led to the October Revolution, the decision of the moderate socialist leaders on October 18 to postpone the opening of the Congress of Soviets from the 20th to the 25th looms fatefully momentous (it was postponed on the grounds that an insufficient number of deputies had arrived in Petrograd). This was wonderfully fortuitous for the Bolsheviks, who were unprepared for and could not have attempted any seizure of power before the 20th even if they had so wished. The five extra days changed everything. They gave time for the further buildup of tensions, for a major struggle for control of the garrison, and for mobilization efforts by the Red Guards. Most of all they gave time for Kerensky's fateful decision to strike at the leftists on the 24th, which precipitated the armed seizure of power before the congress met. Without those events the October Revolution as we know it could not have occurred.

The mobilization of supporters during this period was especially important. A declaration of the transfer of power at the Congress of Soviets, however much expected, would after all be an insurrectionary action. The Bolsheviks and Left SRs could assume that Kerensky's government would try to resist. Therefore, they worked to insure that the Congress of Soviets could successfully take power upon itself and launched a series of measures designed to weaken the government and deprive it of its remaining legitimacy. They undertook to mobilize their own supporters, including a belated effort to create a Petrograd-wide Red Guard organization. They moved to take away the government's remaining authority over the garrison of Petrograd, thus destroying any ability of the government to use it against the seizure of power by the Congress of Soviets. They repeatedly called on workers and soldiers to be ready to defend the revolution and the Congress of Soviets. Seen in this light, as preparation to defend a transfer of power at the Congress of Soviets, the actions in October by the Bolshevik and Left SR leaders, the government, other political figures and local activists have a logic that they lack if one holds to the old myth of careful planning for a Bolshevik seizure of power *before* the congress.

It was as part of the efforts by the Bolsheviks and Left SRs to guarantee that they could successfully declare Soviet power at the congress that the Military Revolutionary Committee (MRC) and its attempt to neutralize government authority in the Petrograd garrison takes on meaning. The idea of the MRC originated in the proposal by a Menshevik member of the Petrograd Soviet on October 9 to form a special committee to work on the problems of the restive mood of the garrison and the defense of Petrograd (a German attack was feared). Trotsky, as chairman of the Soviet, took up the idea and extended it, calling for a "revolutionary defense committee" to familiarize itself with all issues of defense of the capital and to supervise the arming of the workers. The purpose was to defend the city not only against any German threat, but against a "Kornilovite counterrevolution." It took form slowly and held its first meeting only on October 20 (i.e., not before the Congress of Soviets was originally scheduled to open). It selected a five-man leadership executive consisting of three Bolsheviks and two Left SRs, with one of the latter, Pavel Lazimir, as its chairman (he was also the chairman of the Soldiers' Section of the Petrograd Soviet). About the same time the Bolshevik leadership began to realize the MRC's potential as a vehicle for dominating essential armed power in the capital through its authority over the soldiers, and thus the role the MRC could play in enforcing a transfer of power at the Congress of Soviets.

Control of the garrison now became a key point in the developing struggle between the government and the left. Resolutions passed at an MRC-sponsored garrison conference on October 21 promised full support to the MRC and the Petrograd Soviet and called for the Congress of Soviets to take power and to provide peace, land and bread for the people. With this reaffirmation of the garrison's primary loyalty to the Soviet in hand, the MRC, knowing that numerous soviets along the nearby Northern Front and Baltic coast had already asserted authority over local military authorities, pressured the government. The night of October 21 an MRC delegation called on General G. P. Polkovnikov, commander of the Petrograd Military District, and told him that "henceforth orders not signed by us are invalid."[31] Polkovnikov rejected their ultimatum. In response the MRC sent to all garrison units a declaration the next day that denounced Polkovnikov's refusal to recognize the MRC as proof that military headquarters was "a tool of counterrevolutionary forces." Therefore, it declared, protection of the revolution rested with the soldiers under the direction of the MRC. "No orders to the garrison not signed by the Military Revolutionary Committee are valid . . . The revolution is in danger."[32] At the same time the MRC began to send its own commissars to replace the old, Revolutionary Defensist and pro-government ones in key military units, completing the process of transfer from moderate to radical socialist influence. By asserting this authority over the garrison the MRC not only challenged the essence of government authority – command control over the troops – but took a major step toward assuring the success of a proclamation of Soviet power at the Congress of Soviets. If the government could not call on the garrison, it would be helpless to defend itself.

Meanwhile Petrograd was the scene of numerous mass rallies, rumors and self-mobilizations. October 22 had earlier been proclaimed the "Day of the Petrograd Soviet," a day for meetings and demonstrations to raise funds and to consolidate support for the Soviet. Given the tension in the air, it now took on special significance. At mass rallies around the city the Bolsheviks and Left SRs worked to garner popular support for transfer of power to the Soviet. The aroused crowds roared their support. "All around me," wrote Sukhanov of a meeting where Trotsky spoke of the benefits of Soviet power, "was a mood bordering on ecstasy."[33] The MRC sent orators to regimental rallies to appeal directly to the soldiers for their support and to intensify their anger against the government. The prospect of a clash between Soviet demonstrators and Cossacks, who had scheduled a patriotic procession to commemorate the anniversary of the liberation of Moscow from Napoleon, heightened tensions. Rumors that "counterrevolutionaries" would do something that day led some Red Guard units to mobilize themselves and lent an air of nervous expectation. Some of these Red Guards decided to remain on alert until the Congress of Soviets met. The Vyborg district Red Guard staff ordered all units to hold themselves in full fighting readiness. A worker at the Vulkan Factory, F. A. Ugarov, wrote that "after the 'Day of the Soviet' the mood of the workers intensified . . . The bolts of rifles clicked. In the yard of the factory they fitted the trucks with sheet armor and mounted machine guns."[34] By the end of the 22nd everyone was expecting *some* kind of a revolutionary move, whether a classic armed rebellion (fueled by images of the French Revolution, peasant rebellions, and the July Days), an act by the Congress of Soviets, or even a counterrevolutionary putsch – something! A nervous tension rippled through the city.

Petrograd Soviet leaders, emboldened by support shown on the 22nd and having largely completed replacing old military unit commissars with new men – mostly Bolsheviks and Left SRs – escalated their challenge to the government on the 23rd. The MRC announced to the population that to defend the revolution it had sent commissars to military units and important points in the city, and only orders confirmed by them were to be obeyed. That evening the MRC won the allegiance of the garrison of the Peter and Paul Fortress after an all-day meeting where competing orators, including Trotsky, struggled for their allegiance. The fortress occupied the center of the city and its guns loomed over the Provisional Government offices in the Winter Palace across the river. The evening of the 23rd the Petrograd Soviet meeting commended the efforts of the MRC, stating that their continuation would insure the meeting and work of the Congress of Soviets. Indeed, everything done thus far fit within the framework of measures necessary to insure a successful transfer of power at the Congress of Soviets, or a successful defeat of the ever-feared counterrevolution if the latter did strike.

Meanwhile the Kerensky government took what it confidently assumed were sufficient preparations to defeat any attempted overthrow. On October 17 the minister of the interior, Nikolai Kishkin, reported that the government had sufficient reliable forces to put down disturbances once they broke out, but lacked the forces necessary to start an action against the left (a distinction Kerensky should have remembered a week later when he initiated action). Basically the government limited itself to issuing regular calls for public order and assuming that it had sufficient control of the garrison to suppress any armed uprising. How wrongly confident they were was revealed by Kerensky when on the night of October 21–22 he assured General N. N. Dukhonin at Stavka (military front headquarters) that his departure to meet him "was in no way delayed by fear of some kind of unrest, rebellions and the like; it is possible to cope with that sort of thing without me, because everything is organized."[35] Indeed, Kerensky assured the British ambassador, Sir George Buchanan, that "I only wish that they [Bolsheviks] would come out and I will put them down."[36]

Nonetheless, Kerensky, the government members and military commanders in Petrograd finally became alarmed at the trend of events: the massive show of support for Soviet power on the 22nd, the activities of the MRC, the behavior of the garrison and the Red Guards, and the looming Congress of Soviets. They made inquiries about the dispatch of troops from the nearby Northern Front, but these only raised doubts about whether such troops would support the government. Kerensky and the government were confronted with either waiting passively for the Congress of Soviets to declare their replacement or taking some sort of preemptive action. Finally, during the night of October 23–24, the government decided to act. Kerensky proposed arresting the MRC. The government instead agreed to initiate legal proceedings against some MRC members and Bolsheviks, and to close two Bolshevik newspapers in the city. For balance, two conservative papers would be closed also. They ordered military officials to assemble a reliable force at the Winter

Palace. These proposed actions were so minor and inadequate that the government obviously did not comprehend either the popularity of the idea of Soviet power or the very real discontents felt by the populace. They clearly had not understood the fiery rhetoric of the past few days about defending against a counterrevolution. They completely failed to anticipate the firestorm of opposition that their actions would set off. Such minor repressive measures by the government could hardly stop the rising tide of demand for Soviet power, but they could provide the very "counterrevolutionary" action for which the left had been watching. Kerensky unexpectedly handed Lenin his seizure of power *before* the Congress of Soviets.

9 The Bolsheviks take power

The October Revolution: the armed confrontation

As most of Petrograd slept in the pre-dawn hours of October 24, a small detachment of military cadets and militiamen sent by the Provisional Government raided the press where two Bolshevik newspapers were published. They destroyed freshly printed copies of that day's paper, damaged the print beds, sealed the entrances and posted a guard. The alarmed press workers ran with the stunning news to the Smolny Institute, headquarters of the Petrograd Soviet, the Military Revolutionary Committee (MRC) and the Bolshevik Party. Unbeknownst to anyone, including the Bolshevik leaders, the October Revolution had begun. It began not in response to the demands of Lenin or a Bolshevik plan, but in response to the government's ill-conceived decision to launch a minor punitive action against the Bolsheviks.

Officials at Smolny quickly branded the press closure a counterrevolutionary move and summoned the leaders of the MRC, Petrograd Soviet and the Bolshevik and Left SR parties. These (not including Lenin, who remained in hiding) assembled at Smolny to find that, in addition to the account of the printers, reports were coming in from various places around the city of suspicious troop movements. The MRC appealed for support: "Counterrevolutionary conspirators went on the offensive during the night. A treasonous blow against the Petrograd Soviet of Workers' and Soldiers' Deputies is being planned . . . The campaign of the counterrevolutionary conspirators is directed against the Congress of Soviets on the eve of its opening, against the Constituent Assembly, against the people." It then sent "Directive No. 1" to regimental commissars and committees: "You are ordered to bring your regiment to fighting readiness."[1]

The question was what to do next. Some of those present supported starting an armed insurrection immediately. Most, however, including Trotsky, focused instead on defensive measures designed to guarantee that the Congress of Soviets – which it was now clear would have a majority in favor of transfer of power – opened as scheduled the next day. Indeed, the Bolshevik Central Committee meeting which was hastily assembled concerned itself more with various aspects of the general political crisis than with the Provisional Government's actions that morning and their response to it; they did *not* discuss overthrowing the government before the congress met. That afternoon Stalin told a meeting of Bolshevik delegates assembled for the congress that there were two viewpoints within the MRC, "that we organize an uprising at once, and . . . that we first consolidate our forces," and that the Central Committee sided with the latter view. Trotsky's speech to the meeting reinforced Stalin's and stressed that the MRC's ordering of troops to reopen the closed Bolshevik newspapers was a defensive action.[2]

Through the morning and afternoon of the 24th the two opposing sides, each basically acting defensively, each accusing the other of betraying the revolution and each posing as its defender, tried to rally political and military support as the confrontation gradually gained momentum. Their efforts found very different responses. During the morning Kerensky and Petrograd military authorities tried without success to find reliable armed support. Government efforts to exercise authority in the Petrograd garrison were futile. The soldiers showed little enthusiasm for being used by either side, and the minority who did supported the Soviet. The garrison soldiers, when confronted with contradictory orders, usually either followed those coming from the Soviet and MRC commissars or did nothing; either way they were of no use to the government. Orders to send troops from outside the city either were countermanded by army committees or else the troops themselves refused to move after Soviet representatives told them they were being used for counterrevolution. By early afternoon the government managed to assemble only a small force of military cadets, officers, Cossacks and a detachment from one of the women's battalions to protect the Winter Palace and key government and communications buildings.

In contrast the Soviet found swift and vigorous support. Although most of the army garrison stayed in their barracks, some radicalized army units responded to the perceived threat of counterrevolution and came out in response to MRC appeals. Moreover, the actions of the government on the 24th galvanized the already agitated industrial workers and propelled their armed detachments, the Red Guard, into the confused struggle for control of the city. Virtually all Red Guards went into action, either on their own or in conjunction with groups of soldiers. Moreover, their *attitude* was especially important. Among the Red Guards there were no wavering units as there were among the soldiers, no forces that a worried Soviet leadership need fear might support the government. The problem for the MRC was that it exercised little direct control over the Red Guards, and even lacked a clear notion of their size and utility. Nonetheless, the Red Guards and those troops who came out gave the pro-Soviet forces preponderant armed strength in the capital.

The government and political opposition to Soviet power, meanwhile, was crumbling. Kerensky himself spent much of the afternoon of the 24th at the Preparliament trying to build political support. Indeed, virtually the entire political leadership of the country, except the Bolsheviks and Left SRs, spent the afternoon and evening there in fruitless debate. Although Kerensky won applause for denunciations of the Bolsheviks, after an evening of debate the Preparliament passed a resolution that effectively repudiated the Kerensky government – this in a body where most of the radical left representatives were absent. At the same time the moderate socialist leaders could not find any course of action other than issuing another tired resolution calling for restraint and warning of counterrevolution, such as the appeal on the night of October 24–25 that "An armed clash on the streets of Petrograd would untie the hands of the lurking bands of hooligans and pogromists . . . [and] inevitably lead to the triumph of counterrevolutionary elements which have already mobilized their forces for crushing the revolution."[3] They still did not understand the deep popular roots of the demand for Soviet power, still seeing it only in terms of the danger of opening the country to counterrevolution. They still believed more in the phantom of a counterrevolution that had "mobilized" its forces than in the real popular movement.

While the politicians debated, while Kerensky sought support that would never come and while the Soviet and MRC leaders moved slowly to control key points that would be necessary to defend against a nonexistent counterrevolution, groups of armed workers and soldiers began an uncoordinated but decisive struggle for control of the city. Most actions on the 24th were defensive and reactive. Red Guards and pro-Soviet soldiers mobilized to control the bridges over the river after the government endeavored to raise them to inhibit movement. Occupation of railroad stations followed rumors that the government was calling in troops from outside the city. This was mostly a process of push and shove, bluff and counterbluff, the government trying to use "reliable" units to maintain control, while pro-Soviet soldiers and Red Guards strove to take over buildings, bridges and key positions. Haphazardly and little by little, a transfer of armed power in the city took place through a series of nonshooting confrontations between armed groups in which the more determined side prevailed, and determination rested with the supporters of Soviet power. There was remarkably little actual shooting; no one was eager to die for the Provisional Government. By nightfall on the 24th the pro-Soviet forces controlled most of the city.[4]

Despite these successes, the Soviet and MRC leaders were still thinking about warding off a blow from the government and about the transfer of power at the congress. On the evening of the 24th Trotsky told the Petrograd Soviet that "All Power to the Soviets" would be implemented at the Congress of Soviets, and "whether this leads to an uprising or not depends not only and not so much on the Soviets as on those who hold state power in their hands contrary to the unanimous will of the people." He then warned that, "if the sham power [Provisional Government] makes a long-shot attempt to revive its own corpse, then the mass of the people, organized and armed, will give it a decisive rebuff."[5] Colorful imagery aside, this was a more realistic assessment of the situation than was coming from the other side.

Around midnight the gathering revolution shifted from defensive to offensive action. This was connected to two events: (1) a growing realization that the government was much weaker than thought and that the city was coming under the physical control of soldiers and Red Guards rallying to the defense of the Soviet, and (2) the arrival of Lenin at Soviet headquarters. Although he had been ordered by the Bolshevik Central Committee to stay in hiding, near midnight an agitated Lenin, aware that something major was happening in the city, left his hiding place to go to Smolny. Wearing a wig, a cap and a bandage on his face, he set off accompanied by a lone bodyguard. On the way they were intercepted by a patrol of military cadets but, mistaken for a pair of drunks and not recognized, allowed to pass. Then when they arrived at Smolny the Red Guard at the door initially refused them entry for lack of proper credentials. Only with difficulty did Lenin manage to enter what was becoming the headquarters of a revolution.[6]

The conjuncture of the dawning realization of the success of pro-Soviet forces and Lenin's arrival dramatically changed the situation. Lenin had not been part of the cautious defensive reaction of the 24th, and he was the one leader who had consistently urged an armed seizure of power *before* the Congress of Soviets met. Under his pressure and the reality of their growing strength, the Bolshevik Soviet leaders shifted from a defensive posture to the offensive about 2:00 a.m. on the morning of the 25th.[7] The changeover is reflected in the contradictory orders sent to Osvald Dzenis, MRC commissar in the Pavlovsky Regiment, which had occupied the Troitsky Bridge (between the Petro-

Plate 20 A Red Guard detachment on guard duty at the Smolny Institute, Soviet and Bolshevik headquarters during the October Revolution and afterward. *Proletarskaia revoliutsiia vobrazakh i kartinakh* (Leningrad, 1926).

gradsky district and the city center). During the evening of the 24th he set up a checkpoint on the bridge and began arresting government officials trying to cross, only to be reprimanded by the MRC and ordered to stop doing so. About 2:00 a.m. on the 25th he received a new order to strengthen his checkpoint and strictly control movement on the bridge.

About the same time the MRC began to work out an elaborate plan for dispersing the Preparliament, arresting the Provisional Government and taking control of remaining key installations. They dropped the notion of waiting for the Congress of Soviets and commenced a drive to seize control of the city immediately. By the time a cold gray windy day dawned on the 25th, pro-Soviet forces had extended their control to almost all of the city except the Winter Palace. There the members of the Provisional Government still sat behind a small, increasingly dispirited band of defenders, surrounded by a large but disorganized force of Red Guards and insurgent soldiers. The besiegers, however, feared that the government might have determined supporters who would inflict heavy casualties on any attackers and so were reluctant to attack. In fact, neither besiegers nor defenders were eager to risk bloodshed.

By mid-morning on the 25th the situation had progressed to the point at which, at about the same time, the Bolsheviks proclaimed the transfer of power while Kerensky fled the city in search of supporters. Kerensky had tried to find reliable troops in Petrograd and, being unsuccessful, decided to leave the city to seek troops at the front. He had trouble finding a way out of the city – the train stations were occupied by insurgents and the government could not find an automobile of its own – and not until about 11:00 a.m. did he speed past the besieging forces loosely surrounding the Winter Palace. While Kerensky searched for a car, Lenin, at the Smolny Institute, seized the initiative and wrote the announcement of the overthrow of the government, which was immediately printed and spread throughout the city. On his way out of the city, in a borrowed car, Kerensky might have passed the first distribution of the proclamation announcing his overthrow. It read:

To the Citizens of Russia!

The Provisional Government has been overthrown. State power has passed into the hands of the organ of the Petrograd Soviet of Workers' and Soldiers' Deputies, the Military Revolutionary Committee, which stands at the head of the Petrograd proletariat and garrison.

The cause for which the people have struggled – the immediate offer of a democratic peace, the abolition of landlord ownership of land, workers' control over industry, the creation of a Soviet government – this has been assured.

Long live the revolution of workers, soldiers and peasants!

The Military Revolutionary Committee
of the Petrograd Soviet
of Workers' and Soldiers' Deputies.

25 October 1917, 10:00 in the morning.[8]

That afternoon Trotsky opened a meeting of the Petrograd Soviet, where he announced the overthrow of the government and steps taken to secure power in the city. Lenin then emerged, his first public appearance since the July Days, to thunderous applause. The excited deputies and others who had crowded into the hall affirmed the transfer of power.

Trotsky's and Lenin's claims, while substantially true, ignored the inconvenient fact that, excepting Kerensky, the Provisional Government still sat in the Winter Palace behind a small defending force. It was a curiously unmilitary faceoff. The afternoon of the 25th the radical journalist John Reed and three other Americans were able to bluff their way past the besiegers and simply walked into the palace unmolested by defenders. They wandered around the palace talking to various persons before walking back out past besieging Red Guards and soldiers and off to dinner.[9] All through the day and evening new arrivals of Red Guards and soldiers reinforced the besiegers, some of whom left, while some of the palace's military defenders changed their minds and marched away unhindered. During the afternoon a light, wet snow began to fall. Finally, during the late evening besiegers began filtering into the palace in small numbers, rather than actually "storming" it (paintings and motion pictures of a great charge on the palace were later fictional romantizations). Toward midnight on the 25th those filtering in became a steady stream. As one defender described the process, "as long as the groups of Red Guards were small, we disarmed them . . . However, more and more Red Guards appeared, and also sailors and soldiers of the Pavlovsky Regiment. The disarming began to be reversed."[10]

At about 2:00 a.m. on the 26th some of the attackers finally found the way to the room where the government ministers sat. At the sound of approaching insurgents the ministers ordered the cadets guarding the door not to resist, in order to save lives, and seated themselves around a table and waited. The door was suddenly flung open and, in the words of one government minister, "a little man flew into the room, like a chip tossed by a wave, under the pressure of the mob which poured in and spread at once, like water, filling all corners of the room." This was Vladimir Antonov-Ovseenko, one of the Bolshevik leaders of the MRC, who shouted, "In the name of the Military Revolutionary Committee, I declare you under arrest."[11] By the time of the arrest, however dramatic, the city was completely in the hands of pro-Soviet forces and the Congress of Soviets already in session.

One of the curious features of the October Revolution is that while it took place life went on in a fairly normal, if somewhat anxious way in much of the city. Although a scare on the afternoon of the 24th caused shops and schools to close early because of the uncertainty of the bridges, by evening the city resumed its more normal life, with the theaters and cafes open and flourishing. The next day, the 25th, the street cars were running and the shops open. Restaurants and theaters opened again that evening, although they made some concessions to the events in the streets: the waiter at the Hotel France, where John Reed and his friends had dinner after leaving the nearby Winter Palace, "insisted that we move to the main dining room at the back of the house, because they were going to put out the lights in the cafe. 'There will be much shooting,' he said."[12] This seeming normality in the midst of revolution, which many observers commented on, was possible in part because the October Revolution, unlike the February Revolution, April Crisis and July Days, was not characterized by massive street demonstrations. Instead, relatively small groups of soldiers and Red

Guards maneuvered to control key points. It also reflected the extent to which the population of Petrograd had become accustomed to political crises, street disorders, and "much shooting."

By the evening of the 25th it appeared that Lenin had obtained his goal of a transfer of power by a violent act of seizure before the Congress of Soviets. It is worth noting, however, that the transfer of power was in the name of the Petrograd Soviet and affirmed by it. It was not a revolution in the name of the Bolshevik Party, and the multiparty Congress of Soviets was still to be the ultimate legitimizing institution. Transforming a seizure of power in the name of Soviet power into a Bolshevik regime would depend on yet another unforeseeable stroke of luck, this one at the Congress of Soviets, comparable to Kerensky's blunder on the 24th.

The Congress of Soviets

As the armed struggle for control of Petrograd drew toward a close the evening of October 25, the emphasis shifted to the political struggle at the Second All-Russia Congress of Soviets. Events unfolding there that night shaped the nature of the new government in ways no one, not even Lenin, could have foreseen at the time. They gave the Bolsheviks full control of the congress and the new government, contrary to all expectations, and transformed the debate about just what "Soviet power" meant now that it was a reality. They profoundly influenced the outcome of the revolution and the Soviet regime that followed for the next several decades.

The Second All-Russia Congress of Soviets opened at 10:40 p.m., October 25. The opening was delayed by the skirmishing in the city, the Bolsheviks being especially anxious to take the Winter Palace and capture the Provisional Government before it opened. The excited, milling crowd of delegates could no longer be put off, however, and finally the meeting opened amidst the sounds of weapons firing and with the palace still under siege. The Bolsheviks were the largest party, with about 300 of the approximately 650–70 seats (figures for the number of delegates and their party distribution are not precise). To obtain a majority they needed the support of other advocates of Soviet power, especially the about 80–85 Left SRs, who had not yet officially broken with the parent SR Party. Nonetheless, these numbers guaranteed that the new leadership would be from the radical left and predominately Bolshevik. Most participants assumed that the congress would create a new government composed of a coalition of socialist leaders – Soviet power. The main question was its exact composition and how radical it would be. That depended to a large degree on the Left SRs and the Menshevik–Internationalists, who held the balance of power between the Bolsheviks and their moderate Menshevik and SR opponents.

Hardly had the congress begun when the sound of cannons was heard in the distance: the artillery on the Peter and Paul Fortress firing across the Neva River at the Winter Palace (which actually did little physical damage). An excited Martov, speaking for the Menshevik–Internationalists, proposed that, to avoid bloodshed, negotiations begin at once for a united democratic government of all socialist parties. This was endorsed by Anatolii Lunacharsky for the Bolsheviks and Sergei Mstislavsky for the Left SRs, and adopted overwhelmingly. This plan immediately went astray, however. A series of speakers from the SR, Menshevik, Bund and smaller parties rose to condemn the "conspiracy . . . by the Bolshevik Party," which, they charged, preempted the work of the congress and "signals the beginning of civil war and the break-up of the Constituent Assembly and threatens to destroy the Revolution." Calling on congress delegates to join in a decision by Petrograd City Council deputies to march to the Winter Palace to support the Provisional Government and to prevent bloodshed, most Mensheviks and SRs then walked out. Martov, still searching for a compromise between the socialist moderates and radicals, then introduced an eloquent appeal to avoid civil war by forming a government "acceptable to the whole revolutionary democracy" (i.e., to the moderate Mensheviks and SRs as well as the Bolsheviks and radical left) and proposed that the congress suspend its work until this could be attended to.[13]

The Congress of Soviets, however, was now in no mood for negotiations. The speeches and departure of the moderate socialists not only left the Bolsheviks with an absolute majority, but also hardened feelings among those remaining, strengthening the militants and undermining those moderate Bolsheviks who were inclined toward concessions. Trotsky contemptuously rejected compromise: "you are miserable bankrupts, your role is played out; go where you ought to be: into the dustbin of history."[14] After passing a resolution (introduced by Trotsky) declaring that the "withdrawal of the Menshevik and Social Revolutionary delegates from the Congress is an impotent and criminal attempt to disrupt" its work,[15] the truncated congress continued to meet through the night, debating resolutions and receiving a string of encouraging reports. News of the taking of the Winter Palace and arrest of the government ministers buoyed spirits even further. Then came a series of reports of support from key military units. A kind of euphoria, not unlike that of February 27th, set in as the long-discussed declaration of

Soviet power seemed to be succeeding almost effortlessly. Finally, approaching 5:00 a.m. on October 26, Lunacharsky stood to read a proclamation of the assumption of power by the Congress of Soviets which Lenin – who still had not appeared at the congress – had just written. The proclamation not only announced that the Provisional Government was overthrown and that the Congress of Soviets had taken power, but also laid out a basic program which would appeal to most people of the Russian state:

The Soviet Government will propose an immediate democratic peace to all the nations and an immediate armistice on all fronts. It will secure the transfer of the land of the landed proprietors, the crown and the monasteries to the peasant committees without compensation; it will protect the rights of the soldiers by introducing complete democracy in the army; it will establish workers' control over production; it will ensure the convocation of the Constituent Assembly at the time appointed; it will see to it that bread is supplied to the cities and prime necessities to the villages; it will guarantee all the nations inhabiting Russia the genuine right to self-determination.

The Congress decrees: all power in the localities shall pass to the Soviets of Workers', Soldiers' and Peasants' Deputies.

After only brief discussion the congress adopted the proclamation with only two votes in opposition and a few abstentions.[16]

At about dawn on October 26th the exhilarated but exhausted congress delegates and Bolshevik leaders – some of whom had hardly slept for two nights – adjourned to try to sleep a little, to assess the events of the day and to plan for the second session that evening. At about the same time citizens of the capital awoke to quiet streets with little sense that any momentous event had occurred; seemingly yet another round of political turmoil, complete with armed groups in the streets, had been passed through. Proclamations, mostly in the name of the MRC, were posted, and although perhaps unsettling they gave little indication of the great events transpiring.

The most serious activity during the day of the 26th was by the moderate socialist opponents of Soviet power. The Mensheviks and SRs who left the congress in protest went to the Petrograd City Council, where they formed the Committee for Salvation of the Fatherland and the Revolution to oppose the Bolsheviks and the Congress of Soviets. Created primarily by Mensheviks and SRs from the Petrograd City Council, the Soviet of Peasants' Deputies and the old Revolutionary Defensist leadership, this became the initial center of political opposition to the Bolshevik Revolution, both in Petrograd and, through similar groups, in some other cities. The committee immediately issued a proclamation denouncing the Bolshevik actions, appealing to the population to refuse to follow them, and announcing that it was taking the initiative in forming a new government. This set the stage for a political struggle with the Bolsheviks over the next several days.

That evening the Congress of Soviets met for the second time. Lenin and the Bolshevik leaders moved quickly to consolidate their position with three major actions: a decree on peace, a decree on land and the formation of a new government. The first two were extremely important, for the Bolshevik leaders realized that they had to move quickly to address these two pressing problems – failure to do so had helped to bring down the Provisional Government. Lenin, newly emerged from hiding, firmly took leadership and was the main speaker on all three resolutions.

Lenin introduced the decree on peace. It called upon all of the belligerent powers to enter into immediate negotiations for a just peace without annexations or indemnities. It appealed to the workers of France, Britain and Germany to support the Soviet's peace effort.[17] The decree is notable for the absence of Lenin's usual vituperative language attacking Western governments and capitalism and predicting the forthcoming international revolution. Indeed, it was remarkably similar to the Revolutionary Defensists' ideas about a general "peace without annexations or indemnities" that had already been almost universally accepted by public opinion in Russia. The problem was implementation, and neither the decree nor Lenin's speech introducing it addressed what the new government would do if the other powers did not respond, or whether it would consider a separate peace with Germany. For now what was important was a dramatic gesture to secure the loyalty of the weary troops – and especially the Petrograd garrison – as well as taking some sort of step that might actually lead out of the morass of war. What was impossible was to do nothing.

Lenin moved quickly to the land question, surprising the congress with a decree on land which he had written that morning. Action on the land question was absolutely essential to shore up popular support. The first part of the decree abolished landed proprietorship without compensation. "The landed estates, as also all crown, monastery and church lands, with all their livestock, implements, buildings and everything pertaining thereto" were ordered taken over by local land committees and soviets, pending the meeting of the Constituent Assembly. The second part of the decree was made up of a "Peasant Mandate on the Land," a document that had been compiled from 242 peasant mandates brought to the All-Russia Congress of Peasants' Deputies in May by delegates and published in its newspaper. This was one of the fruits of Lenin's reading during the enforced leisure of hiding out after the July

Days. It proclaimed that "Private ownership of land shall be abolished forever; land shall not be purchased, sold, leased, mortgaged or otherwise alienated." All land was to "become the property of the whole people, and shall pass into the use of those who cultivate it." The employment of hired labor was prohibited.[18] The land decree, based on the SR land program, was a masterful political stratagem. First, it ensured the support of the Left SRs for the new government. Second, by incorporating the "Peasant Mandate" Lenin gave the land decree a popular force that was impossible to ignore. Third, it legalized and pushed further the social-economic revolution taking place in the countryside, thus legitimizing the new government in the eyes of the peasants. Whatever the long-term settlement of the land question might be, Lenin argued in defending the decree, "the point is that the peasant should be firmly assured that there are no more landowners in the countryside."[19]

The third major action at the meeting was the formation of a new government and a new Central Executive Committee. The congress approved the new government presented by Lenin, the Council of People's Commissars (Sovnarkom). Selection of this terminology emphasized the revolutionary nature of the new government. Although "council" (soviet) was a conventional term, "commissar" was new to designate a government minister. It was used in 1917 for special emissaries of the Provisional Government and of the soviets, with a revolutionary pedigree reaching as far back as the French Revolution. The use of "commissar" here instead of the traditional "minister" both associated the name of the new government with these popular revolutionary officials and emphasized that a new and different kind of government had come into being. The addition of the term "people's" was radically innovative and even more firmly emphasized the break with the past while asserting the government's close connection to the masses.

The new government was, unexpectedly, made up entirely of Bolsheviks. This had not been envisioned in the many debates about a Soviet government, all of which had assumed some kind of multiparty socialist government. The walkout of the moderates changed that. The Left SRs insisted that they would join the government only as part of a broad socialist coalition, but with the moderates gone such a government was impossible. Therefore, an all-Bolshevik government was formed initially. Lenin became chairman of Sovnarkom and thus head of the government, with Trotsky as people's commissar for foreign affairs. The new government structure was completed when the Congress of Soviets chose a new Central Executive Committee (CEC). The Bolsheviks initially took sixty-two seats, the Left SRs twenty-nine and

ten were divided among the Menshevik–Internationalists and minor
leftist groups. The socialist parties that had withdrawn were unrepre-
sented. The congress stated that the CEC exercised full authority in its
name between congresses, including both general supervision of the
government and the right to replace its members. However, the exact
relationship of the CEC to the Sovnarkom, both approved by the
congress, soon became a source of conflict between the Left SRs (who
were in the CEC but not the Sovnarkom) and the Bolsheviks. Although
the CEC with its non-Bolshevik minority did not seriously impede
Lenin in his exercise of power, its multiparty structure maintained the
image of a government based on a multiparty socialist coalition, a
concept which enjoyed immense popularity as part of the slogan of
Soviet power.

When the Congress of Soviets adjourned in the early morning hours
of the 27th, the new government was extremely insecure, facing several
immediate threats which might unseat it. It confronted a military threat
in the form of an attempt by Kerensky to retake the city with troops
from the front supported by an uprising in the city. It faced pressure
from various quarters for a government based on a broad socialist
coalition; indeed, discussion of reorganizing the government began
immediately. Moreover, it was unclear whether the rest of the country
would accept the Bolshevik Revolution and government; could pro-
Bolshevik forces prevail in Moscow and other major cities? An ill-
defined and multisided struggle to define the future of Russia was
underway. These three main threats to Bolshevik control need to be
examined.

Kerensky and the military threat

Kerensky's attempt to retake the city, using troops commanded by
General N. P. Krasnov and taking advantage of potential armed opposition still in the city, was the first threat to the new government. Kerensky
fled the city during the October Revolution, seeking support from the
front. His odyssey had proven how thoroughly unpopular he was, not
only with the rank-and-file troops but with their officers as well. Finally
he managed to obtain the support of a small Cossack force under
General Krasnov's command. Ironically, these were units of the same
cavalry corps which Kornilov had relied on against Kerensky in August.
This small force set out on October 26 and on the 28th occupied
Tsarskoe Selo near Petrograd's outskirts, despite the presence of a large
"revolutionary" garrison. This revealed how fragile was the military
situation of the new regime, dependent on troops who were favorably

inclined politically but disinclined to any fighting and notoriously changeable. Now, in turn, the weakness of Krasnov's situation became equally apparent as he found himself surrounded by a sea of unfriendly troops who would not fight but whose actions and words undermined the morale and resolution of his own troops.

While Krasnov at Tsarskoe Selo attempted to garner the additional troops necessary for an attack on Petrograd, an uprising by cadets of the military schools broke out in the city under the leadership of General G. P. Polkovnikov and some of the members of the Committee for the Salvation of the Fatherland and Revolution. They apparently planned to coordinate an uprising with the attack of Kerensky and Krasnov's troops, but it became known prematurely when Red Guards captured one of the plotters with details of the plan. This forced the rebels to commence action on the morning of October 29, earlier than intended, seizing the telephone exchange and a few other points. In most cases these cadets were quickly surrounded and disarmed by Red Guards, soldiers and sailors. However, bloody fighting took place when Soviet forces besieged the military school buildings and the cadets fought back. The fighting at the Vladimir Cadet School alone claimed more lives than had the entire October Revolution in Petrograd to that point; by the time fighting ended late on the afternoon of the 29th over 200 men were killed or wounded.

Meanwhile, a force of workers and Baltic Fleet sailors began assembling on Pulkovo Heights to block Krasnov and Kerensky. The workers included not only armed Red Guards but also thousands of men and women who dug trenches and prepared fortifications. When Krasnov surveyed the scene on the 30th, he saw that "all the slopes of Pulkovo Heights were dug up with trenches and black with Red Guards."[20] Facing about 10,000 entrenched opponents, Krasnov nonetheless flung his small force against the Red Guards and sailors. He was repulsed and, finding himself facing a counterattack, withdrew. The leader of the Baltic sailors, Pavel Dybenko, offered the demoralized Cossacks a deal: swap Kerensky for safe passage to their homes in the south. Learning of this Kerensky fled once more, disguised in a sailor's uniform and automotive goggles and utterly discredited. The Bolshevik government was temporarily safe in Petrograd from military attack.

Vikzhel – a Bolshevik government or a broad socialist government

Even as they beat back the immediate military threat, Lenin faced an attempt to alter the political composition of the government which would rob him of the fruits of his audacity and luck. The idea of a multiparty socialist government had broad support, including some within the Bolshevik leadership. It was, moreover, what the workers and soldiers had meant when they demanded Soviet power. The most effective pressure forcing negotiations on the composition of the government came from Vikzhel, the All-Russia Executive Committee of the Union of Railway Workers, which was led by the Left SRs. Their ability to control the movement of troops, foodstuffs and other goods put them in a strategic position to demand that all political groups pay attention. On October 29 Vikzhel issued an appeal, virtually an ultimatum, calling for negotiations. Its appeal, addressed to all soviets and many other workers', soldiers' and peasants' organizations, probably reflected widespread sentiment at the time:

The country is without an organized government, and a bitter struggle for power is in progress. Each of the contending parties is trying to create a government by means of force, and [as a result] brother is killing brother . . . The Provisional Government with Kerensky at its head has proved itself too weak to retain the reins of power. The government of the Soviet of People's Commissars, formed at Petrograd by one party only, cannot expect to be recognized or supported by the country as a whole. It is, therefore, necessary to form a government that will have the confidence of the democracy as a whole and have enough prestige to retain the power until the meeting of the Constituent Assembly . . . The Railwaymen's Union gives notice that it will make use of every means at its disposal, even to complete stoppage of all train movements, to carry out its decision.[21]

With the outcome of Kerensky's attempt to bring troops from the front still in doubt, and uncertain whether Moscow and the rest of the country would accept the new government, the Bolsheviks felt that they needed to accept the proposal. Indeed, the concept found considerable sympathy among a portion of the Bolshevik leadership who not only still assumed that such a government was their objective as revolutionaries, but considered it necessary to preserve the revolution, doubting they could survive on their own.

The next several days saw intense negotiations among the various party groups and Vikzhel, as well as debates within the Bolshevik Party. At first the Mensheviks and SRs took a hard position, demanding repudiation of the seizure of power on October 25 and insisting that the new all-socialist government formed must *not* include Lenin or Trotsky. The negotiators from the Bolshevik side, led by the more conciliatory Bolsheviks such as Kamenev and David Riazanov, apparently seriously considered the latter demand. Indeed, the Bolshevik Central Committee on October 29 – in the absence of both Lenin and Trotsky, it should be noted – endorsed the general drift of the talks and "recognizes the necessity of broadening the basis of the government and the possibility of changes in its composition."[22] Lenin, who had not played a very active role in these discussions, finally involved himself, as did Trotsky. At a Central Committee meeting on November 1 Lenin castigated Kamenev and Riazanov for treating the discussions as anything other than a delaying action while the regime strengthened itself, i.e., warded off the military threat and established control in Moscow. Some Bolshevik Central Committee members, however, such as A. I. Rykov, Riazanov and Kamenev, protested that these were serious negotiations and that an attempt by the Bolsheviks to rule alone would only lead to collapse and the loss of everything gained by the revolution thus far. Trotsky and others insisted that the Bolsheviks must have a solid majority in any new government formed.[23] The Central Committee voted to continue exploring the establishment of a broad socialist government.

Events, however, were working against the advocates of compromise. The defeat of the Kerensky–Krasnov effort removed, at least temporarily, the threat of a military-based overthrow. Prospects for success in Moscow brightened and more and more news came in from other cities and front armies about support for the new government. The Menshevik–SR negotiators overplayed their hand, taking a more intransigent position and demanding greater concessions than their strength justified. Under Lenin's and Trotsky's prodding the Bolshevik leadership hardened its position. Lenin angrily threatened to split the party if need be. On November 2 he introduced a resolution at the party Central Committee meeting attacking the proponents of compromise and arguing that "one cannot renounce a purely Bolshevik government."[24]

The Vikzhel negotiations and the Bolshevik intraparty debates raised fundamental questions about the purposes of power, and especially Lenin's drive for power. The most the Leninists were willing to concede was that the other socialist parties be admitted to the CEC in the same proportion as their original membership in the Second Congress of Soviets. They were not willing to admit them to Sovnarkom, the government. The more conciliatory Bolsheviks, such as Kamenev, wanted to go further and broaden the CEC to include also representatives of various "democratic" institutions: trade unions, some city councils, etc., and perhaps even allow other parties into the government. Either way would have meant a loss of absolute majority for the Bolsheviks had their opponents seized on it. They failed to do so. Lenin was able to maintain successfully his intransigent insistence on keeping a firm grip on power and also kept his own party in line. The Bolshevik government, strengthened by the defeat of its immediate military adversaries in Petrograd and by the failure of the moderates within its own ranks to find an alternative, let the negotiations over Vikzhel's proposed coalition government grind to an inconclusive end in early November. One reason that they could do this was the successful spread of the revolution beyond Petrograd.

The spread of Soviet power

During the same first week of the revolution when the Bolshevik leaders were struggling with armed opponents and demands for broadening the government, they also watched anxiously to see whether or not the rest of the country would support their revolution and government. They initially had little ability to influence that, yet it was critical to their longer-term survival. In February the revolution in Petrograd found a remarkably universal acceptance across the country. By October, however, both state and society had splintered. The authority of the capital over the provinces had weakened, while local political, economic, ethnic and other issues had grown stronger. Therefore, the new revolution called forth a different response than had that of February. Now every major locality made a decision, based on local conditions, often accompanied by fighting, to accept or not to accept Soviet power and the new central government. This stretched out over weeks or even months as the many local "Octobers" took a variety of forms. The local responses to Petrograd's October Revolution depended upon a host of local conditions: the political coloration of the local soviet, the social composition of the community, the vigor of local political leaders, the presence or absence of a garrison, nationality conflicts and other factors. Control of the local soviet was especially important because the soviets, not officials of the Provisional Government or city council, exercised predominant authority locally in most instances.

Soviet power came to the Russian provinces in a complex process, not some simple "triumphal march," as Lenin later termed it and as it was sanctified in Soviet histories. Indeed, it is more accurate to speak of several waves of revolution across Russia after the October Revolution in Petrograd, as "Soviet power" spread between October 1917 and early 1918. We can group that process of soviet revolution into three broad categories for the major cities, based on the speed and manner in which it was established. The first two types were part of the initial consolidation of power; the third was part of the second stage.

In one type of provincial October Revolution the local Bolsheviks and their allies were able to assert Soviet power quickly and with little opposition. In these places the Bolsheviks or a Bolshevik-led coalition usually already controlled the local soviet and through it moved immediately to proclaim Soviet power locally and support for the new government in Petrograd. Red Guards and/or reliable garrison soldiers were on hand to enforce the proclamation. Effective opposition or viable rivals were absent. In this type the local soviet leaders declared Soviet power on October 26 or 27 and made it stick without difficulty. This was especially the pattern in the heavily industrialized towns of the Central Industrial Region north and east of Moscow and in the Urals.

In a second – and more important perhaps – type of city the local Bolsheviks had more difficulty, even though usually controlling the soviet. An armed confrontation normally was involved, sometimes with significant fighting, but with the Soviet–Bolshevik position winning out within two or three days to a week (by about November 2). Cities of this type tended to be larger, to have a more diverse social structure and produced an organized opposition to the new Soviet government. This was typical of the central Volga River cities (Kazan, Samara, Saratov), of some of the larger cities of the Central Industrial Region such as Vladimir and Tver, and for many large cities elsewhere. This group also included Moscow, where the outcome was especially critical to the survival of the new regime. Even within this type there was considerable variation, however.

At Saratov, for example, the Bolsheviks won a clear majority in the city soviet in September and, amidst the rising tensions of mid-October, took steps to further strengthen the soviet's domination of the city through control of food distribution and other measures. During the night of October 26–27, after hearing of events in Petrograd, the Saratov Soviet declared the transfer of power locally to the soviet and began measures to implement this. During the early morning hours its executive committee decreed the removal of the local representative of the Provisional Government, sent its own commissars to the districts of the province, prohibited newspapers from publishing "antisoviet" articles and issued its own land decree. The Saratov Mensheviks and SRs, however, resisted. They controlled the city council and now used it to create a Committee to Save the Revolution. The two sides jockeyed for position and mobilized their support throughout the 27th. Finally on the morning of October 28 the soviet forces – Red Guards and some soldiers from the garrison – surrounded the city council building where the committee defenders had made their stand. After a day of negotiations, shooting began that evening and continued through the night. Finally, at about 6:00 a.m. on the 29th, the city council building defenders surrendered. Casualties were three killed and eighteen wounded. The hungry besiegers literally ate away portions of the barricade, which had been built of boxes of quinces. Soviet power was established.[25]

The quick victory and low casualties in Saratov stand in sharp contrast to the struggle in Moscow. As the largest city of Russia and the old capital, Moscow's response to the events in Petrograd was especially important. Moscow's acceptance of the Bolshevik Revolution would give it an immense boost, whereas a rejection would automatically establish a powerful center of opposition and perhaps doom the Bolshevik regime. The outcome in Moscow hung in the balance for several days, and Moscow was the last city in this second category to establish Soviet power.

The Moscow Bolsheviks clearly were unprepared for a revolutionary seizure of power. They controlled the workers' soviet, but not the separate soldiers' soviet, and so their ability to command support from the garrison was uncertain. Nor had they created a Military Revolutionary Committee to play a role similar to the one in Petrograd. Nor had they done much to strengthen or prepare the Red Guard. Moreover, most of the top Moscow Bolshevik leaders were away in Petrograd for the Second Congress of Soviets and thus not in a position to provide immediate leadership. Indeed, several of them turned out to be among the most vigorous proponents of a broad socialist government. Thus the Moscow Bolsheviks went into the struggle unprepared and with a sense that the actions in Petrograd were unwise, but feeling that once begun the revolution had to be defended lest its defeat allow the always feared conservative counterrevolution to triumph. The Moscow Left SRs and some left Mensheviks supported it on the same grounds. The Moscow Workers' Soviet voted to support the actions of the Petrograd Military Revolutionary Committee (i.e., seizure of power) and to create an MRC in Moscow.

The hesitation and unpreparedness among the Moscow Bolsheviks had its mirror image in a more spirited and effective opposition among opponents of the Bolshevik Revolution. On October 25 (i.e., even before the Winter Palace had fallen), they met at the city council and formed a Committee of Public Safety, the two most important members of which turned out to be V. V. Rudnev, the mayor of the city and a Right SR, and Colonel K. I. Riabtsev, commander of the Moscow Military District. The committee was able to put together a force of about 10,000 trained men.[26]

On the 26th both sides organized their supporters and watched the other, each unwilling to be responsible for starting the fighting. Finally on the 27th Riabtsev took the offensive and troops of the Committee of Public Safety recaptured several railroad and telephone stations which the insurgents had seized earlier. Through the night of the 27th and the 28th Riabtsev's units won additional victories, finally taking the Kremlin from its Bolshevik defenders. This was the high point of the success of the Committee of Public Safety's forces. The pro-soviet forces now rallied. The Red Guards, who bore the brunt of the fighting in Moscow, had begun on October 25 with about 8,500 men, but that swelled to about 30,000 by November 1. Moreover, Red Guard units began arriving from the surrounding industrial cities and towns where Soviet power had been established already. The Red Guards fought with particular tenacity, and by the 29th gained artillery support from the army garrison, only a small part of which participated in the fighting. Fighting from street to street, they gradually drove their opponents back toward the city center around the Kremlin, and on November 2 triumphed completely. The fighting in Moscow was bitter, symbolized (and perhaps sparked) by the shooting down of several dozen pro-soviet men after they surrendered in the Kremlin on October 28. The total number of deaths in Moscow was never established with any precision, but clearly ran to several hundred dead, plus wounded.

The Bolsheviks had triumphed in Moscow, but at a cost much higher than in any other city thus far. Even then, they still faced criticism in the Moscow Soviet, where their allies among the Left SRs, who had supported the MRC during the fighting, made clear that they had done so in the name of a broadly based Soviet government and defense of the revolution. For them the fear that somehow General Kornilov and a complete counterrevolution lurked behind a victory of the moderate socialists and liberals of the Committee of Public Safety propelled them to fight for the MRC and Soviet power. Moscow showed a complex political situation, not a simple Bolshevik versus anti-Bolshevik division, in which the various nuances of the idea of Soviet power played an important role, as did fear of a conservative counterrevolution. The same complex of feelings was prevalent in most larger cities.

Especially critical to the initial consolidation of Soviet power was the attitude of the front soldiers, particularly those of the area nearest Petrograd: the Northern Front, the Baltic Fleet sailors and the Helsinki garrison. Troops of this area, already radicalized, quickly proclaimed support for Soviet power, which they identified as a socialist government that would make peace quickly and implement swift and radical social reforms. The Twelfth Army, occupying the critical area of the approaches to Petrograd, reacted to the events of October 25 by sending a telegram to the Congress of Soviets that night declaring that it was forming an MRC to control power, and ordered Latvian infantry units (strongly pro-Bolshevik) to occupy the main towns between the

Plate 21 Damage to the Kremlin from the fighting during the October Revolution in Moscow. Notice the bullet holes and partly blown-away door. National Archives and Records Administration.

Northern Front and Petrograd. Although an army congress on October 28 proved equally balanced between the Bolsheviks and their opponents, and the congress resolution forbade Twelfth Army soldiers to support either side in the confrontation at Pulkovo, the real beneficiaries of that policy were the Bolsheviks, since it deprived Kerensky and the government of needed military support. The First Army, in the same general area, convened a congress October 30 which was dominated by Bolsheviks, Left SRs and Menshevik–Internationalists and which declared for Soviet power. The Minsk city soviet, heavily influenced by the garrison and nearby front, proclaimed Soviet power immediately. The Baltic sailors and Helsinki garrison quickly declared their support. Within days part of Estonia, unoccupied Latvia and the areas to the rear of the Northern Front and northern part of the Western Front declared support for Soviet power and the revolution in Petrograd. The Bolshevik government thus gained essential security as well as possible armed support in the front and immediate rear areas closest to Petrograd.

While most resolutions supported Soviet power, some were more equivocal. Some criticized the Bolsheviks for causing an armed confrontation but also condemned Kerensky, while endorsing the peace and land decrees of the Congress of Soviets. The 517 Batumsky Regiment resolved on October 29 that "the seizure of power by the Bolsheviks in Petrograd, leading to fratricidal war, was caused by the Provisional Government in deviating from the wishes of the majority of the democracy."[27] Even such mixed responses were valuable to the new regime, however, for they showed the absence of any possible armed support for Kerensky's effort. The situation on other fronts took longer to clarify, as did the long-term attitude of the soldiers toward government authority (see chapter 10).[28]

By November 2, the date of the victory in Moscow, the Bolsheviks had managed to gain control – how secure remained uncertain – of a belt of territory across north-central European Russia, reaching from the Western and Northern Fronts in the west to the Volga and Ural Mountains in the east. However, there were significant regions within this belt where Soviet power had not been established. Moreover, such a map refers to provinces where the major cities had declared for Soviet power, but in some of them most of the rural regions and district towns had not yet been brought under the new authority. There also were pockets outside this belt that had declared Soviet power. In many places where "Soviet power" had been proclaimed, the pre-October local government continued to exist and even function. Soviet power was tenuous at best.

After November 2 the spread of Soviet power effectively stopped for a period of two weeks before resuming again about November 17 in the third wave of declaring for Soviet power (see chapter 10). This pause cannot be explained by political or other events in Petrograd and seems to reflect that the successes of the first week exhausted the supply of cities where the Bolsheviks and left radicals were, before the October Revolution, in a strong enough position to establish power quickly and successfully. Indeed, the area corresponded closely to where the soviets had been under Bolshevik or leftist control *before* the October Revolution. In the rest of the country they had to engage in a more prolonged struggle to secure Soviet power. Nonetheless, the victory in Moscow and other major cities and industrial towns of the Russian heartland and in the northern army and naval forces was essential to the initial consolidations of power and gave the new government an essential breathing space.

By November 2, a week after the Bolsheviks first declared Soviet power, the government had beaten back its immediate military adversaries and seen the acceptance of Soviet power in Moscow and many other cities. This in turn allowed Lenin to let the Vikzhel negotiations die, force into line those Bolshevik leaders who advocated a broader-based government and evade the attempt to force the Bolsheviks to share power. The new "provisional workers' and soldiers' government," as Lenin initially styled it in the announcement of the new government issued by the Second Congress of Soviets on October 26, could now consider itself less "provisional" and turn its attention to longer-term issues, both political and social-economic.

10 The Constituent Assembly and the purposes of power

Having found a little security by early November, Lenin and the Bolsheviks could now look ahead to dealing with a number of political issues such as making peace, the further spread of Soviet power, restructuring government and, ultimately, the Constituent Assembly. They also could devote attention to implementing sweeping social and economic reforms in an attempt to address the aspirations of Russian society. In dealing with all these issues, especially the Constituent Assembly, they confronted the question of the nature and purposes of power, and of the revolution itself.

Peace

One of the first acts of the new regime had been the Decree on Peace, which included a call for an immediate armistice. With one stroke the new leaders bought for themselves broad popular support, especially among soldiers, and moved decisively on the issue that more than any other had undermined their predecessors. Vivid descriptions come down to us of the reactions in the hall at the Second Congress of Soviets as Lenin read the peace decree. The American journalist, Albert Rhys Williams, was there and recalled that "a burly soldier stood, tears in his eyes as he embraced a worker who had risen and was clapping furiously . . . A Viborg man [Vyborg district worker], his eyes hollow from lack of sleep, his face gaunt beneath his beard, looked around the hall, dazed, and, crossing himself, muttered: '*Pust budet konets voine!*' ('May it be the end of the war!')."[1] Still, popular support would quickly wither unless peace could promptly be made a reality.

This was not easily done. Lenin and the Bolshevik leaders had managed, while criticizing the Provisional Government, to avoid spelling out how they would deal with achieving peace. Early in 1917 Lenin sometimes talked about possible "revolutionary war" (especially when charged with favoring a separate peace with Germany). Mostly, however, he simply evaded the issue, often with an assertion that a

258

socialist government in Russia would be enough to spark revolution in Germany and Western Europe and thus make the issue irrelevant. Traditional diplomatic negotiations would not be necessary. The Bolsheviks, like their Revolutionary Defensist predecessors, believed that the revolution in Russia was only the beginning of a general European revolution. Faith in the revolution abroad had been a cornerstone of Lenin's ideological justification for seizing power, and it now became a rock they would cling to in the hard days ahead: the international revolution would come to the aid of the radical Russian Revolution.

Faith in world revolution notwithstanding, the need for practical measures quickly intruded itself, and the breathing space after November 2 allowed the leadership to turn attention again to the peace question. The Bolsheviks' peace decree was generally ignored abroad. Therefore, on November 7 the government ordered General Nikolai Dukhonin, the army acting supreme commander, to begin negotiations with the Germans for an armistice on the Eastern Front. When he refused he was dismissed and front-line regiments were ordered to elect representatives to start armistice negotiations with the enemy troops opposite them. Nikolai Krylenko, the Bolsheviks' newly appointed army commander, sent a team across the lines on November 13 to contact the German command with an armistice proposal. By that time individual military units already were negotiating local armistices, which took hold well before the formal armistice talks began on November 19, much less the full armistice agreement on December 2. These many direct armistices brought an effective end to the war on the Eastern Front.

They also had a remarkable effect on both the troops and the government. For the soldiers, the government's directive on armistice talks sanctioned and legitimized their aspirations to stop all fighting and return home. In return the new Soviet government acquired a legitimacy in the eyes of the soldiers far beyond any conferred by the Congress of Soviets, sweeping aside also the issue of a broad-based socialist government (or even, as events showed, the Constituent Assembly). Moreover, by giving the soldiers themselves responsibility, Lenin implicitly sanctioned the soldiers' self-assertiveness, including taking control of the army from the officers and the remaining Revolutionary Defensist committee leadership. All other political issues and parties paled in significance compared to this mutual legitimization and reinforcement of each others' actions.[2] True, formal peace negotiations dragged on and a peace treaty was not signed until March 3, 1918.[a] For Russian

---

[a] By the harsh terms of the Treaty of Brest-Litovsk, signed on March 3, 1918, Russia lost massive amounts of territory, people, industry and grain-producing regions. The onerous terms perhaps vindicated those political leaders of 1917, of varying political

soldiers, however, the war was over and they began self-demobilization in November and December 1917. With the armistice the war and peace issue ceased, for the first time in 1917, to threaten the government in power with popular opposition. This allowed Lenin to face the serious domestic problems confronting the new regime.

Soviet power: resistance and acceptance

The Bolshevik government faced a serious problem of how to ensure the continued spread of Soviet power, which had basically stopped on November 2. Successes during the first week of the October Revolution exhausted the supply of cities where the Bolsheviks and their leftist allies were, before the October Revolution, in a strong enough position to establish power quickly. In the rest of the country they had to engage in a more prolonged *political* struggle of one to two months before the Soviet/Bolshevik forces prevailed. In these cities the Bolsheviks or radical left bloc did not control the soviet, and/or a strong alternative existed. A frequent feature was strong support for the idea of Soviet power as a government uniting all socialist parties coupled with opposition to the Bolshevik government. This was typical in the provinces south of Moscow and in eastern Ukraine as well as parts of the front. These areas show especially well how complex was the meaning of Soviet power and how varied were the reasons for supporting or opposing the revolution in Petrograd and its new government. The struggle for power in these areas is also significant for the introduction of two other issues. One was the struggle of some nationalities to establish their autonomy or independence, a process further complicated by the Declaration of the Rights of the Peoples of Russia, issued November 2, which many nationality leaders took as sanctioning secession. The other was the "railway war" in which expeditionary units sent from Petrograd and Moscow to enforce the authority of the new government battled with local armed forces opposing it.

Representative of these areas and issues was Kharkov, the major industrial and financial center of eastern Ukraine. In Kharkov, a broad socialist coalition, predominantly leftist Menshevik and Left SR, controlled the soviet. They rejected an effort by local Bolsheviks to declare Soviet power on October 26 was rejected and instead power was temporarily vested in a Military Revolutionary Committee (MRC),

persuasions, who had argued against a separate peace with Germany precisely because of the staggering cost it would have for Russia. The cost to any political regime which did not make peace, however, was loss of power, and that was the one price Lenin was unwilling to pay.

which in turn was made responsible to both the city and the regional soviets (worker, soldier and peasant). This MRC was very different from those in Petrograd and Moscow. It was not a Bolshevik-led vehicle for seizing power, but rather a broadly based organ for holding local power during a time of political uncertainty. It refused to support the former Provisional Government, but it also withheld recognition from the new Bolshevik government. Instead it instituted locally the ideal of an all-socialist government of the type advocated by Vikzhel in Petrograd.[3]

The political situation in Kharkov was made the more complex by the growth of Ukrainian assertiveness. Ukrainian nationalism had not been particularly strong in Kharkov – Ukrainians made up only about a third of the population – but was growing. On November 7 the Ukrainian Central Rada in Kiev issued its "Third Universal," proclaiming the formation of the Ukrainian People's Republic, with the Rada and its General Secretariat as the government of Ukraine. It stopped short of proclaiming full independence, but asserted broad autonomy within a radically decentralized federal state. It also proclaimed sweeping social reforms, including distribution of land to the peasants.[4] Ukrainian nationalists in Kharkov now claimed a major role in local politics and pressed for recognition of the authority of the Ukrainian Central Rada in Kiev as the government for all Ukraine. Since they were for the most part also socialists and because power to the Rada suggested Soviet power (*rada* being the Ukrainian equivalent of *sovet* – soviet), the Ukrainian parties were able to combine the broad concept of "Soviet power" with recognition of the aspirations of Ukrainians as a nationality.

The result was a protracted, multisided struggle for power. Three broad groupings emerged, all represented within the Kharkov city soviet as well as the regional soviet and the MRC. The initially dominant group represented a broad coalition of non-Bolshevik socialists. They accepted most of the radical reforms of the new government in Petrograd, especially land reform, but rejected its armed seizure of power and demanded a broad socialist government. This faction based itself on the Kharkov MRC and its executive body, the *deviatka* (The Nine). The second group comprised the Ukrainians, especially the Ukrainian SRs and SDs, who increasingly rallied around the Kharkov branch of the Rada. They cooperated with the first group on many issues, but demanded greater support for the Central Rada in Kiev and were moving toward extensive national autonomy or even independence. The Bolsheviks were the third group and they launched a major campaign to win support for the declaration of full Soviet power in Kharkov, by which they meant full recognition of Lenin's government as the only government for Russia, including the minority nationality areas. Their main tactic was to gain control of the Kharkov city soviet and through it declare power.

The three groups fought a protracted political battle for support of the population, especially the factory workers and the soldiers of the garrison. Gradually the Bolsheviks managed to obtain reelection of enough soviet deputies to gain a working majority in the Kharkov Soviet with the support of some smaller parties. They attempted to declare Soviet power in November, but did not have the armed force to back that up. Armed strength was divided among the three groups, with the Ukrainians again playing a special role as they undertook to build specifically Ukrainian regiments in the garrison. Finally on December 8 the issue came to a head, forced by the arrival of a Bolshevik expeditionary force – Red Guards, sailors and soldiers – from Petrograd and Moscow. After a night of armed confrontation the Ukrainian forces were neutralized and Soviet power, meaning Bolshevik power, was firmly established in Kharkov.

Similar protracted and complex political struggles played out elsewhere across the country during the two months from mid-November to mid-January 1918. These took place in small towns and rural areas as well as large cities, as is well illustrated by the rural Sychevka district of Smolensk province. There radicalized peasants voted overwhelmingly for the Bolshevik ticket in the Constituent Assembly elections on November 12, giving them a 79.4 percent victory, despite the fact that a Bolshevik party organization was practically non-existent. Clearly, "Bolshevism" stood for radical change rather than a party organization or well-understood party program. To further complicate matters, a few days later on November 20 in Sychevka town, a "United Soviet" was created with sixteen SRs (mostly Left SRs), ten Bolsheviks, and seven non-party in its executive committee. This remained the primary government until May 1918, although other government and quasi-governmental bodies continued to function as well. Elections and political struggles here reinforce the conclusion that political blocs were more important than specific parties, and that "soviet power" at this time meant a call for radical policies rather than support for any given political party.[5]

Particularly important in this process of acceptance or rejection of the October Revolution was the situation in the Cossack lands. The Cossacks were spread among several "hosts" along the southern and eastern edges of European Russia. Two of them, the Orenburg Cossacks under Ataman General A. I. Dutov and the Don Cossacks under Ataman General Aleksei Kaledin, quickly organized to resist a Bolshevik takeover. The situation with the Don Cossacks lands, a large and strategic area south of Moscow, was especially important. The Don Cossacks exhibited strong regional, even incipient nationalist, traits in 1917. They received broad internal autonomy from the Provisional Government, including the right to elect their own ataman (leader). This was General Kaledin, who had been supportive of Kornilov during his attack on the Provisional Government but was not directly involved. On October 30 Kaledin proclaimed a separate Don Republic. The Cossacks were not a direct threat to the new government, but Kaledin's proclamation endangered the further spread of Soviet power south. The Bolsheviks, moreover, believed them to be a threat, in particular as potential supporters of an anti-Bolshevik military force, and decided on action against Kaledin and the Cossacks.

Meanwhile, General Alekseev and some other conservative generals, also assuming the Cossacks to be conservative and defenders of social order, headed for the Don territory in late October and November. There they undertook to create an anti-Bolshevik Volunteer Army, composed as it turned out primarily of Russian officers who were flooding to the region. While sympathetic Don Cossack leaders and popular Cossack suspicion of the Petrograd government provided a certain security within which to organize, the Cossacks generally were hostile to renewed fighting against either Germany or the Soviet government, which was Alekseev's plan. Then on November 30 pro-Soviet workers supported by Black Sea sailors seized control of the Don territory city of Rostov-on-Don, which led to fighting between them and the Cossacks, and in turn to a temporary Cossack–Volunteer Army alliance. Some Kadet Party leaders came to the area also – the party had done well in elections in the Don for the old State Duma – in a bid to exercise political leadership of what they saw as an emerging center of anti-Bolshevik strength. These developments caused immense concern among Soviet leaders, who promptly identified the Don as the center of a new "Kornilovite" counterrevolution (indeed, Kornilov did arrive in December to join the Volunteer Army). Events in the Don Cossack territory, when added to the proclamation by the Ukrainian Rada to be the government authority in neighboring Ukraine, created enormous concern among the Bolsheviks that the southern regions might be the focus of a potent counterrevolution. Continuing the tradition of finding parallels for comparison in the French Revolution, they dubbed the Don territory the *Vendée*[b] of the Russian Revolution.

To deal with these threats and general resistance to Soviet power, the Soviet government in late November organized and sent out a series of

[b] The *Vendée* was a province that became a center of conservative opposition to Paris during the French Revolution.

"echelons," special armed detachments organized and moved along railroads. These detachments usually included a mixture of Red Guards (especially from Moscow or Petrograd), soldiers and Baltic Fleet sailors, in varying proportions. By early December these were concentrated south of Moscow, which represented an area where the revolution was spreading only slowly and where two perceived threats lay: Kaledin's Don Cossacks and the Ukrainian nationalists. Under the direction of Vladimir Antonov-Ovseenko and relying heavily on Left SR-oriented commanding officers, these echelons pushed south and then both west and east into the Ukrainian and Don Cossack areas respectively. They forced the establishment of a Bolshevik government in Kharkov on December 9 and then moved toward Kiev, taking the city on January 26 and driving out the government of the Ukrainian Rada. Antonov simultaneously moved east and attacked the Don territory; his echelons captured the main Don cities in February 1918. Kaledin committed suicide and the Volunteer Army retreated further south (to reemerge later as a major force in the civil war). Success in Ukraine was soon reversed by German intervention, while that in the Don territory rested more on divisions among the Cossacks, especially the unwillingness of recently returned front soldiers to take up arms for either side, than it did on broad support for the Bolsheviks.

Another area of special importance at this time was the military front. The army was already in an advanced state of disintegration by the time of the October Revolution and its weary soldiers were a major source of support for the concept of Soviet power. The Decree on Peace legitimized their yearning for a cessation of hostilities and solidified support for the new regime. Still, the Bolshevik leaders were worried about the army and its future behavior and undertook to try to establish control over the army command. In doing so the Bolsheviks were helped by the complex attitudes and disunity among the highest-ranking officers. Many generals hated the Bolsheviks and refused to have anything to do with the new government. Others, however, reacted differently. Many of the General Staff officers in Petrograd stayed at their offices and did their jobs under the new government in the name of maintaining the army. Some front commanders refused to support Kerensky, thereby effectively supporting the Bolsheviks in the critical period immediately after October 25. General A. V. Cheremisov, commander of the nearby Northern Front, who had reasonably good relations with radical army committeemen, had canceled Kerensky's orders to send troops to help in Krasnov's assault on Petrograd. Trying to find a middle ground between accommodation with a regime they disliked and their sense of duty, and perhaps playing for time, officers such as Cheremisov fell between the stools. Indeed, the Bolsheviks dismissed him November 12.

The Bolsheviks soon turned their attention to the front headquarters, Stavka, at Mogilev. Stavka at first tacitly accepted the new government, if reluctantly; it had little choice if it wanted to maintain even a semblance of army structure and command. General Dukhonin, the acting army commander, moved into open opposition only when ordered to make an armistice. At the same time Stavka became a magnet for various political figures who hoped that it might be the place where a new government could be formed and the Bolsheviks somehow blocked. These hopes came to nothing. Meanwhile Dukhonin's replacement, Nikolai Krylenko, a 32-year-old Bolshevik activist of the Military Organization (and ensign in the army), and a force of Baltic sailors and Red Guards made a slow procession to Mogilev, removing commanders and arranging armistices at places en route. They arrived at Stavka only on November 20. Dukhonin, already under arrest by the local soldiers, was killed by a mob despite Krylenko's efforts to save him. His death marked the end of any danger from the army General Staff, and the final end of the old army.

Meanwhile, the Bolsheviks and Left SRs were waging, and winning, a battle for the allegiance of the front soldiers and their committees. The front soldiers, as we have noted, immediately identified with the Decree on Peace and the armistice that followed. At the same time, however, they supported Soviet power in its original meaning of a government of all the socialist parties. They disliked partisan politics and feared fratricidal armed conflict. They were, therefore, sympathetic to the Vikzhel and similar proposals and often sent delegations to Petrograd demanding socialist unity and warning against civil war. Many committee resolutions condemned both the Provisional Government and the Bolshevik seizure of power, although at the same time they approved of the new government's early steps on land, peace and social issues. Only slowly, in November and December, were Bolshevik and Left SR activists able to manage the reelection of unit committee and army front congresses and set up Military Revolutionary Committees as the new local political authorities. As Allan Wildman noted, those struggles "were fought not on battlefields and streets with guns and armored cars but in countless electoral contests, improvised meetings, newspapers and wrangling debates at army and front congresses stretching over the month of November and early December."[6] The Bolsheviks and their Left SR allies made rapid progress on the Northern and Western Fronts, nearer Petrograd and Moscow, and slower but real gains on the Southwestern and Romanian Fronts. By the end of the year the army as a whole supported the new regime, and certainly was of no possible use to its opponents.

In the major nationality regions the situation was more complex and less favorable to the Bolshevik government, although perhaps also less immediately critical. The October Revolution created new opportunities and dilemmas for nationality movements. Was the new Soviet government just another version of the Provisional Government? Would its nationality policies differ? Should they recognize it or take it as a sign of the further disintegration of Russia and strike out on their own? How did this affect relations with local Russian authorities? In general the October Revolution stimulated nationalist demands for autonomy or even independence, for two reasons: first, because it further weakened the central government and especially its legitimacy; and, second, because it seemed to signal a greater support by the new central government for local self-determination. Lenin and the central Bolshevik leadership had been especially vocal in support of the right to self-determination, and the Declaration of the Rights of the Peoples of Russia on November 2 reinforced this.

Many nationality leaders took the declaration as a green light to assert greater local authority and self-determination, and even to move closer to secession and independence. In November and December most of the major nationalities in a wide arc from Finland in the northwest, reaching south through the Baltic territories and Ukraine, then east across Transcaucasia and Central Asia, and up through the Tatar regions of the Volga and Urals, declared for autonomy within a democratic federal Russian state or full independence. Many of them refused to recognize the new Bolshevik government in Petrograd or did so only conditionally. In most cases this sparked conflict not only with the new Bolshevik government but with local supporters of Soviet power, including local Bolsheviks, as well as with anti-Bolshevik Russians. Sometimes it exacerbated social or ethnic tensions.

In the Baltic region the situation differed by nation. As noted earlier, the Finnish legislature, which had already gone further toward independence than any other national assembly, declared independence after the October Revolution. The Soviet government officially recognized Finnish independence on January 4, 1918, the only region so recognized, although it also supported the Finnish government's socialist opponents in the civil war that soon followed. In Latvia and Estonia the October Revolution provoked a sharp struggle between the Bolsheviks and liberal nationalists. In those parts of Latvia not occupied by Germany the Latvian Social Democratic Party (which had become completely Bolshevik) combined radical social revolution with ethnic identity and was already the strongest party. They projected a future Latvia within a Russian federation, but one with a radical socialist government. Through the Latvian Rifle Regiment in particular they provided much needed early support to the Bolshevik government in nearby Petrograd. In Estonia, in contrast, neither Bolsheviks nor nationalists clearly dominated. The Russian- and Bolshevik-controlled Tallinn Soviet proclaimed Soviet power in Estonia and declared the elected nationalist center, the Maapäev, dissolved. The latter retaliated by declaring itself the supreme political authority in Estonia. The nationalists seemed to be gaining the upper hand by the end of 1917, rallying the middle class, most of the intelligentsia and the peasants, and even portions of the small urban lower classes, around national identity and moderate social reform. The political outcome, however, was still unsettled when German troops occupied the area in February of 1918.

In Ukraine the reaction to news of the October Revolution was very complex, as the discussion of Kharkov suggests. In Kiev a three-cornered struggle began among Ukrainians, pro-Bolshevik forces and supporters of the Provisional Government, each backed by its own armed forces, and fighting ensued. In contrast to Kharkov, the Ukrainian Rada and the Bolsheviks initially cooperated to drive out the supporters of the Provisional Government or a Vikzhel-type solution, but it was an uneasy alliance. The Rada effectively controlled the city. It soon asserted its authority not only in Kiev but in all Ukraine by issuing the "Third Universal" on November 7, stating that "A heavy and difficult hour has fallen upon the land . . . ; the central government has collapsed and anarchy, lawlessness and ruin are spreading throughout the state." It claimed all power in Ukraine until a Constituent Assembly of Ukraine could be convened. The Universal did, however, echo reforms of the new Bolshevik government, declaring confiscation of landlord lands and an eight-hour day in industry, calling for "peace negotiations at once," and other reform measures. It still provided, however, for an autonomous Ukraine in a federal state.[7]

Relations with the Bolshevik government soon deteriorated as the latter moved to assert control in south Russia. It especially feared a Ukrainian–Cossack alliance and on December 4 levied a series of demands on the Rada about relations with the Cossacks. In fact the Petrograd government had already organized armed detachments that were moving south, where they precipitated the Bolshevik takeover in Kharkov (see pp. 260–62). An effort by Kiev Bolsheviks to take power failed, however. Relations between the Central Rada and the Bolshevik government in Petrograd rapidly deteriorated. The latter launched a full military attack on Kiev. The Rada issued a Fourth Universal on January 9, declaring full independence for Ukraine, but the Bolshevik forces soon captured the city. Ukraine descended into complex, multisided warfare.

In Transcaucasia most Georgian, Armenian and Azerbaijani leaders did not recognize the new Bolshevik government. At a meeting of major party leaders in Tbilisi on November 11, Noi Jordania (a Georgian Menshevik) proposed formation of a local government to preserve Transcaucasia until the national political situation was clarified and the Constituent Assembly convened. On November 25 they created a Transcaucasian Commissariat as the temporary government, based on local national-ethnic movements, until the Constitutional Assembly could restructure Russia's political system. The new Commissariat had three Georgians, three Armenians, three Azerbaijanis and two Russians. It was more an attempt to keep order in the region than an assertion of nationalist sentiment.

In Central Asia generally conservative Muslim religious leaders co-operated with nonsocialist Russians against both Muslim reformers and Russian leftists. In Tashkent, where a Left SR- and left Menshevik-led effort at Soviet power failed in September, on October 26 the Russian radicals proclaimed Soviet power and support for the new Petrograd government. The new Tashkent Revolutionary Committee, however, was entirely European- and Left SR-dominated, an island in a more conservative Muslim sea. It rejected allowing native peoples to partici-pate in the new government, and so the Muslim political leaders with-drew to Kokand and set up a rival government for Turkestan. In Kazakh, Tatar, Bashkir and other major Muslim ethnic regions the general trend was for religious-nationality leadership to take advantage of the October Revolution and the Declaration of the Rights of the Peoples of Russia to declare greater autonomy and local control in the unsettled situation, pending the national and in some cases local constituent assemblies.

At first many nationality leaders believed that they could work with the Bolsheviks, given the latter's position on self-determination. However, two factors quickly disillusioned them. First, they realized that the Bolsheviks were in fact centralizers. Second, most local Bol-sheviks (except in Latvia) tended to be hostile to nationalist aspirations and to rely primarily on elements such as Russian emigrants, industrial workers, Russian garrison soldiers and other non-native urban popula-tions (versus the more rural native populations). This soon provoked hostility and in some areas fighting between nationalist and Soviet armed forces. As a result the new regime's control over most major nationality areas was either nonexistent or tenuous, often based on the soviet in one or two large cities having declared for Soviet power, but having little influence outside that city among the majority of the population.

The October Revolution severed the legitimacy and acceptance of the Petrograd government's authority and created political uncertainty in the nationality regions. National organizations, as other local political bodies, took government authority increasingly into their own hands. Based on principles of self-determination and self-rule, they became effectively independent political centers, with or without declaring full independence. Often they saw themselves as performing a holding action until the meeting of the Constituent Assembly and, in some cases, nationality-based local constituent assemblies. Most still looked to some type of autonomy within a federal state, although some were moving toward complete independence, especially as they saw Russia as deteriorating into a chaos they hoped to escape.

By the opening of 1918 the new Soviet government could claim to have the allegiance – or at least nonopposition – of the army and of the local governments of most of the major cities and provincial capitals of the Russian heartland, and to have under its nominal authority much of the non-Russian territory of the old imperial Russian state. That masked two great weaknesses, however. First, control over many areas was tenuous. In most of the areas where Soviet power had been proclaimed that was done in the major cities, which often were quite unrepresentative of the surrounding countryside, whether for social or nationality reasons. Worrisome pockets of resistance still existed, the attitude of the peasants was uncertain and some nationalities, including Ukraine, were moving toward full independence. Indeed, a peculiarity of November–December 1917 is that even as Bolshevik or Bolshevik-led forces secured the spread of the revolution through the provincial capitals of the empire, the villages were at the same time mostly voting for the SRs (right, center and left) and nationality parties in the elections to the Constituent Assembly. Second, the Soviet government still depended on the Left SRs not only centrally but also in many local soviet governments. These SRs still supported a multiparty socialist government, whereas Lenin remained uncomfortable with that idea – and with the Left SRs as allies. Nonetheless, whatever its insecurities, the broad acceptance of the regime during November and December gave a measure of stability and allowed it to address social-economic issues as well as political problems in Petrograd.

Social and economic restructuring

The Russian Revolution was a social as well as a political revolution, and the Bolshevik rise had been based in significant part on their advocacy of radical and swift social revolution. Not surprisingly, therefore, amidst their many problems the Bolshevik leadership moved quickly to carry out a fundamental restructuring of society, supported in most instances by the Left SRs and other radicals. In doing so they also attempted to fulfill the basic aspirations of the working class, soldiers and peasants. The land decree was the first step in that direction. Next the new government issued a dizzying array of economic and social decrees and proclamations during its first weeks. On October 29 the new government decreed a law on the eight-hour work day, one of the primary aspirations of workers since February but never enacted as law by the Provisional Government. On November 2 it issued the "Declaration of the Rights of the Peoples of Russia" (mentioned above), which declared the abolition of all privileges as well as disabilities based on nationality or religion and affirmed the right of self-determination. A decree on November 10 abolished the many social, legal and civil distinctions, ranks and titles that were part of old Russia, giving legal force to the egalitarian social revolution sweeping the country in 1917 (the original motion was introduced by a Left SR and carried into effect a project discussed by the Provisional Government in the summer but not implemented). Church schools were transferred to the People's Commissariat of Education by decree of November 11. On November 22 the old judicial system was abolished and replaced by new "people's courts" composed of individuals either elected or appointed by local soviets. On December 16 a decree abolished all ranks and titles in the army and provided for election of commanders. Decrees of December 16 and 18 made marriage, divorce and registration of births and deaths civil procedures, stripping the church of its control over these matters. Divorce, previously difficult, now became a simple matter of either party applying to the local civil authorities. Full separation of church and state followed by an act of January 20, 1918. The new wave of decrees continued into 1918, bringing the Russian calendar into line with the Western one on February 1/14 and, on a political note, in March renaming the Bolsheviks the Russian Communist Party.[8]

In addition to social changes actually decreed, others were declared to be the intent of the new regime as Bolshevik officials issued proclamations expressing their visions of a new society. On October 29 V. I. Lunacharsky, the new people's commissar of education, declared to "the Citizens of Russia" the regime's determination to introduce "universal, obligatory and free education" in order to "achieve universal knowledge of reading and writing in the shortest possible time," with access to higher education based on ability rather than family wealth.[9] The intention to implement full social insurance against unemployment, illness, injury, old age and other disabilities was announced November 13. The new revolutionary authorities, clearly, were intent on sweeping away the old Russia and starting to fashion a new one. Some Bolsheviks believed that a social and cultural transformation was the very purpose of revolution, without which political changes were meaningless. They hoped to create a whole new proletarian-based culture. Indeed, they saw their project as not merely a revolution in Russia, but the beginning of a worldwide revolutionary process and transformation of humanity.

Economic issues and decrees reinforced the social revolution. The Bolsheviks were committed to creating a socialist society and abolishing private property, but did not agree among themselves on how quickly and by what means that would be accomplished. Lenin and most leaders assumed the state would directly control key sectors, but that for now most private property, including factories, would remain in the hands of its owners but be brought under public supervision and regulation. The focus would be on controlling key institutions such as banks and on creating (and controlling) large syndicates for major industrial sectors (fuel, metallurgy, etc). In this they would build on the already extensive government involvement in managing the economy that had evolved during the war years. This approach was reflected in two of the three main pieces of industrial-economic legislation of the first weeks, the nationalization of banks on December 14 and the creation of the All-Russia Council for the National Economy on December 1. Both were designed to give the government greater control over the economy in order to deal with the immediate economic crisis as well as to shape its longer-term development. Introducing socialism immediately or nationalizing industry were secondary concerns at this stage.[10]

The leaders were pushed toward the latter, however, by the industrial workers' response to the economic crisis as well as their general aspirations. Workers still expected the revolution to address problems of adequate wages, job security, working conditions, workplace dignity and a voice in factory affairs. Central to the concerns of the workers, therefore, was the third major piece of economic legislation, the Decree on Workers' Supervision (*kontrol'*) of November 14. Workers' supervision, as we have seen, gathered force as a popular demand in the late summer and fall. The decree gave the factory committees much more authority vis-à-vis management than previously and real power now rested with them. Many workers, euphoric over "their" government being in power and faced with continuing economic deterioration (sharpened by the end of military orders that followed the Decree on Peace), quickly gave the decree and workers' supervision a more radical meaning. They called for a more extensive and aggressive involvement in the running of the factories and the disposal of their products and resources, even to worker takeover and self-management of the enterprise. One by one, not through a government or Bolshevik plan but in response to specific situations and workers' demands, often to forestall closure, a series of individual enterprises were nationalized in late 1917 and effectively taken over by their workers. Almost all orders for nationalization of factories in late 1917 came from local authorities rather than from the central government, although the former may well have assumed that their actions were in keeping with government policy, given the rhetoric of the radical left in 1917.

Indeed, for many workers and the left wings of the Bolshevik and SR Parties the success of the October Revolution, together with the current economic crisis, demonstrated that it was time to complete the social-economic revolution by dispossessing industrialists, landowners and privileged society in general. They saw broader worker involvement in running the factory as an essential part of the process whereby workers could learn the necessary management skills to take over operation of the socialized factories. They saw it, in the words of the Central Council of Factory Committees on December 7, as "a transitional stage toward organizing the whole life of the country on social lines."[11] Local city soviets issued their own revolutionary social and economic decrees, while Red Guards, peasants and other groups moved to dispossess the old upper and middle classes through thousands of separate acts of property seizure and intimidation. Workers, encouraged by socialist ideas and their own economic plight, pushed the Bolshevik leaders faster than the latter wished to go. For Lenin the factory committees and other kinds of mass activism were useful for the political support they gave (although he did get genuinely enthusiastic about them sometimes), but they could not be the basis for future economic and political authority. Moreover, Lenin and most other Bolshevik leaders stressed the importance of drawing on the skills of the old managers and owners in the current economic crisis and transitional stage; supervision, not replacement, of them was needed. Yet, the regime could not ignore – or fully control – demands of their key constituents at this time, and so followed a rather inconsistent economic policy for the rest of 1917, especially on workers' supervision and nationalization.

Agrarian issues added to the government's economic problems even as it encouraged a fundamental social and economic revolution in the countryside. The Decree on Land had the effect of legitimizing peasant land seizure thus far and of stimulating seizure of the rest. Otherwise the October Revolution had remarkably little effect for the next few weeks on events in the countryside, where the revolution continued on the course already set. Although the Bolsheviks had some misgivings about this process of land seizure by peasants (they preferred state ownership and large farms), their Left SR allies had none and political considerations dictated that at this stage they focus on continuing the destruction of the old order and securing the allegiance of the peasantry. The peasants were left to take ever more control of the countryside and its life and resources. In the short time from the October Revolution to the Constituent Assembly, which presumably would give fuller legal confirmation to land distribution – something not unimportant to the peasants – they proceeded as they had, but with the legal sanction of the land decree. Thus land redistribution was left primarily to the village communes, which dealt with land by their own lights, combining traditional practices with new conditions introduced by 1917 such as broader participation within the village and the active role of returning soldiers. For a short time, until the opening of civil war, the peasants were left to sort out their own affairs and continue their own rural revolution.

Unfortunately the rural land seizures added to the already serious problem of inadequate flow of grain to the markets and cities, since it was the estates and larger producers who marketed the most foodstuffs. Factories sent out groups to trade manufactured goods for food and the government joined them: in the first ten days of November almost 7,000 workers and sailors went out from Petrograd with cloth and tools to exchange for foodstuffs. After the armistice the government began to send goods originally produced for the army to the villages in return for grain.[12] Trade alone, however, was inadequate. The Soviet government, as the Provisional Government before it, had to send armed detachments to grain-producing regions to try to force the shipment of foodstuffs, while reducing urban rations. Food supply remained a serious problem for the regime, threatening its core support, the urban workers and the military garrisons, especially in Petrograd and Moscow.

A dual disillusionment took place at the end of 1917. On the one hand, despite gains such as workers' supervision being enacted into law, worker hopes stimulated by October and establishment of "their" regime faltered as the economy continued to deteriorate. The general welfare of workers, and of all the urban population, declined with the economy. Conditions got worse. At the same time Lenin and the

Bolshevik leaders became disillusioned with the self-activism of the masses – about which Lenin had been uncharacteristically enthusiastic in his writings during the weeks just before October – and turned toward a more typical emphasis on central guidance and control of the economy as well as political control.

The economic problems helped push Lenin and the Bolsheviks toward centralizing and authoritarian measures, which they preferred for ideological reasons anyway. Centralized control, political and economic, was fundamental to the Bolshevik vision – a strong central authority was seen as necessary to direct state political organs and to regulate economic life, including privately owned enterprises. The Bolsheviks, Lenin wrote at the end of September in "Can the Bolsheviks Retain State Power," "are centralists by conviction, by their programme and by the entire tactics of their party."[13] The establishment of the All-Russia Council for the National Economy was a reflection of this. Indeed, in the economy and other areas the Bolsheviks found themselves in a new role after October 25. They had to shift from being opponents of an existing order to defining and defending a new one. Very soon calls for discipline and order filled their speeches. Lenin's November and December speeches and writings contained sentiments such as that the new socialist order would require "a tremendous organizational effort" and called on the population to "devote mind and will . . . to arousing the slumberers and irresolute . . . at this, perhaps the most serious and responsible, moment of the great Russian revolution." He appealed to railway workers: "Comrades, we need your help to get the railways going. Only by joining efforts with you can we overcome the disorder."[14] The new turn toward organization, discipline and public order, as well as simple survival, required creating a new governmental apparatus.

Creating a government: MRC, Sovnarkom, Cheka

Amid all their other problems, the Bolsheviks had to confront the task of the organization of political power, and the even more fundamental question of the purposes of power. These issues were focused around the intertwined problems of creating a government structure while at the same time dealing with the forthcoming Constituent Assembly and other political parties, especially their erstwhile allies, the Left SRs. For Lenin the problem was how to ensure that Soviet power meant Bolshevik power. In facing that he had to answer basic questions about the nature and purposes of political power in the new order, and with those answers rested the future of democracy in Russia.

Success in consolidating power and carrying through a radical social program required the development of an effective government apparatus. Lenin had given little attention to this before taking power. Illuminating, however, was Lenin's "Can the Bolsheviks Retain State Power?," written at the end of September. He argued that the new state would take over the structures of the old system – banks, factories, schools, etc. – and, by changing who controlled them, use them to build a new order. After October Lenin applied this concept to government ministries as well. Indeed, existing government institutions and structures were for the most part retained, although some were extensively transformed. A perusal of government decrees issued in late 1917 is striking for the number that are directed toward taking over existing institutions and infusing them with a new spirit.

For the first two or three weeks after the October Revolution the primary vehicle of revolutionary government was the Petrograd MRC. Its commissars took control of various civil agencies in Petrograd. It confronted the food and other shortages by draconian measures of rationing and requisitioning overseen by its own special commissars. It enforced press censorship and confiscation of presses. It took on the tasks of issuing residency permits for Petrograd, of licensing theatrical performances and of allocating housing, as well as the wide range of tasks of urban government and police. It dealt with anything which involved the possibility of opposition to the new government and even had a special section to arrest suspected counterrevolutionaries and to carry out searches. Its fluid and ever-changing membership, although Bolshevik-dominated, included Left SRs and anarchists, which furthered the image of multiparty government. Part revolutionary-insurrectionary committee, part committee for consolidation of the revolution, part de facto government, it was the key transitional revolutionary power structure for the first weeks of the revolution, until the new Sovnarkom (Council of People's Commissars) could organize itself as a functioning government.

The new government, Sovnarkom, took charge slowly. At first it met irregularly and under tremendous pressure of events, with inexperienced members who lacked a clear notion of how the new government should function. Decisions, not unlike the Petrograd Soviet Executive Committee after the February Revolution, were taken by whatever member of the Sovnarkom or MRC felt competent to do so, sometimes after hurried and informal consultations in crowded offices and hallways. "In the days following the seizure of power the typical people's commissariat consisted of a table, a couple of chairs, and a piece of paper stuck on the wall behind bearing the name of the commissariat."[15] To add to the confusion, MRC, Sovnarkom and Bolshevik Party officials overlapped and all operated out of the same set of offices in the Smolny Institute. Gradually, however, the Sovnarkom began to function as a government executive.

At the same time the state bureaucratic apparatus was brought to heel. When the new people's commissars first went to their ministries they met hostility and passive resistance. Most civil servants refused to recognize the Soviet government; some stayed home but most went to their offices and simply refused to cooperate, quietly ignoring the new decrees and officials. Sometimes they left the room when Bolshevik-appointed officials entered. Often they refused to turn over keys to offices, and some would not even show the new officials where their offices were located. Many apparently felt they could hold out until a "legitimate" government was created by the Constituent Assembly. To deal with this the Bolsheviks used a policy of mixed coercion and incentives. Salaries were modified so as to benefit the lower ranks and induce them to break with the upper ranks, while selective arrest or dismissal of officials removed presumed ringleaders and applied indirect coercion to the rest. The Bolshevik commissars, sometimes backed by Red Guards or sailors, physically set up office in the ministries and gradually began to function. A nationwide strike of government employees in December failed by the end of the year, while the dispersal of the Constituent Assembly in early January removed any hope of waiting the Bolsheviks out in favor of a different government. By early January 1918 the Bolshevik Revolution had successfully taken over the old administrative structure and began using it for new ends. This was essential to Bolshevik success in harnessing the revolutionary turmoil and consolidating power.[16]

The Bolsheviks also quickly turned to repressive measures in the consolidation of power and in building a new government structure. This had profound consequences not only for the immediate task of consolidating power, but for the nature of the state that would result. Lenin had a long history of talking about use of force by a revolutionary government, and immediately after the October Revolution he turned to threats and repressive measures against opponents. The first law issued by the new Sovnarkom, on October 27, instituted press censorship in the name of combating counterrevolution (some papers had already been closed by the MRC). At the same time the MRC, with Lenin's support, readily used force against actual or suspect opponents, who were broadly and vaguely defined. The Bolshevik leaders lumped all nonsocialists (and some socialists) together as enemies quite as readily as Kornilov had lumped most socialists together as "Bolsheviks." Workers who struck against the government's closing of printing presses were treated as enemies as much as were striking civil servants or military opponents.

This trend toward repressive measures alarmed the Left SRs and even some Bolsheviks. As soon as the immediate Kerensky–Krasnov armed threat to the regime was defeated they challenged those policies. A major debate erupted on November 4 in the CEC. Iurii Larin, a recent Bolshevik convert from Menshevism, introduced a resolution revoking the press censorship decree and declaring that "No acts of political repression may be carried out except by authorization of a special tribunal, chosen by the CEC in proportion to the strength of each fraction [party]." It was hardly a ringing declaration of civil rights, but it was enough to set off a major debate. The Left SRs and some Bolsheviks invoked the absurdity of trying to establish democracy and freedom via censorship. Lenin, Trotsky and some other Bolsheviks justified censorship and other repressive measures as essential at the current moment. The Bolshevik-dominated CEC defeated the motion. A Left SR spokesman declared the vote "a clear and unambiguous expression [of support for] a system of political terror and for unleashing civil war." The Left SRs withdrew from the MRC and other quasi-governmental positions which they still held from the time of the October Revolution. More shocking, four Bolshevik people's commissars, linking the debate to the Vikzhel proposal on forming a broad socialist government, resigned their posts, declaring that "a purely Bolshevik government has no choice but to maintain itself by political terror."[17] Lenin, however, held firm and the Bolshevik majority with him. Indeed, the dissident Bolsheviks soon returned to the fold: they lacked a leader who could present an effective alternative to Lenin's view of the party and state.

The Bolsheviks soon moved toward even more repressive measures. On November 28 the Sovnarkom ordered the arrest of leading Kadets, declaring it "a party of the enemies of the people."[18] Some of those arrested had already been elected to the Constituent Assembly, so there were additional political implications. The order sparked another debate in the CEC on December 1. Stanislaw Lapinski of the small Polish Socialist Party charged that "The terror which the . . . [Sovnarkom] is applying against the Kadets will in the nature of things be extended to parties standing to their left [i.e., socialist parties]." Trotsky responded that "You wax indignant at the naked terror which we are applying against our class enemies, but let me tell you that in one month's time at the most it will assume more frightful forms, modeled on the terror of the great French revolutionaries. Not the fortress [imprisonment] but the guillotine will await our enemies."[19]

The turn toward repression required a special organization for that purpose. The new government had, since October 26, relied on the MRC, Red Guards and some soldiers and sailors for this. By early December the political structure had developed to the point at which a new, more permanent organization was needed. On December 6 Sovnarkom, seconded by Lenin in a separate letter, asked Felix Dzerzhinsky, a Polish Bolshevik, to draft proposals for fighting "saboteurs and counterrevolutionaries." The next day Sovnarkom implemented his report with a resolution on creating the "All-Russia Extraordinary Commission for the Struggle with Counterrevolution and Sabotage," generally known simply as the "Cheka" (from the first letter of the second and third words of the name).[20] Although the immediate impulse for it was to create a tool to break the strike of government and white-collar employees, more fundamentally it grew out of Lenin's and the Bolshevik leadership's readiness to use force against opponents. The rhetoric of Lenin, Trotsky and some other Bolsheviks of this period was extremely violent. Physical threats against opponents, class or individual, were a regular part of their statements. The Cheka was the main vehicle for political terror and the origins of the political, or secret, police which under various names became a fundamental part of the later Soviet political system.

The debate over censorship and coercion inevitably raised questions about their implications for the Constituent Assembly. At the CEC meeting of December 1 Isaac Steinberg, in raising objections on behalf of the Left SRs, noted that "The decree [arresting Kadets] suggests a willingness to disrupt the Constituent Assembly."[21] Indeed, Lenin was considering exactly that, for it was the ultimate problem for the Bolsheviks as they struggled with the question of the nature and uses of power, and specifically how to hold on to it and to turn the revolution for Soviet power into a Bolshevik regime.

The Constituent Assembly and the purposes of power

When the new Soviet government was formed in October it had declared itself "provisional" and many of the early decrees and proclamations stated that they were in force until the Constituent Assembly acted. This assumption was shared by Bolsheviks elsewhere also. The Bolshevik leaders of the Saratov Soviet, when declaring Soviet power there, stated that any conflicts among peasants growing out the Saratov Soviet's own land decree would be arbitrated by the soviet, "whose decisions are binding until resolution by the Constituent Assembly."[22] In the first weeks after the October Revolution it was widely assumed by most political activists that the Bolshevik government was temporary, until the Constituent Assembly in January. Lenin, Trotsky and growing numbers of the Bolshevik leadership, however, were not willing to consider their government provisional or to relinquish power. Yet, as returns for the Constituent Assembly elections came in during November they showed that the Bolsheviks would be a distinct minority. How was the circle to be squared? How could the Bolsheviks solidify *this* government and avoid handing over power to rivals at the Constituent Assembly?

Central to the political dilemma facing the regime were the SRs and their peasant supporters. Bolshevik power was urban-based and their claim to authority rested especially on the Second All-Russia Congress of Soviets of Workers' and Soldiers' Deputies, the Petrograd Soviet and other city soviets; most of these did not include the peasants directly. Thus most of the population was outside the formal organizational structure upon which the government was founded. Moreover, the Bolsheviks had to face the reality that the peasants still gave their support primarily to the SRs and that therefore the upcoming Constituent Assembly elections would probably return an SR majority. Although the SR Party was in the process of splitting and the Left SRs generally supported Soviet power and worked with the Bolsheviks, the Left SRs had significant differences with the latter and affinities with their party comrades. Only small shifts in policy by the SR center might result in the Left SRs abandoning the Bolsheviks for the former, and the SR center had indeed shown signs even before the October Revolution of moving toward abandoning coalition with the liberals in favor of some kind of socialist government.

A new All-Russia Congress of Peasants' Deputies, therefore, loomed as both a problem and an opportunity. The All-Russia Congress of Peasants' Deputies in May had elected an executive committee dominated by the center and right wings of the SR Party. Now, after the October Revolution, the SR leaders moved to convene a special peasants' congress so that they could exert more influence on political events. This began with a "preliminary conference" opening in Petrograd on November 10. Most deputies represented soldiers, while the peasant rural districts themselves were underrepresented. This gave the Bolsheviks an important minority presence. The right and left wings of the SR Party, the latter supported by the Bolsheviks, struggled for control of the congress amid credentials challenges, walkouts and returns, and confused and sometimes contradictory resolutions. The proceedings provided ample justification for Lenin's anxiety about the reliability of his Left SR allies. Finally the delegates split into two rival assemblies. The Left SRs and Bolsheviks, with a small majority, declared theirs the legitimate assembly, dubbed the "Extraordinary Congress." When the actual Second Congress of Peasants' Deputies convened on November 26, the disputes and the split into two assemblies were repeated.[23] As a result the Socialist Revolutionary movement splintered beyond repair and in the process undermined its ability to influence decisively the course of the revolution. The Bolshevik–Left SR alliance, in contrast, was reinforced despite the disagreements over censorship and terror.

This facilitated Lenin's effort to solve the problem of how to deal with the peasants and the Socialist Revolutionaries while retaining power. The Bolsheviks and the Left SRs from the "Extraordinary Congress" agreed on November 13 to create a restructured and much enlarged All-Russia Central Executive Committee of Workers', Soldiers' and Peasants' Soviets. This new expanded CEC included 108 representatives from the old CEC elected in October at the Congress of Soviets of Workers' and Soldiers Deputies (101 original and 7 coopted members), an equal 108 from the left-dominated Congress of Peasants' Deputies, 100 from army and navy units and 50 from the trade unions. The new CEC's unwieldy size reduced its ability to challenge Sovnarkom's control of the actual running of government affairs (as it sometimes had done since October). The Bolshevik–Left SR alliance was taken a step further on December 9 when the Left SRs finally joined the Council of People's Commissars, although in a distinctly minority role. This coalition lasted only until April 1918, but during the critical last month of 1917 it strengthened the position of the fledgling government by making it a multiparty, or at least two-party, government. This undermined one of the criticisms of the Bolsheviks, while not seriously threatening Bolshevik control. It also deepened the split within the SRs and thus further weakened the Bolsheviks' main political rivals.

One of the values of the strengthened alliance with the Left SRs was the support the latter gave – unintentionally perhaps – to Lenin's efforts to evade the implications of the forthcoming Constituent Assembly. The notion of a Constituent Assembly, of a freely and democratically elected body that would establish the fundamental laws and form of government for Russia, was a long-held tenet of both liberal and revolutionary parties. After the February Revolution it had been an article of faith for all political groups that a Constituent Assembly must be elected, which would then determine the basic questions of the political future of Russia. All formations of the Provisional Government had included its speedy convocation in their programs, and the Petrograd Soviet regularly endorsed it as well. Resolutions from soldiers, workers and peasants

Plate 22 Reading campaign posters for the Constituent Assembly elections. People voted by party lists, each of which had a number. List number 2, the large poster with the woman in traditional garb, was for the Kadet Party (officially in 1917 "The Party of People's Freedom"). Courtesy of Jonathan Sanders.

consistently, almost ritualistically, included calls for speedy convocation of the Constituent Assembly. One of the sources of weakness of the Provisional Government had been its delay in convening the assembly while insisting that all fundamental questions – such as land reform, status of national minorities, etc. – had to await it. The delay fed popular fears that counterrevolutionaries were trying to block the assembly, and many resolutions for Soviet power linked that to guaranteeing that the Constituent Assembly would meet. The Bolshevik Party had been especially vociferous in attacking the Provisional Government for its slowness in organizing the election, accusing it of attempting to foil the opportunity of the people to express their will though the Constituent Assembly. On October 3 the main Bolshevik newspaper wrote that "In order for the Constituent Assembly to take place . . ., in order for decisions of the Constituent Assembly to be fulfilled . . . the Congress of Soviets . . . [must] take into its hands both power and the fate of the Constituent Assembly."[24] The Provisional Government finally scheduled elections for November 12, but by that time it had been overthrown.

After October 25 some of the Bolsheviks, including Lenin, wanted to cancel the elections, but other leaders successfully opposed such a radical step and the elections were allowed to proceed. The elections in fact probably bought valuable time for the new Bolshevik regime. Many of their opponents were relatively quiescent during November and December precisely *because* of the presumably forthcoming Constituent Assembly. They saw the new Bolshevik government as simply another of the provisional governments that had succeeded each other since February. The Socialist Revolutionaries in particular took this view of the Bolshevik government as temporary. Their newspapers regularly reminded readers that the actions of the Council of People's Commissars, or of local Bolshevik city governments, were only provisional and that power and all final decisions rested with the soon to be convened Constituent Assembly. Without that perception a more vigorous political and even armed opposition to the Bolsheviks almost certainly would have developed earlier than it did. As long as opponents were confident that the Constituent Assembly would meet, probably with a more moderate socialist majority, there was no need to go much beyond rueful hand wringing at the activities of the Bolsheviks, since their government presumably was only temporary. Only the relatively small groups on the political far right who lumped all socialists together and had little prospects for future electoral success had any reason to consider more vigorous opposition, and they wielded little influence at this juncture.

Lenin and the Bolsheviks thus faced a dilemma over the Constituent Assembly. Predictions of their defeat proved well founded. Overall, the Bolsheviks obtained only about a quarter of the votes, the SRs in their various manifestations received just over half, and the remainder was split among the Kadets, nationality candidates and others. For the assembly itself, the breakdown by membership shows that, of about 703–07 members, the SRs had 370–80 (including about 81 Ukrainian SRs), the Left SR Party 39–40, the Bolsheviks 168–75, the Kadets and the Mensheviks each about 17, and nationality candidates about 77–86; the rest were scattered among other parties.[25] These figures by no means represented a solid SR majority, however. Only about 300 of the SRs represented a solid core of support for the SR leadership. Therefore, the SR leaders had to retain the loyalty of the nationalist-oriented SRs and of some of the left-leaning SRs for a working majority. How long they could do so was questionable. Nonetheless, two points were clear. First, the SRs would have a sufficient majority to control the opening and initial work of the assembly, which presumably would then represent the further working out of the democratic parliamentary processes of the Russian Revolution. Second, the Bolsheviks would be an influential minority, but a minority nonetheless, and therefore presumably would have to relinquish government power.

As it became apparent that the Bolsheviks and their left coalition would not prevail, Lenin began to search for a way out of the problem, for he was not willing to relinquish power. Although Lenin had criticized the Provisional Government for not convening the Constituent Assembly and argued that, "if the Soviets were to win [power], the Constituent Assembly would be certain to meet; if not, there would be no such certainty,"[26] now he and the Bolsheviks began to challenge the legitimacy of the Constituent Assembly and to threaten violence against it. Nikolai Bukharin suggested that when it met the left delegates should expel the rest and declare a "revolutionary convention."[27] The idea of a revolutionary convention (inspired by the French revolutionary model) that in some way combined the Constituent Assembly and the forthcoming Third Congress of Soviets was widely discussed. M. S. Uritsky (whom the Bolsheviks put in charge of the elections and such preparations for the Constituent Assembly as were made) put the precarious status of the assembly most clearly: "Shall we convene the Constituent Assembly? Yes. Shall we disperse it? Perhaps; it depends on circumstances."[28] Meanwhile, Lenin prepared the party and public for violence against the Constituent Assembly by publishing a series of "theses" on the assembly in *Pravda* on December 13. He declared a republic of soviets to be "a higher form of democracy" and that because of "the divergence between the elections . . . and the interests of the working and exploited classes," the only function for the Constituent Assembly would be to endorse the Soviet revolution and its actions.[29] The theses left no doubt but that Lenin was prepared to ignore the election results.

Others also began to waver in their commitment to the Constituent Assembly. Most importantly, the Left SRs joined in the talk of dispersal. In some contexts they continued to defend its sanctity, but in others questioned it. The resolution of a congress of the Special Army on November 27 that the Constituent Assembly must defer to Soviet power passed with the help of Left SRs as well as Bolsheviks.[30] More telling, a Left SR party congress on November 28 stated that they would support the Constituent Assembly only if it put into effect the policies of the Second Congress of Soviets. Maria Spiridonova, their firebrand orator, stated that it might be necessary to disperse the assembly. They joined the Bolsheviks in trying to devise mechanisms by which elected deputies might be recalled through actions of local soviets, which they hoped would allow Left SRs to replace right or centrist SRs in many rural districts, and in discussions of purging the assembly of its nonsocialist members and turning it into a "revolutionary convention."[31] On the other side some Kadets, looking at the assembly's composition and the activities of the Bolsheviks, also began to give up on it and to look to alternatives, such as the armed opposition gathering in south Russia.

As the date for the Constituent Assembly neared, with a distinct possibility that it might be dispersed, the opposing sides acted in remarkably different ways. The Bolsheviks not only began a propaganda campaign against the Constituent Assembly, they also took steps to back up any action against the assembly. As Bolshevik delegates arrived they were briefed and sent to factories and barracks to prepare support for dispersing the assembly. Especially reliable military and Red Guard units patrolled the streets, prepared to break up any demonstrations of support for the Constituent Assembly or the Bolsheviks' opponents. The Bolsheviks also had the advantage that their support had been strongest in cities such as Petrograd and among troops of the nearby Northern and Western Fronts and the Baltic Fleet. In contrast the SRs made little effort to prepare physical support. That was admittedly difficult given that their support came primarily from the millions of peasants spread across the vastness of Russia and had sunk to a new low among the garrison soldiery and urban workers. Even so they made little effort to mobilize their still substantial supporters in Petrograd factories and barracks, although they did mount a demonstration of support for the assembly on the day of its opening.

Part of the problem for the Constituent Assembly's adherents was that for the worker, soldier and peasant masses the importance of the assembly had declined. It was still desirable in some vague way, but no longer essential. The soviets – through the Congress of Soviets, the Sovnarkom and local soviets – had already acted to fulfill their main aspirations, making the Constituent Assembly less important, even unnecessary. The Decree on Land had given the peasants land; they did not need the Constituent Assembly to decide that. The soldiers' yearning for peace had been met by the armistice, which validated the new government in their eyes and made the Constituent Assembly less important. For the workers, the new Soviet government had given them "workers' supervision" and various other benefits. For all these key constituencies, what then was the practical purpose of the Constituent Assembly? Moreover, Soviet power and the soviets, central and local, were their institutions, responsible to them and representing their aspirations. The Constituent Assembly, on the other hand, represented all social and political groups and therefore was to be viewed with apprehension; the "bourgeoisie" might somehow yet use it to wrest control of power and nullify their gains.

Nonetheless, the Constituent Assembly opened the afternoon of January 5, 1918, in the Tauride Palace. There was a certain symmetry to the use of the Tauride Palace. It had been the meeting place of the State Duma in 1906, Russia's first attempt at parliamentary government. Then in 1917 it was the focal point of the February Revolution and the birthplace of the Petrograd Soviet and the Provisional Government, when workers and soldiers of a very different frame of mind had also crowded into it. Now, in January 1918, it was a hostile armed camp with an unfriendly "guard" of sailors and Red Guards and the spectators' gallery filled with an antagonistic crowd, some of them drunk and many of them armed. Some of the deputies, again reminiscent of February at the palace, feared that they would not emerge alive. Vladimir Zenzinov, a Right SR, recalled that "We entered the building with heads held high, prepared for death – we were all persuaded that the Bolsheviks would use force . . . many of us were convinced that we would not return home alive."[32]

The Bolsheviks disrupted the Constituent Assembly's beginning when Iakov Sverdlov seized the gavel from the senior deputy who was to open it and instead opened it in the name of the CEC, i.e., the government. The SR majority held firm, however, and elected Victor Chernov president of the assembly. The Bolsheviks then introduced a resolution that would have had the Constituent Assembly limit its authority to working on problems of reorganizing society on a socialist basis and otherwise recognizing the actions of the Council of People's Commissars. This was rejected, and the Bolsheviks and Left SRs walked out. The assembly proceeded to declare Russia a republic, approve the armistice with Germany and issue a land law. Just as business on the land law was being concluded during the early morning hours of January 6, the "guards" assigned by the government insisted that the meeting end because they were tired. Under this pressure Chernov hastened through the vote on the land and other laws, and at 4:40 a.m., after over twelve hours of meeting, the assembly adjourned for the night.[33]

The assembly planned to reconvene at noon, but before then the Bolshevik–Left SR led Central Executive Committee ordered its dissolution and Red Guards prevented the delegates from reentering the meeting hall. Immediate efforts by the SRs to stage demonstrations in support of the assembly were broken up by force, and longer-term efforts on its behalf foundered on popular apathy. The indifference to its fate outside political circles indicated the extent to which the population was politically weary and had little understanding of or care for abstract political symbols or democratic procedures.

The dispersal of the Constituent Assembly effectively marked the end of the revolution. By this action the Bolsheviks announced that they would not be voted from power. If they could not be voted from office, then political struggle was no longer an option and the only alternative was armed opposition. Only by force could they be removed. Civil war was inevitable and would now determine the future of Russia and its peoples.

11   Conclusions

The Russian Revolution of 1917 was a series of concurrent and over-lapping revolutions: the popular revolt against the old regime; the workers' revolution against the hardships of the old industrial and social order; the revolt of the soldiers against the old system of military service and then against the war itself; the peasants' revolution for land and for control of their own lives; the striving of middle-class elements and educated society for civil rights and a constitutional parliamentary system; the revolution of the non-Russian nationalities for rights and self-determination; the revolt of most of the population against the war and its seemingly endless slaughter. People also struggled over differing cultural visions, over women's rights, between nationalities, for domination within ethnic or religious groups and among and within political parties, and for fulfillment of a multitude of aspirations large and small. These various revolutions and group struggles played out within the general context of political realignments and instability, growing social anarchy, economic collapse and the ongoing world war. They contributed to both the revolution's vitality and the sense of chaos that so often overwhelmed people in 1917. The revolution of 1917 propelled Russia with blinding speed through liberal, moderate socialist and then radical socialist phases, at the end bringing to power the extreme left wing of Russian, even European, politics. An equally sweeping social revolution accompanied the rapid political movement. And all of this occurred within a remarkably compressed time period – less than a year.

The February Revolution released the pent-up frustrations and aspirations of the population, who put forward long lists of expectations from the revolution. These, and their fulfillment or nonfulfillment, profoundly shaped the working out of the revolution. Moreover, the people of the Russian Empire quickly organized to fulfill their aspirations. Within a few weeks they created a vast array of organizations for self-assertion: thousands of factory committees, army committees, village assemblies, Red Guards, unions, nationality and religious organizations, cultural and educational clubs, women's and youth organizations, officers' and industrialists' associations, householders' associations, economic cooperatives and others. These many organizations represented genuinely popular movements and gave form to the hopes and aspirations of the peoples of the empire. For all inhabitants of the Russian state, Russian and non-Russians, of whatever class, gender, occupation or other attribute, the revolution stood for the opening of a new era and a better future. The struggle was over how to satisfy often competing visions and conflicting aspirations.

Along with new organizations, new revolutionary language, symbols and rituals emerged to express the ideas and aspirations of the revolution. As Figes and Kolonitskii note, "Words and symbols acted as a code of communication, whose signals served to sanction and legitimize the actions of the crowd, to define the revolution's common enemies, to uphold principles and generate authority for certain leaders."[1] The new revolutionary language and symbols were omnipresent in daily speech, print, dress, demonstrations, and all public functions. They acquired political significance as political parties and other groups struggled to appropriate these symbols and to attach their own programs to them. Success or failure in mastering the new revolutionary vocabulary and symbolism was important in the failure of the liberals and moderate socialists and the success of the radicals and Bolsheviks.

Certain words became shorthand for broad aspirations, fears, and belief systems. They defined both one's own group and the enemy, legitimized one's own actions, and de-legitimized opponents. The most potent positive word was "democracy," with words such as freedom, liberty, and republic close behind. In contrast, "bourgeois" and "bourgeoisie" quickly developed as potent negative terms against which much of the lower classes could be mobilized, as well as terms such as "counter-revolutionaries" and, after August, "Kornilovite." "Dark forces" and "German agents" were used vaguely but widely and effectively to mobilize sentiments against a variety of real and imagined enemies. The vocabulary of class (and, by extension, of class conflict) was especially powerful in 1917 because it could both express an important identity and unite large numbers of people in a common language of political struggle that had broad appeal to all those excluded from the world of wealth and privileges. Particularly striking is the dominance of socialist terminology and its success in framing political discourse during the revolution. "Citizen," with its broadly inclusive connotations of revolutionary unity and a liberated people, was very popular, especially in the early months, but was increasingly challenged by the more exclusive "comrade." Comrade(s), signaling recognition of certain people as democrats, revolutionaries, and socialists, was at once a unifying term for the political left and the lower classes and a way to mark off others to whom the term was not applied – the middle and upper classes, much of educated society, and non-socialists. Other vocabularies of identity – nationality, peasant, soldierly comradeship, gender, youth, etc. – played important mobilizing roles, forging unity and expressing programs of action in a word.

Renaming of places, objects, and people was part of the new revolutionary symbolism. Streets, towns, and naval ships bearing tsarist names were renamed. The naval warship "Alexander II" became "Freedom" and the "Tsarevich" was renamed the "Citizen," for example. Streets and squares were similarly renamed, and some stores adopted the new revolutionary words as names: "Democracy," "Red Flag," amongst others. Some individuals with names reminiscent of the former regime (Romanov, Rasputin, for example), or whose names were otherwise considered unsuitable for the new age, petitioned for a change of name, often choosing one with a revolutionary flavor (Republic, Freedom, Citizen, Democrat).

Sound was an important part of this revolutionary world. Speeches, debates, and shouted slogans of demonstrators were part of daily life. Revolutionary songs and music accompanied most public activity in 1917. In February, demonstrators marched singing songs of protest and unity. Mutinous troops on February 27 and 28 often marched out of their barracks led by their regimental bands. Revolutionary songs were played constantly at public meetings and during demonstrations, and often leaflets with revolutionary songs were handed out. The "Marseillaise" (in both the original French and more militant Russian version) was played constantly and became the unofficial anthem of 1917. When theaters reopened, orchestras often prefaced performances with the Marseillaise, while revolutionary themes, especially celebrations of February, were sometimes inserted into programs. "Concert meetings" combining music and revolutionary speeches became popular. Both the Mensheviks and the Bolsheviks encouraged the "Internationale," an avowedly class protest song, which was little known at first but was played and sung more and more frequently as the year progressed.

A new visual revolutionary symbolism also was everywhere, most conspicuously in the omnipresence of red: red banners, red cockades, red armbands, red ribbons in coat buttonholes or pinned to garments, red draping speakers' platforms, and other displays. Red, the traditional color of revolution since the nineteenth century, became the universal symbol of the Russian Revolution. Even foreign visitors put red ribbons in their suit buttonholes. On the other hand, tsarist symbols, such as the two-headed eagle, were pulled down and destroyed, sometimes in public rituals. On another level, the street behavior of soldiers, from the cutting off of officers' shoulder boards to wearing their own hats and uniforms askew, powerfully symbolized a world turned upside down.

The new revolutionary language and symbols came together especially in the festivals that were so popular during the first months of the revolution. The great March 23 burial of victims of the revolution in Petrograd and the April 18 "May Day" celebrations were the largest and most famous revolutionary festivals; picture postcards of them circulated throughout the country and even abroad. At the former, after massive parades of soldiers and others through Petrograd, 184 people were buried with great ceremony – revolutionary, not religious – at the "Field of Mars" in Petrograd, attended by the leaders of the Provisional Government and the Petrograd Soviet. The location was renamed "Square of the Victims of the Revolution." During the spring, festivals of freedom were held throughout the country. These were festooned in red and accompanied by the Marseillaise and other revolutionary songs and by fervent speeches about freedom and democracy. They almost always included parades in the city, town, or village center, with marchers decked out in their best clothes and carrying red banners inscribed with revolutionary slogans, both traditional ones such as "Land and Liberty" and new ones such as "Long Live a Democratic Republic." They often included ritualistic destruction of tsarist emblems and portraits and swearing of allegiance to the Provisional Government.

The new revolutionary atmosphere was even reflected in moving pictures: 53 of 245 movies made in 1917 had revolutionary themes. Immediately after the February Revolution, film makers produced a rash of films and documentaries about the revolution and revolutionary movement, including ones providing a negative characterization of Nicholas and of Rasputin. By mid-year, however, as the optimism of the early weeks faded, fewer films presented revolutionary themes and movie-makers reverted to standard themes such as romance, melodrama, and mystery. Darker themes of suicide, violence, Satan, and pornography became more prevalent, perhaps reflecting the collapse of the ideals of spring and a growing pessimism about Russia's future.[2]

The new language and symbolism was part of a new era of mass politics ushered in by the February Revolution. Mass activism was central to the major political crises of 1917 and to the revolution's rapid political evolution. It had forced the Duma to go much further than it had intended during the February Revolution. It triggered the April Crisis and formation of coalition government, then demanded the latter's replacement by a Soviet government during the July Days (unsuccessfully), and played an important role in Kornilov's defeat in August. Through elections it radicalized the political composition of city councils, soviets, factory and soldiers' committees, trade unions, and other organizations, and thus helped set the stage for the October Revolution.

This popular activism created a dilemma for educated society. Educated society, and the intelligentsia in particular, believed in democracy and many had an almost mystical belief in "the people." At the same time, they saw the revolution as an opportunity not merely to take the government and its powers away from an inept old regime, but an opportunity to use it to implement long held ideas about the restructuring of society. Ensconced in the leadership of both the government and soviets, they still thought in terms of the old notion of the "consciousness" of the politically educated minority counterposed to the "spontaneity" of the masses, who had yet to learn how to be responsible citizens and understand the broader interests of the state and nation. Both the leaders of the Provisional Government, in all its compositions, and the socialist leaders of the soviets saw themselves as tutors of the people, who could easily be led astray if not properly guided. They feared an anarchism of the masses and saw the Bolsheviks as feeding that tendency. Both liberal and moderate socialist intelligentsia in 1917 were strongly "statist" and increasingly used "interests of state" to defend measures that were unpopular with the masses. Moreover, they saw the state as the mechanism through which their specific policies could be implemented and "enlightenment" brought to the people. This tutorial approach clashed with the ambitions of the mass of the population, who saw themselves as full and equal citizens. Indeed, many people among the lower orders saw the revolution not only as a vehicle for fulfilling specific aspirations, but as a means of throwing off altogether the domination of the upper and middle, educated classes (increasingly lumped together as "the bourgeoisie"). The mass of workers, soldiers, and peasants had an uneasy relationship with their would-be tutors, aware that the educated classes had knowledge and skills that were essential and sometimes had to be sought out, but distrustful and even resentful of them as well.

A central problem facing the political elites in 1917 was establishing a viable government and a new political system through which they could work with the new organizations, gain control over popular self-assertiveness and fulfill popular aspirations. The Duma Committee, the Petrograd Soviet and the Provisional Government created on March 2, as well as local soviets and Public Committees, were initial attempts by political elites to consolidate the popular revolution of February, channel popular self-assertion and direct the revolution's future course along lines of their own preference. The political elites, however, were in turmoil, caught in a sweeping political realignment that recast politics. The February Revolution swept away the old right wing and transformed the liberals into the conservatives of the new era, leaving the socialist parties alone on the left wing of the new political spectrum. At the same time both the left (socialists) and the right (nonsocialists) split into two subfactions, with centrist and more extreme wings.

The realignment on the right focused on the Provisional Government and the Kadet Party, the main liberal party. The initial Provisional Government seemed to represent the triumph of liberal, reform Russia over autocratic Russia. It had achieved the first objective of the revolution – the overthrow of the autocracy. The present task was to consolidate its political gains, namely a constitutional parliamentary government and the guarantee of civil rights. Other goals, such as fundamental social and economic reforms, would await the end of the war. There were, however, significant differences among the liberals of the new government and they were deeply divided, especially on the two issues of the war and relations with the Soviet. Many, symbolized by P. N. Miliukov, the Kadet Party leader and foreign minister, were staunchly committed to continuing the war and strongly opposed the role the Petrograd Soviet was playing in affairs. They became the effective right wing of the new politics. At the same time a more centrist viewpoint quickly emerged which stressed cooperation with the more moderate socialists of the Soviet as well as a willingness to consider a way out of the war other than by total victory. The key members of this grouping were the new minister-president, Prince G. E. Lvov, the left Kadet N. V. Nekrasov and A. I. Konovalov, leader of the small Progressist Party. These were men for whom party labels were less important than a set of shared attitudes toward the political and social issues of the day. This loosely defined center-right bloc quickly came to dominate the first Provisional Government.

The parallel realignment on the left among socialist parties was a continuation of a political recasting that had begun earlier in arguments among socialists about cooperation with the liberals and over their response to the war. The revolution intensified those issues. Two returning political leaders with fundamentally different responses to these issues and conflicting programs of revolutionary action by the Soviet, Irakli Tsereteli and Vladimir Lenin, drove the realignment on the left and Soviet policies.

Tsereteli returned from Siberian exile on March 20 and led a group which forged the Menshevik–SR led bloc of "moderate socialists" under the banner of "Revolutionary Defensism." Composed of the bulk of the SR and Menshevik Parties plus smaller groups such as the Bund and Popular Socialists, this bloc dominated the Petrograd Soviet until September and the Moscow Soviet and most provincial city soviets until about the same time. The key to the Revolutionary Defensist bloc's identity and success was the war issue. With its combination of an active program for obtaining a negotiated general peace and defense of the country until that could be achieved, Revolutionary Defensism struck a responsive chord in the country and especially among soldiers. It also accepted cooperation with the government and thus was able to forge a working arrangement with the center-right Lvov–Nekrasov–Konovalov group. Indeed, although the moderate socialists saw February as the first step in a much more sweeping social as well as political revolution, they also foresaw the difficulties of an immediate socialist revolution and looked toward an indeterminate but prolonged process. They therefore entered into a working arrangement with some of the liberals for a centrist coalition that they hoped would provide temporary political stability as well as major if limited political and social-economic gains. The price, however, was compromise and temporization on issues ranging from the war to land distribution and workers' aspirations. As a result the Revolutionary Defensists soon came under attack from the radical left, which called for a more rapid and sweeping revolution.

The Revolutionary Defensist leaders of the Soviet and the Lvov–Nekrasov–Konovalov bloc in the government had much in common, despite the socialist/nonsocialist division and their disagreements on many specific issues. These men were all members of the small, educated, politically active sector of Russian society and shared many values. They easily spoke the same language of national unity, faith in "the people" and the worldwide significance of the revolution. Their shared values and tacit understandings facilitated cooperation and laid the foundation for the political coalitions and "coalition mentality" that dominated political life until the October Revolution. The overall result of this realignment and centrist cooperation was a new political and governmental system, what one might call the "February System," based on multiparty blocs and quite different from that which anyone would have predicted. This led, from May to October, to a series of "coalition governments," i.e., governments based on a centrist bloc of liberals and moderate socialists that united "all the vital forces of the country," even at the expense of long-held party programs. Moreover, a similar political realignment took place in the major provincial cities, making it a national phenomenon.

Alexander Kerensky soon became the linchpin of the coalition system.

Originally the lone socialist in the government, he quickly joined with the men from the liberal tradition who made up the new center-right around Lvov. Kerensky was the mildest of socialists, however. He stood at the point where moderate socialism blended into the left wing of the liberals and thus was a perfect symbol of the emerging political center and of coalition politics. Kerensky became the essential man, the political hinge on which hung the two wings, left and right, of the new political alignment. This set it up for him to move from being a key member of the Lvov bloc in the first cabinet of the Provisional Government to being, by summer, the government's commanding figure. Kerensky's popularity, even cult, was important because the removal of Nicholas as symbolic as well as actual head of the country, plus the breakdown of coercive power of the state in 1917, created the need for someone with strong personal authority who could symbolize the revolution and state. Kerensky, constantly in the public eye, represented that for the first six months of the Revolution.

The radical left bloc of the general political realignment emerged in opposition to the Revolutionary Defensists, the Provisional Government and the centrist coalition. It was ill defined, disorganized and lacking strong leadership until the return of major political leaders, mostly from abroad. These included Vladimir Lenin of the Bolsheviks, Iulii Martov among the left Mensheviks (Menshevik–Internationalists), Leon Trotsky (who first joined the Interdistrictites and then in July the Bolsheviks) and Mark Natanson and Maria Spiridonova of the Left SRs. Lenin's arrival on April 3 was especially important because it changed the tone of politics. Here was a clear, consistent, and uncompromising opponent of the February System. There were other hard critics, but Lenin differed in two respects: his uncompromising and confident demand for a new order, and the fact that, unlike other critics, he was the leader of a party that could become both the institutional embodiment of his radical posture and a vehicle for working toward the new revolution that he demanded. As a result, even though Lenin was absent from Petrograd during the three and a half months before the October Revolution, he remained a major figure in political calculations, while "Leninist" and "Bolshevik" became generic terms for radicalism regardless of party, catchwords for the general demand for radical change.

The radical left – Bolsheviks, Left SRs, Menshevik-Internationalists, anarchists and others – pressed for more rapid and more sweeping social and economic reforms, demanded more vigorous efforts to end the war, criticized the policies of the Provisional Government and Petrograd Soviet leadership, and increasingly called for the Provisional Government's replacement by an all-socialist government based on the soviets.

Initially the radical left's extremism was out of keeping with the mood of optimism following the collapse of the autocracy. Their oppositional stance, however, positioned these parties and groups to become the beneficiaries of any failures of the government and Soviet leadership to solve the many problems facing the country.

The centrist alliance and February System were tested first of all by the debate over the war and the April Crisis. The war was perhaps the single most important issue of 1917. Its continuation sapped the energies and resources of the country and made it difficult to resolve any of the other problems or meet popular aspirations. It absorbed the attention of political leaders, stimulated broad popular discontent and provoked the first political crisis of the revolutionary regime. The Petrograd Soviet quickly called for an end to the war. This was in part a genuine desire to end the war, but also reflected the extent to which Russian socialists saw the Russian Revolution as an event of world significance. In the words of the Petrograd Soviet's appeal of March 2, the Russian Revolution was not just a national revolution but "the first stage in a world revolution which will end the baseness of war and bring peace to mankind."[3] In contrast, Miliukov and many liberals remained committed to winning the war and viewed the revolution as a domestic affair that did not affect Russia's foreign policy interests.

The socialists therefore launched a concerted attack on Miliukov and the government's war and foreign policy. This criticism undermined the moral as well as physical authority of the first Provisional Government. It also threatened to destroy the fragile political structure created by the February Revolution. The political debate over peace revealed how deeply felt was the popular demand for an end to the war, while the street demonstrations of the April Crisis not only demonstrated popular discontent but also raised the specter of civil war, one of the greatest fears of 1917. As a result the more centrist wings of the liberals and socialists came together to carry out a new political revolution from above in which a coalition of liberals and moderate socialists replaced the original Provisional Government on May 5.

The continued use of the name "Provisional Government" and Lvov's remaining as its head masked the revolutionary nature of the change. The Petrograd Soviet had asserted its predominant power and its socialist leaders now entered the government, something they had earlier refused to do. They brought with them an agenda, however muffled, for a much greater social transformation than the liberals could accept. This set the stage for continued liberal–socialist conflict, only now within as well as outside the government. Moreover, this restructured government proved unable to deal successfully with the war or with the other problems such as the economy. It had no way both to meet the often-conflicting aspirations of the populace *and* hold the coalition together.

The effort of the centrists to guide the revolution was complicated at the center by the existence of two authoritative political institutions, the Provisional Government and the Petrograd Soviet. This created what Russians at the time called *dvoevlastie*, dual authority. Although the coalition government was supposed to end this, it merely transferred the underlying political division to within the government while the institutional dichotomy remained as well. This was because the *dvoevlastie* was not only, or even essentially, an institutional division. Rather, it represented a deep social-political chasm in Russia that divided society broadly into socialists versus nonsocialists, workers versus bourgeoisie, peasants versus landlords, soldiers versus officers. Russians in 1917 saw the revolution very much as a conflict along broad class lines and between the *nizy* (lower classes) and *verkhi* (upper classes). Both found their aspirations incompatible and, fueled by old and new grievances, they struggled for control of the levers of power and, ultimately, of government authority. They did so with full awareness that political authority was a tool for advancing the interests of one group or another.

The *dvoevlastie* at the top found an echo throughout society in conflicts between new revolutionary organizations and established authorities: soldiers' committees against the army command system, local soviets versus city councils, factory committees against factory management and nationalist movements against centralized government were only the most important among a multitude of new popular organizations contesting authority with the government or other hierarchical authorities (new or old). The assertiveness of the new popular organizations hollowed out the government's authority, central and local. At the same time political power passed down to the localities, Russian as well as minority, and to the new popular organizations. Even within Petrograd the Red Guards, city district soviets, unions, workers' and soldiers' committees, and other organizations appropriated authority to themselves and ignored the government's (and sometimes even the Soviet's) orders.

The problems facing the centrist coalition worsened in the summer. The February Revolution had not automatically removed any of the fundamental causes of the revolution except Nicholas and his government. Underlying social and economic problems and the stresses of the war remained. The population expected the Provisional Government to solve these problems and to meet their aspirations, but it could not. Many of the problems were beyond its control, just as many aspirations were unattainable or mutually exclusive. Indeed, the continued deterioration of the economy exacerbated already existent social tensions and the division of society into antagonist social classes. The industrial workers, seeing the gains of spring slip away, sought economic security, greater control over their lives and other improvements that the economic conditions simply could not provide, whatever the intentions of the government. Major nationality groups clamored for autonomy and other rights, becoming ever more assertive. The central government's authority eroded in the provinces. At the same time deteriorating social conditions – crime, public transportation, food shortages, housing and other problems – reinforced the sense of society falling apart.

Moreover, just as social and economic problems increased, the peace program of Revolutionary Defensism stumbled. The attempt of the Revolutionary Defensists to force a peace conference and general peace floundered on the rocks of opposition from Russia's allies. The government and Soviet leaders then made a fateful gamble on a military offensive. This undermined the political base of Revolutionary Defensism. The latter's popularity rested on being a program for defending the country while seeking a quick peace. This the soldiers could accept. As the peace offensive bogged down, however, the coalition government turned toward using the army for a military offensive. This the soldiers would not accept. The basic argument that a military offensive would bring peace nearer was flawed, born of desperation and wishful thinking. It never convinced a war-weary populace. The offensive's unpopularity, compounded by its catastrophic failure, destroyed the prospects for the success of Revolutionary Defensism and the centrist coalition. Workers, soldiers and others turned toward arguments that stressed that they could achieve peace and solve their other problems only through a new revolution that would produce a radically different government more attuned to their needs. This belief came to be summed up by the slogan of "All Power to the Soviets" – Soviet power. Whether such a soviet-based government could in fact solve their problems is another issue, and irrelevant to the point that they *did believe* it in 1917. Their attempt to force the Revolutionary Defensist leaders to accept Soviet power, and implicitly more radical policies, led to the great popular demonstrations known as the July Days.

The July Days have often been called a "dress rehearsal" for the October Revolution. In reality they were more like February than October. The July Days, like the February Revolution, began as popular demonstrations against the war, the economic situation and a government that had lost credibility. Like February, the political parties were active in stimulating discontent but did not plan the actual revolt. Rather, again like February, socialist political leaders, in the July case the Bolsheviks in particular, stepped forward at the end to try to consolidate the popular revolt in the streets (unsuccessfully this time). The July Days and the February Revolution (and the April Crisis), but not the October Revolution, were characterized by massive popular street demonstrations. Such demonstrations were conspicuously absent in the October Revolution, which began and concluded very differently. The similarity with October rested primarily with the popularity of the demand that the Soviet take full power and create a radical revolutionary government, and with the prominent role played by Bolshevik, Left SR and anarchist agitators; it is in this demand for Soviet power and the support from the radical left that the July Days can be called a "prelude" to October.

July and August witnessed contradictory political tendencies. After the July Days the newspaper headlines and editorials, focused on high politics, talked of a conservative political revival and a demand for "order." This turn to the right among political leaders led to the Kornilov Affair. At the same time, however, the small news articles in the inner pages of the newspapers chronicled a leftward drift as workers and soldiers chose more radical leaders for their committees and organizations. The July Days reflected genuine popular discontents and therefore the radical left parties, including the supposedly discredited Bolsheviks, rebounded swiftly among their worker, soldier and urban lower-class and lower middle-class constituencies. These parties supported policies that coincided with popular sentiments, such as opposition to the restoration of the death penalty in the army and the demand for immediate peace and land distributions. Moreover, they provided an explanation of why things had not worked out as expected after February, blaming it on the continued political dominance of the "bourgeoisie" and the economic domination of capitalists and landlords. That argument resonated in the popular mind. The radicals – Bolsheviks, Left SRs, Menshevik–Internationalists, anarchists – articulated the demand for a sweeping change of government and policy and registered rapid gains in worker, soldier and other popular organizations, and even in elections for general city offices.

The moderate socialists, on the other hand, undermined their popular support not only by failed policies, but also because of their opposition to the ideas behind the slogan of Soviet power. By refusing to champion unreservedly worker, soldier and peasant demands and by opposing Soviet power, the Revolutionary Defensists implicitly questioned the legitimacy of the new popular organizations – soviets, factory, soldier and peasant committees and others – as political institutions. They saw these as having important but limited roles at the present. The masses, in contrast, saw them as having a very great present role and could not see any reason why it should not be expanded to include political authority. At the same time the Revolutionary Defensists' involvement in the coalition governments put them in an impossible situation, pushing them away from the more revolutionary aspects of their belief system and toward the politics of compromise in the name of the country's good. They became more accommodating to multiparty, multiclass, all-Russia politics just as the worker and soldier masses were becoming less tolerant and less accommodating to such politics and more supportive of radical, exclusionary politics and social policies.

While cataloging the failures of the Provisional Government and Revolutionary Defensists, we should not lose sight of their successes and, indeed, of the radicalism of the Provisional Government and the "moderates" in 1917. The Provisional Government introduced sweeping reforms, especially but not only in civil rights and freedoms. These were truly remarkable when compared with what had existed in Russia only weeks earlier, and even compared with the world at the time. They attempted to create a democratic and more egalitarian society based on the rule of law rather than arbitrariness, and a political system based on elections and the popular will rather than autocracy or authoritarianism. Their reforms seem timid only in comparison to the even greater demands of an impatient populace and the extraordinary radicalism of Bolshevism and the initial decrees of the Soviet government after the October Revolution. By measuring the Provisional Government against Bolshevism, we measure it against the most radical political party (except anarchists) not only in Russia but perhaps in the world in 1917. That creates a peculiar distortion in evaluating the Provisional Government. This is even more the case if one considers the Revolutionary Defensists and the "moderate socialists." They were hardly moderate by any normal measurement of European socialism of the time, much less in comparison to Russian society before 1917. They were staunch socialists and advocates of a sweeping social-economic transformation that put them on the radical edge of European and world thought of the time. It is only in comparison to the Bolsheviks and their own left wings that they are seen as moderate. Nor should we forget the dilemma of a government or parties committed to sweeping change while preserving some sense of political and social stability, creating democratic institutions and confronted by an all-consuming war. That is a balancing act of the utmost difficulty in the best of times, and these certainly were not that.

The Revolutionary Defensist leaders, having failed in their peace policy, unable to satisfy popular aspirations and tarnished by the

Kornilov Affair, found it impossible to keep control of either the soviets or the Provisional Government. The former began to slip away in August and moved out of their hands even faster in September, while the latter became virtually Kerensky's personal regime. The centrist coalition disintegrated, but neither the moderate socialists nor the liberals could find an alternative and so clung desperately to the idea of coalition government. "Coalition," however, was becoming a source of popular hostility toward the parties supporting it. The urban and soldier masses, thoroughly disillusioned with the February System and fearing the loss of the initial gains of the revolution, sought a leadership committed to more explicitly class-based goals, one that would use the government's resources to help them fulfill their aspirations to the exclusion of rival claimants. At the same time the radical left parties leveled a scathing criticism of the government and Revolutionary Defensist leadership *and* waged a battle for influence in the mass organizations, especially those of the workers and soldiers – the soviets, committees, unions.

The radical left, itself a product of the political realignment of spring and finding its voice especially in the Bolsheviks, Left SRs, Menshevik–Internationalists and anarchists, now moved to take power. At first, in the optimistic early period of the revolution, their radicalism had marginalized them, but soon they were giving voice to popular frustrations and promising a more certain fulfillment of the aspirations of the revolutionary masses. They now presented their own visions of a new and more radical revolution. They pressed for rapid and radical action on the main political and social issues and criticized the inactivity of the coalition government and the moderation of the Revolutionary Defensists. They promised to satisfy fundamental aspirations and endorsed the deepening of social antagonisms as both legitimate and a way to resolve problems. This led to a dramatic surge in popular support for the radical left in the summer and fall that swept them into power under the unifying slogan of "All Power to the Soviets" – Soviet power.

In an ongoing process of debates, agitation and reelection of deputies and leadership in soviets, unions and committees, the left bloc replaced the moderate socialists as the leaders of more and more of these popular organizations. This process has traditionally been described as a series of Bolshevik victories and that is a tempting shorthand for what was in fact a much more complex political situation. The Bolsheviks were only a part, the leading part as it turned out, of a larger radical left bloc that included the Left SRs, Menshevik–Internationalists and anarchists. Many of the resolutions and electoral successes traditionally termed "Bolshevik" were in fact the result of Left SR activity or of the left bloc.

Critical to the rise of the left was the capture of the Petrograd Soviet. This gave the Bolshevik-led left bloc control of the most important political institution in Russia and put them in a position to move to take governmental power. Since they had consistently argued for some kind of all-socialist or soviet-based government, the takeover of the Petrograd Soviet – and of the Moscow and some other city soviets – naturally posed the question: "What are the Bolsheviks planning?"

There is little doubt but that the new leaders of the Petrograd Soviet were planning to use the Second All-Russia Congress of Soviets to declare a transfer of power. The Bolshevik leaders in particular discussed this extensively in party councils and in venues such as the CSNR. There both the more adventuresome demands of Lenin and the cautious appeals of Kamenev and Zinoviev were bypassed in favor of implementing the vastly popular slogan of Soviet power, with the forthcoming congress as the vehicle for achieving it. Such a step would be revolutionary in that it involved overthrowing the existing Provisional Government, and it was in this sense that people talked of a new revolution or a seizure of power. Nor was there any doubt but that such a move would be widely popular and that Red Guards and other activists were preparing to enforce that action. In this scenario the Congress of Soviets would catapult the Bolsheviks and radical left into governmental power, where they would be able to try to carry out the political and social-economic projects that they did, after all, believe in. Their criticism of the moderates was not merely opportunistic. Belief and opportunity dovetailed nicely for the Bolsheviks and other radicals in late 1917.

Nor is there much doubt that the government and other political leaders expected such an attempt to take power. The Left SRs and Menshevik–Internationalists also believed the time had come for some type of new, all-socialist government, through the Congress of Soviets if not through some earlier agency such as the Democratic Conference or other agreement among party leaders. Kerensky appears to have been almost anxious for the Bolsheviks to make a move, foolishly confident that he could crush them and end the threat. The moderate socialists looked on in dismay, still locked in the belief that a Bolshevik attempt to take power would merely open the door to a successful conservative counterrevolution. Some on the political right agreed with this interpretation, but looked forward to it with hope. The question by mid-October seemed to be not so much *would* the Bolsheviks and their allies attempt an overthrow of the Provisional Government by the Congress of Soviets, but what would be the details of the process? What would be the exact nature of the new government? To what extent and how successfully might Kerensky's government resist? Would this spark civil war?

The answer to the question of what would be the result of a declared assumption of power at the Congress of Soviets can never be known, because Kerensky's ill-considered move against Bolshevik newspapers the morning of the 24th opened the way for a transfer of power *before* the congress. All along Bolshevik leaders in Petrograd had been warning Lenin that the workers and soldiers would not come out on behalf of an action by the Bolsheviks, but would in defense of the Soviet and the Congress of Soviets. On October 24–25 they did exactly that. By the time the congress met on the evening of the 25th, power had already been effectively transferred by the workers and soldiers rallying to the defense of the revolution and Soviet against "counterrevolution," capped by Lenin taking advantage of that to proclaim the seizure of power before the congress opened.

In the midst of this seemingly inexorable course of events, the supporting roles of chance and of individual human action are striking. Had the old Revolutionary Defensist leadership not postponed the Congress of Soviets from October 20 to October 25, the Bolsheviks and their allies and supporters would have been even less prepared to take power than they were five days later. A seizure of power before a Congress of Soviets meeting on October 20 would have been virtually impossible even had they intended one (which they did not): the preparations were not there. Nothing resembling the confrontation of the Military Revolutionary Committee with the military authorities on October 21–23 or the psychological and physical preparation for revolution that took place during the "Day of the Petrograd Soviet" on October 22 was planned or possible in the days before October 20. Yet those were essential to any transfer of power, and were key events in the October Revolution that happened.

More critically, the October Revolution would not have commenced nor ended as it did without Kerensky's decision on the 24th. It was Kerensky's attack on Bolshevik newspapers that forced the issue of Soviet power before the congress met, galvanized its supporters and gave Lenin the revolution which he otherwise had little hope of getting. Indeed, Kerensky's action had more to do with the launching and outcome of the October Revolution than did Lenin's own unsuccessful attempt to plot a Bolshevik seizure of power before the Congress of Soviets. Kerensky's blunder provoked the armed struggle that transferred power before the congress met. This changed the nature of the transfer of power and altered the role of the Congress of Soviets and the essential character of the revolution. It gave Lenin the seizure of power before the congress that he had so long, and unsuccessfully, demanded. Kerensky, not Lenin, began the October Revolution. It allowed Lenin to turn a revolution for Soviet power into a Bolshevik Revolution.

Moreover, once the congress opened Lenin found himself the recipient of yet another unpredictable stroke of luck: the walkout of the moderate socialists because of the armed struggle in the streets that Kerensky's action had provoked and that Lenin had seized upon to proclaim Soviet power. That walkout left the Bolsheviks in a majority rather than merely a plurality. Therefore Lenin could proceed relatively unhindered in the steps of the next few weeks, exercising his iron determination to hold power in the face of pressures to share and compromise.

Given the opposition from both the Left SRs and the Kamenev-type moderates within the Bolshevik Party to many of Lenin's and Trotsky's authoritarian measures in the days after October 25, one could speculate on a very different outcome had the transfer of power come as a result of a vote at the Congress of Soviets for a multiparty, all-socialist, Soviet-based government. Without the prior street conflict and the resulting Lenin-inspired declaration of the seizure of power on the morning of the 25th, before the Congress of Soviets met, the congress would have performed quite differently. There would have been no grounds for the walkout by the Menshevik and SR moderates, ever larger portions of which were moving toward accepting some form of all-socialist government. Had they remained at the congress and participated in formation of a new Soviet-based, all-socialist government structure, it would have been a very different government from the one formed after their walkout (and presumably the future of Russia would have been different as well). The October Revolution was a complex mixture of powerful long-term forces moving toward a radical government of some type and of unpredictable events of the moment that shaped its specific form and outcome.

Central to understanding the October Revolution is recognizing that it was carried out in the name of Soviet power, of "All Power to the Soviets." Popular support for it was based on an assumption that such a change of government would allow fulfillment of aspirations for peace, workers' supervision, land distribution, nationality autonomy and other demands. The extensive popular support for Soviet power and the Bolsheviks, Left SRs and other radicals in the fall of 1917 cannot be doubted. Ever since 1917, however, there have been repeated efforts to deny that, primarily for political reasons. Some Russian opponents simply were unwilling to acknowledge the erosion of their own support and its shift to the radicals, a view taken over into much Western writing on the revolution. Others later tried to deny that the Bolsheviks had widespread popular support in 1917, suggesting that to accept it is to legitimize the dictatorship and Stalin system that followed. Such arguments are transparently wrong. The Bolsheviks (and Left SRs) did have widespread popular support in the fall of 1917; that the Bolsheviks lost large portions of it in 1918 and that they soon became dictatorial does not negate the fact of support in October 1917. Nor does the fact that much of their support in 1917 was for a concept of Soviet power very different from what later developed in the Soviet Union nullify the reality of that support. Neither, on the other hand, does the fact of popular support for Soviet power in 1917 legitimize the dictatorship that later emerged. Extensive popular support for the Bolsheviks and Soviet power, especially in the urban centers and the army, was a reality of 1917, without moral implications pro or con for regimes created later in different circumstances.

Events after the October Revolution, in contrast, had a much greater influence on the nature of the regime to follow. Lenin now faced the daunting task of turning Soviet power into Bolshevik power. Although that would be completed only in the cauldron of civil war, it was the early efforts by the Bolsheviks to do so that not only consolidated their tenuous grip on power but transformed the revolution into civil war and the regime into a dictatorship. The immense popularity of the idea of Soviet power allowed the new government both to handily defeat the initial armed opposition and to witness the successful spread of Soviet power across much of Russia and through the army by the beginning of the new year. However, the meaning of Soviet power and the purposes of power had not yet been fully defined. Only with difficulty did Lenin overcome a serious effort during the first week after the October Revolution to force him to share political power through a broad multiparty socialist government, which it had been commonly assumed Soviet power involved. At the same time Lenin and Trotsky worked to polarize opinion and parties and to strengthen the Bolshevik hold on power. They did this in part through swift movement to meet popular aspirations by the land decree, the armistice, extension of workers' authority in management of factories and other measures. At the same time they tightened control through censorship, the formation of the Cheka, repressive measures against the Kadet Party and other actions to suppress opposition. Thus began the descent toward dictatorship and civil war.

The final act in marking the end of the revolution and the onset of civil war was the dispersal of the Constituent Assembly. The elections to the Constituent Assembly and its forthcoming convocation kept alive the notion not only of a future broad multiparty socialist government, but a sense that Lenin's government was only another temporary – provisional – government. This muted early physical opposition to the new government. It also presented Lenin and the radical left with their great dilemma. Throughout 1917 they had criticized the Provisional Government for delay in convening the Constituent Assembly. Indeed, the Bolsheviks had argued that only Soviet power could guarantee that the assembly would meet. The Constituent Assembly was for most political leaders the goal of the political revolution and the supreme authority through which the people would speak authoritatively on social as well as political issues. For Lenin, however, it became an obstacle to retaining political power.

As predicted, the elections in November gave the Bolsheviks only about a quarter of the seats, while the SRs held a majority. However unstable that SR majority might be, it would control the Constituent Assembly in its opening stages. Any government coming out of the assembly would be a coalition, probably the broad socialist coalition that the slogan "All Power to the Soviets" was thought to mean. Lenin had successfully evaded precisely such a socialist coalition thus far. Accepting it meant yielding power, and this Lenin was unwilling to do. His unwillingness led him and other Bolsheviks and some Left SRs to denigrate the assembly's importance and to prepare action against it. This came on January 6 when the Constituent Assembly was forcibly closed after one meeting. Dispersal was not essential for maintenance of a socialist government, or even "Soviet power," but it was if Lenin and Trotsky were to hold power and for such a radical government as they envisioned.

Dispersing the Constituent Assembly was one of the most fateful decisions Lenin was ever to make. The results for the Bolsheviks, Russia and the world were of a significance almost impossible to exaggerate. For the Bolsheviks, in the immediate situation it appeared merely that they had avoided a serious threat to their hold on power. More fundamentally, however, it revealed that the party had irrevocably set itself upon the course of dictatorial rule and that those members who had protested that tendency in November had given up their "constitutional illusions," as Lenin derisively called them. The party would cling to power at any price and take the road of authoritarian government and dictatorship.

The consequences for Russia were even more profound. By this act Lenin and his party announced clearly that they were abandoning the long-held intelligentsia commitment to the people's right to express through the ballot their wishes on fundamental political issues. More specifically, the dispersal of the Constituent Assembly was an announcement by the Bolsheviks that they would not give up governmental authority peacefully, via elections, but could be removed only by force. To the misfortune of millions of people, this meant that civil war was inevitable. The Bolsheviks' declaration that they could not be voted out of office meant that their opponents, of whatever political persuasion, could no longer carry on a merely political struggle within the context of the revolution of 1917. They either had to retire permanently to the sidelines or take to the field with arms. The dispersal of the Constituent Assembly effectively marked the end of the Russian Revolution of 1917; a brutal civil war would now decide the fate of Russia.

Nor was that the end of it, for the long-run repercussions were equally great. On January 6 the Tauride Palace witnessed not merely the end of the Russian Revolution, but the destruction of the democratic and constitutional hopes that had fitfully resided there since 1906 and which appeared to have finally been realized in the heady days of spring 1917. The Bolsheviks' decision to abandon the electoral politics of 1917 and rule by force laid the foundations of the political culture of the Soviet Union. The legacy of this decision still haunts post-Soviet Russian society in its struggles to revive the democratic hopes of 1917.

Moreover, the outcome of the Russian Revolution profoundly affected the entire globe via the enormous and varied influences the Soviet state and communism had on the world in the following decades. The extent to which the later Soviet Union was shaped by the revolution or by other events of Russian history are still vigorously debated. Yet, there can be no doubt but that the path toward dictatorial government taken by the Bolsheviks and their supporters in the winter of 1917–18 sent Russia and the world on a very different historical route than if a more democratic, pluralistic regime had emerged from the Russian Revolution of 1917.

Notes

1 THE COMING OF THE REVOLUTION

1 Christian L. Lange, *Russia, the Revolution and the War: An Account of a Visit to Petrograd and Helsingfors in March, 1917* (Washington, D.C., 1917), ii.

2 *The Nicky–Sunny Letters*, 100, 145, 454.

3 Rogger, *Russia*, 106–07.

4 Quoted ibid., 107–08.

5 Joseph Bradley, "Voluntary Associations, Civic Culture, and *Obshchestvennost'* in Moscow," in Clowes, Kassow and West, *Between Tsar and People*, 136–37.

6 Samuel D. Kassow, James L. West and Edith W. Clowes, "Introduction: The Problem of the Middle in Late Imperial Russian Society," in Clowes, Kassow and West, *Between Tsar and People*, 1–2.

7 John Channon, "The Peasantry in the Revolutions of 1917," in Frankel, Frankel and Knei-Paz, *Revolution in Russia*, 117.

8 Knox, *With the Russian Army*, 270.

9 Quoted in Kowalski, *The Russian Revolution*, 20.

10 Wildman, *End of the Russian Imperial Army: The Old Army*, 95.

11 On the parastatals and their role, see Holquist, *Making War, Forging Revolution*, pages 4 and 21–27 in particular, but the theme runs throughout the book. I borrow this term from him.

12 Program in Golder, *Documents*, 134–36.

13 *The Nicky–Sunny Letters*, 456, letter of December 14, 1916. Emphasis in the original.

14 Ibid., 429, letter of October 31, 1916.

15 See the discussion of the role of rumors about Rasputin's activities and about German treason in delegitimizing Nicholas in popular opinion, in Figes and Kolonitskii, *Interpreting the Russian Revolution*, 9–29.

16 Speech in Golder, *Documents*, 154–66.

17 "Aleksandr Ivanovich Guchkov rasskazyvaet," *Voprosy istorii* 7–8 (1991), 205.

18 Quoted in Golder, *Documents*, 116.

19 Hughes, " 'Revolution Was in the Air!,' " 93.

20 Quoted in Hasegawa, *The February Revolution*, 201.

21 Engel, "Not By Bread Alone," 712–16. Engel explores the extensive role of women, especially soldiers' wives, in popular disturbances during the war.

22 Report in Vernadsky, *Source Book*, III, 877.
23 Report ibid., 867–68.
24 Quoted in Hasegawa, *The February Revolution*, 201.
25 Report in Vernadsky, *Source Book*, III, 868.
26 Koenker and Rosenberg, *Strikes and Revolution*, 58.
27 Longley, "The Mezhraionka," 626.
28 On socialist party activities in Petrograd on the eve of the revolution, see especially Melancon, *The Socialist Revolutionaries*, 190–225. I am grateful to Melancon for sharing with me as yet unpublished material that included recent archival research.
29 *The Nicky–Sunny Letters*, 315.

2 THE FEBRUARY REVOLUTION

1 The figures for the number of strikers and factories closed for this period vary. These are from Hasegawa, *The February Revolution*, 204, 208. Steve Smith, *Red Petrograd*, 52, cites 132 factories for January 9 and 58 for February 14, which would suggest a larger number of workers. Other figures exist, reflecting the difficulty of accurate measurement. Koenker and Rosenberg, *Strikes and Revolution*, 66, cite 137,000 strikers for January 9, while police reports say 59,000 for February 14.
2 V. M. Zenzinov, "Fevral'skie dni," *Novyi zhurnal* 34 (1953), 188–211, 35 (1953), 208–40; quote on 198.
3 I. Gordienko, quoted in Burdzhalov, *Russia's Second Revolution*, 106.
4 See Hasegawa, *The February Revolution*, 221–22, for a discussion of the figures, as well as a detailed account of the spread through the factories.
5 Quoted in Burdzhalov, *Russia's Second Revolution*, 118.
6 Just what was planned or not planned for February 23 has long been a source of debate. For a discussion of the issues and historiography surrounding the role of the socialist parties on the 23rd and after, see Melancon, *The Socialist Revolutionaries*, 116–72, and the debate in a series of articles: Melancon, "Who Wrote What and When"; James White, "The February Revolution and the Bolshevik Vyborg District Committee"; Longley, "The Mezhraionka"; and Melancon, "International Women's Day." See also Hasegawa, *The February Revolution*, 215–31, and Longley, "Iakovlev's Question," in Frankel, Frankel and Knei-Paz, *Revolution in Russia*, 365–87.
7 As quoted in Hasegawa, *The February Revolution*, 225.
8 Quoted in Burdzhalov, *Russia's Second Revolution*, 117.
9 Quoted in Hasegawa, *The February Revolution*, 233.
10 A. P. Peshekhonov, "Pervyia nedeli (Iz vospominanii o revoliutsii)," *Na chuzoi storone* 1923, no. 1, 272.
11 Melancon, *The Socialist Revolutionaries*, 252–56. Hasegawa, *The February Revolution*, 215–310, and Melancon, *The Socialist Revolutionaries*, 226–75, give the best day-by-day accounts of the revolution, but do not always agree on interpretation. See also Burdzhalov, *Russia's Second Revolution*, for the best Soviet-era account, which is valuable but must be used with caution.

See also the articles in n. 6 above. A detailed memoir account is Sukhanov, *The Russian Revolution*, I, 1–160.

12 Quoted in Melancon, *The Socialist Revolutionaries*, 259.

13 There are several accounts of this incident, in some of which the police commander was killed by a Cossack's saber cut, but all agree that the Cossacks attacked the police.

14 Quoted in Lincoln, *Passage Through Armageddon*, 333.

15 As quoted ibid., 327.

16 For details on the shootings, see Hasegawa, *The February Revolution*, 268–70. He says that only training detachments fired that day. See also Wildman, *End of the Russian Imperial Army: The Old Army*, 139.

17 In Golder, *Documents*, 267.

18 *Izvestiia revoliutsionnoi nedeli*, no. 2, Feb. 28. Newspapers ceased publication after the morning of the 25th, leaving the city without news reports of events. A committee of journalists managed to put together this small newspaper on the 27th, which became the main source of printed information for the next few days. Gradually newspaper publication resumed, but it was fundamentally changed by the appearance of a large number of socialist newspapers and the disappearance of some of the old conservative ones.

19 On the Duma Committee, see the documents in Browder and Kerensky, *Russian Provisional Government*, I, 39–62, as well as translated memoir accounts by Miliukov (*The Russian Revolution*), Shulgin (*Days of the Russian Revolution*) and Kerensky (*The Catastrophe, The Crucifixion of Liberty, Prelude to Bolshevism*, and *Russia and History's Turning Point*). For a historical account, see Hasegawa, *The February Revolution*, 348–60.

20 On the formation of the Soviet, see Hasegawa, *The February Revolution*, 313–47. See also the documents in Browder and Kerensky, *Russian Provisional Government*, I, 70–76, and the memoir accounts of Sukhanov, *The Russian Revolution* (especially), and Mstislavskii, *Five Days*.

21 At the All-Russia Conference of Soviets, as quoted in Galili, *Menshevik Leaders*, 46–47.

22 *Izvestiia revoliutsionnoi nedeli*, no. 6, March 2.

23 *Izvestiia revoliutsionnoi nedeli*, no. 7, March 3.

24 On the formation of the Provisional Government two especially valuable sources are the accounts of two of the chief negotiators, Miliukov, *The Russian Revolution*, I, 26–37, and Sukhanov, *The Russian Revolution*, I, 114–57. A selection of documents, including the announcement of the government's composition and program and the Soviet declaration of support, is in Browder and Kerensky, *Russian Provisional Government*, I, 117–38. Rosenberg, *Liberals*, 52–56, has a good discussion of the Kadets' role, and Hasegawa, *The February Revolution*, 519–45, provides a detailed account.

25 Phillips, " 'A Bad Business,' " 134–38.

26 The following draws primarily on the excellent detailed account found in Hasegawa, *The February Revolution*, 431–515, which not only explores the events carefully but demolishes numerous myths surrounding them.

3 POLITICAL REALIGNMENT AND THE NEW POLITICAL SYSTEM

1 Rosenberg, "Social Mediation," 175.
2 The fullest account of the Constituent Assembly as an issue in the revolution is L. G. Protasov, *Vserossiiskoe Uchreditel'noe sobranie: istoriia rozhdeniia i gibeli* (Moscow, 1997). In English see his article, "The All-Russian Constituent Assembly and the Democratic Alternative," and Radkey, *Russia Goes to the Polls.*
3 Nabokov, *Nabokov and the Russian Provisional Government,* 87. Nabokov, a Kadet and close to Miliukov, was head of the Provisional Government's chancellery and thus in an excellent position to observe it and its members.
4 "Iz dnevnika gen. V. G. Boldyreva," *Krasnyi arkhiv* 23 (1927), no. 4, 260.
5 *Petrogradskii sovet rabochikh i soldatskikh deputatov v 1917 godu. Protokoly, stenogrammy i otchety, rezoliutsii, postanovleniia obshchikh sobranii, sobranii sektsii, zasedanii Ispolnitel'nogo komiteta i fraksii 27 fevralia–25 oktiabria 1917 goda,* ed. B. D. Gal'perina, O. N. Znamenskii and V. I. Startsev, vol. I (Leningrad, 1991), 234, 260.
6 On the Kadets and the liberals in the revolution, see especially Rosenberg, *Liberals.* There are two biographies of Miliukov, both focusing on the pre-1917 period, by Stockdale, *Miliukov and the Quest for a Liberal Russia,* and Riha, *A Russian European.* See also the accounts by Miliukov, *The Russian Revolution,* and Nabokov, *Nabokov and the Russian Provisional Government.*
7 Quoted in Browder and Kerensky, *Russian Provisional Government,* III, 1258–59.
8 Quoted in Francis King, "Between Bolshevism and Menshevism," 2.
9 Price, *Dispatches,* 44 (written June 13).
10 Ibid., 105–06.
11 V. B. Stankevich, *Vospominaniia 1914–1919* (Berlin, 1920), 78.
12 For the Tsereteli group's establishment of ascendancy in the Soviet and its composition, see Wade, *The Russian Search for Peace,* 17–25. On the Siberian Zimmerwaldist origins of what became Revolutionary Defensism, see Wade, "Irakli Tsereteli and Siberian Zimmerwaldism," and Galili, "The Origins of Revolutionary Defensism."
13 Lenin, *Collected Works,* XXIV, 21–24.
14 For Lenin and the Bolshevik party during this period, see Rabinowitch, *Prelude,* 32–53; Service, *Lenin,* II, 149–76; Harding, *Leninism,* 89–90.
15 Information on the Left SRs and Mensheviks is mostly scattered in works on the SR and Menshevik Parties. On the Left SRs, see Melancon, "The Left Socialist Revolutionaries," and also his entry in *Critical Companion to the Russian Revolution,* 291–99, and material in Melancon, *The Socialist Revolutionaries,* and in Radkey, *Agrarian Foes* and *The Sickle Under the Hammer.* A detailed study of the Left SRs is Lutz Hafner, *Die Partei der linken Sozialrevolutionäre in der russischen Revolution von 1917–1918* (Cologne: 1994). On the left wing of the Mensheviks and the Menshevik–Internationalists, see material scattered through Galili, *The Menshevik Leaders*; Basil, *The Mensheviks*; Getzler, *Martov* and "Iulii Martov." See also Francis King, "Between Bolshevism and Menshevism," on the Social-Democrat Internationalists.

16 On the anarchists, see especially Paul Avrich, "The Anarchists in the Russian Revolution," *The Russian Anarchists* and (as editor) *The Anarchists in the Russian Revolution*.

17 Tseretelli [Tsereteli], "The April Crisis," Part 3, 316.

18 Sukhanov, *The Russian Revolution*, I, 33.

19 Quoted in Radkey, *Agrarian Foes*, 225.

20 Shulgin, *Days of the Russian Revolution*, 113.

21 On Kerensky and his popularity, see Figes and Kolonitskii, *Interpreting the Russian Revolution*, 76–96.

22 In Golikov, "The Kerensky Phenomenon," 52.

23 Chernov, *The Great Russian Revolution*, 174.

24 Kerensky figures prominently in almost all memoirs of and histories about the revolution, published several volumes of memoirs himself, and is the subject of a biography by Richard Abraham, *Alexander Kerensky: The First Love of the Revolution*. See also articles by Kolonitskii ("Kerensky," in *Critical Companion to the Russian Revolution*, 138–49) and Golikov ("The Kerensky Phenomenon").

25 In an interview with Oliver Radkey, given in Radkey, *Agrarian Foes*, 218.

26 Quoted in Browder and Kerensky, *Russian Provisional Government*, III, 1265.

27 *Izvestiia*, June 27. This was in a proclamation approved at the congress.

28 Golder, *Documents*, 325–26.

29 *Rech'*, March 23. This was the newspaper of the Kadet Party.

30 The declaration is in Browder and Kerensky, *Russian Provisional Government*, II, 1045–47; a series of documents regarding foreign policy and the dispute over it are in II, 1042–1101, and III, 1226–48. For a detailed account of the controversy and the April Crisis, see Wade, *The Russian Search for Peace*, 9–43.

31 Quoted in Browder and Kerensky, *Russian Provisional Government*, II, 1098.

32 Quoted ibid., 1100.

33 Miliukov, *The Russian Revolution*, I, 92.

4 THE ASPIRATIONS OF RUSSIAN SOCIETY

1 Irina Sergeevna Tidmarsh, in Horsbrugh-Porter, *Memories of Revolution*, 63.

2 Quoted in Khalid, *Politics of Muslim Cultural Reform*, 247.

3 There is a vast literature on the industrial workers in the revolution, not only in Russian but in English and other languages as well. For the workers' aspirations as well as for other material on them I have drawn primarily on my own research and writings (particularly *Red Guards and Workers' Militias* and "*Rajonnye Sovety*"), but have drawn also on S. A. Smith (*Red Petrograd* and "Craft Consciousness"), Koenker (*Moscow Workers* and "Urban Families"; Koenker and Rosenberg, (*Strikes and Revolution*), Rosenberg ("Russian Labor" and "Workers"); Rosenberg and Koenker, ("Limits of Formal Protest"), Shkliarevsky (*Labor*), Mandel (*Petrograd Workers and the Fall of the Old Regime* and *Petrograd Workers and the Soviet Seizure of Power*), and the relevant sections of works such as Keep (*The Russian Revolution*),

Ferro (*The Russian Revolution* and *October 1917*), Suny (*Baku*) and Raleigh (*Revolution on the Volga*) as well as others. All of these works give guidance to the Russian-language literature.

4 Service, "The Industrial Workers," in Service, *Society and Politics*, 148–49.

5 Ferro, *The Russian Revolution*, 112, gives a detailed analysis of worker aspirations based on the content of resolutions passed at factory meetings in March. Workers' aspirations are also discussed in the works mentioned in n. 3 of this chapter.

6 S. A. Smith, *Red Petrograd*, 70.

7 Ibid., 55.

8 Mandel, *Petrograd Workers and the Fall of the Old Regime*, 97.

9 Raleigh, "Political Power in the Russian Revolution: A Case Study of Saratov," in Frankel, Frankel and Knei-Paz, *Russia in Revolution*, 45.

10 On workers' supervision, see especially Shkliarevsky, *Labor in the Russian Revolution*, 1–29, and Rosenberg, "Workers," but also the books on the Petrograd workers by Smith, *Red Petrograd*, and Mandel, *Petrograd Workers and the Fall of the Old Regime* and *Petrograd Workers and the Soviet Seizure of Power*, and Koenker on Moscow, *Moscow Workers*, as well as Avrich, "The Bolshevik Revolution" and "Russian Factory Committees."

11 Keep, *The Russian Revolution*, 97.

12 On the district soviets, see Wade, "The *Rajonnye Sovety* of Petrograd."

13 On the Red Guards, see Wade, *Red Guards and Workers' Militias*.

14 On the *zemliachestva*, see especially Hickey, "Urban *Zemliachestva*," Melancon, "Soldiers," and James White, "Sormovo."

15 *Vestnik gorodskogo samoupravleniia*, June 29.

16 S. A. Smith, *Red Petrograd*, 202.

17 Account of Colonel Engelhardt, to whom they made the statement, quoted in Hasegawa, *The February Revolution*, 399.

18 This and following quotations from Order No. 1 are from the document given in Browder and Kerensky, *Russian Provisional Government*, II, 848–49.

19 Quoted in Wildman, *End of the Russian Imperial Army: The Old Army*, 222. Wildman gives the best account of the revolution in the army and I draw heavily on him.

20 Ferro, *The Russian Revolution*, 130–35, examines the content of soldier resolutions; see also his "Russian Soldier in 1917." Howard White, "1917 in the Rear Garrisons," examines attitudes there.

21 On the army committees, see the two volumes by Allen Wildman on *The End of the Russian Imperial Army*, but especially *The Old Army*, 246–90, on their origins.

22 Quoted in Wildman, *End of the Russian Imperial Army: The Old Army*, 245.

23 Account of meeting in Denikin, *Russian Turmoil*, 178–80.

24 Wildman, *End of the Russian Imperial Army: The Old Army*, 345.

25 Mawdsley, *Russian Revolution and the Baltic Fleet*, 12–21, and Saul, *Sailors in Revolt*, 64–80.

26 Melancon, "Soldiers," 184–85.

27 This threefold division and the following section draw heavily on Orlovsky, "Lower Middle," and on Howard White, "The Urban Middle Class," in Service, *Society and Politics*, 64–85. See also Galili, "Commercial-Industrial

Circles in Revolution: The Failure of 'Industrial Progressivism,'" in Frankel, Frankel and Knei-Paz, *Revolution in Russia*, 188–216.

28 Orlovsky, "Lower Middle," 258, 264.

29 Hickey, "Discourses of Public Identity," 636.

30 *Zhenskii vestnik* in October, 1914, quoted in Meyer, "Impact of World War I on Women's Lives," 212.

31 Stites, *Women's Liberation Movement*, 291–95; Edmondson, *Feminism*, 166–68. Edmondson gives detailed studies of Russian feminists, and Stites examines both feminism and the Russian women socialists.

32 A good concise description of the Marxist approach is in Clements, *Daughters of Revolution*, 37–41. For a detailed account of the socialists and women, see Stites, *Women's Liberation Movement*.

33 Clements, *Bolshevik Women*, 130; McKean, *St. Petersburg Between the Revolutions*, 331.

34 Clements, *Bolshevik Women*, 131.

35 Donald, "Bolshevik Activity," 155.

36 Barbara Clements, *Bolshevik Women*, 135–47, gives a perceptive and nuanced discussion of the political activism of women Bolsheviks and the roles they did and did not play. For an intriguing account of the activities of one prominent woman political and feminist activist in 1917, see Norton, "Laying the Foundations of Democracy in Russia." Many prominent women socialists of 1917 have biographies and/or memoirs, including Kollontai, Krupskaia, Spiridonova, Inessa Armand, Alexandra Balabanova, Ekaterina Breshko-Breshkovskaia, Emma Goldman and Vera Zasulich, while Clements, *Bolshevik Women* has biographies of several slightly less prominent activists. Information on other female political figures is scattered through general party histories. Tyrkova is unique in being the only liberal to leave behind a memoir of the revolution (*From Liberty to Brest-Litovsk*); none have been the subject of biographies. Bibliographic references for these and other works by or on women in 1917 are available in Frame, *Russian Revolution*.

37 Clements, "Working-Class and Peasant Women," 217–24, has a good discussion of this phenomenon.

38 Koenker and Rosenberg, *Strikes and Revolution*, 316.

39 Clements, *Daughters of Revolution*, 33.

40 Donald, "Bolshevik Activity," 146.

41 *Rabochaia gazeta* and *Pravda* carried brief accounts of their meetings and demands in the April issues especially. There is little published on the *soldatki*, but Engel, "Not by Bread Alone," discusses them for the war years and Donald, "Bolshevik Activity," 141–42, has information on them in 1917.

42 *Rabochaia gazeta*, no. 9, March 16.

43 On the Women's Battalion, see particularly Stockdale, "My Death for the Motherland" and Abraham, "Mariia L. Bochkareva and the Russian Amazons of 1917," as well as Bochkareva's own story: Maria Botchkareva, *Yashka: My Life as a Peasant, Exile and Soldier* (New York and London, 1919).

44 Koenker, "Urban Families," 294.

45 Josephson, "Gor'kii, Science and the Russian Revolution," 25.
46 Mikhail V. Shkarovskii, "The Russian Orthodox Church," in *Critical Companion to the Russian Revolution*, 416–28, and George Kosar, "Russian Orthodoxy in Crisis and Revolution: The Church Council of 1917–1918." Ph.D. dissertation, Brandeis University, 2004.
47 Hickey, "Discourses of Public Identity," 629–30.
48 Holquist, *Making War, Forging Revolution*, 47, 111.

5 THE PEASANTS AND THE PURPOSES OF REVOLUTION

1 Browder and Kerensky, *Russian Provisional Government*, I, 244. On the rural policies of the Provisional Government, see especially Gill, *Peasants and Government*. Atkinson, *End of the Russian Land Commune*, 117–48, discusses the policies of both the government and the main political parties. Browder and Kerensky, *Russian Provisional Government*, I, 243–316, and II, 523–614, give a good selection of the decrees of the Provisional Government and other documents regarding the peasants and the Provisional Government.
2 Browder and Kerensky, *Russian Provisional Government*, I, 245.
3 Retish, "Creating Peasant Citizens," 51. Much of the rest of this paragraph is drawn from Retish's article.
4 On the evolution of expanding government control over food supply and the economy, see Holquist, *Making War, Forging Revolution*, especially chapters 1–3.
5 Ibid., II, 615, 618–21, gives basic documents. Most works on the peasants discuss this issue, but see also Lih, *Bread and Authority*, especially 57–137.
6 Keep, *The Russian Revolution*, 179.
7 Ibid., 172.
8 Peasant violence is notoriously difficult to classify and categorize. Old figures based on reports from local Provincial Government officials are much too low and have been revised upward by more recent investigations. See the discussion of this issue in Perrie, "The Peasants," in Service, *Society and Politics*, 13–19, Channon, "The Peasantry in the Revolutions of 1917," in Frankel, Frankel and Knei-Paz, *Revolution in Russia*, 106–10, and Figes, *Peasant Russia*, 47–61. See also Holubnychy, "The 1917 Agrarian Revolution," 14–16; Keep, *The Russian Revolution*, 186–89; Gill, *Peasants and Government*, 157–90.
9 Figures vary. Compare the charts in Holubnychy, "The 1917 Agrarian Revolution," 10; Perrie, "The Peasants," 16; Gill, *Peasants and Government*, 190.
10 Manning, "Bolsheviks without the Party," 41–48.
11 Figes, *Peasant Russia*, 52.
12 Browder and Kerensky, *Russian Provisional Government*, II, 621–22.
13 Quoted in Keep, *The Russian Revolution*, 200–01.
14 As quoted ibid., 211–12.
15 For discussion of this, see especially ibid., 210–14, and Stites, *Revolutionary Dreams*, 181–83.
16 Perrie, "The Peasants," 27.

17 Channon, "The Peasantry in the Revolutions of 1917," 172.
18 Quoted in Figes, *Peasant Russia*, 51.
19 Browder and Kerensky, *Russian Provisional Government*, II, 562–63.
20 Quoted in Radkey, *Agrarian Foes*, 365.
21 Keep, *The Russian Revolution*, 215.
22 Figes, *Peasant Russia*, 57.
23 Ibid., 56.
24 On the peasants' congresses, see especially Keep, *The Russian Revolution*, 223–47.
25 Ibid., 229–34, 244–47, gives details on the struggle between the two organizations.

6 THE NATIONALITIES: IDENTITY AND OPPORTUNITY

1 For good discussions of the problems of ethnic identity and nationality as motive forces in the revolution, see the several works by Suny in the further reading section and also Stephen Jones, "The Non-Russian Nationalities," in Service, *Society and Politics*, 35–63, and the references in both to the general literature on national identity.
2 I. G. Tsereteli, *Vospominaniia o fevral'skoi revoliutsii* (Paris, 1963), II, 89.
3 Speech in Browder and Kerensky, *Russian Provisional Government*, III, 1460.
4 Statement ibid., 1716.
5 McNeal, *Resolutions*, I, 225–26.
6 On Lenin's and the Bolsheviks' nationality policy, see especially the passages in Harding, *Leninism* and *Lenin's Political Thought*, and in Service, *Lenin*.
7 Reshetar, *Ukrainian Revolution*, 53.
8 Browder and Kerensky, *Russian Provisional Government*, I, 370–402, has many documents on the Ukrainian movement and Russian reactions to it, including samples of these resolutions.
9 Hunczak, *Ukraine*, 382–95, gives the four Universals issued by the Rada in 1917–January 1918 defining its status vis-à-vis the Russian state.
10 Cited in Browder and Kerensky, *Russian Provisional Government*, I, 386.
11 Quoted in Reshetar, *Ukrainian Revolution*, 81.
12 Guthier, "Popular Base," 40. Guthier provides a number of tables elucidating ethnic numerical relationships and their relation to political behavior.
13 Pipes, *Formation*, 63.
14 *Den'*, May 12, in Browder and Kerensky, *Russian Provisional Government*, I, 340.
15 On Finland, see especially Upton, *Finnish Revolution*, and Alapuro, *State and Revolution in Finland*.
16 Ezergailis' works on Latvia are the fullest treatment of either people during the revolution. Page, *Formation of the Baltic States*, devotes material to both Latvia and Estonia, as well as Lithuania, during 1917, but focuses on the post-1917 period. On Estonia in 1917, see Arens, "The Estonian Maapaev" and "Soviets in Estonia," and also his essay in *Critical Companion to the Russian Revolution*, and Aun, "The 1917 Revolutions." See Lehti, "The Baltic League," and Parming, "Population and Ethnicity," on the Baltic region generally and also the essays in Elwood, *Reconsiderations*.

17 Suny, *Revenge*, 57.
18 There is not a history devoted exclusively to 1917 in Muslim regions or in Transcaucasia as a whole. The most detailed study of a portion of the area is Suny, *The Baku Commune*. See also his "Nationalism . . . Baku and Tiflis." Especially insightful are Khalid, "Tashkent 1917" and *Politics of Muslim Cultural Reform*. For other Muslim areas, see the sections on 1917 in Zenkovsky, *Pan-Turkism and Islam in Russia*, Carrère d'Encausse, *Islam and the Russian Empire*, Rorlich, *The Volga Tatars*, Swietochowski, *Russian Azerbaijan*, Kazemzadeh, *Struggle for Transcaucasia*, Allworth, "Search for Group Identity in Turkistan" and Pipes, *Formation*.
19 Speech quoted in Zenkovsky, *Pan-Turkism and Islam in Russia*, 147. The Resolution of the congress is in Browder and Kerensky, *Russian Provisional Government*, II, 409–11.
20 The following discussion of Tashkent is drawn primarily from Khalid, "Tashkent 1917." See also Pierce, "Toward Soviet Power in Tashkent."
21 Carrère d'Encausse, "The Fall of the Tsarist Empire," 214.
22 Suny, "Nationalism . . . Baku and Tiflis," 253.
23 Hickey, "Revolution on the Jewish Street," 828. On Jews in the revolution, in addition to Hickey's article, see Abramson, *A Prayer for the Jews*, 33–66, John D. Klier, "The Jews," in *Critical Companion to the Russian Revolution*, 693–705, and the four essays by Lionel Kochan in Shukman, *Blackwell Encyclopedia of the Russian Revolution*, 207–11. All give suggestions for further reading.
24 See Holquist, *Making War, Forging Revolution*, especially pages 47–142.
25 On Siberian regionalism, see Pereira, "The Idea of Siberian Regionalism" and "Regional Consciousness in Siberia," and Rupp, *The Struggle in the East*, 2–6.

7   THE SUMMER OF DISCONTENTS

1 Sukhanov, *The Russian Revolution*, I, 341.
2 The peace offensive is detailed in Wade, *The Russian Search for Peace*, 51–88.
3 *Vserossiiskoe soveshchanie sovetov rabochikh i soldatskikh deputatov* (Moscow, 1927), 40.
4 Miliukov, *The Russian Revolution*, I, 96.
5 Denikin, *Russian Turmoil*, 142.
6 *Izvestiia*, May 2.
7 *Den'*, May 30.
8 *Delo naroda*, May 14; *Izvestiia*, May 17. Emphasis in original.
9 V. S. Voitinskii, *K chemu stemitsia koalitsionnoe pravitel'stvo* (Petrograd, 1917), 3–10.
10 *Pravda*, April 29.
11 Quoted in Browder and Kerensky, *Russian Provisional Government*, II, 936.
12 Kerensky, *The Catastrophe*, 195.
13 See Wildman, *End of the Russian Imperial Army*, *passim*, for materials on the army committees. The following discussion of the committees and Bolshevik influence follows in general Wildman's detailed study. See also the

examination of evolving soldier attitudes by Buldakov, "Soldiers and Changes."

14 Wildman, *End of the Russian Imperial Army: The Old Army*, 38.
15 Quoted in Wildman, *End of the Russian Imperial Army: The Road*, 53.
16 Quoted ibid., 47–48.
17 Rabinowitch, *Prelude*, 68–69. He gives the best description of the events of June 10–18.
18 Denikin, *Russian Turmoil*, 273.
19 Browder and Kerensky, *Russian Provisional Government*, II, 967.
20 Sukhanov, *The Russian Revolution*, II, 430.
21 The most thorough account of the July Days is Rabinowitch, *Prelude*, 135–205. See also the memoir account of Sukhanov, *The Russian Revolution*, II, 425–59.
22 Rabinowitch, *Prelude*, 175.
23 Miliukov, *The Russian Revolution*, I, 202.
24 Flenley, "Industrial Relations," 192, citing *Delo naroda*, July 25.
25 The industrial crisis and the fundamental conflict between employer and worker outlooks, and the "rationality" of both, is well discussed in Flenley, "Industrial," 185–94.
26 Wade, *Red Guards and Workers' Militias*, 253.
27 Ibid., 141.
28 Suny, *The Baku Commune*, 111–12.
29 A good discussion of the food supply problem is in Lih, *Bread and Authority*, 56–126. See also Struve, *Food Supply*, and especially the section on rationing cards, 169–73.
30 Lih, *Bread and Authority*, 79; he provides a good description of the phenomenon on 76–81.
31 Browder and Kerensky, *Russian Provisional Government*, III, 1277.
32 Ibid., II, 660.
33 Ibid., 677.
34 In addition to my own reading of newspapers from 1917, this draws heavily, especially for specifics, from Hasegawa, "Crime," and an unpublished paper on crime in Smolensk kindly lent to me by Michael Hickey.
35 *Rabochaia gazeta*, June 22.
36 On the issue of "German gold" to the Bolsheviks, which was a cornerstone of anti-Bolshevik propaganda in 1917 and of the Provisional Government's order for the arrest of Lenin and some other Bolsheviks after the July Days, see Lyandres, *The Bolsheviks' "German Gold" Revisited*.
37 As quoted in Lih, *Bread and Authority*, 99. The "bony hand of hunger" referred to a phrase used in a speech by the industrialist Pavel Riabushinsky in August, which created a furor and fed conspiracy theories when, as here, misused. Riabushinsky had said that it would result from leftist policies.
38 In Steinberg, *Voices of Revolution*, 199.
39 Ibid., 102.
40 McAuley, *Bread and Justice*, 34–37 (quote, 36–37).
41 All three quotations from Browder and Kerensky, *Russian Provisional Government*, III, 1423–24 (bracketed material in Tsereteli quote mine).
42 Ibid., 1407, 1414.

43 Ibid., 1440.
44 Quoted in Rosenberg, *Liberals*, 201.
45 Quoted ibid.
46 In Browder and Kerensky, *Russian Provisional Government*, III, 1437.
47 Quoted in Rosenberg, *Liberals*, 222.
48 An extensive selection of the speeches at the conference and related documents is in Browder and Kerensky, *Russian Provisional Government*, III, 1451–1522.
49 The Kornilov Affair, especially the question of what each person intended, was incredibly complex, with plots within plots, garbled communications and general distrust. Good accounts which try to unravel it are Munck, *The Kornilov Revolt*, Ascher, "The Kornilov Affair," Asher, "The Kornilov Affair," and James White, "The Kornilov Affair." Wildman examines the military role in his book on the Russian army and in "Officers of the General Staff and the Kornilov Movement," in Frankel, Frankel and Knei-Paz, *Revolution in Russia*, 76–101. There is a very extensive set of documents and memoir selections in Browder and Kerensky, *Russian Provisional Government*, III, 1527–1614. Kerensky presented his own account in *Crucifixion of Liberty* and in later memoirs; Kornilov never wrote his account (he died the next year).
50 Browder and Kerensky, *Russian Provisional Government*, III, 1589.

8 "ALL POWER TO THE SOVIETS"

1 The Bolsheviks have been the subject of an immense literature. For studies of the party leading up to and during the October Revolution, see especially the two books by Alexander Rabinowitch, *Prelude* and *Bolsheviks*, and Robert V. Daniels, *Red October*. On Lenin especially, see Robert Service, *Lenin*, and Neil Harding, *Lenin's Political Thought*. Adam Ulam, *The Bolsheviks*, provides another look at Lenin and the party.
2 On the origins and nature of Lenin's new vision of the state, see Service, *Lenin*, 143–71, and Harding, *Lenin's Political Thought*, II, esp. 71–168 (a shorter treatment is his "Lenin, Socialism and the State in 1917," in Frankel, Frankel and Knei-Paz, *Revolution in Russia*, 287–303).
3 Lenin, *Collected Works*, XXV, 368–69. This was published on September 24 but written a few days earlier.
4 Melancon, *The Socialist Revolutionaries*, 282. On the Left SRs, Menshevik–Internationalists and other radicals, see the references in chapter 3, n. 14.
5 Avrich, *The Russian Anarchists*, 145–46.
6 Koenker, *Moscow Workers*, 202–10; Radkey, *Agrarian Foes*, 363, 443.
7 *Ekonomicheskoe polozhenie Rossii nakanune Velikoi Oktiabr'skoi sotsialisticheskoi revoliutsii* (Moscow, 1957), II, 351–52.
8 Ibid., 319. The deteriorating supply situation and its ramifications are a major thread running through the history of 1917. See especially Pethybridge's fine summary in *The Spread of the Russian Revolution*, esp. 1–56 and 83–110, and the books by Lih, *Bread and Authority*, and McAuley, *Bread and Justice*. Browder and Kerensky, *Russian Provisional Government*, II, 615–708, offer documents on the economic situation.

9 Quoted in Lih, *Bread and Authority*, 111.

10 Suny, *The Baku Commune*, 115.

11 Price, *Dispatches*, 75.

12 Suny, *The Baku Commune*, 131–34.

13 Rieber, *Merchants and Entrepreneurs*, 412.

14 *Ekonomicheskoe polozhenie*, II, 163–64.

15 *Fabrichno-zavodskie komitety Petrograda v 1917 godu. Protokoly* (Moscow, 1979), 490–92.

16 Hasegawa, "Crime," 243–44.

17 Reed, *Ten Days That Shook the World*, 49.

18 *Volia naroda*, September 20, as given in Browder and Kerensky, *Russian Provisional Government*, III, 1641–42, slightly modified.

19 Quoted in Rabinowitch, *Bolsheviks*, 201.

20 Lenin, *Collected Works*, XXVI, 19. Emphasis Lenin's.

21 Ibid., 82. Emphasis Lenin's.

22 Ibid., 21.

23 McNeal, *Resolutions*, I, 284–86.

24 Ibid., 288–89.

25 Ibid.

26 The debates at the Petersburg Committee are in *Pervyi legal'nyi Peterburgskii komitet bol'shevikov v 1917 godu. Sbornik materialov i protokolov zasedanii Peterburgskogo komiteta RSDRP(b) i ego Ispolnitel'noi komissii za 1917 g.* (Moscow and Leningrad, 1927), 316.

27 On the congress and its role in the coming of the October Revolution see especially James White, "Lenin, Trotskii and the Arts of Insurrection," 117–39.

28 Quoted in Daniels, *Red October*, 94.

29 Quoted ibid.

30 On the Left SRs on the eve of the October Revolution, see Melancon, "The Left Socialist Revolutionaries," esp. 67–69.

31 Quoted in Rabinowitch, *Bolsheviks*, 241.

32 *Petrogradskii voenno-revoliutsionnyi komitet. Dokumenty i materialy* (Moscow, 1966), I, 63.

33 Sukhanov, *The Russian Revolution*, II, 584.

34 S. I. Tsukerman, "Petrogradskii raionnyi sovet rabochikh i soldatskikh deputatov v 1917 godu," *Krasnaia letopis'*, 1932, no. 3, 64. See Wade, *Red Guards and Workers' Militias*, 192–94, for the Red Guard mobilization on the eve.

35 Browder and Kerensky, *Russian Provisional Government*, III, 1744.

36 Buchanan, *My Mission to Russia*, II, 201.

9   THE BOLSHEVIKS TAKE POWER

1 *Petrogradskii voenno-revoliutsionnyi komitet*, I, 84, 86.

2 Rabinowitch, *Bolsheviks*, 252–54.

3 In Browder and Kerensky, *Russian Provisional Government*, III, 1785.

4 For descriptions of the struggle in the streets, see Wade, *Red Guards and Workers' Militias*, 196–207, and Rabinowitch, *Bolsheviks*, 249–300.

5 Quoted in Daniels, *The Russian Revolution*, 131–32.
6 This episode is especially well described in Daniels, *Red October*, 158–61.
7 Rabinowitch, *Bolsheviks*, 268–69.
8 *Petrogradskii voenno-revoliutsionnyi komitet*, I, 106.
9 Reed, *Ten Days That Shook the World*, 114–18.
10 Quoted in *Oktiabr'skoe vooruzhennoe vosstanie. Semnadtsatyi god v Petrograde* (Leningrad, 1967), II, 366.
11 Quoted in Rabinowitch, *Bolsheviks*, 300. In addition to the account of the siege and arrest of the government in Rabinowitch, Daniels, *Red October*, 187–96, also gives a good account of the taking of the palace and arrest of the government ministers.
12 Reed, *Ten Days That Shook the World*, 118–19.
13 Wade, *Documents of Soviet History*, I, 2–5.
14 Sukhanov, *The Russian Revolution*, II, 640.
15 Wade, *Documents of Soviet History*, I, 3–4.
16 Ibid., 4–5.
17 Lenin, *Collected Works*, XXVI, 249–53.
18 Ibid., 257–61.
19 Ibid., 261.
20 P. Krasnov, "Na vnutrennem fronte," *Arkhiv russkoi revoliutsii* 1922, no. 1, 166.
21 Bunyan and Fisher, *The Bolshevik Revolution*, 155–56.
22 McNeal, *Resolutions*, II, 42.
23 The debate is given in *The Bolsheviks and the October Revolution: Minutes*, 129–35.
24 McNeal, *Resolutions*, II, 45.
25 On October in Saratov, see Raleigh, *Revolution on the Volga*, 276–91, and Wade, *Red Guards and Workers' Militias*, 231–38.
26 On Moscow, see especially Koenker, *Moscow Workers*, 329–55.
27 Quoted in Wildman, *End of the Russian Imperial Army: The Road*, 314.
28 On the October Revolution at the front, see ibid., 308–402.

10 THE CONSTITUENT ASSEMBLY AND THE PURPOSES OF POWER

1 Albert Rhys Williams, *Journey into Revolution*, 132.
2 For the armistice actions of the front-line troops and its effect on their relations with the government, see Wildman, *End of the Russian Imperial Army: The Road*, 379–405. On early Soviet diplomacy and the armistice itself, see Debo, *Revolution and Survival*, Kennan, *Soviet–American Relations*, and Wheeler-Bennett, *The Forgotten Peace*.
3 For a discussion of the revolution in Kharkov and this third type of "October Revolution," see Wade, "Revolution in the Provinces" and "Ukrainian Nationalism."
4 All four Universals of 1917–January 1918 are in Hunczak, *Ukraine*, 387–91.
5 Manning, "Bolsheviks without the Party," 51–58, describes the fascinating complex history of the district.

6 Wildman, *End of the Russian Imperial Army: The Road*, 310.

7 Hunczak, *Ukraine*, 387–91.

8 For a sampling of the kinds of social and economic legislation of the immediate post-October period, see Wade, *Documents of Soviet History*, I, 19–71, and Bunyan and Fisher, *The Bolshevik Revolution*, 276–315.

9 Wade, *Documents of Soviet History*, I, 16.

10 On Bolshevik economic ideas and policies, including workers' supervision, see Remington, *Building Socialism*, esp. 39–50, and Service, *Lenin*, 298–302. See also the references on workers' supervision in chapter 4, n. 10.

11 Quoted in S. A. Smith, *Red Petrograd*, 212.

12 Lincoln, *Passage Through Armageddon*, 473; Channon, "The Bolsheviks and the Peasantry," 620.

13 Lenin, *Collected Works*, XXVI, 116.

14 Ibid., 364, 368, 385.

15 Rigby, *Lenin's Government*, p. 40.

16 Ibid., chapters 1–4, gives the most detailed account of the attempt to build the new central government apparatus, and this section draws heavily on that. See also Duval, "The Bolshevik Secretariat and Yakov Sverdlov" and "Yakov M. Sverdlov and the All-Russian Central Executive Committee of Soviets."

17 The debate and resolutions are in Keep, *Debate*, 69–78.

18 *Izvestiia*, November 29.

19 The debate is in Keep, *Debate*, 173–81.

20 Lenin's statement and the resolution are in Wade, *Documents of Soviet History*, I, 62–64. On the origins of the Cheka, see Leggett, *The Cheka*, 7–18, and Gerson, *Secret Police*, 19–23.

21 Keep, *Debate*, 174.

22 Wade, *Documents of Soviet History*, I, 15.

23 On the peasants' congress, see Radkey, *The Sickle Under the Hammer*, 203–57, and Keep, *The Russian Revolution*, 436–45.

24 *Rabochii put'*, no. 26, October 3. *Pravda* was closed down after the July Days and until the October Revolution the main Bolshevik newspaper came out under this name.

25 Radkey, *Election*, esp. 12–22 and 78–80. Party numbers were not precise.

26 Lenin, *Collected Works*, XXV, 196–98.

27 Quoted in Schapiro, *1917*, 82.

28 Quoted in Chamberlin, *The Russian Revolution*, I, 368.

29 Lenin, *Collected Works*, XXVI, 379–83.

30 Wildman, *End of the Russian Imperial Army: The Road*, 355.

31 For a brief discussion of these efforts and of the broader attempt to subvert the results of the elections, see Swain, *Origins of the Russian Civil War*, 74–82, and Schapiro, *1917*, 80–82.

32 Vladimir Zenzinov, *Iz zhizni revoliutsionnera* (Paris, 1919), 99.

33 An extensive account of the Constituent Assembly meeting is in Radkey, *The Sickle Under the Hammer*, 386–416.

11 CONCLUSIONS

1 Figes and Kolonitskii, *Interpreting the Russian Revolution*, 3. The following section draws heavily on Figes and Kolonitskii, as well as upon Stites, *Revolutionary Dreams*, Frame, "Theatre and Revolution in 1917," and B. I. Kolonitsii, *Simboly vlasti i bor'ba za vlast: k izucheniiu politicheskoi kul'tury Rossiiskoi revoliutsii 1917 goda* (S.-Peterburg, 2001).

2 V. B. Aksenov, "1917 god: sotsial'nye realii i kinosiuzhety," *Otechestvennaia istoriia*, 2003, no. 6: 8–21

3 Declaration of March 2, given in Golder, *Documents*, 340–43.

Further reading

The following gives an extensive list of further reading. Only English-language works are included, as explained in the preface. Special attention should be drawn to several books that contain large number of articles on 1917 which are not listed separately but which contribute important essays on the revolution. Especially valuable are the collection edited by Robert Service and that edited by Frankel, Frankel and Knei-Paz. Special note should also be taken of the many short essays in *Critical Companion to the Russian Revolution* as well as two earlier encyclopedias of the revolution edited by Harold Shukman and by George Jackson and Robert Devlin. Somewhat older but with still valuable essays are the collections edited by Elwood and Pipes. These works contain a wealth of material which should not be overlooked by the interested reader just because the many essays cannot be listed separately. Some of them are cited in the endnotes. Extensive bibliographies on the revolutionary era are those of Murray Frame and Jonathan Smele.

Abraham, Richard. *Alexander Kerensky: The First Love of the Revolution*. New York, 1987.

"Mariia L. Bochkareva and the Russian Amazons of 1917." In *Women and Society in Russia and the Soviet Union*, ed. Linda Edmondson, 124–44. Cambridge, 1992.

Abramson, Henry. *A Prayer for the Government: Ukrainians and Jews in Revolutionary Times, 1917–1920*. Cambridge, MA, 1999.

Abrosimov, T. A. "The Composition of the Petersburg Committee of the RSDRP(b) in 1917." *Revolutionary Russia* 11, no. 1 (1998): 37–44.

Acton, Edward. *Rethinking the Russian Revolution*. London, 1990.

Alapuro, R. *State and Revolution in Finland*. Berkeley, 1988.

Allworth, E. "The Search for Group Identity in Turkistan, March 1917–September 1922." *Canadian–American Slavic Studies* 17, no. 4 (1983): 487–502.

Anweiler, Oskar K. *The Soviets: The Russian Workers, Peasants and Soldiers Councils, 1905–1921*. Trans. R. Hein. New York, 1974.

Arens, Olavi. "The Estonian Maapaev During 1917." In *The Baltic States in Peace and War, 1917–1945*, ed. V. Stanley Vardys and Romuald J. Misiunas, 19–30. University Park, PA, 1978.

"Soviets in Estonia 1917–1918." In Ezergailis and von Pistohlkors, *Die baltischen Provinzen Russlands*, 294–319.

Ascher, Abraham. "The Kornilov Affair." *Russian Review* 12, no. 4 (1953): 235–52.

Ascher, Abraham, ed. *The Mensheviks in the Russian Revolution*. London, 1976.

Asher, Harvey. "The Kornilov Affair: A History and Interpretation." *Russian Review* 29, no. 3 (1970): 286–300.

Ashworth, Tony. "Soldiers Not Peasants: The Moral Basis of the February Revolution of 1917." *Sociology* 26 (August 1992): 455–70.

Atkinson, Dorothy. *The End of the Russian Land Commune 1905–1930*. Stanford, CA, 1983.

Aun, Karl. "The 1917 Revolutions and the Idea of the State in Estonia." In Ezergailis and von Pistohlkors, *Die baltischen Provinzen Russlands*, 286–93.

Avrich, Paul. "The Anarchists in the Russian Revolution." *Russian Review* 26, no. 4 (1967): 341–50.

"The Bolshevik Revolution and Workers' Control in Russian Industry." *Slavic Review* 22 (1963): 47–63.

The Russian Anarchists. Princeton, 1967.

"Russian Factory Committees in 1917." *Jahrbücher für Geschichte Osteuropas* 11 (1963): 161–82.

Avrich, Paul, ed. *The Anarchists in the Russian Revolution*. London, 1973.

Badcock, Sarah. "'We're for the Muzhiks' Party!' Peasant Support for the Socialist Revolutionary Party During 1917." *Europe-Asia Studies*, 53, no. 1 (2001): 133–49.

Basil, John D. *The Mensheviks in the Revolution of 1917*. Columbus, OH, 1983.

Blank, S. "The Bolshevik Party and the Nationalities in 1917: Reflections on the Origin of the Multi-National Soviet State." *Sbornik* 9 (1987): 9–14.

The Bolsheviks and the October Revolution: Minutes of the Central Committee of the Russian Social-Democratic Labour Party (Bolsheviks), August 1917–February 1918. Trans. Anne Bone. London, 1974.

Borys, Jurij. "Political Parties in the Ukraine." In Hunczak, *Ukraine*, 128–58.

Boyd, J. R. "The Origins of Order No. 1." *Soviet Studies* 19, no. 3 (1968): 359–72.

Brinton, Maurice. *The Bolsheviks and Workers' Control, 1917–1921: The State and Counterrevolution*. Montreal, 1975.

Brovkin, Vladimir N. *The Mensheviks After October: Socialist Opposition and the Rise of the Bolshevik Dictatorship*. Ithaca, 1987.

Browder, Robert Paul and Alexander F. Kerensky, eds. *The Russian Provisional Government, 1917: Documents*. 3 vols. Stanford, CA, 1961.

Bryant, Louise. *Six Red Months in Russia*. New York, 1918.

Buchanan, George. *My Mission to Russia and Other Diplomatic Memories*. 2 vols. London, 1923.

Buldakov, V. P. "Scholarly Passions Around the Myth of 'Great October': Results of the Past Decade." *Kritika: Explorations in Russian and Eurasian History*, 2, no. 2 (2001): 295–305.

"Soldiers and Changes in the Psychology of the Peasantry and the Legal and Political Consciousness in Russia, 1914–1923." *The Soviet and Post-Soviet Review*, 27, Nos. 2–3 (2000): 217–40.

Bunyan, James and H. H. Fisher, eds. *The Bolshevik Revolution 1917–1918: Documents and Materials*. Stanford, CA, 1934; reprinted 1961, 1965.

Burdzhalov, E. N. "Revolution in Moscow." *Soviet Studies in History* 26 (1987–88): 10–100.

Russia's Second Revolution: The February 1917 Uprising in Petrograd. Trans. and ed. Donald J. Raleigh. Bloomington, 1987.

Carr, Edward Hallett. *The Bolshevik Revolution, 1917–1923.* 3 vols. London, 1950–53.

Carrère d'Encausse, Hélène. "The Fall of the Tsarist Empire." In *Central Asia: A Century of Russian Rule,* ed. Edward Allworth, 207–23. New York, 1967.

Islam and the Russian Empire: Reform and Revolution in Central Asia. Trans. Quintin Hoare. Berkeley, 1998.

Chamberlin, William Henry. *The Russian Revolution, 1917–1921.* 2 vols. New York, 1935; reprint, Princeton, 1987.

Channon, John. "The Bolsheviks and the Peasantry: The Land Question During the First Eight Months of Soviet Rule." *Slavonic and East European Review* 64, no. 4 (1988): 593–624.

Chase, William and J. Arch Getty. "The Moscow Bolshevik Cadres of 1917: A Prosopographical Analysis." *Russian History* 5 (1978): 84–105.

Chernov, Victor. *The Great Russian Revolution.* New Haven, 1936.

Clements, Barbara Evans. *Bolshevik Feminist: The Life of Aleksandra Kollontai.* Bloomington, 1979.

Bolshevik Women. Cambridge, 1997.

"Working-Class and Peasant Women in the Russian Revolution, 1917–1923." *Signs: Journal of Women in Culture and Society* 8, no. 2 (1982): 215–35.

Clowes, Edith W., Samuel D. Kassow and James L. West, eds. *Between Tsar and People: Educated Society and the Quest for Public Identity in Late Imperial Russia.* Princeton, 1991.

Cohen, Stephen F. *Bukharin and the Bolshevik Revolution: A Political Biography, 1888–1938.* New York, 1973.

Collins, D. N. "Kabinet, Forest and Revolution in the Siberian Altai to May 1918." *Revolutionary Russia* 4, no. 1 (1991): 1–27.

"A Note on the Numerical Strength of the Russian Red Guard in October 1917." *Soviet Studies* 24, no. 2 (October 1972): 270–80.

"The Russian Red Guard of 1917 and Lenin's Utopia." *Journal of Russian Studies* 30 (1976): 3–12.

Corney, Frederick. *Telling October: Memory and the Making of the Bolshevik Revolution.* Ithaca and London, 2004.

Critical Companion to the Russian Revolution, 1914–1921. Ed. Edward Acton, Vladimir Iu. Cherniaev and William G. Rosenberg. Bloomington, 1997.

Cross, Truman B. "Purposes of Revolution: Chernov and 1917." *Russian Review* 26, no. 4 (1967): 351–60.

Cumming, C. K. and Walter W. Pettit, eds. *Russian–American Relations, March, 1917–March, 1920: Documents and Papers.* New York, 1920.

Daniels, Robert V. *The Conscience of the Revolution: Communist Opposition in Soviet Russia.* Cambridge, MA, 1960.

Red October: The Bolshevik Revolution of 1917. New York, 1967.

Daniels, Robert V., ed. *The Russian Revolution.* Englewood Cliffs, NJ, 1972.

Debo, Richard K. *Revolution and Survival: The Foreign Policy of Soviet Russia, 1917–1918.* Toronto, 1979.

Denikin, Anton Ivanovich. *The Russian Turmoil: Memoirs Military, Social, and Political.* London, 1922.

Dmitriev, Mikhail E. "Riazan Diocese in 1917." *Russian Studies in History,* 38, no. 2 (Fall 1999): 66–82.

Donald, Moira. "Bolshevik Activity Amongst the Working Women of Petrograd in 1917." *International Review of Social History* 27, no. 9 (1982): 129–60.

"'What Did *You* Do in the Revolution, Mother?': Image, Myth and Prejudice in Western Writing on the Russian Revolution." *Gender and History* 7, no. 1 (April 1995): 85–99.

Dune, E. M. *Notes of a Red Guard.* Trans. Diane Koenker and S. A. Smith. Urbana, 1993.

Duval, Charles. "The Bolshevik Secretariat and Yakov Sverdlov: February to October 1917." *Slavic and East European Studies* 122 (1973): 47–57.

"Yakov M. Sverdlov and the All-Russian Central Executive Committee of Soviets (VTsIK): A Study in Bolshevik Consolidation of Power." *Soviet Studies* 31, no. 1 (1979): 3–22.

Edmondson, Linda Harriet. *Feminism in Russia, 1900–1917.* Stanford, CA, 1984.

Elwood, Ralph Carter, ed. *Reconsiderations on the Russian Revolution.* Cambridge, MA, 1976.

Engel, Barbara Alpern. "Not By Bread Alone: Subsistence Riots in Russia During World War I." *Journal of Modern History* 69 (1997): 696–721.

Evtuhov, Catherine. "The Church in the Russian Revolution: Arguments for and Against Restoring the Patriarchate at the Church Council of 1917–1918." *Slavic Review* 50 (1991): 497–511.

Ezergailis, Andrew. "The Latvian 'Autonomy' Conference of 30 July 1917." *Journal of Baltic Studies* 8, no. 2 (1977): 162–71.

The Latvian Impact on the Bolshevik Revolution: The First Phase, September 1917 to April 1918. New York, 1983.

The 1917 Revolution in Latvia. New York, 1974.

"The Provisional Government and the Latvians in 1917." *Nationalities Papers* 3, no. 1 (1975): 1–18.

Ezergailis, Andrew and Gert von Pistohlkors, eds. *Die baltischen Provinzen Russlands zwischen den Revolutionen von 1905 und 1917.* Cologne and Vienna, 1982.

Farnsworth, Beatrice. *Aleksandra Kollontai: Socialism, Feminism and the Bolshevik Revolution.* Stanford, CA, 1980.

Feldman, Robert S. "The Russian General Staff and the June 1917 Offensive." *Soviet Studies* 19, no. 4 (1968): 526–43.

Ferro, Marc. *Nicholas II: Last of the Tsars.* New York, 1993.

October 1917: A Social History of the Russian Revolution. London, 1980.

The Russian Revolution of February 1917. Englewood Cliffs, NJ, 1972.

"The Russian Soldier in 1917: Patriotic, Undisciplined and Revolutionary." *Slavic Review* 30 (1971): 483–512.

Figes, Orlando. *Peasant Russia, Civil War: The Volga Countryside in Revolution, 1917–1921.* Oxford, 1989.

A People's Tragedy: The Russian Revolution. New York, 1997.

"The Russian Revolution and Its Language in the Village." *Russian Review* 56, no. 3 (1997): 323–45.

Figes, Orlando and Boris Kolonitskii. *Interpreting the Russian Revolution: The Language and Symbols of 1917.* New Haven and London, 1999.

Fitzpatrick, Sheila. *The Russian Revolution.* 2nd edn. Oxford, 1994.

Fleishauer, J. "The Agrarian Program of the Russian Constitutional Democrats." *Cahiers du monde russe et soviétique* 20 (1979): 179–201.

Flenley, Paul. "Industrial Relations and the Economic Crisis of 1917." *Revolutionary Russia* 4, no. 2 (1991): 184–209.

Florinsky, Michael T. *The End of the Russian Empire.* New York, 1961.

Frame, Murray, comp. *The Russian Revolution, 1905–1921: A Bibliographic Guide to Works in English.* Westport, CT, 1995.

"Theatre and Revolution in 1917: The Case of the Petrograd State Theatres." *Revolutionary Russia,* 12, no. 1 (June 1999): 84–102.

Francis, David Rowland. *Russia from the American Embassy, April, 1916–November, 1918.* New York, 1921.

Frankel, Edith Rogovin, Jonathan Frankel and Baruch Knei-Paz, eds. *Revolution in Russia: Reassessments of 1917.* Cambridge, 1992.

Friedgut, Theodore. *Iuzovka and Revolution.* 2 vols. Princeton, 1994.

Gaida, Fedor A. "February 1917: Revolution, Power, and the Bourgeoisie." *Russian Studies in History,* 41, no. 4 (Spring 2003): 9–30.

"The Provisional Government's Mechanism of Power (March–April, 1917)." *Russian Studies in History,* 41, no. 4 (Spring 2003): 52–72.

Galili, Ziva. *The Menshevik Leaders in the Russian Revolution: Social Realities and Political Strategies.* Princeton, 1989.

"The Origins of Revolutionary Defensism: I. G. Tsereteli and the 'Siberian Zimmerwaldists.'" *Slavic Review* 41 (September 1982): 454–76.

Gerson, Leonard. *The Secret Police in Lenin's Russia.* Philadelphia, 1976.

Getzler, Israel. "Iulii Martov: The Leader Who Lost His Party in 1917." *Slavonic and East European Review* 72, no. 3 (1994): 424–37.

Kronstadt, 1917–1921: The Fate of a Soviet Democracy. Cambridge, 1983.

Martov: A Political Biography of a Russian Social Democrat. Cambridge, MA, 1967.

Nikolai Sukhanov: Chronicler of the Russian Revolution. London, 2002.

Geyer, Dietrich. *The Russian Revolution.* Trans. Bruce Little. New York, 1987.

Gill, Graeme. *Peasants and Government in the Russian Revolution.* London, 1979.

Gleason, William. *Alexander Guchkov and the End of the Russian Empire.* Philadelphia, American Philosophical Society Transactions, no. 73, part 3, 1993.

Golder, Frank Alfred, ed. *Documents of Russian History, 1914–1917.* Gloucester, MA, 1964; reprint of 1927 edn.

Golikov, A. G. "The Kerensky Phenomenon." *Russian Studies in History* 33, no. 3 (1994–95): 43–66.

Gorky, Maxim. *Untimely Thoughts: Essays on Revolution, Culture and the Bolsheviks, 1917–1918.* London, 1968.

Got'e, I. V. *Time of Troubles: The Diary of Iurii Vladimirovich Got'e, Moscow, July 8, 1917 to July 23, 1922.* Trans. T. Emmons. Princeton, 1988.

Guthier, Steven L. "The Popular Base of Ukrainian Nationalism in 1917." *Slavic Review* 38, no. 1 (1979): 30–47.

Haimson, Leopold H. "The Mensheviks After the October Revolution." *Russian Review* 38, no. 4 (1979): 456–73; 39, no. 2 (1980): 181–207; 39, no. 4 (1980): 462–83.

"The Problem of Social Stability in Urban Russia." *Slavic Review* 23, no. 4 (1964): 619–42; 24, no. 1 (1965): 1–22.

Harding, Neil. *Leninism*. Durham, NC, 1996.

Lenin's Political Thought: Theory and Practice in the Democratic Revolution. 2 vols. New York, 1977, 1981.

Hasegawa, Tsuyoshi. "The Bolsheviks and the Formation of the Petrograd Soviet in the February Revolution." *Soviet Studies* 29, no. 1 (1977): 86–197.

"Crime, Police, and Mob Justice in Petrograd During the Russian Revolutions of 1917." In *Religious and Secular Forces in Late Tsarist Russia: Essays in Honor of Donald W. Treadgold*, ed. Charles E. Timberlake, 241–71. Seattle, 1992.

The February Revolution: Petrograd 1917. Seattle, 1981.

"Gosudarstvennost', Obshchestvennost', and Klassovost': Crime, the Police, and the State in the Russian Revolution in Petrograd. *Canadian-American Slavic Studies*, 35, no. 2–3 (2001): 157–88.

Hedlin, Myron. "Zinoviev's Revolutionary Tactics in 1917." *Slavic Review* 34, no. 1 (1975): 19–43.

Heenan, Louise Erwin. *Russian Democracy's Fateful Blunder: The Summer Offensive of 1917*. New York, 1987.

Hemenway, Elizabeth Jones. "Nicholas in Hell: Rewriting the Tsarist Narrative in The Revolutionary *Skazki* of 1917." *Russian Review*, 60, no. 2 (2001): 185–204.

Hickey, Michael C. "Discourses of Public Identity and Liberalism in the February Revolution: Smolensk, Spring 1917." *Russian Review* 55, no. 4 (1996): 615–37.

"Local Government and State Authority in the Provinces: Smolensk, February–June 1917." *Slavic Review* 55, no. 4 (1996): 863–81.

"Moderate Socialists and the Politics of Crime in Revolutionary Smolensk." *Canadian-American Slavic Studies*, 35, no. 2–3 (2001): 189–218.

"Paper, Memory and a Good Story: How Smolensk got its 'October'." *Revolutionary Russia*, 13, no. 2 (2000): 1–19.

"Peasant Autonomy, Soviet Power and Land Distribution in Smolensk Province, November 1917–May 1918." *Revolutionary Russia* 7, no. 1 (1996): 14.

"Revolution on the Jewish Street: Smolensk, 1917." *Journal of Social History* 31, no. 4 (Summer 1998): 823–50.

"The Rise and Fall of Smolensk's Moderate Socialists: The Politics of Class and the Rhetoric of Crisis in 1917." In Donald J. Raleigh, ed., *Provincial Landscapes: Local Dimension of Soviet Power, 1917–1935*, 14–35. Pittsburgh, 2001

"Urban *Zemliachestva* and Rural Revolution: Petrograd and the Smolensk Countryside in 1917." *Soviet and Post Soviet Review* 23, no. 2 (1996): 143–60.

Himka, John-Paul. "The National and the Social in the Ukrainian Revolution of 1917–1920: The Historiographical Agenda." *Archiv für Sozialgeschichte* 34 (1994): 95–110.

Hogan, Heather. "Conciliation Boards in Revolutionary Petrograd: Aspects of the Crisis of Labor–Management Relations in 1917." *Russian History* 9 (1982): 49–66.

Holquist, Peter. *Making War, Forging Revolution: Russia's Continuum of Crisis, 1914–1921.* Cambridge, MA: 2002.

Holubnychy, Vsevolod. "The 1917 Agrarian Revolution in the Ukraine." In *Soviet Regional Economics: Selected Works of Vsevolod Holubnychy*, ed. I. S. Koropeckyi, 3–65. Edmonton, 1982.

Horsbrugh-Porter, Anna, ed., *Memories of Revolution: Russian Women Remember.* London and New York, 1993.

Hosking, Geoffrey. *The Russian Constitutional Experiment: Government and Duma, 1907–1914.* Cambridge, 1973.

Hughes, Michael. "'Revolution Was in the Air!': British Officials in Russia During the First World War." *Journal of Contemporary History* 31, no. 1 (1996): 75–97.

Hunczak, Taras, ed. *The Ukraine, 1917–1921: A Study in Revolution.* Cambridge, MA, 1977.

Husband, W. B. "Local Industry in Upheaval: The Ivanovo–Kineshma Textile Strike of 1917." *Slavic Review* 47, no. 3 (1988): 448–63.

Jackson, George and Robert Devlin, eds. *Dictionary of the Russian Revolution.* New York, 1989.

Janke, Arthur E. "Don Cossacks and the February Revolution." *Canadian Slavonic Papers* 10, no. 2 (1968): 148–65.

"The Don Cossacks on the Road to Independence." *Canadian Slavonic Papers* 10, no. 3 (1968): 273–94.

Johnston, Robert H. *Tradition Versus Revolution: Russia and the Balkans in 1917.* Boulder, CO, 1977.

Jones, David R. "The Officers and the October Revolution." *Soviet Studies* 28, no. 2 (1976): 207–23.

Josephson, Paul R. "Maksim Gor'kii, Science and the Russian Revolution." *Soviet and Post-Soviet Review* 22, no. 1 (1995): 15–39.

Kaiser, Daniel H., ed. *The Workers' Revolution in Russia, 1917: The View from Below.* Cambridge, MA, 1987.

Kamenetsky, Ihor. "Hrushevsky and the Central Rada." In Hunczak, *Ukraine*, 33–60.

Katkov, George. *Russia 1917: The Kornilov Affair: Kerensky and the Break-up of the Russian Army.* London, 1980.

Kazemzadeh, Firuz. *The Struggle for Transcaucasia, 1917–1921.* New York, 1951.

Keep, John L. H. *The Russian Revolution: A Study in Mass Mobilisation.* London, 1976.

Keep, John L. H., ed. *The Debate on Soviet Power: Minutes of the All-Russian Central Executive Committee of Soviets, Second Convocation, October 1917–January 1918.* Oxford, 1979.

Kennan, George Frost. *Soviet–American Relations, 1917–1920.* 2 vols. Princeton, 1956, 1958.

Kerensky, Alexander. *The Catastrophe: Kerensky's Own Story of the Russian Revolution.* New York, 1927.

The Crucifixion of Liberty. New York, 1934.

The Prelude to Bolshevism: The Kornilov Rebellion. New York, 1919.

Russia and History's Turning Point. New York, 1966.

Khalid, Adeeb. *The Politics of Muslim Cultural Reform: Jadidism in Central Asia.* Berkeley, 1998.

"Tashkent 1917: Muslim Politics in Revolutionary Turkistan." *Slavic Review* 55, no. 2 (1996): 270–97.

King, Francis. "Between Bolshevism and Menshevism: The Social-Democrat Internationalists in the Russian Revolution." *Revolutionary Russia* 7, no. 1 (1996): 1–18.

King, Richard Douglas. *Sergei Kirov and the Struggle for Soviet Power in the Terek Region, 1917–1918.* New York, 1987.

Kingston-Mann, Esther. *Lenin and the Problem of Marxist Peasant Revolution.* New York and Oxford, 1983.

Knei-Paz, Baruch. *The Social and Political Thought of Leon Trotsky.* Oxford, 1979.

Knox, Sir Alfred William Fortescue. *With the Russian Army, 1914–1917.* London, 1921.

Kochan, Lionel. "Kadet Policy in 1917 and the Constitutional Assembly." *Slavonic and East European Review* 45 (1967): 83–92.

Koenker, Diane. *Moscow Workers and the 1917 Revolution.* Princeton, 1981.

"Urban Families, Working-Class Youth Groups, and the 1917 Revolution in Moscow." In *The Family in Imperial Russia: New Lines of Historical Research,* ed. D. L. Ransel, 280–304. Urbana, 1978.

Koenker, Diane and William G. Rosenberg, *Strikes and Revolution in Russia, 1917.* Princeton, 1989.

Kolonitskii, Boris. "Antibourgeois Propaganda and Anti-'Burzhui' Consciousness in 1917." *Russian Review* 53, no. 2 (1994): 183–96.

"Democracy in the Political Consciousness of the February Revolution." *Slavic Review* 57, no. 1 (1998): 95–106.

"The 'Russian Idea' and the Ideology of the February Revolution." In *Empire and Society: New Approaches to Russian History,* ed. Teruyuki Hara and Kimitaka Matsuzato, 41–72. Sapporo, 1997.

Kowalski, Ronald I. *The Russian Revolution: 1917–1921.* New York, 1997.

Leggett, George. *The Cheka. Lenin's Political Police: The All-Russian Extraordinary Commission for Combating Counter-Revolution and Sabotage.* Oxford and New York, 1981.

Lehti, Marko. "The Baltic League and the Idea of Limited Sovereignty." *Jahrbücher für Geschichte Osteuropas* 45, no. 3 (1997): 450–65.

Lenin, V. I. *Collected Works.* 45 vols. Moscow, 1960–70.

Lieven, Dominic. *Nicholas II: Twilight of the Empire.* New York, 1994.

Lih, Lars T. *Bread and Authority in Russia, 1914–1921.* Berkeley, 1990.

Lincoln, W. Bruce. *Passage Through Armageddon: The Russians in War and Revolution, 1914–1918.* New York, 1986.

Longley, David A. "The Divisions in the Bolshevik Party in March 1917." *Soviet Studies* 24, no. 1 (1972–73): 61–76.

"The Mezhraionka, the Bolsheviks and International Women's Day: In Response to Michael Melancon." *Soviet Studies* 41 (1989): 625–45.

"Officers and Men: A Study of the Development of Political Attitudes Among the Sailors of the Baltic Fleet in 1917." *Soviet Studies* 25, no. 1 (1973): 28–50.

Lyandres, Semion. *The Bolsheviks' "German Gold" Revisited: An Inquiry into the 1917 Accusations.* The Carl Beck Papers in Russian and East European Studies 1106. Pittsburgh, 1995.

"On the Problem of 'Indecisiveness' Among the Duma Leaders During the February Revolution: The Imperial Decree of Prorogation and the Decision to Convene the Private Meeting of 27 February 1917." *Soviet and Post-Soviet Review* 24 (1997): 115–28.

McAuley, Mary. *Bread and Justice: State and Society in Petrograd, 1917–1922.* Oxford, 1991.

McCauley, Martin. *The Russian Revolution and the Soviet State, 1917–1921: Documents.* London, 1975.

McDaniel, Tim. *Autocracy, Capitalism, and Revolution in Russia.* Berkeley and London, 1988.

McKean, Robert B. *St. Petersburg Between the Revolutions: Workers and Revolutionaries, June 1907–February 1917.* New Haven and London, 1990.

McNeal, Robert H., ed. *Resolutions and Decisions of the Communist Party of the Soviet Union.* Vol. I, ed. Ralph C. Elwood; vol. II, ed. Richard Gregor. Toronto, 1974.

Mally, Lynn. *The Culture of the Future: The Proletkult Movement in Revolutionary Russia 1917–1922.* Berkeley, 1990.

Mandel, David. *Petrograd Workers and the Fall of the Old Regime: From the February Revolution to the July Days, 1917.* London, 1983.

The Petrograd Workers and the Soviet Seizure of Power: From the July Days 1917 to July 1918. London, 1984.

Manning, Roberta. "Bolsheviks Without the Party: Sychevka in 1917." In Donald J. Raleigh, ed., *Provincial Landscapes: Local Dimensions of Soviet Power, 1917–1935,* 36–58. Pittsburgh, 2001

Marot, John Eric. "Class Conflict, Political Competition and Social Transformation: Critical Perspectives on the Social History of the Russian Revolution." *Revolutionary Russia* 7 (1994): 111–63.

Mawdsley, Evan. *The Russian Revolution and the Baltic Fleet: War and Politics, February 1917–April 1918.* London, 1978.

Mayzel, Matitiahu. *Generals and Revolutionaries. The Russian General Staff During the Revolution: A Study in the Transformation of the Military Elite.* Osnabruck, 1979.

Melancon, Michael. "From Rhapsody to Threnody: Russia's Provisional Government in Socialist-Revolutionary Eyes, February–July 1917." *Soviet and Post-Soviet Review* 24 (1997): 27–80.

"International Women's Day, the Finland Station Proclamation, and the February Revolution: A Reply to Longley and White." *Soviet Studies* 42, no. 3 (1990): 583–89.

"The Left Socialist Revolutionaries and the Bolshevik Uprising." In *The Bolsheviks in Russian Society,* ed. Vladimir Brovkin, 59–80. New Haven, 1997.

The Socialist Revolutionaries and the Russian Anti-War Movement, 1914–1917. Columbus, OH, 1990.

"Soldiers, Peasant-Soldiers, Peasant-Workers and Their Organizations in Petrograd: Ground-Level Revolution in the Early Months of 1917." *Soviet and Post-Soviet Review* 23, no. 2 (1996): 161–90.

"The Syntax of Soviet Power: The Resolutions of Local Soviets and Other Institutions, March–October 1917." *Russian Review* 52, no. 4 (1993): 486–505.

"Who Wrote What and When?: Proclamations of the February Revolution in Petrograd, 23 February–1 March 1971." *Soviet Studies* 42, no. 3 (1988): 479–500.

Melancon, Michael and Alice K. Pate, eds. *New Labor History: Worker Identity and Experience in Russia, 1840–1918.* Bloomington, IN, 2002.

Meyer, Alfred G. "The Impact of World War I on Women's Lives." In Barbara Evans Clements, Barbara Alpern Engel and Christine D. Worobec, eds., *Russia's Women: Accommodation, Resistance, Transformation,* 208–24. Berkeley, 1991.

Miliukov, P. N. *The Russian Revolution.* Trans. Richard Stites and Gary Hamburg. 3 vols. Gulf Breeze, FL, 1978–87.

Mstislavskii, Sergei. *Five Days Which Transformed Russia.* Trans. E. K. Zelensky. London, 1988.

Munck, J. L. *The Kornilov Revolt: A Critical Examination of the Sources and Research.* Aarhus, 1987.

Nabokov, Vladimir. *Nabokov and the Russian Provisional Government, 1917.* Ed. Virgil Medlin and Steven Parsons. New Haven, 1976.

The Nicky–Sunny Letters: Correspondence of the Tsar and the Tsaritsa, 1914–1917. (Reprint of *The Letters of the Tsar to the Tsaritsa, 1914–1917* [1929] and *The Letters of the Tsaritsa to the Tsar, 1914–1916* [1923].) Gulf Breeze, FL, 1970.

Norton, Barbara T. "The Establishment of Democracy in Russia: The Origins of the Provisional Government Reconsidered." *History of European Ideas* 11 (1989): 181–88.

"Laying the Foundation of Democracy in Russia: E. D. Kuskova's Contribution, February–October 1917." In *Women and Society in Russia and the Soviet Union,* ed. Linda Edmondson, 101–23. Cambridge, 1992.

"Russian Political Masonry and the February Revolution of 1917." *International Review of Social History* 28 (1983): 240–58.

Orlovsky, Daniel. "Corporatism or Democracy: The Russian Provisional Government of 1917." *Soviet and Post-Soviet Review* 24 (1997): 15–26.

"The Lower Middle Strata in Revolutionary Russia." In Clowes, Kassow and West, *Between Tsar and People,* 248–68.

"Reform During Revolution: Governing the Provinces in 1917." In *Reform in Russia and the USSR: Past and Prospects,* ed. Robert O. Crummey, 100–25. Urbana and Chicago, 1989.

Page, Stanley W. *The Formation of the Baltic States: A Study of the Effects of Great Power Politics upon the Emergence of Lithuania, Latvia and Estonia.* Cambridge, MA, 1959.

"Lenin's April Theses and the Latvian Peasant-Soldiery." In *Reconsiderations on the Russian Revolution*, ed. R. C. Elwood, 154–72. Cambridge, MA, 1976.

Paleologue, Maurice. *An Ambassador's Memoirs*. Trans. F. A. Holt. 3 vols. 2nd edn. London, 1923.

Pares, Bernard. *My Russian Memoirs*. London, 1931.

Parming, Tonu. "Population and Ethnicity as Intervening Variables in the 1905/1917 Revolutions in the Russian Baltic Provinces." In Ezergailis and von Pistohlkors, *Die baltischen Provinzen Russlands*, 1–19.

Pearson, Raymond. *The Russian Moderates and the Crisis of Tsarism 1914–1917*. London, 1977.

Pereira, N. G. O. "The Idea of Siberian Regionalism in Late Imperial and Revolutionary Russia." *Russian History* 20, nos. 1–4 (1993): 163–78.

"Regional Consciousness in Siberia Before and After October 1917." *Canadian Slavonic Papers* 30, no. 1 (1988): 112–33.

White Siberia: The Politics of Civil War. Montreal, 1996.

Pethybridge, Roger W. "Political Repercussions of the Supply Problem in the Russian Revolution of 1917." *Russian Review* 29, no. 4 (1970): 379–402.

The Spread of the Russian Revolution: Essays on 1917. London, 1972.

Phillips, Hugh. "'A Bad Business': The February Revolution in Tver." *Soviet and Post-Soviet Review* 23, no. 2 (1996): 123–42.

"The Heartland Turns Red: The Bolshevik Seizure of Power in Tver." *Revolutionary Russia*, 14, no. 1 (2001): 1–21.

Pierce, Richard A. "Toward Soviet Power in Tashkent, February–October 1917." *Canadian Slavonic Papers* 17, no. 2/3 (1975): 261–69.

Pipes, Richard. *The Formation of the Soviet Union: Communism and Nationalism, 1917–1923*. Revised edn. Cambridge, MA, 1964.

Pipes, Richard, ed. *Revolutionary Russia*. London, 1968.

Pitcher, Harvey. *Witnesses to the Russian Revolution*. London, 1994.

Price, Morgan Phillips. *Dispatches from the Revolution: Russia 1915–1918*. Durham, NC, 1998.

My Reminiscences of the Russian Revolution. London, 1921.

Procyk, Anna. "Russian Liberals and the Nationality Question During the Revolution." *Ukrainian Quarterly*, 53, no. 4 (1997): 323–34.

"The Russian Provisional Government and Ukraine." *Ukrainian Quarterly*. Vol. 54, no. 3–4 (1998): 257–68.

Protasov, L.G. "The All-Russian Constituent Assembly and the Democratic Alternative." *Russian Studies in History* 33, no. 3 (1994–95): 66–93.

Rabinowitch, Alexander. *The Bolsheviks Come to Power: The Revolution of 1917 in Petrograd*. New York, 1976.

"The Evolution of Local Soviets in Petrograd, November 1917–June 1918: The Case of the First City District Soviet." *Slavic Review* 46, no. 1 (1987): 20–37.

Prelude to Revolution: The Petrograd Bolsheviks and the July 1917 Uprising. Bloomington, 1968.

Radkey, Oliver H. *The Agrarian Foes of Bolshevism: Promise and Default of the Russian Socialist Revolutionaries, February to October 1917*. New York, 1958.

The Election to the Russian Constituent Assembly of 1917. Cambridge, MA, 1989.

The Sickle Under the Hammer: The Russian Socialist Revolutionaries in the Early Months of Soviet Rule. New York, 1963.

Raleigh, Donald J. *Revolution on the Volga: 1917 in Saratov*. Ithaca and London, 1986.

"Revolutionary Politics in Provincial Russia: The Tsaritsyn 'Republic' in 1917." *Slavic Review* 40, no. 2 (1981): 194–209.

Read, Christopher. *From Tsar to Soviets: The Russian People and Their Revolution, 1917–1921*. New York, 1996.

Reed, John. *Ten Days That Shook the World*. London, 1977 (first published in 1919).

Remington, Thomas F. *Building Socialism in Bolshevik Russia: Ideology and Industrial Organization 1917–1921*. Pittsburgh, 1984.

Reshetar, John S. *The Ukrainian Revolution, 1917–1920*. Princeton, 1952.

Retish, Aaron B. "Creating Peasant Citizens: Rituals of Power, Rituals of Citizenship in Viatka Province, 1917." *Revolutionary Russia*, 16, No. 1 (June 2003): 47–67.

Rieber, Alfred J. *Merchants and Entrepreneurs in Imperial Russia*. Chapel Hill, NC, 1982.

Rigby, T. H. *Lenin's Government: Sovnarkom 1917–1922*. London, 1979.

Rogger, Hans. *Russia in the Age of Modernisation and Revolution 1881–1917*. London, 1983.

Roobol, W. H. *Tsereteli: A Democrat in the Russian Revolution. A Political Biography*. The Hague, 1976.

Rorlich, Azade-Ayse. *The Volga Tatars: A Profile in National Resilience*. Stanford, CA, 1986.

Rosenberg, William G. "The Democratization of Russia's Railroads in 1917." *American Historical Review* 86 (1981): 983–1008.

Liberals in the Russian Revolution: The Constitutional Democratic Party, 1917–1921. Princeton, 1974.

"The Problem of Market Relations and the State in Revolutionary Russia." *Comparative Studies in Society and History* 36 (1994): 356–86.

"Russian Labor and Bolshevik Power After October." *Slavic Review* 44, no. 2 (1985): 205–38.

"The Russian Municipal Duma Elections of 1971: A Preliminary Computation of Returns." *Soviet Studies* 21, no. 2 (1969–70): 131–63.

"Social Mediation and State Construction(s) in Revolutionary Russia." *Social History* 19, no. 2 (1994): 169–88.

"Workers and Workers' Control in the Russian Revolution." *History Workshop* 5 (1978): 89–97.

"The Zemstvo in 1917 and Its Fate Under Bolshevik Rule." In *The Zemstvo in Russia: An Experiment in Local Self-Government*, ed. Wayne S. Vucinich, 383–422. Cambridge, 1982.

Rosenberg, William G. and Diane Koenker. "The Limits of Formal Protest: Workers' Activism and Social Polarization in Petrograd and Moscow, March to October, 1917." *American Historical Review* 2 (1987): 296–326.

Rudnytsky, Ivan L. "The Fourth Universal and Its Ideological Antecedents." In Hunczak, *Ukraine*, 186–219.

Rupp, Sue Zayer. *The Struggle in the East: Opposition Politics in Siberia, 1918*. The

Carl Beck Papers in Russian and East European Studies 1304. Pittsburgh, 1998.

Sack, A. J. *The Birth of Russian Democracy.* New York, 1918.

Sanborn, Joshua A. *Drafting the Russian Nation: Military Conscription, Total War, and Mass Politics, 1905-1925.* DeKalb, 2003.

Sanders, Jonathan. *Russia 1917: The Unpublished Revolution.* New York, 1989.

Sargeant, Elena. "Reappraisal of the Russian Revolution in Contemporary Russian Historiography." *Revolutionary Russia* 10, no. 1 (1997): 35–54.

Saul, Norman E. *Sailors in Revolt: The Russian Baltic Fleet in 1917.* Lawrence, KS, 1978.

Schapiro, Leonard. *1917: The Russian Revolutions and the Origins of Present-Day Communism.* Hounslow, 1984.

Selunskaia, N. B. "Levels of Technology and the Use of Hired Labor in the Peasant and Manorial Economy of European Russia in 1917." *Russian Review* 47, no. 4 (1988): 409–23.

Service, Robert. *The Bolshevik Party in Revolution: A Study in Organisational Change, 1917-1923.* London, 1979.

Lenin: A Biography. London, 2000.

Lenin: A Political Life. 3 vols. London, 1985–94.

The Russian Revolution 1900-1929. 2nd edn. Basingstoke and London, 1991.

Service, Robert, ed. *Society and Politics in the Russian Revolution.* Basingstoke and London, 1992.

Shkliarevsky, Gennady. *Labor in the Russian Revolution: Factory Committees and Trade Unions, 1917-1918.* New York, 1993.

Shklovsky, Viktor. *A Sentimental Journey: Memoirs, 1917-1921.* Trans. Richard Sheldon. Ithaca and London, 1984.

Shlapentokh, Dmitry. *The Counter-Revolution in Revolution: Images of Thermidor and Napoleon at the Time of the Russian Revolution and Civil War.* New York, 1999.

Shukman, Harold, ed. *The Blackwell Encyclopedia of the Russian Revolution.* Oxford, 1988.

Shulgin, V. V. *Days of the Russian Revolution: Memoirs from the Right, 1905-1917.* Trans. B. F. Adams. Gulf Breeze, FL, 1990.

Siegelbaum, Lewis. *The Politics of Industrial Mobilization in Russia, 1914-1917.* London and New York, 1983.

Slusser, Robert H. *Stalin in October: The Man Who Missed the Revolution.* Baltimore and London, 1987.

Smele, Jonathan D. *The Russian Revolution and Civil War, 1917-1921: An Annotated Bibliography.* London and New York, 2003.

Smith, Nathan. "The Role of Russian Freemasonry in the February Revolution: Another Scrap of Evidence." *Slavic Review* 27, no. 4 (1968): 604–08.

Smith, S. A. "Craft Consciousness, Class Consciousness: Petrograd 1917." *History Workshop* 11 (1981): 33–58.

Red Petrograd: Revolution in the Factories, 1917-1918. Cambridge, 1983.

"Writing the History of the Russian Revolution After the Fall of Communism." *Europe–Asia Studies* 46 (1994): 563–78.

Snow, Russell E. *The Bolsheviks in Siberia, 1917–March 1918.* Rutherford, NJ, 1975.

Spence, Richard. *Boris Savinkov, Renegade on the Left*. Boulder, CO, 1991.

Startsev, V. I. "Lenin in October of 1917." *Soviet Studies in History* 27, no. 2 (1988–89): 86–113.

"The Question of Power in the October Days of 1917." *Soviet Studies in History* 27, no. 2 (1988–89): 36–55.

"Russian Masons in the Twentieth Century." *Russian Studies in History* 34, no. 4 (Spring 1996): 59–95.

Steinberg, Mark D. *The Fall of the Romanovs: Political Dreams and Personal Struggles in a Time of Revolution*. New Haven, 1995.

Voices of Revolution, 1917. New Haven, 2001.

Stites, Richard. *Revolutionary Dreams: Utopian Vision and Experimental Life in the Russian Revolution*. New York and Oxford, 1989.

The Women's Liberation Movement in Russia: Feminism, Nihilism, and Bolshevism, 1860–1930. Princeton, 1978.

Stockdale, Melissa Kirschke. *Paul Miliukov and the Quest for a Liberal Russia, 1880–1918*. Ithaca, 1996.

"'My Death for the Motherland is Happiness': Women, Patriotism, and Soldiering in Russia's Great War, 1914–1917." *American Historical Review*, 109, no. 1 (February 2004): 78–116.

Stojko, Wolodymyr. "Ukrainian National Aspirations and the Russian Provisional Government." In Hunczak, *Ukraine*, 4–32.

"The Ukrainian Central Rada and the Bolsheviks." *Ukrainian Quarterly*, vol. 54, nos.3–4 (1998): 269–81.

Stone, Norman. *The Eastern Front 1914–1917*. London, 1975.

Struve, P. B. *Food Supply in Russia During the World War*. New Haven, 1930.

Sukhanov, N. N. *The Russian Revolution 1917: A Personal Record*. 2 vols. Trans. J. Carmichael. London, 1955.

Suny, Ronald Grigor. *The Baku Commune, 1917–1918: Class and Nationality in the Russian Revolution*. Princeton, 1972.

"Nationalism and Social Class in the Russian Revolution: The Cases of Baku and Tiflis." In *Transcaucasia. Nationalism and Social Change: Essays in the History of Armenia, Azerbaijan, and Georgia*, ed. Suny, 241–60. 2nd edn. Ann Arbor, MI, 1996.

"Nationality and Class in the Russian Revolutions of 1917: A Reexamination of Social Categories." In *Stalinism. Its Nature and Aftermath: Essays in Honor of Moshe Lenin*, ed. Nick Lampert and Gabor Rittersporn, 211–41. Armonk, NY, 1992.

The Revenge of the Past: Nationalism, Revolution, and the Collapse of the Soviet Union. Stanford, CA, 1993.

"Revision and Retreat in the Historiography of 1917: Social History and Its Critics." *Russian Review* 53 (1994): 155–82.

"Toward a Social History of the October Revolution." *American Historical Review* 88 (1983): 31–52.

Swain, Geoff. "Before the Fighting Started: A Discussion on the Theme of 'The Third Way.'" *Revolutionary Russia* 4, no. 2 (December 1991): 210–34.

The Origins of the Russian Civil War. London, 1996.

Swietochowski, Tadeusz. *Russian Azerbaijan, 1905–1920*. Cambridge, 1985.

Thompson, John H. *Revolutionary Russia, 1917*. 2nd edn. New York, 1989.

Tirado, Isabela A. *Young Guard: The Communist Youth League, Petrograd 1917–1920*. Westport, CT, New York and London, 1988.

Tribunskii, Pavel A. "The Riazan Zemstvo in the February Revolution." *Russian Studies in History*, 38, no. 2 (Fall, 1999): 48–65.

Trotsky, L. D. *History of the Russian Revolution*. 3 vols. New York, 1932.

Tseretelli [Tsereteli], I. "Reminiscences of the February Revolution: The April Crisis." *Russian Review* 14 (1955): 93–108, 184–200, 301–21; 15 (1956): 37–48.

Tyrkova-Williams, Ariadna. *From Liberty to Brest-Litovsk*. London, 1919; reprint, Westport, CT, 1977.

Ulam, Adam. *The Bolsheviks*. New York, 1965.

Uldricks, Teddy J. "The Crowd in the Russian Revolution: Towards Reassessing the Nature of Revolutionary Leadership." *Politics and Society* 4, no. 3 (1974): 397–413.

Upton, Anthony F. *The Finnish Revolution 1917–1918*. Minneapolis, 1980.

Varneck, E. "Siberian Native Peoples After the February Revolution." *Slavonic and East European Review* 21 (1942–44): 70–88.

Vernadsky, George, ed. *A Source Book for Russian History From Early Times to 1917*. Vol. III. New Haven, 1972.

Volobuev, P. V. "The Mensheviks in the Fall of 1917: Decisions and Consequences." In *The Bolsheviks in Russian Society*, ed. Vladimir Brovkin, 43–58. New Haven, 1997.

Von Hagen, Mark. *Soldiers in the Proletarian Dictatorship: The Red Army and the Soviet Socialist State, 1917–1930*. Ithaca and London, 1990.

"The Russian Imperial Army and the Ukrainian National Movement in 1917." *Ukrainian Quarterly*, vol. 54, no. 3–4 (1998): 220–56.

Von Laue, Theodore. "Westernization, Revolution and the Search for a Basis of Authority: Russia in 1917." *Soviet Studies* 19, no. 2 (October 1967): 156–80.

Why Lenin? Why Stalin?: A Reappraisal of the Russian Revolution, 1900–1930. Philadelphia, 1964 and later edns.

Wada, Haruki. "The Russian February Revolution of 1917." *Annals of the Institute of Social Science*, no. 15 (1974): 72–94.

Wade, Rex A. "Argonauts of Peace: The Soviet Delegation to Western Europe in the Summer of 1917." *Slavic Review* 26, no. 3 (1967): 453–67.

Documents of Soviet History, vol. I, *The Triumph of Bolshevism, 1917–1919*. Gulf Breeze, FL, 1991.

"Irakli Tsereteli and Siberian Zimmerwaldism." *Journal of Modern History* 39, no. 4 (December 1967): 425–31.

"The *Rajonnye Sovety* of Petrograd: The Role of Local Political Bodies in the Russian Revolution." *Jahrbücher für Geschichte Osteuropas* 20 (1972): 226–40.

Red Guards and Workers' Militias in the Russian Revolution. Stanford, CA, 1984.

"The Revolution in the Provinces: Khar'kov and the Varieties of Response to the October Revolution." *Revolutionary Russia* 4, no. 1 (1991): 132–42.

ed. *Revolutionary Russia; New Approaches*. New York and London, 2004

The Russian Search for Peace, February–October 1917. Stanford, 1969.

"Ukrainian Nationalism and Soviet Power: Kharkiv, 1917." In *Ukrainian Past, Ukrainian Present*, ed. Bohdan Krawchenko, 70–83. New York, 1993.

Warth, Robert A. *The Allies and the Russian Revolution: From the Fall of the Monarchy to the Peace of Brest-Litovsk*. Durham, NC, 1954.

Nicholas II: the Life and Reign of Russia's Last Monarch. Westport, CT, 1997.

White, Howard. "Civil Rights and the Provisional Government." In *Civil Rights in Imperial Russia*, ed. Olga Crisp and Linda Edmondson, 287–312. Oxford, 1989.

"1917 in the Rear Garrisons." In *Economy and Society in Russia and the Soviet Union, 1860–1930*, ed. L. Edmondson and P. Waldron, 152–68. Basingstoke and London, 1992.

White, James D. "The February Revolution and the Bolshevik Vyborg District Committee (in Response to Michael Melancon)." *Soviet Studies* 41, no. 4 (1989): 603–24.

"The Kornilov Affair: A Study in Counter Revolution." *Soviet Studies* 20, no. 2 (1968–69): 187–205.

Lenin: The Practice and Theory of Revolution. London, 2001.

"Lenin, Trotskii and the Arts of Insurrection: The Congress of Soviets of the Northern Region, 11–13 October 1917." *Slavonic and East European Review*, 77, no. 1 (January 1999): 117–39.

The Russian Revolution, 1917–1921: A Short History. New York, 1994.

"The Sormovo–Nikolaev Zemlyachestvo in the February Revolution." *Soviet Studies* 31, no. 4 (1979): 475–504.

Wildman, Allan K. *The End of the Russian Imperial Army: The Old Army and the Soldiers' Revolt (March–April 1917)*. Princeton, 1980.

The End of the Russian Imperial Army: The Road to Soviet Power and Peace. Princeton, 1987.

Williams, Albert Rhys. *Journey into Revolution: Petrograd, 1917–1918*. Chicago, 1969.

Williams, Beryl. *The Russian Revolution 1917–1921*. Oxford, 1987.

Wood, Alan. *The Russian Revolution*. 2nd edn. London, 1986.

Zeman, Z. A. B., ed. *Germany and the Revolution in Russia, 1915–1918: Documents from the Archives of the German Foreign Ministry*. London, 1958.

Zemelis, Sigurds. "Latvia on the Way to October." In Ezergailis and von Pistohlkors, *Die baltischen Provinzen Russlands*, 257–64.

Zenkovsky, Sergei A. *Pan-Turkism and Islam in Russia*. Cambridge, MA, 1960.

Znamenskii, O. N. "The Petrograd Intelligentsia during the February Revolution." *Soviet Studies in History* 23, no. 1 (1984–85): 39–55.

Zohrab, I. "The Socialist Revolutionary Party, Kerensky and the Kornilov Affair: From the Unpublished Papers of Harold W. Williams." *New Zealand Slavonic Journal* (1991): 131–61.

Index

NEW APPROACHES TO EUROPEAN HISTORY